The Second Coming of the Lord

The Second Coming of the Lord

Gerald N. Lund

DESERET
BOOK

SALT LAKE CITY, UTAH

© 2020 GNL Enterprises, LP

All rights reserved. No part of this book may be reproduced in any form or by any means without permission in writing from the publisher, Deseret Book Company, at permissions@deseretbook.com or P. O. Box 30178, Salt Lake City, Utah 84130. This work is not an official publication of The Church of Jesus Christ of Latter-day Saints. The views expressed herein are the responsibility of the author and do not necessarily represent the position of the Church or of Deseret Book Company.

DESERET BOOK is a registered trademark of Deseret Book Company.

Visit us at DesertBook.com

Library of Congress Cataloging-in-Publication Data

Names: Lund, Gerald N., author.
Title: The second coming of the Lord / Gerald N. Lund.
Description: Salt Lake City, Utah : Deseret Book, [2020] | Includes bibliographical references and index. | Summary: "Noted Latter-day Saint author Gerald N. Lund examines Restoration and earlier prophecies about the Second Coming of the Lord Jesus Christ"—Provided by publisher.
Identifiers: LCCN 2020022743 | ISBN 9781629728209 (hardback)
Subjects: LCSH: Second Advent. | End of the world. | The Church of Jesus Christ of Latter-day Saints—Doctrines. | Mormon Church—Doctrines.
Classification: LCC BT886.3 .L86 2020 | DDC 236/.9—dc23
LC record available at https://lccn.loc.gov/2020022743

Printed in the United States of America
Lake Book Manufacturing, Inc., Melrose Park, IL

10 9 8 7 6 5 4 3 2 1

CONTENTS

Preface vii

PART I: LIVING IN THE LAST DAYS
 1. A Lesson from History 3
 2. "Be Not Troubled" 10
 3. Voice of Warning, Voice of Promise 20
 4. The Covenant and the Covenant People of the Lord 32
 5. The Gathering of Israel in the Latter Days 45

PART II: HOW SOON THE END?
 6. "It Is Nigh, Even at the Doors" 57
 7. The Signs of the Times 68
 8. The Seven Seals of the Apocalypse 78
 9. The Angels of Judgment 90
 10. The Times of the Gentiles 102

PART III: THE DREADFUL DAY
 11. "The Great and Dreadful Day of the Lord" 123
 12. "The Devil Shall Have Power over His Own Dominion" 129
 13. "There Shall Be Wars and Rumors of Wars" 138
 14. Natural Disasters, Famine, Plague, Pestilence 156
 15. By a Thread: The United States in Prophecy 169

PART IV: THE GREAT DAY
 16. An American Zion 187
 17. The Law of Consecration and Stewardship 201
 18. The New Jerusalem: Land of Peace, City of Refuge, Place of Safety 209

- 19. Life in the City of Zion 221
- 20. The City of Zion 230
- 21. The Lost Tribes of Israel 242
- 22. The Return of the Lost Ten Tribes 255
- 23. Adam-ondi-Ahman 268

PART V: THE WINDING-UP SCENES

- 24. A War to End All Wars 283
- 25. The Battle of Armageddon 298
- 26. "Then Shall They Know" 311
- 27. Great and Marvelous Changes 325
- 28. He Comes! 331
- 29. He Shall Reign 348
- 30. Caught Up to Meet Him 359
- 31. The Great Millennial Day 371

PART VI: "IF YE ARE PREPARED YE SHALL NOT FEAR"

- 32. Watch and Be Ready 387
- 33. Increase in Knowledge 398
- 34. Temporal Preparation 410
- 35. Strengthen the Bridges:
  Preparing Ourselves Spiritually 425

  Epilogue 443
  Bibliography 448
  Index 451

PREFACE

BEGINNINGS

In the summer of 1969, my wife and I and our four young children packed our station wagon and a trailer and headed for California. After five years as a seminary teacher, I was going to be an institute instructor at a junior college in Southern California. It was a big step for us, and we were both excited and a little apprehensive. Our five years there proved to be a wonderful experience for us. It also led to something totally unexpected.

Early in my seminary career, I developed an interest in prophecy and the signs of the times and began collecting quotes and scriptures on the subject. That only intensified as I began teaching institute classes. Seminary and institute teachers are often asked to speak at various Church functions—firesides, youth conferences, etc. Because of my interest, I often chose to speak on prophecy and the signs of the times.

In doing so, an interesting thing began to happen. Often people would come up afterward and ask how they could get copies of the quotes I had used. When I explained that I had drawn most of them from sources in the Brigham Young University library, they were disappointed that the quotes weren't more readily accessible. Their next question was often, "So, why don't you write a book about this?"

At first I brushed it off. I wasn't an author and had no aspirations to be one, so writing a book on the subject had not occurred to me. But the thought did intrigue. One night, on the way home from a fireside, my wife asked what I thought about that frequent question. When I told her I found the idea intriguing but intimidating, she brushed that aside with a three-word response: "Just do it."

Fortunately, I had already done most of the research, and so I set to work immediately. Several months later, I sent off a manuscript to a publisher in Salt Lake City, and in 1971, *The Coming of the Lord* was published. I had become an author.

It is ironic to me that this happened fifty years ago now. And to my great surprise, the book has been in continuous print ever since. It has been gratifying to know that this is a gospel topic of great interest to many people over multiple generations.

Over those next five decades, my interest in prophecy and the signs of the times only increased. And even though the book was still in print, I began wondering if I should consider doing an updated version of the book. Two oft-asked questions kept that idea on my mind.

The first question: "Have you considered updating *The Coming of the Lord*?" That was easy. Yes, I had been thinking about it for some time. People encouraged me to do so. But the second question took me aback at first. "So, if you do update it, how will it be different?"

There were several answers to that, but two were the most compelling. As already noted, the book had been published in 1971. David O. McKay, the ninth President of the Church, was the prophet when I started writing. He died before I had finished the book. One of the primary objectives I had when I first wrote the book was to heavily emphasize the scriptural passages on this topic and to see what prophets—*ancient and modern*—had said about it.

Our current prophet, President Russell M. Nelson, is the *seventeenth* President of the Church—which means that we have had *eight* additional prophets! And in addition to the prophets themselves, think how many additional Apostles and counselors in the First Presidency we have had in the last fifty years. This means that there was a treasure trove of new prophetic commentary that hadn't been available when I wrote the book. That was a huge factor in my decision to update it.

The second reason may not be quite so compelling, but it is an important one nevertheless. As the years passed and I mentioned to people who asked that I was considering doing a major revision, they asked me one question again and again: "What would you do differently in the new edition?" I mentioned the amount of new material there was, but there was something else too. And it has to do with the relationship between history and prophecy.

A colleague of mine in the Church Educational System once noted that history and prophecy were different ends of the same timeline. He also noted that the line between the two was constantly shifting. Meaning, what had once been prophecy was now history. In other words, some of the things I discussed in *The Coming of Lord* were treated as prophetic promises, whereas in this new edition, some of those same things will now be discussed as history, or history in the process of being fulfilled. That change is of no small significance.

Here is one dramatic example of that. As a boy in my teens, I had always planned on serving a mission. My friends and I often speculated about where our mission calls might take us. A question often heard at that time was, "Do you think we will ever see missionaries called to Russia?" The most common answer was, "Not likely. Not until after the Millennium begins."

Well, we were wrong! Russia began letting the Church have a legal presence in the country in the early 1990s. As we shall see in this book, that "history" has continued to the point where we have a number of faithful Church congregations there, and recently, President Nelson announced that a temple will be built in one of the major cities of Russia.

There is a dynamic synergy between history and prophecy—a synergy that we shall see again and again throughout the book.

UNFOLDING PROPHECY

This brings me to one last introductory point before we turn to some practical considerations about the book. After years of gathering and filing material on prophecy and the signs of the times, I formally began work on this new edition. Not long after that, we also chose a new title for it: The first edition was *The Coming of the Lord*. This edition is titled *The Second Coming of the Lord*.

I began writing this book in mid-October 2018. I naively projected that I could finish the book in about nine months. This turned out to be a woefully short estimation. I finally submitted the manuscript to Deseret Book on December 16, 2019, having taken five months longer than I had originally planned.

But to my great surprise, that delay has turned out to allow the Lord to give us a sweet, tender mercy. If I had met my original goal, you would be reading a very different preface from the one you are reading now. For in that short space of less than four months between the submission of the manuscript to be edited and the return of the edited manuscript for me to review, the whole world has been turned upside down. And, if anything, that is an understatement.

On New Year's Eve, 2019, just two weeks after I finished the manuscript, a health official in China informed the World Health Organization (WHO) that they had found a cluster of forty-one patients in the city of Wuhan, in the People's Republic of China. All were exhibiting mysterious "pneumonia-like" symptoms. They suspected that the outbreak was connected to a "wet market" (large markets where live seafood, poultry, and other animal products are butchered and sold). They didn't have a name for it yet, but soon two new words would enter the world's vocabulary: *coronavirus* and *COVID-19*.

As I write this preface, that was not even four months ago. Yet here is a sampling of the profound impact COVID-19 has had on the world in general, and members of The Church of Jesus Christ of Latter-day Saints specifically:

- Eleven days after that first announcement, China reported its first death from the unknown infection. As I do the final review of this preface, about five months later, the number of people infected with the virus has passed ten million, and over five hundred thousand deaths have resulted from it. (By the time readers receive the printed book, the numbers will likely be much higher than that.)
- It is estimated that about one-third of the world's population (almost two billion people) are currently under some kind of quarantine or "stay-at-home" orders.
- In March, the U.S. State Department issued a level four emergency—the highest possible—warning against travel of U.S. citizens to other countries, especially Europe. About this same time, the U.S. Center for Disease Control (CDC) recommended no gatherings of more than fifty people anywhere in the United States. Numerous countries immediately followed suit.
- Around the world, literally millions of stores, businesses, churches, restaurants, schools, parks, medical facilities, daycare centers, and recreational areas were closed or tightly restricted the number of their visitors.
- Major public events of all kinds were canceled or postponed, including all levels of athletic events, from high school to professional sports, and virtually all public and private schools were closed. Movie theaters, concert venues, conventions, corporate training seminars, national parks, cruise lines, and many other venues were shut down.
- For the first time since World War II, the Olympic Games, scheduled to be held in Tokyo in the summer of 2020, were postponed for one year.
- Along with coronavirus and COVID-19, "social distancing" became a new addition to the global vocabulary.
- In compliance with governmental recommendations, The Church of Jesus Christ of Latter-day Saints asked that all general meetings of their

members that involved more than six people moved to be held electronically or by families at home. This included all Sunday meetings, weekday activities, stake conferences, youth conferences, camps, leadership meetings, and general conference.
- On February 14, France announced the first death caused by the virus in Europe. A short time later, the European Union asked all of its twenty-seven member states—more than five hundred million citizens—to close their borders to incoming visitors and be confined to their homes unless there were compelling reasons to go out.
- Global stock and bond markets have seen the largest drop since the Great Depression in the 1930s. At this time, thirty million people in the United States had filed for unemployment benefits, the largest number since the Great Depresssion.
- Tens of thousands of full-time missionaries of The Church of Jesus Christ of Latter-day Saints were brought home for reassignment or were released early. Others were given the option to wait twelve to eighteen months and then decide whether to return to the mission field. Some are now returning on a limited basis.
- With some countries threatening to close their airports and many airline flights being canceled, the Church chartered multiple 747 jumbo jets to evacuate missionaries safely back to the United States. All returning missionaries were asked to go into fourteen-day quarantine to minimize the risk of them being infected or of spreading infection.
- All Missionary Training Centers around the world were closed, and the training of new missionaries went online.
- Panic-buying began all across the United States and in many other places around the world. People lined up for blocks as stores limited the numbers who could be inside at one time and the number of key items that an individual could purchase.
- With the virus threat rapidly increasing in the United States, by early April governors of virtually every state imposed some kind of lockdown or stay-in-place orders for their state's populations.
- On March 18, in the midst of everything else, a 5.7-magnitude earthquake struck in the western part of the Salt Lake Valley. It was the strongest earthquake in the region since 1992. A few days later, a 6.5 earthquake struck in northern Idaho, the strongest in that area in fifty years. On May 15, 2020, a 6.5-magnitude earthquake struck along the eastern side of the Sierra Nevada mountains. It was the largest earthquake in that area in 65 years. Numerous minor aftershocks have been

felt since. Though no deaths were reported, and the damage was serious but not catastrophic, it was one more thing for people to worry about.
- In the Church, the restrictions affected the performance of sacred ordinances for many members. Sacrament meetings were canceled and home worship took their place, and bishops were instructed to ensure that all members had the opportunity to receive the sacrament at least once a month. It was recommended that baptisms be postponed if possible. If not, attendance at the service could not exceed four people.
- For the first time in the history of the Church, all temples were closed until further notice, directly affecting temple sealings and ordinance work for the dead.
- Other major religious services and observances have been affected around the world. The Church of the Holy Sepulchre in Jerusalem, where many Christians believe Christ was buried, closed its doors to visitors for the first time in 800 years. The entire city of Bethlehem, site of the Savior's birth, was closed to visitors and remains closed as of this writing. Easter services all around the world were canceled, broadcast via technology, or limited to some degree. Saudi Arabia asked the millions of pilgrims who normally come to Mecca in celebration of the birth of the prophet Mohammed to stay at home this year. Significant religious sites all around the world are closed.
- The April 2020 general conference for members of The Church of Jesus Christ of Latter-day Saints was held and broadcast around the world as scheduled. However, only those who were actually participating were invited to be physically in attendance. And they maintained the recommended "social distance" of six feet apart throughout the conference.
- Nevertheless, the 190th conference of The Church of Jesus Christ of Latter-day Saints celebrated a jubilee year, the 200th anniversary of Joseph Smith's First Vision. Three especially remarkable things took place during the conference. (1) An official proclamation on the Restoration was shared by the First Presidency and the Quorum of the Twelve. It is only the sixth official proclamation in the history of the Church. (2) A Hosanna Shout honoring the bicentennial anniversary of the First Vision was led by President Russell M. Nelson. All members of the Church were invited to participate. Normally, the Hosanna Shout is given only during temple dedicatory services. (3) Along with seven other new temples, two temples were announced that were remarkable firsts. The first temple to be built in a country

where there is Muslim majority in their population was announced to be built in Dubai, in the United Arab Emirates. A temple will also be built in Shanghai, in the People's Republic of China. China has several congregations of native Chinese members of the Church. With this announcement, they will no longer be required to leave the country to receive their temple ordinances.

We could add numerous other examples of the drastic changes that have come since the beginning of the year 2020. We are living in a time of great suffering, great tribulation, great disruption, and social upheaval.

Or, to put it another way, we are becoming witnesses to the unfolding of some of the signs of the times. Prophecies given centuries or even millennia ago are now unfolding right before our eyes. This has profoundly affected billions of people in all nations. And yet, in the case of *The Second Coming of the Lord*, there has also been this small, tender mercy, which has allowed us to make it part of our study. And there is another upside to what is happening.

As all of this has unfolded with breathtaking speed, over and over again we have heard people try to describe their feelings about what is happening. Here are a few of the expressions I have heard or read about. And these are not coming from only members of the Church, or even believing Christians.

- "I think God is giving us a wake-up call. In our family, we're already making a list of things that we need to start doing differently when this is over."
- "I expected that having all of my children home for weeks at a time, being schooled online, would prove to create all kinds of family conflicts and family crises. We have had some of those, but we are also seeing incredible things happen. Our family is spending time together like we have never done before. My daughter recently told me that she has become best friends with her older brother, who she clashed with so much before."
- Families are talking about the sweetness of home worship meetings with the sacrament and "virtual dinners," where extended families stay in their own homes but eat together and talk together through electronic media.
- Every day we read of accounts of people from all walks of life being kinder to others, sacrificing to ease the burdens of others. Exceptional examples of that are the medical people putting their own lives at risk to minister to the needs of others.

- One man said, "Things have been happening so rapidly in the last few weeks that a day seems like a week, a week feels like a month, and it seems like forever ago when we first learned of the virus. I can barely keep up with it, and yet, I am grateful for life and health and family like I have never been before."
- A friend told me, "Some people are calling it a 'wake-up call,' but I think a better description would be to think of it as a 'shot across the bow.' It feels like this is the Lord's way of telling us to reevaluate our priorities and change direction where necessary."
- One young adult simply said: "What is the Lord trying to teach us through all of this?"

I conclude this portion of the preface with the words of our living prophet, President Russell M. Nelson. He gave this message in general conference just over a month ago. It seems particularly relevant to our discussion here in this preface and to the overall purpose of this book:

> In the past several weeks, most of us have experienced disruptions in our personal lives. Earthquakes, fires, floods, plagues, and their aftermaths have disrupted routines and caused shortages of food, staples, and savings. Amidst all of this, we commend you and thank you for choosing to hear the word of the Lord during this time of turmoil by joining with us for general conference. The increasing darkness that accompanies tribulation makes the light of Jesus Christ shine ever brighter. Just think of the good each of us can do during this time of global upheaval. Your love of and faith in the Savior may very well be the catalyst for someone to discover the Restoration of the fulness of the gospel of Jesus Christ (Nelson, "Hear Him," *Ensign*, May 2020).

A WORD ABOUT PROPHETS AND PROPHECY

At the head of the Church are fifteen men who make up the Council of the First Presidency and the Quorum of the Twelve Apostles. We regularly and separately sustain those fifteen men as "prophets, seers, and revelators." The Hebrew word for *prophet* means "one who speaks for the Lord." A revelator is "one who dispenses revelation." But a seer brings additional gifts to us. The word literally means, "one who sees, or a see-er." In the Book of Mormon we learn that "a seer is a revelator *and* a prophet also; and *a gift which is greater can no man have*, except he should possess the power of God" (Mosiah 8:16; see also D&C 107:92).

God has spoken, is speaking, and will continue to speak to us through the Spirit and through His servants the prophets. This is a gift of inestimable worth to those who live in the last days. Though the title this book carries is *The Second Coming of the Lord*, it is much more than a book that focuses only on the actual return of Jesus Christ. It is an examination of the prophecies about the Second Coming and the events leading up to it. These events include what the Savior Himself called the "signs of the times, and the signs of the coming of the Son of Man" (D&C 68:11; see also D&C 45:39).

Our ancient and modern prophets and seers teach us how we can "abide the day of his coming" (D&C 61:39). I love that word—*abide*. It conveys so much more than "surviving" the day of His coming, or "enduring" the day of His coming. It conveys peace, calm, rest, and safety.

So in this book, my primary purpose will be to share with readers what the prophets, seers, and revelators of both ancient and modern times have taught us so that we can wisely prepare ourselves and our families for what lies ahead. I recognize that there are other outstanding gospel scholars and other General Authorities and General Officers of the Church who have taught valuable concepts and given us important insights on this topic. But, as you shall see, the vast majority of the quotations I have chosen to use in this book come from the scriptures and from those who have been sustained as prophets, seers, and revelators by the Church and its members.

With that said, however, it is important to keep two additional things in mind. First, while those whom we sustain as prophets, seers, and revelators are given the gift of seership, they themselves are quick to point out that what they have said, even over the pulpit, does not constitute the official doctrines of the Church. Nor does what they say carry the same weight as canonized revelations.

The Brethren often remind us that they are not perfect and that the apostolic office does not make them infallible. President Dallin H. Oaks, of the First Presidency, reminded us that the declaration of official doctrine for the Church comes only from the full body of the First Presidency *and* the Quorum of the Twelve, i.e., all fifteen of those we sustain as prophets, seers, and revelators. Speaking of other writings about Church doctrine, he said:

> As to all of these, the wise cautions of Elders D. Todd Christofferson and Neil L. Andersen in earlier general conference messages are important to remember. Elder Christofferson taught: "It should be remembered that not every statement made by a Church leader, past or present, necessarily constitutes doctrine. It is commonly understood in the Church that a statement made by one leader on a

single occasion often represents a personal, though well-considered, opinion, not meant to be official or binding for the whole Church." In the following conference, Elder Andersen taught this principle: "The doctrine is taught by all 15 members of the First Presidency and Quorum of the Twelve. It is not hidden in an obscure paragraph of one talk." The family proclamation, signed by all 15 prophets, seers, and revelators, is a wonderful illustration of that principle (Oaks, "Trust in the Lord," *Ensign*, November 2019).

If that principle is true of those who are called to the holy apostleship, it certainly has even more direct application to me as an author. This book is a product of my own interest in prophecy and the Second Coming. I was not asked by the leadership of the Church to write this book, nor was it written under their direction in any way. It represents *my own interpretations* of the scriptures and the words of our prophets.

Therefore, though I often use quotations from our Church leaders, readers should understand that I am not suggesting that these somehow *prove* that my interpretations or conclusions on the subject are the correct ones. They are cited only to offer further clarification on the topic for the readers to consider.

The same principle applies in those places where we talk about timing of events or try to draw inferences about what the original writer intended. Though I try to use words like "it seems," or "it is possible," or "perhaps what is meant here is," and similar phrases, sometimes I may speak as though what I am saying is conclusive, or the only possible interpretation to be drawn. Please know that this is not my intent. In my own mind, I see this book as a *joint exploration* between author and reader, not a collection of infallible declarations and conclusions.

A FEW LAST CONSIDERATIONS

Here are a couple of practical things for readers to consider as they begin this book. First, though this book is organized in a logical and sequential order of concepts and topics, it does not need to be read in order. In a way, each chapter stands alone, so you the reader should feel free to browse wherever your interests take you.

Next, I warn you in advance. Much of what you will read in this book is dark, grim, and in some places actually quite gruesome. When Elijah appeared to Joseph Smith and Oliver Cowdery in the Kirtland Temple, he noted that from his visitation they could know that the "*great* and *terrible* day of the Lord is near, even at the doors" (D&C 110:16).

That is important to remember. It is a dual scenario that the prophets present to us. Some of it is glorious beyond our ability to grasp. But some is downright dreadful. We shall not spend an inordinate amount of time on the more awful things, but neither can we simply ignore them because we find them disconcerting. After all, it is the Lord who chose to reveal them to us.

One aspect of human nature is that we seem to be more fascinated by or are more focused on the negative sides of life. So, sometimes, we get into conversations where all we talk about are the dreadful things happening, and we grow gloomier and more depressed the longer it goes.

But here is an interesting lesson we can draw from the scriptures and the words of our modern prophets. Note the table of contents. One section of this book is dedicated to the dreadful things we find in the prophecies. It has five chapters in it. But the next section focuses on the great side of what is coming. And there are *eight* chapters in that section. That provides a good model of how the Lord teaches us about the future, and how we should remember to view the future too.

As a final point of clarification, except where noted, italics in scriptures and quotations have been added for emphasis and do not appear in the original sources.

May you find as much inspiration and revelation and application in the reading of this book as I did in the writing of it.

–Gerald N. Lund
Alpine, Utah
May 2020

Part I

Living in the Last Days

CHAPTER 1

A Lesson from History

I want our members to know that the Restoration is a continuing process. And we have a lot to do before the Lord will come again. He wants Israel to be gathered and the world to be made ready for the Second Coming of the Lord. So all I know is that there's a lot of work to be done. And we're going to do it, we're going to receive those instructions when it's needful and try to respond to each instruction as it comes. (Russell M. Nelson, *Church News*, September 8, 2019, 28)

AND WHEN YOU SEE JERUSALEM ENCOMPASSED WITH ARMIES

During the last week of His mortal ministry, Jesus and the Twelve were in Jerusalem for the Passover. One day, as they were on the Temple Mount, His disciples commented on the wonders of the magnificent structures that constituted the complex there. The crown jewel was the temple itself.

What Jesus said next must have come as a profound shock. He told them that they would see the day when these great buildings would be thrown down and not one stone would be left standing upon the other (see Matthew 24:1–2; Mark 13:2; Luke 21:6; see also JS—Matthew 1:2).

As they left the Temple Mount and ascended the Mount of Olives, Jesus stopped, perhaps to rest for a moment, for it was a strenuous climb. From that vantage point the Temple Mount lay directly before them. Peter, James, John, and Andrew came to Jesus. "Tell us," they said, "when shall these things be? and what shall be the sign when all these things shall be fulfilled?" (Mark 13:3–4).

What followed is known as the Olivet Discourse. In it, the Savior not only prophesied about the fall of Jerusalem, which would occur in their lifetime (A.D. 66–70)[1], but He spoke of the distant future as well. Matthew, Mark, and Luke all recorded part of that discourse. In our dispensation, Jesus gave us additional information on what He said that day.

While he was working on the Joseph Smith Translation of the Bible (JST), the Prophet made substantial changes to Matthew 24. These were eventually published separately in the Pearl of Great Price as Joseph Smith—Matthew. Somewhere about that same time—perhaps when working on the JST—the Prophet Joseph received a revelation that is now section 45 in the Doctrine and Covenants. In that revelation, the Lord shared some of what He had shared with His disciples, but this account also added information not found in the New Testament accounts (see D&C 45:15–60). Taken together, these five versions of the Olivet Discourse provide a remarkable prophecy uttered by the Savior a short time before His death.

In Luke's account, Jesus said: "When ye shall see Jerusalem *compassed* [or encircled] *with armies,* then know that the *desolation* thereof is nigh. Then *let them which are in Judea flee to the mountains;* and *let them which are in the midst of it depart out;* and let not them that are in the countries enter thereinto. For these be the days of vengeance" (Luke 21:20–22).

There had always been tension between the Romans and the Jews of Judea since the Romans had conquered the area about 66 B.C. But by A.D. 65, things had deteriorated badly. Various rebel groups attacked two Roman fortresses and slaughtered the garrisons there. The Roman governor unleashed his legionnaires on the populace in Caesarea. By the end of the day, 20,000 Jewish citizens were dead. From there, it quickly escalated into full-scale war.

The Romans had four legions (about 25,000 men) garrisoned in Caesarea, about eighty miles northwest of Jerusalem. As the rebellion quickly spread, Cestius Gallus, the general in command of the legions, reacted quickly, but unwisely. He set off for Jerusalem with only one legion, with auxiliary forces, and about 7,000 men. The Zealots ambushed them in a narrow pass, but Gallus fought his way through without heavy losses and pushed on to Jerusalem. There he laid the city under siege, completely

---

1 Throughout this book we shall use the traditional B.C. and A.D. designations. B.C. stands for "Before Christ." However, A.D. does not mean "After Death," as some suppose, but *Anno Domini,* "the year of our Lord" in Latin. Though A.D. is often used after the year, technically it should precede it. In consideration of those who are not Christian, modern scholars began using B.C.E., "before the common era," and C.E., "common era," as neutral designations.

surrounding—or *encompassing*—the city with his troops, ensuring that no one could escape. Then the Romans settled in to starve the Jews out.

A short time later, something quite astonishing happened. The besieged citizens of Jerusalem awoke one morning to find the Romans packing up their gear and setting fire to their camps and excess equipment. No one knows exactly why Gallus suddenly decided to withdraw. His army wasn't under any immediate threat and he was prepared for a long siege, so this development stunned the Jews. Soon thousands of cheering and jeering citizens lined the walls and watched their hated enemy disappear.

One would think that Gallus had learned a lesson from his previous encounter with the Jewish rebels, but that was not so. The Zealots raced ahead to the same narrow pass and fell on Gallus's troops as they entered the narrow defile. The fighting was so fierce, and his losses so heavy, Gallus commanded his demoralized men to abandon anything they could not carry, including goods, weaponry, and even catapults and battering rams. By the time he finally broke free and reached Caesarea, virtually all of his legion—about 6,000 men—were dead. Worse, the spoils of war would be used to great advantage by their enemy when the Romans finally returned.

Flavius Vespasian, a battle-hardened general, and his son Titus returned the next spring with something Judea had never before seen—an entire Roman *army,* seven full legions and numerous auxiliary troops. That was about 60,000 men, fully equipped with the engines of war, all of them veterans eager to avenge the humiliating defeat of the previous fall.

For the next two and a half years, Vespasian and Titus methodically moved southward, through Galilee, Samaria, and Judea, crushing the rebellion as they went. When Vespasian was called back to Rome to become emperor, he left Titus to finish what they had started. When Titus finally reached Jerusalem the following spring, he put his troops to work building a siege wall around the city. Soldiers patrolled the wall day and night. No one was allowed in or out of the city. All supplies were cut off. Jerusalem was under full siege. And this time, there would be no pulling back.

Very quickly, conditions in the city became unbearable. People died by the hundreds every day. Houses and buildings quickly filled with decaying corpses. Disease spread quickly. Any who tried to escape were crucified in the sight of the besieged. Finally, on September 26, A.D. 70, Titus breached the final citadel. After nearly three years of siege, Jerusalem fell. What followed was horrific. Josephus, an ancient historian and a witness to the war, said that 1,100,000 Jews—over ninety percent of the population—were killed, and the remainder were sold into slavery. After the slaves were sorted out, the soldiers put the rest of the population to the sword, and the Temple Mount ran with blood.

Titus ordered that everything on the Temple Mount be leveled so the Jews would not feel compelled to try to reclaim their holy place. And thus, as Jesus had foretold, not one stone of the temple remained standing upon another.

PROPHECY AND THE FUTURE

So why begin a book on the last days and the Second Coming of Christ with such a horrible tragedy that occurred two millennia ago? It is because this voice from the past holds an important lesson for our day. This is a good example of where prophecy can become more sure than history.

The famous Spanish philosopher George Santayana (1863–1952) once said, "Those who cannot remember the past are condemned to repeat it." About 3,000 years ago, Moses noted that the way to tell a true from a false prophet was if the prophecy came to pass (see Deuteronomy 18:20–22). In this case, the Savior's prophecy of the fall of Jerusalem was fulfilled in the most gruesome detail.

When Christ made that prophecy in the spring of A.D. 33, we don't know with exactness how many followers had joined "The Church of Jesus Christ of Former-day Saints." Nor do we know how many of them were residents of Jerusalem. Luke records that a short time after Christ was taken up into heaven, Peter met with about 120 disciples in Jerusalem (see Acts 1:15). This was not quite two months after Christ's death. Jesus had experienced much greater success in Galilee than in Jerusalem, so it is unlikely that 120 constituted all that had been converted to Christ and had been baptized by that time.

What we do know is that however many members there were when Christ died, this was about to change dramatically. Note the following from Luke's account in the book of Acts, which describes what happened in the next few months in Jerusalem:

- On the day of Pentecost (fifty days following Passover), after Peter and the Apostles spoke in tongues and flames of fire hovered over their heads, "about three thousand souls" were baptized (Acts 2:41). In our modern organizational terminology, that was a full stake in one day! But these were Jews from all over the empire who had come for Passover, so it is likely some of them left and returned to their

homeland, where they would seed the coming gospel effort when the Apostles took the word to the world.
- As they continued to preach, the Lord "added to the church daily" (Acts 2:47).
- A short time later, those that believed the word included about 5,000 men (see Acts 4:4). Surely some of their families were converted as well.
- Not long after that, "believers were the more added to the Lord, *multitudes* both of men and women" (Acts 5:14).
- And finally we read: "And the word of God increased; and the number of the disciples *multiplied in Jerusalem greatly;* and a *great company of the priests* were obedient to the faith" (Acts 6:7).

From the standpoint of doing missionary work, Jerusalem provided an extremely rich harvest of souls. It appears that within a year of Christ's death, there were ten thousand or more Christians in Jerusalem. But how many must there have been thirty-three years later when war with Rome broke out? It is possible that when Cestius Gallus laid siege to the city in A.D. 66, the number of Christians in Jerusalem could have been twenty thousand or more.

When the Romans packed up and disappeared, how many of those early converts remembered the Savior's warning: "When ye shall see Jerusalem compassed with armies . . . then let them which are in Judea flee to the mountains" (Luke 21:20–21)?

Unfortunately, there are no contemporary records of what happened to the Christians during that great war. But two early Christian historians did speak of it much later. About A.D. 325, a Christian scholar named Eusebius wrote an extensive history of the early Christian Church. In his work, Eusebius made reference to the war between Rome and the Jews:

> The members of the Jerusalem church by means of an oracle [something spoken through revelation or inspiration], given by revelation to acceptable persons there [i.e., persons who "accepted" his word], were ordered to leave the city before the war began and settle in a town in Peraea called Pella (Eusebius, Book III, 5:4).

About a century later, another ancient Christian historian stated:

> [There was an] exodus from Jerusalem when all the disciples went to live in Pella because Christ had told them to leave Jerusalem and to go away since it would undergo a siege. Because

of this advice they lived in Perea after having moved to that place (Epiphanius, *Panarion*, 29, 7, 7–8).

Pella was one of the cities in the Decapolis, a Roman district on the east side of the Jordan River, a few miles southeast of the Sea of Galilee. Since it was east of the Jordan, it was not caught up in the Roman conquest of the province. This was probably not the only place they fled to if their numbers were as substantial as the evidence suggests. But where they went is secondary to the fact that they were not in Jerusalem when Titus returned, because they remembered the Master's prophecy and were miraculously delivered.

How we would love to know exactly how many Christians were saved at that time. How we would love more details on exactly how that came about and what difficulties they may have faced during their exodus. But even without those details, we have a powerful lesson on the purpose and the value of prophecy.

PREPARATION AND SEPARATION

One day, as I was in the process of organizing the resources about the Second Coming I had been collecting over the years, one of my sons came to visit with his family. As the children played, he and I began talking about this project I was just beginning. He noted that he had recently read a New Testament passage in the JST Appendix. He was troubled by the implications it holds for all of us today who claim membership in the Church. Two verses had particular impact on him: "And that servant who knew his Lord's will, and prepared not for his Lord's coming, neither did according to his will, shall be beaten with many stripes. . . . For unto whomsoever much is given, of him shall much be required; and to whom the Lord has committed much, of him will men ask the more" (JST Luke 12:56–57). My son then observed, "It seems like most authors tend to focus on the specific signs found in the prophecies in somewhat of an academic approach. But what the Lord cares most about is our *preparation* for what is coming. We know the future holds a great *separation* of the righteous from the unrighteous. So, I'm wondering if in addition to compiling lists of what is going to happen, we focus on that preparation. For it is *preparation that gets us ready for the coming separation.*"

It was one of those clarifying moments. I knew that he had put his finger on something important. I am constantly hearing from people who are anxious and troubled about the future. Evidence that the world is quickly unraveling is all around us. And all the time people ask me, "What do we do? How do we protect our families? What is going to happen to us? How long can this go on?"

This book is about the future as seen primarily through the eyes of God's prophets, seers, and revelators. The future, as noted in the preface, will be both great and dreadful. At the very time of the writing of this book, we are seeing evidence on every side of a deepening and widening separation between those who are striving to be faithful to their covenants and those who are embracing the world with ever-intensifying eagerness.

We feel and see all around us a growing sense of hostility against age-old principles and values. We are witnessing a spread of evil and pervasive wickedness that not only chills the soul but creates an inner longing to separate ourselves and our families from the world and find places of peace, safety, and refuge.

As we shall see, the prophecies are clear. There is a coming separation of the righteous from the wicked, of the clean from the unclean, of the just from the unjust. And if we are not preparing for it now—both temporally and spiritually—then we may find ourselves separated from the very peace, safety, and refuge for which we so desperately long. In the gospel we are taught how to ready ourselves for that separation from the world:

1. "If ye are prepared ye shall not fear" (D&C 38:30).
2. "Be not troubled" (D&C 45:35).

In a recent talk to young single adults at Utah State University, Elder Jeffrey R. Holland spoke in glowing terms of the blessings and promises of this generation and how to maintain hope in days of darkness:

> We are indeed the most blessed people in the history of the world. Truly we live in a magnificent day . . . in this, the last and greatest dispensation in the history of the world. . . . In the entire history of humankind, there have never been so many advantages bestowed on one era in so many different ways. . . . The world is challenging and will get more challenging, but it is possible to be cheerful because the victory has already been won. Never again will the priesthood keys and true doctrine of Jesus Christ be taken from the earth. . . . Zion isn't "where" we live, it's "how" we live. This responsibility to build Zion is a prophetic mandate, what President Russell M. Nelson calls "the gathering of Israel" (Holland, *Church News*, October 6, 2019, 5–6).

CHAPTER 2

"BE NOT TROUBLED"

Today, the Lord's work in The Church of Jesus Christ of Latter-day Saints is moving forward at an accelerated pace. The Church will have an unprecedented, unparalleled future. . . . Remember that the fulness of Christ's ministry lies in the future. The prophecies of His Second Coming have yet to be fulfilled. We are just building up to the climax of this last dispensation when the Savior's Second Coming becomes a reality. . . . The time is coming when those who do not obey the Lord will be separated from those who do. . . . The choice to come unto Christ is not a matter of physical location; it is a matter of individual commitment. . . . Spiritual security will always depend upon how one lives, not where one lives. (Russell M. Nelson, "The Future of the Church: Preparing the World for the Savior's Second Coming," *Ensign*, April 2020)

A WORLD OF WICKEDNESS

It is hard to estimate the number of people who have lived in relative peace, freedom, prosperity, and stability in this state we call mortality. One reason for that is because the records tend to focus on the tragic side of human history. What is clear is that the weight of historical evidence suggests that times of peace, safety, prosperity, freedom, and the other desirables of human life may be in the minority. For example, consider these questions:

- How many full-scale wars have been fought since the time of Adam and Eve?
- How many people have lived in slavery under tyrants and dictatorships?
- How many people have been killed by their fellow human beings?

- How many times has adultery or fornication been committed throughout history?
- How many infants have died through abortion, neglect, malnutrition, or infanticide?
- How many people have spent their entire lives in crushing poverty?
- How many people have been victimized by predators of all kinds?
- How many people have been victims of sexual crimes?
- How many lives have been ruined by addiction to alcohol, drugs, pornography, etc.?

These are depressing questions. They remind us of the terrible wickedness that has prevailed in much of the history of the world. Why is that so? How does that fit into God's plan?

One of the most chilling scriptures about Satan and his minions is recorded by Enoch. After seeing that "the power of Satan was upon all the face of the earth" (Moses 7:24), Enoch then had a vision: "And he beheld Satan; and he had a great chain in his hand, and it veiled the whole face of the earth with darkness; and he looked up and laughed, and his angels rejoiced" (Moses 7:26).

> *There has never been a time like this in the history of the world. Never!*
>
> RUSSELL M. NELSON,
> "HOPE OF ISRAEL," WORLDWIDE
> DEVOTIONAL FOR YOUTH, JUNE 3, 2018

That reaction is almost incomprehensible to us. The questions above give us a small glimpse into the immense human suffering that this world has seen, but when Satan looked on those same horrific scenes, he looked up and laughed! And his followers rejoiced! That gives us just a glimpse into the depths of their evil.

GOD IS AT THE HELM

While serving as a General Authority Seventy, I had one of those unexpected teaching moments that life presents to us. This was when the financial crash was in full swing and our country was experiencing the most drastic drop in the economy since the Great Depression. Every day there were new announcements. The stock market crash. The collapse of the housing market. Major banks, mortgage companies, retirement funds, and investment houses were failing. There was talk of massive government bailouts. Unemployment was skyrocketing. A dark cloud had settled over the country and was spreading to other nations.

In the fall of 2007, my assignment as a General Authority Seventy was in Salt Lake City, working in the Church Office Building. One day I went down to a small cafeteria in the basement of the Church Administration Building that is reserved for General Authorities. After getting my food, I saw that four of my colleagues in the Seventy were seated at a table for six, just starting to eat. They invited me to join them. We spoke briefly about our various assignments, but soon the talk turned to the current financial crisis. It didn't take long for our conversation to become quite bleak in tone. One of the brethren had a grandchild who had recently graduated with an MBA but was having no luck in finding employment. Another reported that a grandchild was unsure about wanting to get married and bring children into the world.

About that time, as this cloud of gloom settled over our lunch table, Russell M. Nelson, then Elder Nelson of the Twelve, came into the lunchroom with a tray of food. Seeing that we had a vacant spot at our table, he joined us. He ate quietly for a time as our conversation went right on in that same sense of discouragement. Finally, one of the brethren said, "They're talking about the possibility of the whole government of the United States failing. Then what shall we do?"

Elder Nelson, who hadn't said much since sitting down, laid down his fork and looked at us directly. His expression was very sober as he spoke quietly, saying something like this: "Brethren, the Lord chose the United States of America as the place for the Restoration of the gospel in our dispensation. He did that so we would have a base of religious freedom that would sustain the work of the Restoration. Also, the financial affluence and the political stability of the United States makes it possible for our Church to take the gospel to the world. That is a task that is not yet finished. Brethren, the Lord is at the helm. He will not let this work fail."

That was more than ten years ago, but I still vividly remember two things. First, how sheepish we felt for letting ourselves become so negative. And the second was the lesson taught: God is in control. Why then do we fear? It was a profound teaching moment, and I have reminded myself of that day often when I have found myself growing discouraged and pessimistic. God is at the helm!

> *One of your important responsibilities is to help prepare the world for the Second Coming of the Savior.*
>
> NEIL L. ANDERSEN,
> "PREPARING THE WORLD FOR THE SECOND COMING," *ENSIGN*, MAY 2011

"WHY ARE YE FEARFUL, O YE OF LITTLE FAITH?"

President Nelson's counsel that "God is at the helm" brings to mind a lesson taught by the Master. While crossing the Sea of Galilee one night, a violent storm descended. It must have been particularly dangerous, for these were fishermen who dealt with such storms all the time, but this one was violent enough that they were terrified. And, to their great dismay, Jesus slept through it all. Finally, they awakened Him: "Lord, save us: we perish."

Sometimes that's how we feel when the world rages around us and our lives rock back and forth so violently that we feel like we are going under. Surely there are people around the world with that experience during the COVID-19 crisis. But from the disciples' experience on the Sea of Galilee there is a great lesson for us. Once awakened, Jesus looked at the storm raging around them and said unto them, "Why are ye fearful, O ye of little faith?" (Matthew 8:23–26). What happened next is the key teaching moment. "Then he arose, and rebuked the winds and the sea; and there was a great calm." His disciples learned a great lesson that night, one that applies with equal power to us as we face the current and coming storms of life. "But the men marvelled, saying, What manner of man is this, that even the winds and the sea obey him?" (Matthew 8:26–27).

LIVING IN THE LAST DAYS

So what does the future hold for those who are living in the last days of the world's history? Since I wrote *The Coming of the Lord* those many years ago, questions about the future and what it holds for us have come up all the time. In recent years, with world conditions deteriorating at an ever-increasing pace, the questions are still with us. Many are deeply concerned. Many are anxious about current conditions and the future and what that means for them and their families. Here are a few of the questions I hear most frequently:

Question: *Do you think the world today is more wicked than it has ever been?*

Answer: No, not yet. There is a lot happening out there that is deeply troubling, but a look at history, both secular and scriptural, shows that there have

> *There never was a generation of the inhabitants of the earth in any age of the world who had greater events awaiting them than the present.... And an age fraught with greater interest to the children of men than the one in which we live never dawned since the creation of the world.*
>
> WILFORD WOODRUFF,
> *JOURNAL OF DISCOURSES*, 18:111

been times when things were much, much worse. For example, think of the flood in the time of Noah. The Northern Kingdom grew so wicked in the time of Isaiah that the people were taken into captivity by the Assyrians and never returned. About a hundred years later, the Southern Kingdom of Judah suffered the same end, this time under the hands of Babylon. Lehi's colony was warned in advance and fled, but the rest of the nation ceased to exist for a time. It happened yet a third time, with even greater fury, when the Holy Land was ravaged by the Romans and the Lord's chosen people were scattered for almost two millennia.

We remember the Jaredites, a mighty civilization in the Americas, who came to their end in a prolonged war where they fought down to one last, single survivor. Mormon described the evil and depravity of his people in these words to his son, Moroni:

> Many prisoners [were taken] . . . there were men, women, and children. And the husbands and fathers of those women and children they have slain; and they feed the women upon the flesh of their husbands, and the children upon the flesh of their fathers. . . . For behold, many of the daughters of the Lamanites have they taken prisoners; and after depriving them of that which was most dear and precious above all things, which is chastity and virtue . . . they did murder them in a most cruel manner, torturing their bodies even unto death; and after they have done this, they devour their flesh like unto wild beasts, because of the hardness of their hearts; and they do it for a token of bravery (Moroni 9:7–10).

Yes, we see much wickedness all around us. Yes, we have much to be concerned about. But, as a world, we have not yet reached those depths of iniquity and depravity.

Question: *Are things going to get worse than they are now?*

Answer: Absolutely! Sorry, but the prophecies are very clear on that. Part III of this book is titled, "The Dreadful Day." In that section we shall explore the terrible things that are coming in greater detail—war, natural disasters, fire, plague, famine, etc. These are the signs of the times that the Lord has given us so that we can be prepared and "be not troubled."

While we are powerless to alter the fact of the Second Coming and unable to know its exact time, we can accelerate our own preparation and try to influence the preparations of those around us.

DALLIN H. OAKS,
"BE NOT DECEIVED," *ENSIGN*, MAY 2004

"Be Not Troubled"

As noted in the Preface, the first edition of *The Coming of the Lord* was written in 1969–70. Here is just a small sampling of statistics that indicate how things have changed since that time:

- In 1970 there were about 2.5 million refugees who had been forcibly driven from their homes around the world. In 2020 that number had risen to 70.8 million, a 28-fold increase! It is estimated that as many as half of that number are children.
- In 1968, 85% of all children in the United States were living with two married parents. In recent years (2018), about one-third of children live with an unmarried parent.
- In 1970, 193,000 abortions in the United States were reported to the Center for Disease Control. In 2017 that number had risen to 882,000, a 457% increase.[1] Worldwide, reports indicate there may be as many as 46,000,000 abortions each year.
- In the United States and many other first-world countries, marriage rates are dropping significantly as the rate of cohabiting couples goes up. One study showed that about two-thirds of couples surveyed had lived in a cohabitation relationship at least once.
- In the world today, an estimated one-third of the world's 7.7 billion people—about 2.5 billion—currently live under totalitarian governments.

The changes in our society in the last fifty years are stunning and alarming and will be discussed further in Chapter 7, "The Signs of the Times." Is humanity showing signs of learning from their disastrous mistakes and returning to higher levels of righteousness? No. The history of civilizations shows that once a people begin that downward spiral, evil and wickedness typically increase until it eventually hastens their destruction or subjugation.

Question: *Is there anything to look forward to in the future?*

Answer: Of course! The prophecies make it clear that humanity is not going to be extinguished in one last final conflagration as some in the world would have us believe. Nor will we somehow evolve until we spontaneously become the ideal society. But for all the gloomy outlook, some of the most exciting events in the history of the world are yet to come, including such things as the covenant gathering of millions upon millions of the house of Israel on both sides of the veil. There will be places of peace, refuge, and safety for the

---

[1] In the United States, the number of abortions is dropping, but much of that is attributed to drops in pregnancy rates.

Saints of the most high in these terrible times. The city of New Jerusalem will be built in America. Ancient Israel will have its own homeland again and Jews from all over the world will continue to gather there. The lost tribes will return to their promised lands. There will be a great priesthood conference and sacrament meeting in the Valley of Adam-ondi-Ahman. And, greatest of all, the Son of Man will return in all of His glory, at which time the wicked will be thrown down, and a thousand years of peace and righteousness will come in.

Question: *Do you think any of us now living on the earth will live long enough to see these wondrous things come to pass?*

Answer: Absolutely! No question about that. In fact, we can say with supreme confidence that *all* of us will still be living when these marvelous things come to pass. We can say this because the question did not ask how many of our *bodies* would still be alive when these things come to pass. Every person now alive will still be living when He comes. Without exception! Just not in our mortal bodies.

> *My beloved brothers and sisters, fear not. Be of good cheer. The future is as bright as your faith.*
>
> Thomas S. Monson,
> "Be of Good Cheer,"
> Ensign, May 2009

Do we really think that it is only those who are living on the earth who are preparing for the Second Coming? Joseph Smith is the head of this dispensation. Surely he and all of his successors are heavily involved in whatever preparations are being made in the spirit world. President Ezra Taft Benson taught:

> On the other side of the veil, the righteous are taught their duties preparatory to the time when they will return with the Son of Man to earth when He comes again, this time to judge every man according to his works. These righteous spirits are close by us. They are organized according to priesthood order in family organizations as we are here; only there they exist in a more perfect order (Benson, *Teachings*, 35–36).

Question: *How do I prepare myself and those I love so that we can face what is coming with greater faith and brighter hope, and help others to do the same?*

Answer: That, of course, is the key issue, and Part VI of this book will focus on that very question. There we shall see that spiritual preparation is the most critical part of preparing. If we are spiritually ready, then what is coming will be a "great day" for us, even though we may pass through much trouble and tribulation before then.

If we are not spiritually ready, then it will be a terrible day for us even if we have enough food and water storage for forty years, or live in an underground bunker that can withstand a direct nuclear blast, or have moved to some isolated place in the mountains where we think we will be safe.

Remember this promise: "If ye are prepared ye shall not fear" (D&C 38:30). President Boyd K. Packer explained:

> We live in troubled times—very troubled times. We hope, we pray, for better days. But that is not to be. The prophecies tell us that. We will not as a people, as families, or as individuals be exempt from the trials to come. No one will be spared the trials common to home and family, work, disappointment, grief, health, aging, ultimately death. What then shall we do? That question was asked of the Twelve on the day of Pentecost. Peter answered, "Repent, and be baptized every one of you in the name of Jesus Christ for the remission of sins, and ye shall receive the gift of the Holy Ghost." We need not live in fear of the future. We have every reason to rejoice and little reason to fear. If we follow the promptings of the Spirit, we will be safe, whatever the future holds. We will be shown what to do (Packer, *Mine Errand from the Lord*, 399–400).

SUMMARY AND CONCLUSIONS

How tragic that people of faith would be fearful of the future! Remember the Savior's rebuke on the Sea of Galilee. Even though the disciples were career fishermen, the seas became so rough that they feared for their lives. I think it is safe to suppose that some things in the future (and even in the present) will be so rough that we too shall cry out, "Lord, save us! We perish."

In their case, Jesus immediately calmed the seas. In our case, that may not always happen. But just as they found comfort in His words, let us take comfort in His numerous promises to us. For example:

> *In a season of increasing tumult in the world . . . , the Spirit promised has produced a sense of optimism about what lies ahead, even as the commotion in the world seems to increase.*
>
> HENRY B. EYRING,
> "FEAR NOT TO DO GOOD,"
> *ENSIGN*, NOVEMBER 2017

- The command to "fear not" is found ninety-six times in the scriptures.
- "Be not afraid" is found twenty-eight times.
- "Be not troubled" is found five times.
- "Do not fear," three times.
- "Ye shall not fear," four times.
- "Be of good cheer," thirteen times.

That is a total of 149 admonitions from the Lord. Surely that should give us some inkling of how strongly the Lord feels about this. And that is not all.

Here are some promises from our modern-day prophets that should also bring us great comfort and hope:

> Our Savior and Redeemer, Jesus Christ, will perform some of His mightiest works between now and when He comes again. We will see miraculous indications that God the Father and His Son, Jesus Christ, preside over this Church in majesty and glory. But *in coming days, it will not be possible to survive spiritually without the guiding, directing, and comforting influence of the Holy Ghost. . . . I plead with you to increase your spiritual capacity to receive revelation* (Russell M. Nelson, "Revelation for the Church, Revelation for Our Lives," *Ensign,* May 2018).

> A few weeks ago our youngest son and his wife and family stopped to see us. The first one out of the car was our two-year-old grandson. He came running to me. . . . He hugged my legs, and I looked down at that smiling face and those big, innocent eyes and thought, "What kind of a world awaits him?" . . . Everywhere we go fathers and mothers worry about the future of their children in this very troubled world. But then a feeling of assurance came over me. . . . The fear of the future was gone. That bright-eyed, little two-year-old can have a good life—a very good life—and so can his children and his grandchildren, even though they will live in a world where there is much of wickedness (Boyd K. Packer, "The Dawning of a Better Day," *Ensign,* May 2004).

> As evil increases in the world, there is a compensatory spiritual power for the righteous. As the world slides from its spiritual moorings, the Lord prepares the way for those who seek Him, offering them greater assurance, greater confirmation, and greater confidence in the spiritual direction they are traveling. . . . My brothers and sisters, as evil increases in the world, there is a compensatory

power, an additional spiritual endowment, a revelatory gift for the righteous. This added blessing of spiritual power does not settle upon us just because we are part of this generation. It is willingly offered to us; it is eagerly put before us. But as with all spiritual gifts, it requires our desiring it, pursuing it, and living worthy of receiving it (Neil L. Andersen, "A Compensatory Spiritual Power for the Righteous," BYU Education Week, August 2015).

CHAPTER 3

VOICE OF WARNING, VOICE OF PROMISE

Son of man, I have made thee a watchman unto the house of Israel: therefore hear the word at my mouth, and give them warning from me. When I say unto the wicked, Thou shalt surely die; and thou givest him not warning, nor speakest to warn the wicked from his wicked way, to save his life; the same wicked man shall die in his iniquity; but his blood will I require at thine hand. Yet if thou warn the wicked, and he turn not from his wickedness, nor from his wicked way, he shall die in his iniquity; but thou hast delivered thy soul. (Ezekiel 3:17–19)

A DUAL VOICE

An important concept for our study of prophecy has to do with what the Lord refers to as His voice. This is not a description of the *sound* of His voice, but rather what that voice says to us. In the opening section of the Doctrine and Covenants, the Lord speaks of His voice six different times, three of which occur in the first four verses (see D&C 1).

- It is the voice of Him who dwells on high, whose eyes are upon all (v. 1).
- His voice is unto all, and there is none who can escape it (v. 2).
- It is a voice of warning to all people, and it comes from the mouth of His disciples (v. 4).
- His voice is unto the ends of the earth so that all who will hear may hear (v. 11)
- All things the Lord says will be fulfilled; whether it be from His voice directly, or through the voice of His servants—it is the same (v. 38).

Here are a few of the warnings He gives us in that section:

- There is no eye that shall not see, no ear that shall not hear, nor heart not penetrated (v. 2).
- The rebellious shall feel deep sorrow, for their iniquities will be made known to all (v. 3).
- His voice is to all men through the voice of His disciples, and none shall stay them (vv. 4–5).
- His wrath shall be poured out upon the wicked without measure (v. 9).
- The anger of the Lord is kindled and shall fall upon the earth's inhabitants (v. 13).
- Those who will not hear the voice of the Lord shall be cut off from among the people (v. 14).
- Those who don't repent shall have the light taken from them (v. 33).
- The day is near when peace shall be taken from the earth and the devil shall have power over his dominion (v. 35).

> *It is my testimony that we are facing difficult times. We must be courageously obedient. My witness is that we will be called upon to prove our spiritual stamina, for the days ahead will be filled with affliction and difficulty. But with the assuring comfort of a personal relationship with God, we will be given a calming courage. From the Divine so near we will receive the quiet assurance.*
>
> JAMES E. FAUST,
> "THAT WE MIGHT KNOW THEE,"
> ENSIGN, JANUARY 1999

Interwoven throughout that section is another voice, though the Lord doesn't specifically name it as He did the voice of warning. But it is clearly there. It is a voice of promise:

- His servants shall go forth, and none can stay them (v. 5).
- As those servants go forth, there is power given to them (v. 8).
- The Lord will recompense all according to their work and how they have treated others (v. 10).
- The Lord is nigh (v. 12).
- The Lord called Joseph Smith (v. 17). This was so that the weak things could break down the strong; that all could speak in the name of the Lord; that faith might increase; that His everlasting covenant might be fulfilled; and that the fulness of His gospel could be preached to the world (vv. 19–23).
- The Lord shall have power over His Saints and reign in their midst (v. 36).
- Though heaven and earth may pass away, His word will not pass away (v. 38).

In this preface to the Doctrine and Covenants, we see very clearly the voice of warning and the voice of promise. This pattern of speaking with two voices is found throughout the revealed word of God. And usually, both voices speak with great clarity and specificity.

THE LAST SERMON OF MOSES

As he neared the end of his mortal life, Moses was camped with the children of Israel on the plains of Moab, across the River Jordan from the promised land. They were preparing to enter that land after forty years of wandering. After forty years, Moses's people were about to get their original homeland back. By this time, the Lord had told Moses that he would *not* be the one to lead his people into the promised land. The Lord had decreed that Joshua would be the one to take them home.

Moses had already written what are now the first four books of the Old Testament. Now he wrote what could be called a summary of his ministry. It is the book of Deuteronomy. Near the end of this book, he gave what could be termed his "final sermon" to his people. He called on them to renew the covenant they had made with the Lord near Mount Sinai, then concluded with a discourse on the blessings of keeping the law and the consequences of turning away from it (see Deuteronomy 28). Though written more than two thousand years ago, what Moses taught his people provides an interesting model of the voice of warning and voice of promise for us today.

Deuteronomy 28 is divided into two basically parallel sections: The first part outlines the blessings—both temporal and spiritual—that come from obedience to the laws of God. The second part describes the consequences—what Moses called "cursings"—that come as the natural result of disobedience. In both cases, he began with a brief general statement, then gave specific examples. Here, in summary form, are the two messages. This will serve as a model for much of what will be discussed in this book.

> *In another revelation the Lord declares that some of these signs are His voice calling His people to repentance.*
>
> DALLIN H. OAKS,
> "BE NOT DECEIVED," *ENSIGN*, MAY 2004

THE PROMISES

"And it shall come to pass, *if thou shalt hearken diligently unto the voice of the Lord* thy God, to observe and to do all his commandments which I command thee this day, that the Lord thy God will set thee on high above all nations of the earth: And *all these blessings* shall come on thee, and overtake thee, *if thou shalt hearken* unto the voice of the Lord thy God."

- They will be blessed—in the city, in the field, in the fruit of their bodies [families], and the fruit of their flocks [their livelihood].
- They will be blessed in their basket [their daily needs] and their stores [their long-range needs].
- They will be blessed when they come in and go out from their homes [their daily lives].
- The Lord will smite their enemies and all nations will fear them.
- He will bless them in all they set their hands to, opening up His treasures to them.
- He will cause the heavens to rain and bless all the work of their hands.
- They shall prosper to the point that they can lend money to other nations and not borrow (an interesting way to describe great prosperity).
- All of these things will come if they hearken to His commandments (vv. 1–14).

Then comes a huge "but."

> *The world will not glide calmly toward the Second Coming of the Savior. The scriptures declare that "all things shall be in commotion." Brigham Young said, "It was revealed to me in the commencement of this Church, that the Church would spread, prosper, grow and extend, and that in proportion to the spread of the Gospel among the nations of the earth, so would the power of Satan rise."*
>
> NEIL L. ANDERSEN,
> "SPIRITUAL WHIRLWINDS,"
> ENSIGN, MAY 2014

THE CURSES

"But it shall come to pass, *if thou wilt not hearken* unto the voice of the Lord thy God, *to observe to do* all his commandments and his statutes which I command thee this day; that *all these curses* shall come upon thee, and overtake thee:"

- The Lord will send cursing and vexing and rebuke them *in all they set their hands to do*, until they are destroyed.
- He will make pestilence cling to them until their crops have been consumed.

- He will curse them with a consumption [in Hebrew, a "wasting disease"], along with other severe health conditions.
- He will smite them with the sword [warfare].
- The heavens will become as brass and drought will destroy their crops.
- They will be smitten by their enemies, carried off into all the kingdoms of the earth; many dead will be left for the fowls of the air [complete social chaos].
- The Lord will smite them with madness and blindness and astonishment [loss of good judgment].
- They will have other nations come into the lands and utterly overthrow their peaceful and stable lives.
- They shall be taken to nations they have never known and there be ridiculed and detested [their nation shall cease to exist].
- They shall serve their enemies and come down very low (vv. 15–45).

Moses then concluded his sermon with a very specific and detailed prophecy about what the future held for them if they turned away from the covenant. He promised them this would follow if they didn't serve the Lord with "joyfulness, and with gladness of heart" (v. 47). What followed was a remarkably detailed prophecy that would be fulfilled in full, not just once, but several times.

- Moses described an invasion of their lands from a fierce nation that comes from afar.
- The invaders would lay the land waste and besiege Israel's high walls.
- In the siege, conditions would become horrific beyond belief, even to the point that some adults would resort to eating their own children (vv. 48–62).

In A.D. 66, a rebellion broke out among the citizens of Judea. Flavius Josephus, a Jewish captive, was allowed to be an eyewitness of much of the war so that he could make a history of it for the Roman generals. He described in awful detail the horrors that he saw firsthand during the siege of Jerusalem: mass crucifixions, widespread starvation, endemic disease, houses and buildings filled with the dead, a stench that left the air barely breathable. In his record, Josephus also included a vivid and gruesome account of cannibalism (see Josephus, "War of the Jews," Book VI, iii:3–4).

Moses concluded his prophecy with a precise description of how it all would end, summing it up in these words: "And ye shall be left few in number, . . . And the Lord shall scatter thee among all people, from the one end of the earth even unto the other; and there thou shalt serve other gods. . . . And among these nations shalt thou find no ease. . . . And thy life shall hang in doubt before thee; and thou shalt fear day and night, and shalt have none assurance of thy life" (Deuteronomy 28:62–66). That is a grim warning of the horrific consequences of them turning away from God.

Josephus provides us an eyewitness account of how accurate Moses's prophecies were. When the Romans conquered Judea, they killed an estimated 1.1 million citizens (about 90% of the population) and sold the rest (about 100,000) off to slavery, scattering them across the width and breadth of the empire.

But what is even more astonishing is that the prophecy of Moses was fulfilled two other times prior to that. When the Northern Kingdom fell prey to the Assyrian Empire in 721 B.C., the conditions were the same. Assyria was a fierce nation from afar. No mercy was shown to the people. The city was put under siege. The people endured horrific conditions, including widespread starvation.

Jerusalem, the capital of the Southern Kingdom of Judah, was less than fifty miles from Samaria. After defeating Israel, Assyria moved south and laid siege to Jerusalem. However, Judah had not fallen as far into idolatry and wickedness, and a miracle occurred when some kind of scourge fell on the Assyrian army, and thousands of them died overnight (see Isaiah 37:33–38). They withdrew, leaving Jerusalem intact.

One would think the tragedy of Israel and such a miraculous escape would have taught Judah a powerful lesson. But as the years went on, Judah gradually turned away from the Lord as well. By this time, the Babylonians had conquered Assyria and were the new bullies of the Middle East. It should come as no surprise that Babylon also fits Moses's description perfectly. They too were a fierce nation from afar. They too laid siege to the city, showing no mercy. Here too the people suffered under the most terrible conditions (it was at this time that Lehi was warned to take his family and flee from Jerusalem).

> *Prophets see ahead. They see the harrowing dangers the adversary has placed or will yet place in our path. Prophets also foresee the grand possibilities and privileges awaiting those who listen with the intent to obey.*
>
> Russell M. Nelson,
> "Stand as True Millennials,"
> *Ensign*, October 2016

Still the people did not turn to the Lord. So, in 587 B.C., King Nebuchadnezzar returned, and this time there was no mercy. The prophet Jeremiah, who was in Jerusalem, became an eyewitness to this national tragedy. He described what he saw in these terrible words:

> Their visage is blacker than a coal [a result of the famine]; they are not known in the streets: their skin cleaveth to their bones; it is withered, it is become like a stick. *They that be slain with the sword are better than they that be slain with hunger:* for these pine away, stricken through for want of the fruits of the field. The hands of the pitiful women have sodden [to boil, cook, bake, roast] their own children: they were their meat in the destruction of the daughter of my people (Lamentations 4:8–10).

Those are horrific images that make us recoil at the very thought of them. Why would the Lord have Jeremiah record them? And why would later prophets include that record as part of the Bible? We can see that it provides dramatic confirmation of the Lord's prophetic warnings, but must it be so graphic?

Some people would say, "Well, that's the nature of the Old Testament. It is a violent book because they were a primitive people." But this kind of prophetic commentary is not unique to the Old Testament. The Savior Himself gave solemn warning of the coming war with Rome (see Matthew 24:21; see also JS—M 1:18).

In the Book of Mormon, three of the great prophets of America—Ether, Mormon, and Moroni—described in vivid detail the total destruction of their civilizations. They felt compelled to raise a warning voice for our day.

The prophet Ether took two full chapters to describe the final destruction of the Jaredites, describing women and children being put in the battle lines (see Ether 15:15), millions of war deaths (see Ether 15:2), and a great nation fighting down to one last, sole survivor (see Ether 15:15–32).

The prophet Mormon experienced a whole lifetime of warfare, becoming

---

I do not wish to be an alarmist. I do not wish to be a prophet of doom. I am optimistic. I do not believe the time is here when an all-consuming calamity will overtake us. I earnestly pray that it may not. There is so much of the Lord's work yet to be done. We, and our children after us, must do it. . . . Are these perilous times? They are. But there is no need to fear. We can have peace in our hearts and peace in our homes.

Gordon B. Hinckley,
"The Times in Which We Live,"
Ensign, November 2001

the commanding general of the Nephite armies at age sixteen. He was a man of great faith, but here is how he described his day:

> And it is impossible for the tongue to describe, or for man to write a perfect description of the horrible scene of the blood and carnage which was among the people, both of the Nephites and of the Lamanites. . . . And now behold, I, Mormon, do not desire to harrow up the souls of men in casting before them such an awful scene of blood and carnage as was laid before mine eyes; but . . . all things which are hid must be revealed upon the house-tops . . . therefore I write a small abridgment, daring not to give a full account of the things which I have seen (Mormon 4:11; 5:8–9).

Why did he feel compelled to share that with us? Because he had seen our day (see Mormon 8:34–41). Therefore he was directed by the Spirit to raise a voice of warning in our day.

When Elijah appeared to Joseph Smith and Oliver Cowdery in the Kirtland Temple and conferred the keys of the sealing power upon them, he said that his coming was evidence that "the great and dreadful day of the Lord" had come (D&C 110:16). "Great" and "dreadful" clearly suggest two "voices" in the scripture. With the *voice of promise* our Father teaches us doctrines and principles that will bring us peace, prosperity, and joy in this world as well as the next. Here are a few examples:

- "Learn of me, and listen to my words; walk in the meekness of my Spirit, and you shall have peace in me" (D&C 19:23).
- "Learn that he who doeth the works of righteousness shall receive his reward, even peace in this world, and eternal life in the world to come" (D&C 59:23).
- "For thus saith the Lord—I, the Lord, am merciful and gracious unto those who fear me, and delight to honor those who serve me in righteousness and in truth unto the end" (D&C 76:5).

The other is a *voice of warning,* wherein we are informed of things that may bring us harm or lead to destructive behaviors. Here are some examples of those scriptures:

- "They who are filthy shall be filthy still; . . . and they shall go away into everlasting fire, prepared for them; and their torment is as a lake of fire and brimstone, whose flame ascendeth up forever and ever and has no end" (2 Nephi 9:16).

- "Wo unto him that has the law given, . . . that wasteth the days of his probation, for awful is his state!" (2 Nephi 9:27).
- "Wo unto him that spurneth at the doings of the Lord; yea, wo unto him that shall deny the Christ and his works!" (3 Nephi 29:5).
- "The time soon cometh that the fulness of the wrath of God shall be poured out upon all the children of men" (1 Nephi 22:16).

A short time ago, a person who is deeply faithful and a diligent student of the scriptures made this thoughtful observation: "I know that there are warnings to us throughout the scriptures, and I can see why the Lord gives those to us and why we need to take note of them. But I believe that if we are trying to motivate people to change their lives for the better, focusing on positive promises is a stronger force for motivating change than stressing the negative consequences, which bring guilt and shame. Counseling studies have shown that while warnings of negative consequences can motivate some to change, the negative approach often has the opposite effect. It discourages rather than encourages. It de-motivates instead of motivating. It can easily lead people to lose hope and give up rather than motivate them to try harder and change."

That is a thoughtful and compelling argument, and there is much wisdom in the counsel not to be too negative (remember the example of President Nelson's counsel that "God is at the helm"). But if that is the case, then why is it that there are so many warnings—and some of them pretty grim warnings—from the Lord? Are these psychological studies something that the Lord has overlooked somehow? Why doesn't He just focus on the positives? Or why does the Lord specifically ask His elect to also raise a warning voice?

> *You are living in the "eleventh hour." The Lord has declared that this is the last time that He will call laborers into His vineyard to gather the elect from the four quarters of the earth. And you were sent to participate in this gathering. . . . This is part of your identity and your purpose as the seed of Abraham.*
>
> Russell M. Nelson,
> "Becoming True Millennials,"
> worldwide devotional for young adults, January 10, 2016

- "The voice of warning shall be unto all people, by the mouths of my disciples, whom I have chosen in these last days" (D&C 1:4).
- "And let your preaching be the warning voice, every man to his neighbor, in mildness and in meekness" (D&C 38:41).
- "Every man should . . . lift a warning voice unto the inhabitants of the

- earth; and declare both by word and by flight that desolation shall come upon the wicked" (D&C 63:37).
- "Behold, I sent you out to testify and warn the people, and it becometh every man who hath been warned to warn his neighbor" (D&C 88:81).

> *All dispensations have had their perilous times, but our day will include genuine peril.*
>
> Howard W. Hunter,
> *Teachings*, 200

An interesting question comes to mind in this discussion. Which of these two voices does the Lord use most frequently in the scriptures? Are there more verses of warning or of promise? We don't have that information, and it would be a huge task to go through every verse in the four standard works to determine that.

WHY THE WARNING VOICE?

Here are some things to consider about the warning voice. These are simple concepts but are important for us to keep in mind:

- If someone knows of imminent danger and cannot stop it from happening, then warning others of that danger is the responsible thing to do. Actually, it is more than that. It is also the *loving* thing to do, for it shows love and concern for others. This is a principle we see being implemented all around us. We put the skull and crossbones on dangerous household agents. We post warnings on cigarettes about cancer risks. We put up signs marking dangerous curves or narrow bridges or railroad crossings. We list the ingredients of food so we can make wise choices about what we eat. No reasonable person would suggest that this is a negative approach. It is the responsible thing to do.
- The fact that someone knows of danger and warns us of it *does not* suggest they are being too negative. It is the threat of danger that is the negative, not the warning. If a highway flagman leaves his post and fails to stop traffic when the road crew is about to do some blasting ahead, he would be criminally liable for his neglect.
- Warning others of danger is the loving thing to do because it empowers them to take action to avoid the danger and its consequences. Therefore, the logical response toward someone who raises a warning voice should be gratitude, not irritation and condemnation.

- If a person rejects a warning or simply ignores it and subsequently suffers loss or damage, no reasonable person would blame the one who raised the warning voice for causing the tragedy.
- The more specific the warning voice is about the nature of the danger, the more helpful it is, and the more likely it is that people will heed the warning. This explains why some prophecies describe awful, horrible things.
- The combination of a voice of warning and a voice of promise provides a strong motivation to move forward toward positive goals.

In the gospel, promises and warnings can motivate us to seek greater light and greater knowledge so that we can draw down the powers of heaven and greater joy and happiness.

Note this thoughtful explanation by one of our Church Presidents:

> Success in righteousness, the power to avoid deception and resist temptation, guidance in our daily lives, healing of the soul—these are but a few of the promises the Lord has given to those who will come to His word. Does the Lord promise and not fulfill? Surely if He tells us that these things will come to us if we lay hold upon His word, the blessings can be ours. And if we do not, then the blessings may be lost. However diligent we may be in other areas, certain blessings are to be found only in the scriptures, only in coming to the word of the Lord and holding fast to it as we make our way through the mists of darkness to the tree of life (Ezra Taft Benson, *Teachings*, 359–60).

The motivation for raising the warning voice is love—love of God and love of fellowman. To warn is to care. . . . It can be urgent, as when we warn a child not to put his or her hand in a fire. It must be clear and sometimes firm. On occasion, warning may take the form of reproof, . . . but always it is rooted in love.

D. TODD CHRISTOFFERSON,
"THE VOICE OF WARNING,"
ENSIGN, MAY 2017

SUMMARY AND CONCLUSIONS

The Lord is not only a loving, caring Heavenly Father, but a wise one as well. He cares for His children and wants us to be happy and safe and cherished and fulfilled and free. Everything in His plan is designed to accomplish this purpose. But moral agency, which is the ability and the right to choose between moral alternatives—or opposites, as Lehi called them—is also a factor. This is part of the required equation: choice comes with consequences. We can and will learn that lesson through our own experience. As the saying goes, "Good judgment comes from experience, and experience comes from poor judgment."

To close this discussion on the voice of warning and the voice of promise, consider the words of President James E. Faust of the First Presidency:

> I wish to sound a voice of warning to this people. I solemnly declare that this spiritual kingdom of faith will move forward with or without each of us individually. No unhallowed hand can stay the growth of the Church nor prevent fulfillment of its mission. Any of us can be left behind, drawn away by the seductive voices of secularism and materialism. To sustain faith, each of us must be humble and compassionate, kind and generous to the poor and the needy. Faith is further sustained by daily doses of spirituality that come to us as we kneel in prayer. It begins with us as individuals and extends to our families, who need to be solidified in righteousness. Honesty, decency, integrity, and morality are all necessary ingredients of our faith and will provide sanctuary for our souls (Faust, "The Shield of Faith," *Ensign*, May 2000).

CHAPTER 4

THE COVENANT AND THE COVENANT PEOPLE OF THE LORD

The gathering . . . is an item I esteem to be of the greatest importance to those who are looking for salvation in this generation, or in these what may be called "the latter times," as all the prophets that have written, from the days of righteous Abel down to the last man, that has left any testimony on record, for our consideration, in speaking of the salvation of Israel in the last days, goes directly to show that it consists in the work of the gathering. (Joseph Smith, "Letter to the Elders of the Church, 16 November 1835," p. [209], *The Joseph Smith Papers*)

THE COVENANT AND A COVENANT PEOPLE

Another reality that is crucial to our understanding of the prophecies is the concept of a people who make a covenant with God and become His chosen people. We will speak often of the house of Israel in this book, and if we don't understand the covenant they made, we cannot understand why they play such a role in His plan, even now with what lies ahead for us.

What is a covenant? And what does that covenant have to do with Jesus Christ and His Second Coming? We talk a lot about covenants in the Church, and often we hear the word defined as a "two-way promise between God and a person." That is not incorrect, but a more accurate word might be *contract*. A contract is an agreement between two or more parties wherein both agree to certain conditions in return for certain benefits. A contract could be described as an "if-then" agreement. In its simplest form, contracts look like this:

If you do this and this and this,

Then I will do this and this and this in return.

The contract is fulfilled only when both parties meet their obligations. A covenant with the Lord follows that same pattern. As the Lord Himself has plainly stated, "I, the Lord, am bound when ye do what I say; but when ye do not what I say, ye have no promise" (D&C 82:10).

However, there are important differences in the covenants we make with our Heavenly Father and His Only Begotten Son and even the best of worldly contracts. Here are some of the most important differences:

- Since God is perfect in every aspect of His being and attributes, *He sets all of the conditions of the contract.* Our part is to accept those conditions, knowing that all will be for our good.
- In this world's contracts, negotiation and compromise are allowed and expected. For the reasons mentioned above, that doesn't happen in our covenants with God.
- One thing we often forget is that while the Father and the Son will always fulfill Their part of the covenant, if we fulfill ours, They also get to determine all aspects of when Their side of the agreement will be fulfilled. As the Lord Himself put it so succinctly: "It shall be in his own *time*, and in his own *way*, and according to his own *will*" (D&C 88:68).

> *We are leading toward one objective for each individual member of the Church. That is for all to receive the ordinances of the gospel and make covenants with our Heavenly Father so they may return to his presence. That is our grand objective. The ordinances and covenants are the means to achieving that divine nature that will return us into his presence again.*
>
> Howard W. Hunter,
> *Teachings*, 218

Because of Their perfections—perfect love, perfect knowledge, perfect power, and so on—Their promises will always be fulfilled if we fulfill ours. But we must always remember to be very careful that we don't start thinking we can tell God how best to answer our prayers, or when they need to be answered.

If we lose sight of these three important principles, we can begin to view God as if He were a divine vending machine. If we put in enough quarters—go to church, pay tithing, say our prayers, read the scriptures, etc.—then we can punch a button and His obligation will be to make sure the candy drops into our hands.

We cannot emphasize that point enough. In our covenant-making and covenant-keeping arrangement with the Father and the Son, let us always remember those three conditions: "In his own time, and in his own way, and according to his own will."

In the partaking of the sacrament each Sunday we see how this covenant process works:

IF we covenant to . . .

- Take upon us the name of Christ
- Always remember Him
- And keep His commandments

THEN God promises that . . .

- We will always have His Spirit to be with us.

Here are some other examples of scriptural "if-then" clauses:

- "If ye keep my commandments, ye shall abide in my love" (John 15:10).
- "Be thou humble; and the Lord thy God shall lead thee by the hand, and give thee answer to thy prayers" (D&C 112:10).
- "Learn that he who doeth the works of righteousness shall receive his reward, even peace in this world, and eternal life in the world to come" (D&C 59:23).

> *Most of us find ourselves at this moment on a continuum between a socially motivated participation in gospel rituals on the one hand and a fully developed, Christlike commitment to the will of God on the other. Somewhere along that continuum, the good news of the gospel of Jesus Christ enters into our heart and takes possession of our soul. It may not happen in an instant, but we should all be moving toward that blessed state.*
>
> D. TODD CHRISTOFFERSON,
> "FIRM AND STEADFAST
> IN THE FAITH OF CHRIST,"
> *ENSIGN*, NOVEMBER 2018

Note that in each of these references, and dozens of others just like them, there are no other conditions required. We don't have to be rich, well educated, or from a good family. The fulfillment of the promises is conditioned only on our willingness to strive to meet our part of the covenant.

Through the Restoration scriptures we know that this covenant-making process began in the premortal world when the Father laid out His plan for us. In order to continue on to the next step—mortality—we had to covenant that we would accept the Father's plan and the redemptive power of Christ's Atonement to make it work. We also know that moral agency was given to all of us so that we were "free to choose between liberty and eternal life, . . . or to choose captivity and death" (2 Nephi 2:27).

One thing the scriptures make clear is this: It is one thing to *receive* a covenant. It is quite another to *keep the covenant.*

THE ELECT OF GOD

One of the interesting words we find in the scriptures is "elect." *Elect* means chosen, preferred, or favored over another. And that is how it is used by the Lord. And, by the way, it is always the Lord who designates His elect. It is not a self-selection process.

Before His death, Jesus warned His disciples of false prophets who would, if possible, "deceive the very elect, . . . according to the covenant" (JS—M 1:22). Note the connection between being an elect person and making a covenant. In a revelation given specifically to Emma Smith, the Savior told her, "Thy sins are forgiven thee, and thou art an elect lady, whom I have called" (D&C 25:3). She didn't give herself that title. He called her an elect lady.

When the Lord called some of the first missionaries of the latter days to take the gospel to the world, He told them that they were "called to bring to pass the gathering of mine elect," saying that they were found in "the four quarters of the earth" (D&C 29:7; 33:6). "Mine elect" reminds us that it was the Lord that did the choosing.

Where did the calling and election of these future members take place? We know that in the premortal world we were offered the opportunity to make covenants with the Lord. We don't know how that was done or exactly what those covenants were, but we know that some of those premortal spirits were so firm in their commitment to the covenant that they were called to become leaders in the work of the Lord when they came to earth. Abraham saw them and called them "noble and great ones" (Abraham 3:22).

Moses made this observation: "When the most High divided to the nations their inheritance, when he separated the sons of Adam, *he set the bounds of the people according to the number of the children of Israel*" (Deuteronomy 32:8). That is a fascinating statement. In God's plan for His children, a determining factor in that placement was the number of the children of Israel. This seems to be a reference to a determination made in the premortal world. Paul may have been thinking of Moses's statement when, after affirming that God made the world and all things therein, he said, "And hath made of one blood all nations of men for to dwell on all the face of the earth, *and hath determined the times before appointed, and the bounds of their habitation*" (Acts

17:26). Paul taught a similar doctrine to the Ephesians when he taught that God the Father chose who would become members of the Church "before the foundation of the world" (Ephesians 1:4).

Finally, in a vision of the spirit world, President Joseph F. Smith learned that the first five Presidents of the Church, along with other "choice spirits" (*choice* is another word for *elect*) were chosen to be held back so they could take part in "laying the foundations of the great latter-day work" (D&C 138:53).

President Russell M. Nelson has often spoken about gathering Israel on *both* sides of the veil, meaning those we gather to the Church in this life and those we gather to the covenant in the spirit world. Perhaps there is a third possibility for gathering Israel.

We believe that faithful and righteous parents who have been sealed together for eternity in the covenant will be privileged to have some of those elect in the premortal world sent into their families, so they are "born in the covenant" and grow up in the covenant. That would give those of us living on the earth right now three possibilities for "gathering" the Lord's elect to the covenant.

1. Those who are blessed to find an eternal spouse and be sealed in the temple can gather spirits from the premortal world into their homes. They can even pray that if it be the Lord's will, the Father will send one of those elect souls to them. *That's the premortal side of the veil.*

2. Missionaries from The Church of Jesus Christ—those formally called and lay members who invite friends and family to hear the gospel message—can reach out to those who either were the elect in the premortal life or who will become the elect in this mortal life and bring them to the covenant. *This happens in this mortal world, which is between the two veils.*

3. We can participate in doing family history work and see that the ordinance work is done for those who are part of the Lord's elect but never had the chance to enter the covenant in mortality. Surely there are millions there who are ready to accept the covenant and become the elect of God. *That's the postmortal side of the veil.*

These are our three areas of labor.

THE AGE OF THE PATRIARCHS AND ABRAHAMIC COVENANT

Our next focus will be on those who have been called to be the Lord's covenant people in this life, for this is how the Lord takes the covenant to people of the world.

We know that while Adam and Eve were still in the Garden of Eden, the Lord put them (two of the elect in the premortal world) under covenant, a covenant that they kept faithfully throughout their lives. We know from the temple that they were given the same covenants we still make today. Though we are given very few details of how they worshiped and were organized, we do know that in those days, the presiding prophets of God's kingdom were patriarchs, not Presidents of the Church as we have them.

The line of authority was passed from faithful patriarch to faithful patriarch down to the time of Abraham, a period of about 2,000 years (see Genesis 5:3–32; D&C 107:40–52). Today we call that organizational structure the Patriarchal Order of the Priesthood.

Abraham was a direct descendant of the patriarchs and received the patriarchal authority through Melchizedek (see Genesis 14:18–20; D&C 84:14). He passed that authority on to Isaac and Jacob. Later in Abraham's life, the Lord appeared to him and established a covenant with him. Because of his faithfulness to the covenant, Abraham was given three distinct promises, which have come to be known as the Abrahamic covenant. President Russell M. Nelson explained these promises:

> After Abraham withstood the severe trial commanded of God in which Abraham was willing to offer his special son, Isaac, the Lord personally appeared and made a covenant with Abraham. Included were the following assurances:
> 1. Christ would come through the lineage of Abraham.
> 2. Abraham's posterity would receive certain lands as an inheritance.
> 3. All the nations of the earth would be blessed through his seed.
> These divine declarations are known as the Abrahamic covenant (Nelson, *Perfection Pending*, 201).

In the book of Abraham we get additional detail about this covenant. We learn that Abraham was not only promised that his seed would bless all nations but that they would be as numberless as the stars in the heavens or the sands of the sea. He was also told that his lineage would be given the priesthood and the responsibility to take the gospel to the world (see Abraham 2:9–11).

THE HOUSE OF ISRAEL—A NEW NAME FOR THE LORD'S COVENANT PEOPLE

With the Abrahamic covenant came a change in the way the covenant people were organized. And that brought about a change in name as well.

Abraham and Sarah finally had Isaac when Sarah was ninety and Abraham was a hundred. Isaac and Rebekah had twin boys, Jacob and Esau. Jacob's name was later changed by the Lord to Israel, which means "God prevails." Jacob had twelve sons through four wives, and these eventually became known as the twelve tribes of Israel, or the house of Israel. This family, or tribal organization, began to shape how the gospel covenant was to be taken to the world.

Why does all of this matter in a book on the Second Coming? The Church now has congregations in over 180 countries. Every one of its members is now a member of modern Israel. In their patriarchal blessings, members are told from which tribe of Israel their spiritual blessings shall come. Their children and grandchildren and great-grandchildren are born under the Abrahamic covenant. And their sons and daughters are serving missions of their own and taking the gospel to the lost sheep of the house of Israel in every nation. And they come home and do ordinance work for the dead in the temples. All of this is how the gathering of covenant Israel takes place.

As we speak further of the gathering of Israel, it will be helpful to understand the many terms that are used in connection with the house of Israel and the gathering.

SOME TERMS RELATED TO THE HOUSE OF ISRAEL

Covenant people (also called the *chosen people*). This is a generic term for the people the Lord has chosen, is choosing, or will yet choose to carry out His work among the other peoples of the earth and in the spirit world. That contractual, covenant relationship is between God and a defined group of people. This does not imply that they are superior to others, nor always more righteous. In many cases they are considered part of the house of Israel by blood lineage without regard to whether they are keeping the covenants or not.

House of Israel (also the *house of Jacob, children of Israel*). From Abraham onward, this became the formal name of the Lord's covenant people. Anciently, it referred only to the descendants of the twelve tribes. Then gradually it began to take on other meanings. Today, The Church of Jesus Christ of Latter-day Saints consider all members to be literal and covenant descendants of the house of Israel. We are comfortable doing so because the scriptures confirm that language: "Blessed are ye if ye continue in my goodness, a light unto the Gentiles, and through this priesthood, *a savior unto my people Israel*" (D&C 86:11; see also D&C 136:22).

The Covenant and the Covenant People of the Lord

Israel, Israelite. Generally, if we are speaking of Old Testament peoples, we mean the original house of Israel. In modern times, the Jewish citizens of Israel do not call themselves Israelites, but Israelis. In almost all uses of these terms outside the Church they refer to ancient Israel or the State of Israel, though not their citizens. However, over the centuries these terms took on new, and in some cases, very different meanings. These include:

- *Blood Israel.* This refers to literal descendants of one of the twelve tribes, whether they recognize those blood ties or not. In the first years of its existence, Blood Israel was almost always defined by one's genealogical ties to a specific tribe. That grew less important as time went on after they inhabited the promised land. Though each tribe was given an assigned territory, these were not independent nations but more like a loose confederation of states or provinces, as we see in the U.S. and Canada. While recognized as independent territories, the boundaries were sometimes undefined, and movement between tribal lands was not restricted. Tribes were not required to live within the boundaries of their specific territory, and intermarriage and other social interactions between the various tribes were common. That doesn't mean they lost their tribal identity, but it became less important than while they were in the wilderness.

  To further complicate the idea of what constitutes Blood Israel, consider this. Abraham, Isaac, and Jacob lived about 4,000 years ago. Demographers say that a new generation comes along about every twenty years on average. That means that Abraham now has about 200 generations of descendants. And in all that time they have been migrating, emigrating, immigrating, warring with each other, trading with each other, marrying each other, and so on. With that in mind, it is very possible that if all people could accurately trace their genealogy back that many generations, it would be rare to find someone who didn't have at least one genealogical tie back to the twelve tribes. And it would likely be very common to find people who had ties back to *all* twelve tribes. This conclusion has direct implications for the lineage we are given in our patriarchal blessings, which we shall discuss in a moment.

- *Land Israel.* When the Israelites under Joshua's leadership conquered the promised land, the land was divided up between the tribes in a loose confederation that called itself Israel. So its citizens were Israelites, no matter where they came from or which tribe they came through.

- *Political Israel.* As just noted, the twelve tribes called themselves Israel when they settled the promised land. Around 900 B.C., a major political schism occurred after the death of King Solomon. When it couldn't be resolved, the country split into two separate political entities:
- The *Kingdom of Israel*, also called the *Northern Kingdom*, included ten of the twelve tribes. They too called themselves Israelites. Its capital was Samaria. Ephraim was the most prominent tribe and controlled the royal line, so "Ephraim" was sometimes used as a nickname for the Northern Kingdom. However, it is a mistake to think this division was strictly tribal. Many members of the northern tribes went south to the other kingdom, and vice versa. The tribal identity was still honored, but it was no longer the defining political identity.
- The *Southern Kingdom*, consisting of two tribes, was called the *Kingdom of Judah*, since Judah was the prominent tribe there and also controlled the royal line. Its capital was Jerusalem. By extension, their citizens were called Jews, no matter what their tribal lineage was. We do the same. We call ourselves Americans first and then Hispanics, African Americans, and so on.

As part of the political identity, Ephraim and Judah, who had been the two most dominant tribes even back in the wilderness, now became "cousin" nations, and were often fierce competitors, even going to war with each other. Thus the ancient prophets often spoke of the "envy" or "enmity" between Judah and Ephraim (see Isaiah 11:11–13, Ezekiel 37:21–22).

Although it has now been about 3,000 years since this division occurred, ironically the prophecies tell us that in the last days, the two tribes that will lead out in the gathering of Israel and the events leading up to the Second Coming are Ephraim and Judah. This is made more interesting because Joseph Smith was not only of the tribe of Ephraim, but "a pure Ephraimite," suggesting that his bloodline back to Ephraim was pretty strong.

Another consideration has to do with patriarchal blessings, which began early in the Church's history. We are now approaching the 200-year anniversary of the organization of the Church. Though the Church does not publish statistics on tribal lineage designations as given in patriarchal blessings, there is no question that a very large majority of all Church members since those early days have been told that their lineage comes through the tribe of Ephraim. Is that part of Ephraim leading out? We shall answer that further on.

- *True Israel is covenant Israel.* This term is the most relevant for our discussion here. To understand this we have to ask a question. Simply put, it is this: In God's eyes, what constitutes true Israel? Being born into His covenant people? No. Blood Israel? Land Israel? These do not define true Israel. For example, during His mortal ministry, the Savior rebuked the Pharisees for believing that simply being born into the covenant family automatically meant they were God's favored people (see John 8:39).

Nephi gives one of the clearest statements on this principle: "For behold, I say unto you that as many of the Gentiles as will repent *are the covenant people* of the Lord; and as many of the Jews [the house of Israel] as will not repent shall be cast off; for *the Lord covenanteth with none save it be with them that repent and believe in his Son,* who is the Holy One of Israel" (2 Nephi 30:2).

> *President Russell M. Nelson's [counsel is] to begin with the end in mind. For us, the end is always on the covenant path through the temple to eternal life, the greatest of all the gifts of God.*
>
> DALLIN H. OAKS,
> "WHERE WILL THIS LEAD?,"
> ENSIGN, MAY 2017

True Israel depends on three things: *What we do. How we act. What we are!*

This principle applies to members of The Church of Jesus Christ of Latter-day Saints as well. Note this clear and firm definition of what it means to be a true member of the Church: "Behold, this is my doctrine—*whosoever repenteth and cometh unto me,* the same is my church" (D&C 10:67).

- *Gentile.* From the Hebrew word *goy,* plural *goyim.* The word means "nations." Anciently it was used to designate anyone who was not of the house of Israel. For ancient Israel, people were divided into two groups: those who were of the house of Israel by bloodline, and anyone else. Today it is mostly used by Jewish people to describe non-Jews.
- *Jew (generic).* This is an example of a term that can be confusing because its uses have changed over time. Usually we think of a "Jew" as meaning someone of Jewish heritage or someone who practices Judaism. And in many cases that is correct. But because the term also became a political title—a citizen of Judea—as well as a tribal name, things changed. When the Northern Kingdom of Israel was taken to Assyria, the Kingdom of Judah was the only remaining identifiable remnant

of Israel. And so "Jew" became a generic term for what was left of the house of Israel, for that's where all the known Israelites were found.

Because Lehi's colony came from the Kingdom of Judah, for them, "Jew" now had two meanings: a descendant of the tribe of Judah and a citizen of Judah. And they took that terminology with them to America. Very often, when Nephi and the other writers use the term "Jews and Gentiles," we may think they are referring to the tribe of Judah, or Jews as we call them today. But in reality, the term "Jews" is used as another title for the house of Israel. An excellent example of that is found in the title page of the Book of Mormon. There are also places in the Book of Mormon where the word is used to refer to the tribe of Judah, so readers need to study the context carefully to understand what the writer meant.

- *Remnants of the house of Israel.* This is a phrase we find frequently throughout all four standards works. A "remnant" is defined as a small portion of something that is left over or separated from the rest. Typically it is used in one of two ways:
- *Remnant of Jacob.* Jacob's name was changed to Israel, so this is just another way of saying remnants of the house of Israel.
- *Remnant of the seed of Joseph* (see Alma 46:23–24; 46:27). This is a different remnant. Joseph was the eleventh son of Jacob. As noted, his two sons, Ephraim and Manasseh, took his place and became separate tribes. We also know that Lehi was from the tribe of Manasseh, so generally the "remnant of Joseph" refers to the descendants of Book of Mormon peoples, such as the Lamanites, which may include some of the Polynesian peoples. Since many members of the Church have been designated as being from the tribe of Ephraim, the "remnant of Joseph" could in some cases include members of the restored Church.
- *Covenant lineage (patriarchal blessings).* This brings us to one last concept that is pivotal to our understanding of the covenant people. As we discuss this, remember what we said about the blood of Abraham now being found in a large majority of the world's population. As noted, it is likely that many members of the Church have the blood of numerous tribes—even all twelve—in their DNA. So what are we to make of that? The answer is simple, and also helps us understand why patriarchs are instructed to declare a lineage in all patriarchal blessings. Elder Eldred G. Smith, who was Patriarch to the Church for many, many years, taught that in our

patriarchal blessings we are given a "lineage of blessing" through one of the twelve tribes of Israel:

> It is the responsibility of the patriarch to designate the line of Israel *which you receive in your blessings*. These are the choice blessings that make you a part of the Church. You are entitled to this original blessing that was given down through the ages of time, that you would be a great part of this choice lineage (Eldred G. Smith, "Patriarchal Blessing," Lectures in Theology: "Last Message Series," University of Utah Institute of Religion, April 30, 1971, 3).

As also discussed, the vast majority of patriarchal blessings have designated Ephraim as the covenant line from the beginning of the Church.

> The leaders of our people from the beginning have looked forward to this great day when *Ephraim* would be gathered and would stand in his place to crown the tribes of Israel. In an epistle issued by the First Presidency in October, 1852, the following appears: "The invitation is to all, of every nation, kindred and tongue, who will believe, repent, be baptized, and receive the gift of the Holy Ghost, by the laying on of hands, Come home: come to the land of Joseph, *to the valleys of Ephraim*." . . . We are now gathering the children of Abraham who have come through the loins of Joseph and his sons, *more especially through Ephraim,* whose children are mixed among all the nations of the earth (in Joseph Fielding Smith, *Doctrines of Salvation* 3:253).

SUMMARY AND CONCLUSIONS

The concept of a covenant being at the heart of a covenant people is so simple as to be redundant, and yet it is so profound that we must keep it ever in mind. President Russell M. Nelson has spoken much about the gathering of Israel in his ministry, even saying that it is one of the most important things happening right now in the world. In doing so, he has also focused on the importance of the covenant, which is at the heart of a chosen people. Here is a brief sampling of the emphasis he has given to this concept:

> Adam and Eve, Noah and his wife, Abraham and Sarah, Lehi and Sariah, and all other devoted disciples of Jesus Christ—since the world was created—have made the same covenants with God. They have received the same ordinances that we as members of the Lord's restored Church today have made: those covenants that we

receive at baptism and in the temple (Nelson, "Come, Follow Me," *Ensign*, May 2019).

While some aspects of that covenant have already been fulfilled, the Book of Mormon teaches that this Abrahamic covenant will be fulfilled only in these latter days! It also emphasizes that we are among the covenant people of the Lord. Ours is the privilege to participate personally in the fulfillment of these promises. What an exciting time to live! (Nelson, "The Gathering of Scattered Israel," *Ensign*, November 2006).

God has always asked His covenant children to do difficult things. Because you are covenant-keeping sons and daughters of God, living in the latter part of these latter days, the Lord will ask you to do difficult things. You can count on it—Abrahamic tests did not stop with Abraham (Nelson, "Becoming True Millennials," worldwide devotional for young adults, January 2016).

With that background as context for our studies, let us now move to a subject that is mentioned literally hundreds of times in prophecy—the gathering of Israel in the last days.

CHAPTER 5

THE GATHERING OF ISRAEL IN THE LATTER DAYS

These surely are the latter days, and the Lord is hastening His work to gather Israel. That gathering is the most important thing taking place on earth today. Nothing else compares in magnitude, nothing else compares in importance, nothing else compares in majesty. And if you choose to, if you want to, you can be a big part of it. You can be a big part of something big, something grand, something majestic! When we speak of the gathering, *we are simply saying this fundamental truth: every one of our Heavenly Father's children, on both sides of the veil, deserves to hear the message of the restored gospel of Jesus Christ. They decide for themselves if they want to know more. . . . Think of it! Of all the people who have ever lived on planet earth, we are the ones who get to participate in this final, great gathering event. How exciting is that!* (Russell M. Nelson, "Hope of Israel," worldwide devotional for youth, June 3, 2018)

GATHERING ISRAEL: AN INTEGRAL PART OF THE RESTORATION OF ALL THINGS

The above statement by President Nelson was given to the youth of the Church in a worldwide broadcast by President Nelson and his wife, Wendy. If I may, I would like to share a personal note about that broadcast, as I believe it represents the feelings that other members of the Church may have had at that time.

This event took place just three months after President Nelson had been sustained and set apart as the seventeenth President of The Church of Jesus Christ of Latter-day Saints. Although it was billed for the youth of the

Church, there was a lot of excitement about the broadcast, and I wanted to hear what President Nelson had to say.

After some preliminary welcoming remarks, he challenged the youth to do "the necessary spiritual work" that would bring personal revelation. But what came next took me aback a little. "Now, we would like to talk with you about *the greatest* challenge, *the greatest* cause, and *the greatest* work on earth. And we want to invite *you* to be part of it" ("Hope of Israel," worldwide broadcast for youth, June 3, 2018). President Nelson spoke to the theme of the gathering, and what he said took me completely by surprise.

He began with, "These surely are the latter days, *and the Lord is hastening His work to gather Israel.*" What came next was stunning. "*That gathering is the most important thing taking place on earth today. Nothing else compares in magnitude, nothing else compares in importance, nothing else compares in majesty.*"

I remember thinking, "He's talking to the *youth* of the Church about the gathering of Israel? That's a pretty mature topic for adults, let alone for youth as young as twelve and thirteen." I pushed those thoughts aside and listened intently as he went on and asked them if they would like to be part of the work of the gathering. As he concluded his remarks, he emphasized yet again the importance of his topic: "My dear extraordinary youth, you were sent to earth at this precise time, *the most crucial time in the history of the world*, to help gather Israel. *There is nothing happening on this earth right now that is more important than that. There is nothing of greater consequence. Absolutely nothing.*"

> *Missionary work is not just one of the 88 keys on a piano that is occasionally played; it is a major chord in a compelling melody that needs to be played continuously throughout our lives if we are to remain in harmony with our commitment to Christianity and the gospel of Jesus Christ.*
>
> Quentin L. Cook,
> "Be a Missionary All Your Life,"
> Brigham Young University
> 2006–2007 Speeches, 7

My mind was reeling as he finished. I knew that the gathering of Israel was important, but *nothing* matches it in magnitude, importance, majesty, and consequence? I knew that it was important, but the *most* important? What about the Atonement? What about missionary work? What about temples and temple ordinance work? Aren't they all more important than the gathering of Israel?

But then came a teaching moment as I asked myself again, "More important than the Atonement?" Of course not—not in the eternal scope of things. But President Nelson didn't say that. He said that the gathering of Israel was the most important thing happening *on earth* right now. And why is it more important than anything else happening? Because only as people gather to the covenant does the Atonement become a reality in their lives. More important than missionary work? Of course. The whole purpose of missionary work is to invite people to come into the covenant. And that's true on both sides of the veil. When we consider it, every doctrine, every principle, every part of the organization of the Church, every blessing of the gospel won't do the people of the world one bit of good until they are gathered to the Church where they will find those doctrines, where they will have access to those ordinances, and where they can become the Lord's true covenant people.

That night was a marvelous teaching moment for me. I had learned something profound that I had not considered before. The gathering of Israel is of prime importance in our task to prepare the Church and the world for the Second Coming of Jesus Christ precisely because that is how we get people into the covenant so they can enjoy all the blessings of the gospel.

BRINGING THE CHILDREN OF ABRAHAM BACK TO THE FOLD

Russell M. Nelson is not the only prophet who has suggested that the gathering of Israel is one of the greatest things to ever happen. We earlier cited the prophet Jeremiah, who said that the day would come when we would no longer talk about the day when Moses brought Israel out of Egypt, but of the Lord bringing back the ten tribes from the north (see Jeremiah 16:14–15). He then described how it was possible that the return of Israel could be so important:

> Behold, the days come, saith the Lord, that I will make a new covenant with the house of Israel, and with the house of Judah: Not according to the covenant that I made with their fathers, . . . which my covenant they brake. . . . But this shall be the covenant that I will make with the house of Israel; After those days, saith the Lord, *I will put my law in their inward parts, and write it in their hearts; and will be their God, and they shall be my people* (Jeremiah 31:31–33).

That last verse is a wonderful description of true Israel, covenant Israel. Ezekiel, a contemporary of Jeremiah who was taken captive to Babylon, also described the gathering in our time:

> I will even gather you from the people, and assemble you out of the countries where ye have been scattered, and I will give you the land of Israel. . . . And I will give them one heart, and I will put a new spirit within you; and I will take the stony heart out of their flesh, and will give them an heart of flesh: That they may walk in my statutes, and keep mine ordinances, and do them: and they shall be my people, and I will be their God (Ezekiel 11:17, 19–20).

While the resurrected Lord was visiting the Nephites in America, He too spoke of the gathering as the time when a renewed Israel, a covenant people, would return, including the descendants of Father Lehi:

> I will remember the covenant which I have made with my people; and I have covenanted with them that I would gather them together in mine own due time, that I would give unto them again the land of their fathers for their inheritance, which is the land of Jerusalem, which is the promised land unto them forever, saith the Father. And it shall come to pass that the time cometh, when the fulness of my gospel shall be preached unto them; and they shall believe in me, that I am Jesus Christ, the Son of God, and shall pray unto the Father in my name. . . . *Verily I say unto you, I give unto you a sign, that ye may know the time when these things shall be about to take place—that I shall gather in, from their long dispersion, my people, O house of Israel, and shall establish again among them my Zion* (3 Nephi 20:29–31; 21:1).

Four months after President and Sister Nelson spoke to the youth of the Church, President Nelson again spoke of the gathering of Israel, this time in the women's session of general conference:

> This gathering is the greatest challenge, the greatest cause, and the greatest work on earth today! It is a cause that desperately needs women, because women shape the future. *So tonight I'm extending a prophetic plea to you, the women of the Church, to shape the future by helping to gather scattered Israel* (Nelson, "Sisters' Participation in the Gathering of Israel," *Ensign*, November 2018).

The gathering of Israel is found virtually everywhere in the scriptures. In the Topical Guide, under such headings as "Apostasy of Israel," "Israel, Bondage of, in Egypt," "Israel, Bondage of, in Other Lands," "Israel, Gathering of," "Israel, Mission of," and "Israel, Scattering of," there are more than six hundred references on the scattering and gathering of Israel.

Those references make it clear that one of the primary reasons The

Church of Jesus Christ of Latter-day Saints was organized in this dispensation was to provide the doctrines, the priesthood keys, the covenants, and the ordinances required to gather Israel back into the covenant fold. We often speak of eternal families as one of God's greatest gifts to us. But isn't that what the gathering of Israel is all about? Bringing individuals into the covenant so they can become part of their own eternal family? Is there anything of greater significance than that?

THE DISPENSATION OF THE FULNESS OF TIMES

President Nelson told the youth that we are living in the most crucial time in the history of the world. Through the Prophet Joseph Smith, the Lord taught that our time is unique in the history of the world. To Elder Thomas B. Marsh, who was President of the Quorum of the Twelve at that time, the Lord said that the First Presidency and the Twelve have the power of the priesthood "given, for the last days and for the last time, in the which is the dispensation of the fulness of times." Then the Lord said, "How great is your calling" (D&C 112:30, 33). Three years later, Joseph Smith, then in Nauvoo, was taught more about this dispensation:

> It is necessary in the ushering in of the dispensation of the fulness of times, which dispensation is now beginning to usher in, that a whole and complete and perfect union, and welding together of dispensations, and keys, and powers, and glories should take place, and be revealed from the days of Adam even to the present time. And not only this, but those things which never have been revealed from the foundation of the world, but have been kept hid from the wise and prudent, shall be revealed unto babes and sucklings in this, the dispensation of the fulness of times. . . . I deign to reveal unto my church things which have been kept hid from before the foundation of the world, things that pertain to *the dispensation of the fulness of times* (D&C 128:18; 124:41).

This is a sweeping, all-encompassing statement. To better understand why this is so, we have to understand what a dispensation is and how our dispensation is different than all the others.

The word *dispensation* comes from the verb "to dispense," meaning "to give out, to distribute, to allot." In terms of gospel dispensations, it means a time when a fulness of the gospel is given to people through the leadership of God's prophets.

But our dispensation is different from all others in that it includes all that was given to previous dispensations as well as many new things. The Apostle Paul taught this in his day: "In the dispensation of the fulness of times he [the Lord] might *gather together in one all things in Christ,* both which are in heaven, and which are on earth; even in him" (Ephesians 1:10). Joseph Smith described it in these words:

> The work of the Lord in these last days, is one of vast magnitude and almost beyond the comprehension of mortals. Its glories are past description, and its grandeur unsurpassable. It is the theme which has animated the bosom of prophets and righteous men from the creation of the world down through every succeeding generation to the present time; and it is truly the dispensation of the fulness of times, when all things which are in Christ Jesus, whether in heaven or on the earth, shall be gathered together in Him, and when all things shall be restored, as spoken of by all the holy prophets since the world began; for in it will take place the glorious fulfillment of the promises made to the fathers, while the manifestations of the power of the Most High will be great, glorious, and sublime (Joseph Smith, *Teachings,* 512).

It is our privilege to live in the last days. It is our privilege to live in this, the last dispensation. But with that privilege comes great obligation. Ours is the dispensation to prepare the world, and especially the covenant people of the Lord, for the Second Coming and the ushering in of a thousand years of peace and righteousness. And we cannot do that until we gather them in from the premortal, mortal, and spirit world. That fact alone validates President Nelson's statement that this is the most crucial time in the history of the world.

The dispensation of the fulness of times will be unique in many ways, but here are several of the most important:

First, ours is the first truly *global* dispensation. Never before has the gospel gone to the entire world at the same time.

Second, every other dispensation has seen a dispersion of the Lord's covenant people. This was both a literal dispersion as they migrated ever outward and a spiritual dispersion as they left the covenant. That is being reversed now, and our dispensation is a dispensation of gathering.

Third, we live in a time of great wickedness. This has happened in every dispensation, but ours will see wickedness more widespread, more pervasive, more violent, more enslaving, and more truly evil than the world has ever seen before. We have no idea how many people were killed in the flood of Noah's time. But at no time in history has the world population come even close to the 7.2 billion who live on earth right now. That not only means more wickedness in sheer numbers but also more death when the cleansing judgments come.

Fourth, the good news is that we shall bring more of Abraham's seed back to the covenant than any other dispensation.

President Nelson taught: "This dispensation of the fulness of times was foreseen by God as the time to gather, both in heaven and on earth. . . . This dispensation of the fulness of times would not be limited in time or in location. It would not end in apostasy, and it would fill the world" (Nelson, *Ensign*, November 2006).

A NEW APPROACH IN THE GATHERING OF ISRAEL

This dispensation necessarily started out small and grew slowly. It took 117 years for the Church to reach its first million members. Now there are over 16 million members. Of necessity, the work of gathering in the 1800s was limited to small areas in the eastern half of the United States. When driven out several times, Church members moved into the vastness of the western United States and found a permanent home. But that didn't stop our missionaries from going to countries all over the world to gather people to the covenant. An indicator of their success is that at one time in Nauvoo in the 1840s, there were more people speaking English with a British accent than there were speaking with an American one.

From the new center in Utah, missionary work continued to spread throughout much of the world. During that time, the call to gather involved a physical relocation of families wherever possible. The call from Church leaders was to come to Zion—meaning to where the Church headquarters were located. Eventually tens of thousands of Saints came to the Great Basin areas of North America. They came on foot, by wagon and handcart, and eventually

> *I am very convinced that because of what is going on out in the world, the Lord is sending in His reserves, those spirits held in abeyance until the final days of the dispensation of the fulness of times, when wickedness would so overcome the world that there would be little hope. He sends them into the homes of the Latter-day Saints—young men and young women. They are better prepared and more powerful spiritually than we ever were to meet what is ahead for this Church.*
>
> BOYD K. PACKER,
> "ONE IN THINE HAND,"
> ADDRESS AT NEW MISSION PRESIDENTS' SEMINAR, JUNE 22, 2005

by railroad. By the time the transcontinental railroad was finished in 1869, an estimated 70- to 80,000 Latter-day Saints had gathered to the American West, representing a phenomenal growth in those first fifty years of the Church's existence.

But by the late nineteenth century and the early decades of the twentieth century, the First Presidency began calling on members to stay in their home countries and build up the Church there. Though many still felt the pull to come to Zion, congregations in Europe, Central and South America, the Pacific Islands, and Asia were established. Still, up until the 1960s, the stakes of Zion—one of the surest signs of Church strength and stability—were still mostly found in the western third of the United States and Canada.

About that time, something of great significance took place. There was a formal and official change in policy related to the gathering. In 1977, President Spencer W. Kimball, then President of the Church, held a series of conferences in South America, which was a strong indicator of the growth that was taking place there and elsewhere. Elder Bruce R. McConkie of the Twelve was asked to accompany him. In a conference in Lima, Peru, in February of that year, Elder McConkie spoke of the gathering of Israel and described how it was undergoing a major change. Here are some excerpts from that seminal address:

> The gathering of Israel and the establishment of Zion in the latter days is divided into three periods or phases. The first phase is past; we are now living in the second phase; and the third lies ahead. Prophecies speak of them all. If we do not rightly divide the word of God, as Paul's expression is, we will face confusion and uncertainty. If on the other hand we correctly envision our proper role and know what should be done today, we shall then be able to use our time, talents, and means to the best advantage in building up the kingdom and preparing a people for the second coming of the Son of Man.
>
> The three phases of this great latter-day work are as follows:
>
> Phase I—From the First Vision, the setting up of the kingdom on April 6, 1830, and the coming of Moses on April 3, 1836, to the secure establishment of the Church in the United States and Canada, a period of about 125 years.
>
> Phase II—From the creation of stakes of Zion in overseas areas, beginning in the 1950s, to the second coming of the Son of Man, a period of unknown duration.
>
> Phase III—From our Lord's second coming until the kingdom is perfected and the knowledge of God covers the earth as the waters

cover the sea, and from then until the end of the Millennium, a period of 1,000 years.

With that historical foundation established, Elder McConkie then described the process of gathering that prevailed in the Church at that time and would continue to do so from that point to the Second Coming of Christ:

> We are living in a new day. The Church of Jesus Christ of Latter-day Saints is fast becoming a worldwide church. Congregations of Saints are now, or soon will be, strong enough to support and sustain their members no matter where they reside. Temples are being built wherever the need justifies. We can foresee many temples in South America in process of time. [As of this writing there are seventeen operating temples in South America, with several more announced or under construction.]
>
> Stakes of Zion are also being organized at the ends of the earth. In this connection, let us ponder these truths: A stake of Zion is a part of Zion. You cannot create a stake of Zion without creating a part of Zion. Zion is the pure in heart; we gain purity of heart by baptism and by obedience. A stake has geographical boundaries. To create a stake is like founding a City of Holiness. Every stake on earth is the gathering place for the lost sheep of Israel who live in its area.
>
> The gathering place for Peruvians is in the stakes of Zion in Peru, or in the places which soon will become stakes. The gathering place for Chileans is in Chile; for Bolivians it is in Bolivia; for Koreans it is in Korea; and so it goes through all the length and breadth of the earth. Scattered Israel in every nation is called to gather to the fold of Christ, to the stakes of Zion, as such are established in their nations (McConkie, "Come: Let Israel Build Zion," *Ensign*, May 1977).

On their return to Salt Lake City, President Kimball asked that Elder McConkie's talk be published in the May 1977 edition of the *Ensign*, along with the April 1977 general conference addresses, even though the talk had not been given in general conference.

SUMMARY AND CONCLUSIONS

With a context of the true gathering of Israel well established in our minds, we are prepared to begin our focus on what the prophets have said about the last days and the Second Coming of the Lord Jesus Christ. Our current prophet obviously has a great sense of urgency about this work.

Speaking to a gathering of Saints in early September 2019, President Nelson said: "There are exciting things ahead, and there is more to come. This work is moving forward at an accelerating pace. I can hardly wait to bounce out of bed each morning and see what the new day will bring" (*Deseret News*, September 2, 2019, A5).

Part II

How Soon the End?

CHAPTER 6

"It Is Nigh, Even at the Doors"

There is a lot of difficulty in the world. What's the world coming to? Will it survive? We had a family meeting a year or two ago. There was much worry and foreboding: "Will the world hold together?" When they asked me to speak, I said, "I want you to buy two spruce trees, Colorado blue spruce, just little seedlings. The reason I choose those is because they are the slowest growing tree I know of. Plant them about thirty feet apart. Then buy a hammock and wait for the trees to grow. When they grow, you can swing in the hammock between the trees. Will the world still be there? Oh, yes. You will be able to marry and give in marriage, you'll be able to have a family, see your children and grandchildren as we have done, and now, as we are doing, welcome great-grandchildren. The world will still be here and you will be somebody. You'll be in the right place!" (Boyd K. Packer, Mine Errand From the Lord: Selections From the Sermons and Writings of Boyd K. Packer, 400)

NOT EVEN THE ANGELS

After His Resurrection, Jesus returned to be with His followers for a time. Some have called this time His forty-day postmortal ministry because Luke tells us that he was "seen of them forty days" (Acts 1:3). We are told only a little about what He did during that time other than that He spoke "of the things pertaining to the kingdom" (Acts 1:3).

In His last meeting with the disciples, they asked Him a question that we would all like the answer to: "Lord, wilt thou at this time restore again the kingdom to Israel?" (Acts 1:6). His answer should not surprise us: "It is not for you to know the times or the seasons, which the Father hath put in his own power" (Acts 1:7). He then told them to stay in Jerusalem until they received the Holy Ghost, which He had promised to them earlier and which would come on the day of Pentecost (see Acts 2). And with those words, "while they beheld, he was taken up; and a cloud received him out of their sight" (Acts 1:9). What happened next would be shared with His current and future followers for many generations to come:

> And while they looked steadfastly toward heaven as he went up, behold, two men stood by them in white apparel; which also said, Ye men of Galilee, why stand ye gazing up into heaven? this same Jesus, which is taken up from you into heaven, shall so come in like manner as ye have seen him go into heaven (Acts 1:10–11).

We are not told who was there on that occasion, or even how many. We can assume it included the Apostles, though there were only eleven of them now. (They would choose a replacement for Judas not long after this experience.)

Knowing human nature as we do, it is likely that it wasn't long before questions started to come up, such as, "If He is coming again, when will that be?" "Will we have any indicators, any signs, that it is growing near so we can prepare for it?" "If so, what are those signs?" "Will we then be taken up into heaven?" "How do we prepare ourselves for that day?" These were questions that would be asked for centuries to come, and that are still being asked by believers all around the world even now.

And again, knowing human nature as we do, it shouldn't surprise us that it wasn't long before some people decided that the time had arrived. From the Apostle Paul, we learn that this happened within a few decades of the Savior's ascension. On his third missionary journey, Paul had stopped in Thessalonica, in the province of Macedonia, and had found success there. It is likely that he and other missionaries would have taught that Christ was coming again sometime in the future. Some years later, Paul received word that the Thessalonians were having some serious problems. Someone was teaching that the return of the Master was about to happen. For those early

---

I know that many of you have wondered in your hearts what all of this means regarding the end of the world and your life in it. Many have asked, "Is this the hour of the Second Coming of the Savior and all that is prophesied surrounding that event?"

JEFFREY R. HOLLAND, "PREPARING FOR THE SECOND COMING: TERROR; TRIUMPH; AND A WEDDING FEAST," BYU DEVOTIONAL, SEPTEMBER 12, 2004

Saints, most of whom had converted from paganism and were like little children when it came to gospel understanding, this would have been electrifying news. From what Paul wrote to them, it is clear that they were so convinced that they would be caught up to meet Him that they had put everything else aside, including leaving their occupations, and were sitting around waiting to be taken up at any moment. Paul rebuked them sharply. He said they had become little more than "busybodies" (see 2 Thessalonians 3:10–12).

> *Be watchful and be sober, looking forth for the coming of the Son of Man, for he cometh in an hour you think not.*
>
> D&C 61:38

Paul then clearly taught them that Christ's return would not come before there had been a "falling away" in the Church (see 2 Thessalonians 2:1–4). The Greek word Paul used there was *apostasia*, which means a defection from the faith. As we know, other prophets had spoken of a time of great apostasy in the Church and foretold that there would be a restoration of the true Church sometime in the latter days (see, for example, Acts 3:21).

We do not have record of how the Thessalonians responded to Paul's correction. But we do know that they were not the last believers who would be lured into thinking that they were the favored ones.

The idea that Christ will soon come down from the heavens in all His glory is so wonderful, so sensational, that virtually every generation since has wondered if their generation would be the ones to see it actually happen. Here is just a small sample of the dozens of times this has happened:

- Three early and distinguished Christian theologians, after a careful study of the prophecies, predicted that the Millennium would begin in A.D. 500. It didn't.
- In A.D. 536, a cataclysmic volcanic eruption in Iceland plunged large areas of the world into near darkness for eighteen months, bringing crop failure, disease, bitter cold, and many deaths. It was widely believed that this was proof that the world was coming to an end and, therefore, Christ's coming would follow shortly thereafter. This didn't happen.
- An esteemed mathematician calculated that the Millennium would start at 8:00 a.m. on October 19, 1533. It didn't.
- In 1534 an unusual alignment of the planets was seen as a sign of the

- end of times by a group of Protestants. They took control of an entire city and proclaimed it to be the New Jerusalem. Jesus never came.
- In the early history of the Church, some members were influenced by George Miller and Ann Lee, respective founders of the Adventist and Shaker movements and, like the Thessalonians, began to wait for His coming. Section 49 of the Doctrine and Covenants was given to refute those teachings. In that revelation the Lord said that the "time is nigh at hand," but that "the hour and the day no man knoweth, neither the angels in heaven, *nor shall they know until he comes*" (D&C 49:6–7). The other churches and a few of the Saints rejected the revelation when it was presented to them.
- A modern and tragic example made world headlines in the early 1990s. A group calling themselves the Branch Davidians, led by David Koresh, who claimed he was the Anointed One, gathered together and prepared for Christ's return. When federal agents moved in to seize illegal weapons, fire broke out. Seventy-four people, including Koresh, died. He wasn't the Anointed One.
- As the twenty-first century approached, people all around the world were certain that the year 2000 would usher in the Millennium. Now, twenty years later, we are still waiting.
- In 2012, the Mayan calendar made world headlines. The Mayan calendar used a complex system of three interacting calendars. Modern scholars interpreted it to mean that on December 21 of that year, what the Mayans called a "Great Cycle" of one of its "long counts" would come to an end, triggering massive natural disasters. If readers don't remember any of those disasters occurring on that day, it is not because their memory is faulty.

Ironically, none of this seems to discourage zealous followers of the Messiah from making new predictions and new calculations. When it is pointed out that Jesus said no one would know the day, they brush that aside, claiming that they have studiously examined the scriptural record

> *People often ask the Apostles, "When is the Second Coming going to be?" I've got the answer. "I don't know." It won't be today or tomorrow, because there is much work that needs to be done before that can come. All I know for sure is that we are a day closer today than we were yesterday.*
>
> Russell M. Nelson,
> *Teachings*, 351

and under the inspiration of heaven have finally "figured it out," notwithstanding the word of the Lord.

"THE TIME SOON COMETH"

When the angel Moroni came to Joseph Smith in the fall of 1823, after telling him about a record written upon gold plates, he cited several Bible prophecies. Here are excerpts from Joseph's account: "He quoted the eleventh chapter of Isaiah, saying that it was *about to be fulfilled.* He quoted also the third chapter of Acts, twenty-second and twenty-third verses, . . . He said that that prophet was Christ; but the day had not yet come . . . but *soon would come.* He also quoted the second chapter of Joel, from the twenty-eighth verse to the last. He also said that this was not yet fulfilled, but was *soon to be.* And he further stated that the fulness of the Gentiles *was soon to come in*" (JS—H 1:40–41).

> *We live . . . in the days preceding the Lord's Second Coming, a time long anticipated by believers through the ages. We live in days of wars and rumors of wars, days of natural disasters, days when the world is pulled by confusion and commotion.*
>
> Neil L. Andersen,
> "Thy Kingdom Come,"
> Ensign, May 2015

Four different times we have angelic testimony that the end times are soon to come or about to be fulfilled. And that is not all. When Joseph Smith and Oliver Cowdery received additional keys of the priesthood from Moses, Elias, and Elijah in the Kirtland Temple, Elijah declared, "By this [the coming of the three messengers] ye may know that the great and dreadful day of the Lord *is near, even at the doors*" (D&C 110:16). The Lord says that the time is near in about fifteen other places in scripture.

In the parable of the ten virgins, Christ taught that the bridegroom, who represents Christ, comes "at midnight" (Matthew 25:6). In a revelation given in October 1830, the Lord declared that it was "the eleventh hour" (D&C 33:3), a seeming reference to the parable. The Lord added that this would be the *last time* He called laborers into the vineyard (D&C 33:3; see also Jacob 5:62–63; D&C 24:19; 43:28; 95:4).

In the preface to the Doctrine and Covenants the Lord tells us that "the *day speedily cometh;* the hour is not yet, but is *nigh at hand,* when peace shall be taken from the earth" (D&C 1:35). The Savior personally declares in numerous places that "*I come quickly*" (D&C 33:18; 34:12; 35:27; 39:24; 41:4; 49:28; and multiple others). He also says, "Behold, I will *hasten my work* in its time" (D&C 88:73). Early in the history of the Church the Lord said, "The day *soon cometh* that ye shall see me, and know that I am" (D&C 38:8). The phrase "soon cometh," referring to His coming, is found in nine other places.

So it seems we have a dilemma. Over and over the Lord has indicated that the time of the end is near and that the day of His coming will be soon. And yet most of those scriptural passages are now almost two hundred years old, but we are still waiting for their fulfillment. So how are we to interpret words like "close," "quickly," "soon," "hasten," and "speedily"? This is why some, including some faithful Church members, claim that we have no reason to believe that the Second Coming is not still five or six hundred years away, and that we are working ourselves up into a dither over nothing.

To understand these prophecies, we need to consider some things about time, such as how we perceive time and how we are interpreting the pertinent scriptural terminology. In doing so, perhaps many of these seeming contradictions can be explained.

A PROBLEM WITH HOW WE PERCEIVE TIME

Here are some things to consider as we contemplate issues related to time and the future:

1. *We must be careful that we don't assume that our interpretation of what a word or phrase means is the right one, or the only one.* For example, let's examine more closely what Moroni said to Joseph Smith on September 21, 1823. He quoted the eleventh chapter of Isaiah, saying that it was *about to be fulfilled.* Some people assume that is a reference to Christ's Second Coming. But a reading of that chapter shows that while there are references to things that are still in the future for us—e.g., the return of the ten tribes (see Isaiah 11:16)—most of the chapter has reference to other things, such as the raising up of a prophet in the latter days, the Restoration of the kingdom of God, and the beginning of the gathering in of the house of Israel. We now know that the prophet was Joseph Smith and that the kingdom is The Church of Jesus Christ of Latter-day Saints. In other words, Joseph's call was being fulfilled even as Moroni spoke, and the promise that the kingdom of God was to be restored to the earth again was less than seven years away. That certainly qualifies as "about to be fulfilled."

As another example, Moroni cited Joel and said that "this was not yet fulfilled, but was *soon to be*." Here is part of that passage: "And it shall come to pass afterward, that I will pour out my spirit upon all flesh; and your sons and your daughters shall prophesy, your old men shall dream dreams, your young men shall see visions" (Joel 2:28). Again, if we assume that is something that will happen only after the Savior comes again, then it is still in the future for us. But if we consider that when the Church was restored, the gift of the Holy Ghost was once again available to its members and revelation began to be poured out upon the people, then that too was just a few short years away from its fulfillment.

In summary, Moroni wasn't just talking about things that we are still awaiting. Some things were, as Elijah put it, truly "at the doors" (D&C 110:16).

2. *In our day and age, we perceive time and deal with the passage of time much differently than most other generations did.* In this day, time is so intertwined in our daily lives that we rarely even think about the concept of time itself. Here are some examples of that:

- Unlike our ancestors of ages past, our *measurement of time* is very precise. Some Olympic events are measured down to a thousandth of a second. Atomic clocks can measure a millionth of a second. We constantly measure our lives in hours, minutes, and occasionally even seconds, whereas centuries ago, people measured their time in days, weeks, seasons, and years.
- Because of that, our lives are filled with devices that track time for us. They are almost omnipresent. The next time we change to or from daylight saving time, count the number of clocks that must be adjusted to reflect that time change. We are usually not aware of how much our lives are influenced by time.
- But millions, even billions, of people have lived—and still do!—using only the sun, the moon, and the stars to mark the passage of time.

A good example of different views of time is found in King Benjamin's final sermon. Quoting the words of an angel, Benjamin told his people that "the time cometh, and *is not far distant*, that with power, the Lord . . . shall come down from heaven among the children of men. . . . And he shall rise . . . from the dead" (Mosiah 3:5, 10). King Benjamin was speaking in 124 B.C., which means that Christ's birth was still over a century away. And the visit of the resurrected Christ to the Nephites was still 158 years in the future! This difference in our perception of time is a reality that we have to take into account.

3. *Time is a constant, but our perception of time is relative and can vary from one moment to another.* Here's a simple example of this fact. A

person—let's call her Sally—gets a twenty-minute break twice each day during her eight-hour shift at her workplace. After a while, she notices how quickly that time passes. Barely has she sat down, it seems, when her break time is over. Then one day she has an idea. She finds a place to sit where there is a wall clock right above her. As she rests, she frequently glances up at the time, and to her surprise, the time seems to pass much more slowly. She knows that it actually doesn't, but it *feels* like it does, and so thereafter that is where she takes her breaks.

Though we may not consciously think of this phenomenon, we have all experienced it. For example, when we are under a tight deadline on an important task, we are dismayed at how rapidly time races by. On the other hand, when we are anxiously waiting for something important to happen, we may feel that the hours are dragging on. Older people often say things like, "That was twenty years ago now, but it seems just like yesterday." Often, two individuals going through the same experience will perceive the passage of time very differently—for example, a boy and girl on their first date.

4. *We are taught that God does not experience or perceive time in the same way humans do.* We don't fully understand how this is possible, but there are several scriptures that teach that God perceives time differently than we do. A question was once put to Joseph Smith about time: "Is not the reckoning of God's time, angel's time, prophet's time, and man's time, according to the planet on which they reside?" What Joseph said about God and time is intriguing: "The angels . . . reside in the presence of God, on a globe like a sea of glass and fire, *where all things for their glory are manifest, past, present, and future, and are continually before the Lord*" (D&C 130:4, 6–7).

In the presence of God all things are manifest (which means "made clear"), including what is *past, present,* and *future,* and are continually before the Lord. That is a mind-blowing concept, for in this life, time comes to us in a linear fashion. We can remember the past and imagine the future, but we can only experience the present. And that moment we call "the present" is always, inexorably moving forward. But what Joseph taught seems to suggest that God is *above* the timeline, not *on* it. Thus He can look "down" on us and see our past, our present, and our future simultaneously. This would explain one of His divine attributes, that He is an all-knowing Being. Understanding that concept is very difficult for us, for we are what might be called "time blind." Therefore, we need to be cautious about making sweeping generalizations about time as we perceive it.

This idea about God and time is confirmed in other scriptures. When Alma was teaching Corianton—the son who had committed fornication while serving as a missionary—he made this statement: *"All is as one day with God, and time only is measured unto men"* (Alma 40:8).

In the opening verses of one of the revelations the Savior gave through Joseph Smith, the Savior described Himself in various ways—Lord God, Jesus Christ, the Great I AM, Alpha and Omega—and then He said that He was "the same which looked upon the wide expanse of eternity, and all the seraphic hosts of heaven, before the world was made; the same *which knoweth all things, for all things are present before mine eyes"* (D&C 38:1–2).

"Present" is an interesting word because it has two definitions. One is related to space. In that sense, to be present means to be "here." But the word is also related to time, and in that sense it means "now." Could it be that both meanings of present were meant in this statement by the Savior, that all things are *here* to Him and all time is *now* to Him?

That is a mind-boggling concept, but it is interesting that Albert Einstein proposed a similar idea in his theory of relativity. He said that as a person begins to accelerate until he or she approaches the speed of light, two things happen. All space begins to *contract* until it becomes "here" to that person, and all time begins to *contract* until it becomes "now" to that person. Trying to comprehend how that is possible is enough to give us a headache, but physicists have confirmed Einstein's theory. And that seems to confirm what the scriptures teach us about God and time.

EARTH TIME, KOLOB TIME, AND GOD'S TIME

In his second general epistle to the early members of the Church, Peter wrote: "Be not ignorant of this one thing, that one day is with the Lord as a thousand years, and a thousand years as one day" (2 Peter 3:8). The world has puzzled over that statement ever since.

Fortunately, as is often the case, we are given clarifying information in modern scripture. Through the Urim and Thummim, Abraham was taught that Kolob is a celestial body that God said was "near unto me" (Abraham 3:3). Abraham was also taught that one revolution of Kolob (its orbit, we presume) was "a day unto the Lord, after his manner or reckoning," but was "one thousand years" in our time reckoning (Abraham 3:4). This not only confirms what Peter said but enlightens us further on its meaning.

So why does this matter to us in this discussion on how soon the coming of the Son of Man will be? Because it gives us another perspective—God's perspective—on time. We now know that it is not only our perception of time that influences how we experience it, but also where we are in space—another thing Einstein postulated. More importantly, we now have a precise comparison of our time and God's time. So with that, let's do some mathematical conversions from the "Lord's time" to "our time."

- If one of the Lord's "days" is 1,000 of our years, then one of his "weeks" would be 7,000 of our years. (This idea of the earth existing for only a "week" is found in the book of Revelation, which will be discussed in the next chapter.)
- On that same scale, our coming Millennium would last for only *one* of the Lord's days. This gives more meaning to a phrase from one of our hymns: "Beautiful, bright Millennial *day*" (*Hymns*, no. 52). It also helps us better understand why the Millennium is sometimes called the "Day of the Lord" (see, for example, 2 Nephi 12:2; D&C 2:1; 43:20) and why the Lord could say that He is coming "tomorrow" (D&C 64:24).
- On that same scale, one "hour" of the Lord's time would be 41.7 years of our time on earth.
- One "minute" of the Lord's time would be 254 of our "days," or about two-thirds of a year.

With those comparisons, let us now make some extrapolations between our time and God's time. Hopefully, this will change how we think of words such as "soon," "quickly," "nigh," and so on. As noted above, most of these phrases are found in revelations that were given almost 200 years ago, which is several complete "lifetimes" for us. But consider this:

- The current lifespan of a person in the United States is about seventy-nine years. In the Lord's time, that's not quite two hours.
- If we use Kolob time, 200 of our years—the time since these revelations were given—is only 2.9% of the total time of the earth's 7,000 years of existence.
- If a family had a daughter serving an eighteen-month mission, and she had only 2.9% of her time left, she would be home in fifteen days. We would not think it odd if the mother said that her daughter would be home "very soon."
- If a person were serving a twenty-year term of service in the military and would be released in seven more months (2.9% of the total time), it would not surprise us if he or she referred to the required time of enlistment as being "nearly over."

SUMMARY AND CONCLUSIONS

While this is all very interesting, I hope it gives us a new perspective on the scriptural use of "time" terminology. As noted, there are some who ask a different question. It goes something like this: "Every generation since the time of Christ has had people who were absolutely certain that Christ would come in their day. Here we are, two thousand years later, and we still hear that same claim. What hard evidence do we have that we're not just like all the others and that His coming is not still five or six hundred years in the future?"

It is a good question. And before answering it, we need to make one thing clear. We are not suggesting that the Second Coming could happen any day now—or even next year. There are still too many things left to be done. However, the pace of prophetic fulfillment is increasing, and our prophets, seers, and revelators keep reminding us that the time for preparation is here.

When it comes to the idea that Christ's coming is still another five or six hundred years off, we have scriptural evidence that suggests otherwise. In fact, the Lord has given us a very specific time indicator that we shall explore in the next chapter.

CHAPTER 7

THE SIGNS OF THE TIMES

The only safety we have as members of this church is to do exactly what the Lord said to the Church in that day when the Church was organized. We must learn to give heed to the words and commandments that the Lord shall give through His prophet, "as he receiveth them, walking in all holiness before me; . . . as if from mine own mouth, in all patience and faith" (D&C 21:4–5). There will be some things that take patience and faith. You may not like what comes from the authority of the Church. It may contradict your political views. It may contradict your social views. It may interfere with some of your social life. But if you listen to these things, as if from the mouth of the Lord Himself, with patience and faith, the promise is that "the gates of hell shall not prevail against you; yea, and the Lord God will disperse the powers of darkness from before you, and cause the heavens to shake for your good, and his name's glory" (D&C 21:6). (Harold B. Lee, *Teachings*, 526)

THE TIMES IN WHICH WE LIVE

In the chapter on the voice of warning, we noted that sometimes we are warned of danger or other problems through visual cues such as traffic signs or warning labels. These inform us of possible risk and allow us to take appropriate action to protect ourselves or those we love. In the scriptures we find similar warnings, which are called the "*signs* of the times" or "the *signs* of the coming of the Son of Man" (D&C 68:11; 45:39).

Noah Webster's *American Dictionary of the English Language*, which was published in 1828, is particularly valuable to help us understand the meaning of words as they were used at the time of Joseph Smith. We're not suggesting that Joseph Smith used that dictionary—we have no evidence of that. But we know that word usage can change dramatically over time as cultural norms change, so it is instructive to see what a word typically meant at the time it was used.

Webster's first definition of the word *sign* states that it is "a token; something by which another thing is shown or represented, . . . [something that] indicates the existence or approach of something else" (Webster, s.v. "sign"). Note especially that last phrase, that a sign is something that indicates the approach of something else. Here is an example of that.

Back in the fifties and sixties, following World War II and the Korean War, the United States was fully engaged in what was known as the Cold War. The primary foe in that "war" was the Union of Soviet Socialist Republics, or the USSR, with Russia as its head. Numerous countries in Europe were under Communist domination. The rights of their citizens were severely curtailed. It was the time of the Berlin Wall, which divided Germany. The nightly news was filled with images of barbed wire, political prisoners, closed borders, guard towers with machine gun emplacements, and tanks rumbling through the streets of major cities.

> *These signs of the Second Coming are all around us and seem to be increasing in frequency and intensity. . . . We are living in the prophesied time "when peace shall be taken from the earth," when "all things shall be in commotion," and "men's hearts shall fail them." There are many temporal causes of commotion, including wars and natural disasters, but an even greater cause of current "commotion" is spiritual.*
>
> DALLIN H. OAKS,
> "PREPARATION FOR THE SECOND COMING," *ENSIGN*, MAY 2004

I graduated from high school in the mid-fifties, so those scenes were very much a part of my growing-up years. As noted earlier, one of the topics of conversation common in the Church then was if we would see the Church established in the USSR in our lifetimes, and the common response was no. And yet . . .

- In 2010, President Thomas S. Monson dedicated a temple in Kyiv, Ukraine, the first temple in the former USSR.
- Elder Russell M. Nelson of the Quorum of the Twelve Apostles, on assignment from the First Presidency, organized the Moscow Russia Stake in June 2011—the first stake in Russia and the second in the former Soviet Union.

- In general conference, April 2018, President Russell M. Nelson announced the first temple in Russia, at a site yet to be determined.

Each of these was an astonishing development.

Many centuries ago the prophet Amos made this sweeping statement: "Surely the Lord God will do nothing, but he revealeth his secret unto his servants the prophets" (Amos 3:7). And in the Book of Mormon, we learn, "A *seer* can know of things which are past, and also of things which are to come, and by them . . . *shall secret things be made manifest, and hidden things shall come to light, and things which are not known shall be made known* by them" (Mosiah 8:17).

So it was with Russia. To my surprise, some years after I had completed *The Coming of the Lord*, I discovered a statement by Elder Melvin J. Ballard, of the Quorum of the Twelve. Back in 1930, just as the Great Depression began, and half a century before the breakup of the Soviet Empire, Elder Ballard spoke about Russia in general conference. This was just nine years after the Russian revolution that brought Joseph Stalin to power. In other words, it was right at the height of Russia's power as one of the world's greatest totalitarian states:

> I am sure also that God is moving in Russia. Much as we are disturbed over the tyranny and the oppression that is waged against religion in that land today, it is not a new thing, for that has been the order for ages. *But I can see God moving also in preparing the way for other events that are to come.* The field that has gone to wild oats needs to be plowed up and harrowed and prepared for a new seed. So in Russia. It may seem appalling to us, but it is God breaking up and destroying an older order of things [viz, the brutal reign of the czars], and the process will be the accomplishment of God's purposes *within a very short period of time,* which normally may have taken generations. *But that people will come back,* for I bear witness that there are thousands of the blood of Israel in that land, and God is preparing the way for them (Melvin J. Ballard, in Conference Report, April 1930, 157).

What I have learned in my further studies is that there wasn't just one prophecy about Russia. Just a few months after the end of World War II, with Russia now a major world power, President George Albert Smith made this remarkable statement. Note the specificity of his prophecy:

> This gospel must be preached in all the world. We must preach the gospel to the South American countries which we have scarcely

touched. We must preach the gospel to every African section that we haven't been in yet. We must preach the gospel to Asia, and I might go on and say in all parts of the world where we have not yet been permitted to go. *I look upon Russia as one of the most fruitful fields for the teaching of the gospel of Jesus Christ.* And if I am not mistaken, it will not be long before the people who are there will desire to know something about this work (George Albert Smith, *Teachings*, 151).

Fifteen years after that, while serving as President of the Church, David O. McKay also spoke about Russia's future:

Can you not see many yet need to hear the truth, . . . Jews as well as Gentiles! India and China both awaking, Russia enveloped with communism—*a new religious freedom must come,* God will overrule it, for *that people must hear the truth,* and truth in its simplicity. *Truly there is much for this Church to do in the coming century!* (McKay, *Church News*, May 28, 1960, 9).

"SUMMER IS NIGH, BE NOT TROUBLED"

Here's an interesting lesson on the signs of the times from the Savior Himself. In chapter 1, we talked about what is called the Olivet Discourse. This was the Savior's prophetic discourse on the future that He gave to His disciples in Jerusalem shortly before His death. In section 45 of the Doctrine and Covenants, we find another account of the Olivet Discourse. After listing the signs of the times that would come in the last days, the Savior said, "And now, when I the Lord had spoken these words unto my disciples, *they were troubled*" (D&C 45:34).

That is not surprising, but it does lead modern readers to exclaim: "*They were troubled?* Much of what Jesus foretold would not happen until our day. If they were troubled with what they saw, what does that mean for those of us who are living in the actual times of which Jesus prophesied?"

What the Savior said next was not just for the Twelve back then, but for our day too: "And I said unto them: *Be not troubled,* for when all these things shall come to pass, ye may know that the promises which have been made unto you shall be fulfilled" (D&C 45:35). Then He explained how it is that we can "be not troubled."

Ye look and behold the fig trees, and ye see them with your eyes, and ye say when they begin to shoot forth, and their leaves are yet tender, that summer is now nigh at hand; Even so it shall be in that day *when they shall see all these things,* then shall *they know that the hour is nigh.* And it shall come to pass that he that feareth me shall be looking forth for the great day of the Lord to come, even for the signs of the coming of the Son of Man (D&C 45:37–39).

Jesus likened the signs of the times to the leaves of a fig tree. To better understand that metaphor, we need to understand why the Savior would pick the fig tree over other trees. Here is what a Christian minister, who spent much of his life in the Holy Land, taught about the nature of the fig tree: "The fig-tree comes into foliage later than the almond, apricot, and peach trees, and when its tender leaves are unsheathed, and expand and deepen in colour, it is a sign that summer days are at hand" (George M. Mackie, *Bible Manners and Customs*, 51).

As cited earlier, when Elijah came to the Kirtland Temple, he said this: "By this ye may know that the *great* and *dreadful* day of the Lord is near, even at the doors" (D&C 110:16). This is the same phrase that Malachi used when he prophesied of Elijah's coming (see Malachi 4:5).

The Hebrew word that is translated as "dreadful" can imply what we think of as true fear and dread, but it also connotes more of a sense of awe, reverence, and astonishment than actual fear. That is an important difference, for as terrible as these things may be, when we know that the Lord's prophets have warned us of them—sometimes centuries in advance—it provides a powerful confirmation that the Lord knows all things and will prepare His people for them. And in that knowledge we can "be not troubled."

Again, Webster's dictionary of American English is helpful. The primary sense of the word *trouble* in 1828 was "to turn or to stir, to whirl about, as in the Latin *turbo,* a whirlwind. . . . To agitate, to disturb, to put into confused motion" (*Webster's Dictionary, 1828,* s.v. "trouble").

In modern use, *troubled* is usually a milder word, conveying a sense of unease, worry, or discomfort, but not wild panic or hopelessness. It seems that the Lord is *not* saying, "Don't be concerned about what is coming," but rather, "Don't be so troubled by it that you are paralyzed with fear and lose your faith." Elder Neal A. Maxwell said a similar thing:

> After the Savior had spoken of some of the specific signs of His second coming, He gave to His disciples, and to us all, the parable of the fig tree. When the fig tree puts forth its leaves, He said, we may know that "summer is nigh." Similarly, we may be warned by certain accumulating signs that His second coming is nigh. The "summer" Jesus cited is upon us. We must neither complain of the

heat nor let that heat, . . . wither our individual tree of testimony, because we will surely feel the heat of that summer sun in our individual lives as the prophesied developments occur on this planet (Maxwell, *We Will Prove Them Herewith*, 78).

When the Savior said to His disciples and then again to us, "Be not troubled," He was not suggesting that we be all smiles and laughter in the face of the world collapsing around us. But He has promised us again and again that He will preserve His people and that we need not fear (see, for example, 1 Nephi 22:17, 19, 22), and it is with this perspective that we can "be not troubled."

President Dallin H. Oaks put things in perspective with this counsel:

> Four matters are indisputable to Latter-day Saints: (1) The Savior will return to the earth in power and great glory to reign personally during a millennium of righteousness and peace. (2) At the time of His coming there will be a destruction of the wicked and a resurrection of the righteous. (3) No one knows the time of His coming, but (4) the faithful are taught to study the signs of it and to be prepared for it (Oaks, "Preparation for the Second Coming," *Ensign*, May 2004).

There are many signs of the times found in the scriptures that have come from ancient and modern prophets. Some are dreadful and some are great, just as Elijah said. But all are meant to instruct us, warn us, and give us courage and hope for the future. In 2015, Elder Neil L. Andersen gave some examples of signs we see all around us:

> My brothers and sisters, we live in very interesting times. Here are some selected statistics from recent studies:
>
> Worldwide there has been a 35 percent increase in terrorist attacks in the past year.
>
> In 2013, 41 percent of all births in the United States were to unmarried women, compared to 18 percent thirty-five years ago.
>
> Adult Americans claiming no religious affiliation increased from 16 percent in 2007 to 23 percent in 2014.
>
> Nearly seven in ten Americans say doctors should be legally allowed to assist terminally ill patients in committing suicide.
>
> There are now more than 43 million refugees worldwide, displaced from their homes because of conflict or persecution.
>
> And how about this very recent concerning headline: "California College Will Now Ask Students to Pick from Six [Different] Genders" in their application for admission. And this one: "Another

Day, Another Mass Shooting in America." Finally, this sobering headline: "Why Selling Baby Parts Should Shock No One." . . . As I said, we live in very interesting times, yet marvelous times. . . . These are days of looking forward, of beautiful anticipation. These are our days (Andersen, "A Compensatory Spiritual Power for the Righteous," BYU Education Week devotional, August 18, 2015, 2–3).

Much of this book will provide detailed discussions on the various signs of the time that have been given to us. We shall group them into two general categories, as suggested by Elijah—the great and the dreadful. But before leaving our topic, let us examine a lesser-known sign of the time that gives us a good example of how signs can specifically help us to "watch, therefore, that ye may be ready" (D&C 50:46). This has to do with rainbows.

THE BOW IN THE CLOUD

When Noah and the other seven members of his family were finally able to leave the ark and start their new lives, Noah built an altar and offered sacrifices to the Lord. "And the Lord said in his heart, I will not again curse the ground any more for man's sake; . . . neither will I again smite any more every thing living, as I have done. While the earth remaineth, seedtime and harvest, and cold and heat, and summer and winter, and day and night shall not cease" (Genesis 8:21–22).

God then blessed Noah and his family. He also reestablished the covenant with them. We are taught some of this in the book of Genesis, but the Joseph Smith Translation of Genesis contains several additions that are directly related to the last days. One of these has to do with rainbows.

The Lord said:

> This shall be *the token of the covenant* I make between me & you. And for . . . perpetual generation & *I will set my bow in the cloud. And it shall be for a token of a covenant between me & the earth.* And it shall come to pass, when I bring a cloud over the earth, that *the bow shall be seen in the cloud;* And I will remember my covenant which I have made between me & you for every living creature of all flesh. And the waters Shall no more become a flood to destroy all flesh ("Old Testament Revision 2," p. 31, *The Joseph Smith Papers*; https://www.josephsmithpapers.org/paper-summary/old-testament-revision-2/38; see also JST, Genesis 9:15–25).

This is a fascinating passage with much material that was lost from the

Bible and restored in our day, and it gives us a sign of the times not found elsewhere in the scriptures. The token is what the Lord called "the bow in the cloud," or what we more commonly call a rainbow.

The rainbow is a lovely and beautiful symbol, for not only is it a thing of great beauty, but in what we might call the "physics" of rainbows we find parallel spiritual lessons. The rainbow shines forth only under two conditions: (1) enough moisture in the air; and (2) sunshine coming at it from the right angle. The rain or moisture could be likened to the storms of life, which are necessary for growth and progression. The sunshine comes when the clouds are beginning to break up, signifying the light of the Lord is brightening our day again.

The insights Joseph Smith gained from the translation of Genesis were of such significance to him that he spoke of them several times. These comments are a blessing to us, for they expand our knowledge and understanding of this phenomenon as well. For example:

> The Lord deals with this people as a tender parent with a child, communicating light and intelligence and the knowledge of his ways, as they can hear it. The inhabitants of the Earth are asleep, they know not the day of their visitation. *The Lord hath set the bow in the cloud for a sign that while it shall be seen, seed time and harvest, summer and winter shall not fail,* but when it shall disappear, woe to that generation, for behold the end cometh quickly ("History, 1838–1856, volume D-1 [1 August 1842–1 July 1843]," p. 1556, *The Joseph Smith Papers*; https://www.josephsmithpapers.org/paper-summary/history-1838-1856-volume-d-1-1-august-1842-1-july-1843/199).

Here are some things of note we learn from what he said:

- Joseph introduced this sign as evidence of the loving and tender concern of our Heavenly Father for His children.
- He also made it clear that in our time it will be as though the inhabitants of the world are in a deep sleep, unaware of the judgments facing them.
- This is why the Lord set the rainbow as a token. In addition to being a token of the covenant God, it was given as an important sign of the times to help us know and prepare for what is coming.
- Note the verb Joseph used in that quote. He said that the bow will "disappear." One natural way for the bow to disappear would be if

there were no rain. If that condition lasted for very long, it could also bring an end to seedtime and harvest.

Thus the token of the rainbow carries with it both a promise and a warning. The promise is that as long as the rainbow is seen, we shall have seedtime and harvest, i.e., there will not be famine. But if there are no rainbows, it suggests that the natural weather cycles will end for a time, and that could have widespread, devastating effects.

A few months before his martyrdom, on March 10, 1844, Joseph again spoke to the Saints about the rainbow:

> I have asked of the Lord concerning his coming & while asking the Lord he gave a sign & said in the days of Noah I set a bow in the heavens as a sign & token that in any year that the bow should be seen the Lord would not come, but there should be seed time & harvest during that year, but whenever you see the bow withdraw, it shall be a token that there shall be famine pestilence & great distress among the nations ("Discourse, 10 March 1844, as Reported by Wilford Woodruff," p. [212], *The Joseph Smith Papers*; https://www.josephsmithpapers.org/paper-summary/discourse-10-march-1844-as-reported-by-wilford-woodruff/8).

In content, this statement is much the same as the first, but there are four small yet significant differences:

- First, Joseph actually quotes the words of the Lord here. He is not paraphrasing.
- In this quote, a specific time span is noted. The Lord says "in any *year* that the bow should be seen," things will continue as normal, suggesting that this may not be a permanent change to the weather. This language could also suggest that this might happen more than once.
- Note that the Lord chose a different verb than Joseph used in recording his insights. Joseph said the bow would *disappear*, but the Lord said the bow would "*withdraw*."
- Here the Lord is more specific on what "woes" will follow. He uses three terms: famine, pestilence, and great distress among the nations. Those would be the natural result of prolonged drought. No rain means a drought. Drought withers and weakens the food crops, which often brings "pests" such as locusts or crickets. They further devastate the food supply, causing famine. Famine drastically affects every aspect of human life, bringing misery and woes. Famine lowers the body's natural resistance, increasing the probability of sickness, disease, and

death—a good definition of great distress. In prolonged famine, even the wealthier classes suffer.
- When Joseph Smith spoke again of the bow on another occasion, he added the word "wars" to this list of consequences (See "Discourse, 10 March 1844, as Reported by Franklin D. Richards," p. [34], *The Joseph Smith Papers*; https://www.josephsmithpapers.org/paper-summary/discourse-10-march-1844-as-reported-by-franklin-d-richards/3). That too could be a natural result of drought—going to war for food, or preying on an enemy too weak to resist.

SUMMARY AND CONCLUSIONS

Though some signs of the times can be troublesome and depressing, nevertheless they forewarn us and give us an opportunity to prepare. However, there are two things to keep in mind when we speak of these signs. First, if we do not know what the signs are, then they are of no worth to us. Therefore we should make it a regular part of our scripture study to watch for, record, and learn from the signs of the times. Remember, there are many signs of the times given in scripture that are not specifically identified as such. Second, if we are aware of the signs of the times but take no action to prepare for them, then they cannot fulfill their purpose. Note this observation from President Jedediah M. Grant, a member of the First Presidency with Brigham Young:

> Why is it that the Latter-day Saints are perfectly calm and serene among all the convulsions of the earth—the turmoils, strife, war, pestilence, famine and distress of nations? It is because *the spirit of prophecy has made known to us that such things would actually transpire upon the earth*. We understand it, and view it in its true light. We have learned it by the visions of the Almighty (Grant, *Improvement Era*, February 1915, 285–86).

By watching and studying the signs of the times—or event markers—as given to us through the Lord's prophets, seers, and revelators, we can remain calm and serene in the midst of the most troubling times. It is in knowing the signs of the times that we can "be not troubled."

CHAPTER 8

THE SEVEN SEALS OF THE APOCALYPSE

And I saw in the right hand of him that sat on the throne a book written within and on the backside, sealed with seven seals. And I saw a strong angel proclaiming with a loud voice, Who is worthy to open the book, and to loose the seals thereof? And no man in heaven, nor in earth, neither under the earth, was able to open the book, neither to look thereon. And I wept much, because no man was found worthy to open and to read the book, neither to look thereon. And one of the elders saith unto me, Weep not: behold, the Lion of the tribe of Judah, the Root of David, hath prevailed to open the book, and to loose the seven seals thereof. (Revelation 5:1–5)

THE BOOK OF REVELATION

Before we begin our study of the book of Revelation, it will be helpful to see how the Lord views the book that He gave to John the Beloved on the Isle of Patmos somewhere around A.D. 100. Surprisingly, it is from the Book of Mormon that we get this perspective. It comes from a passage written by Nephi about 600 B.C.

After his father reported a remarkable dream he'd had about the tree of life, Nephi had a great desire to see the things his father had seen. The Lord answered his prayer, showing him much of what Lehi had witnessed. But in addition, the Lord opened up a vision of the future to Nephi. Basically, this vision rolled out in chronological order, beginning with the mortal ministry of Christ and going up to what is for us the present day, where Nephi saw what he called the church of the Lamb. Note how he described it:

And it came to pass that I beheld the church of the Lamb of God, *and its numbers were few,* because of the wickedness and abominations of the whore who sat upon many waters [the great and abominable church]; *nevertheless, I beheld that the church of the Lamb, who were the saints of God,* were also upon *all the face of the earth; and their dominions upon the face of the earth were small, because of the wickedness of the great whore whom I saw.* . . . And it came to pass that I, Nephi, beheld the power of the Lamb of God, that it descended upon the saints of the church of the Lamb, and upon the covenant people of the Lord, *who were scattered upon all the face of the earth* (1 Nephi 14:12, 14).

That accurately describes our time and our day, as we shall see in a moment. But what has this got to do with the book of Revelation?

A MAN NAMED JOHN

At that point in the vision, the angel who was with Nephi broke in. "Look!" he commanded. Nephi did, and this was what he saw:

And I looked and beheld a man, and he was dressed in a white robe. And the angel said unto me: Behold one of the twelve apostles of the Lamb. *Behold, he shall see and write the remainder of these things.* . . . *And he shall also write concerning the end of the world* (1 Nephi 14:19–22).

At first, it sounds like Nephi's vision had come to an end. But that was not so. The vision would continue, but Nephi would not write about it in his record. That assignment was to go to someone else. The angel continued: "The things which thou shalt see hereafter *thou shalt not write; for the Lord God hath ordained the apostle of the Lamb of God that he should write them.* . . . And I, Nephi, heard and bear record, that *the name of the apostle of the Lamb was John,* according to the word of the angel" (1 Nephi 14:24–25, 27).

> *The book which John saw represented the real history of the world—what the eye of God has seen, what the recording angel has written.*
>
> ORSON F. WHITNEY,
> *SATURDAY NIGHT THOUGHTS*, 11

What an important piece of information that is, for it verifies that the New Testament book we know as "the Revelation of Saint John the Divine" was written under the direction of the Lord.

The book of Revelation, as it is more commonly called, has stirred up much controversy. It is filled with esoteric symbolism and imagery, some of which seems almost bizarre to the Western mind. Part of that comes from the culture of the Middle East, but another factor is that others have tampered with the book through the centuries, as the angel explained to Nephi: "At the time they [John's writings] proceeded out of the mouth of the Jew, . . . *the things which were written were plain and pure, and most precious and easy to the understanding of all men*" (1 Nephi 14:23).

Fortunately for our day, the Lord has raised up prophets again and revealed His will and purposes to them.

THE BOOK WITH SEVEN SEALS

Because it is very esoteric and often obscure, the book of Revelation has inspired many attempts to explain its true meaning, some of which are quite insightful, some of which border on the bizarre. Not long after the Church was organized, the Lord told Joseph Smith that due to poor translators, careless copyists, or corrupt priests who changed the text, the Bible had many errors in it (see Joseph Smith, *Teachings*, 207). Joseph was instructed to begin another "translation" of the Bible. This would not be a translation from ancient languages, but would be more like a revision of the existing text through inspiration and revelation. Joseph immediately began work on what is now called the Joseph Smith Translation.

What is now section 77 of the Doctrine and Covenants is unique in that it asks fifteen questions about the book of Revelation. This likely was given as Joseph was working on John's writings. Some students of the Doctrine and Covenants have expressed disappointment that Joseph asked only fifteen questions, suggesting that they could have come up with a hundred or more. But the fifteen questions Joseph asked under inspiration provide an important key to our understanding of the book.

> *The seven thousand years, corresponding to the seven seals of the Apocalyptic volume are as seven great days during which Mother Earth will fulfill her mortal mission, laboring six days and resting upon the seventh, her period of sanctification. These seven days do not include the period of our planet's creation and preparation as a dwelling place for man. They are limited to Earth's "temporal existence," that is, to Time, considered as distinct from Eternity.*
>
> Orson F. Whitney,
> *Saturday Night Thoughts*, 11

A key is a small thing, of little use for anything other than what it was designed to do—open a lock. However, it is a good analogy as it relates to John's writings. The book of Revelation is like a large room, richly decorated and amply furnished, but available only to those with the key to open the door that provides entry.

Our purpose here is not to examine each of the fifteen questions, but to examine the question of timing in the Lord's plans. And three of the questions Joseph asked are specifically about the Lord's timing.

The opening three chapters of Revelation contain John's description of a personal visitation from the Savior and seven short epistles to branches of the Church that seem to have been under John's leadership. Then, starting in chapter 4, John was caught up into heaven. The remainder of the book of Revelation is his description of what he saw thereafter.

In chapter 4, John saw God the Father on His throne in the celestial kingdom, with various heavenly beings surrounding Him. John saw that the Father held a "book" in His right hand. This was almost certainly a scroll, since bound books were not yet invented. The edge of the scroll was sealed with seven seals. These were dabs of hot wax poured on the paper and stamped with an official insignia so as to ensure that the letter or document would not be read by unauthorized persons.

In the vision, an angel asked if anyone present was able to "open" the book, or break the seals. But no person in heaven, on earth, or under the earth—which pretty well covers it!—was found worthy to open the book. Sensing that this book was highly significant, John began to weep (see Revelation 5:1–4), but an angel told John not to weep and called his attention to another Personage that could open the book. That person was described with three different titles: the Lion of the tribe of Judah, the root of David, and the Lamb which had been slain. All of these are Old Testament titles of the Messiah, or Jesus Christ. The Savior then stepped forth, took the book from the Father, and prepared to open the seals one by one.

Seeing this, a great hymn of joy broke out in heaven (see Revelation 5:5–14). The remainder of the book of Revelation is John's description of what he saw as the seven seals were opened one by one. As mentioned, we shall examine only three of the fifteen questions.

> Q. What are we to understand by the book which John saw, which was sealed on the back with seven seals?
>
> A. We are to understand that it contains the revealed will, mysteries, and the works of God; the hidden things of his economy [or

plan] concerning this earth during the seven thousand years of its continuance, or its temporal existence (D&C 77:6).

- "Mysteries," as used in the scriptures, typically means sacred things of importance that are not generally shared or understood by the world.
- The word "economy" in Joseph Smith's time did not convey financial matters as it does now. Then, the word meant "the management, regulation and government of a family or the concerns of a household" (Webster's, s.v. "economy").
- The phrase "the seven thousand years of its continuance, or its temporal existence" makes it clear that the Lord is not talking about the age of planet earth or of that time when it will become a celestial kingdom after the Millennium. The word *temporal* had two primary meanings at that time: "Pertaining to this life, this earth, or this body," or "measured by or limited by time" (ibid., s.v. "temporal"). This 7,000 years of the world's existence confirms what we learned from both Peter and Abraham, that a day with the Lord is like a thousand of our years.
- A second important point is that, unlike much of the world, we do not believe that this earth and its inhabitants will keep multiplying for untold generations until they either destroy themselves or the sun burns out and everything ceases to exist.

The next question in D&C 77 equally sheds light on the Lord's timing for the last days.

However, before examining what John saw in his vision, we need to briefly discuss the concepts of precision and exactness when it comes to numbers in the scriptures. This is particularly relevant to our discussion on the seven seals of Revelation.

The first problem we encounter concerns numbers that seem to represent a precise point in the past. For example, about 4000 B.C. is widely accepted in Christianity and other religions as the date of the Fall of Adam (see Bible Dictionary, "Chronological Tables"). But the operative word here is "about." We need to remember that we don't know the exact day or even the precise year that Adam fell. Therefore, this date is only an approximation. Nevertheless, it is still a useful approximation.

A second problem with numbers in the scriptures is that some of them are what we call "round numbers." That is especially true in the Bible. In the early centuries of human history, a substantial number of people could not read, write, or do more than basic arithmetic. So the use of "round numbers" was very common then, much more than it is today. A preeminent Bible scholar described round numbers in this way:

> Round numbers; exact tens, hundreds, thousands, etc.; must often have been used by the Israelites on the understanding that they were only approximately accurate; and in the same way smaller numbers were sometimes used indefinitely for "a few." . . . In addition to hundreds, thousands, and ten thousands, the most common number used in the approximate way is "forty": people constantly live or reign for "forty years" or multiples of forty (James Hastings, *Dictionary of the Bible*, 658).

We're not saying that we can't rely on the numbers given in the scriptures—just that we can't assume they are always used with the same precision we use today.

There is a third peculiarity about the use of numbers in the scriptures. A few numbers (and their multiples) carry *symbolic* significance in addition to their *numerical* significance. Here are some that are especially significant:

The number *three* is closely connected with the concept of the Godhead and also the Atonement of Jesus Christ. We see this number occurring again and again in the accounts of the week of the atoning sacrifice in Christ's life. The betrayal price was thirty pieces of silver. Jesus prayed three times in the Garden of Gethsemane. Peter denied Him three times that night. After the Resurrection, Peter was able to affirm his love for the Savior three times. Pilate declared Christ innocent three times. Jesus went before three tribunals: the Sanhedrin, Pilate, and King Herod. There were three crosses on Calvary. Pilate wrote the declaration that Jesus was king of the Jews in three languages. Christ was crucified in the third hour of the day, and died at the ninth hour. And, of course, He was resurrected after three days in the tomb. This is not to suggest that they were only symbolic and not real numbers, only that they can carry symbolic significance too.

Our word *seven* comes from the Hebrew *sheva*, which also means seven. But the root of the Hebrew word connotes "wholeness, completeness, and perfection." This may be why we have seven days in a week. Many things in the Mosaic Law were done seven times to signify they were completing the requirements of the covenant. The Sabbath was the seventh day of the week of creation and became the day for rest and spiritual restoration.

We have already seen that forty can be an approximate number. But it is also often used to signify a time of trial, proving, or testing. Two well-known examples are Israel's wandering in the wilderness for forty years and Jesus's temptation in the wilderness for forty days and nights. It is also interesting that Moses's life is divided into three segments of forty years each—his time as a prince of Egypt, his time as a shepherd in the deserts of Sinai, and his time as the prophet of God. Again we wish to make our point clear. A round number often means that it is an approximation, but that doesn't mean that it is *always* or *only* an approximation. Some numbers also carry symbolic significance, but in most cases those number are also literal numbers. With that understanding in place, let us return now to our discussion of the seven seals.

Q. What are we to understand by the seven seals with which it was sealed?

A. We are to understand that the first seal contains the things of the first thousand years, and the second also of the second thousand years, and so on until the seventh (D&C 77:7).

Here is another powerful key to help us explore the "room" we call the book of Revelation. From chapter 6 on, John records what he was shown when each of the seven seals was opened. One might expect that each of the seven seals would get the same amount of page space. They do not. To understand the significance of that difference, we have to use our present dating system, remembering what we have said about precision and exactness.

Since we do not know exactly when Adam and Eve were expelled from the garden, we shall use the letter *c*, which is the abbreviation for *circa*, the Latin word for "around" or "about," to remind us that we do not know the exact years. In this reckoning, "day one" would be c. 4000–3000 B.C. The second "day" would be c. 3000 B.C. to 2000 B.C., and so on.

The fifth seal, c. A.D. 1 to 1000, includes the life of Christ and the rise of the Christian Church. The sixth seal, c. A.D. 1000 to 2000, includes such things as the Age of Enlightenment, the settlement of the New World, and the opening of the day of Restoration. It is also the "day" in which a large number of current Church members were born.

The final "day," known as the Millennium, will be c. A.D. 2000 to 3000. Thereafter, the earth will become a celestial kingdom for those who have been faithful to their covenants.

It is as simple as that. This is what the Lord has revealed about our earth and the time of its temporal existence.

With that said, we again note that we must be very careful about being too rigid in deciding what the Lord did or did not intend here with these numbers. At first glance, the answers the Lord gave to Joseph Smith seem very clear and unambiguous. What could be plainer than to say that the earth's temporal existence will last for 7,000 years, or a "week" in Kolob time? And He specifically tells us that each "day" will last one thousand of our years. The language seems simple, straightforward, and unambiguous.

But as we have shown in this chapter, it may not always be as simple as that. For example, here are some questions we should ask ourselves:

- Since "thousand" is one of the common "round numbers" found in the Bible, can we automatically assume that the Lord is saying that there will be exactly 7,000 years of 365 days each? Even if it were a hundred years more or less than that, we more literal-minded moderns would be comfortable referring to each "day" as being a thousand years in length.
- As also noted, the number seven is often used symbolically to represent fulness, completeness, and even perfection. Saying that the earth's temporal existence lasts for seven thousand years could suggest the fulness or completeness of its time and purpose. Is it precisely seven thousand years? Possibly. Could it mean "about seven thousand years"? That's possible too, and the key point is that we must be careful not to assume that we know exactly what the Lord meant here.
- The Lord says that each "day" of the earth's existence will be a thousand years. Is that a precise declaration or another approximate one? Suppose, for example, that one of those "days" were actually one thousand and ten years in length, and the next "day" were only nine hundred and ninety years in length. It would be a normal thing even for us to round them off and say that each was a period of a thousand years.

We have taken the time to make this point to remind us that we must be careful when we assume we know precisely what the Lord meant in these passages. And this is a solemn reminder to those who think they can use these scriptures to calculate with great precision where we are on the divine timeline of history, and from that, determine how soon some future events will occur. Some attempt to do this even though the Lord has made it abundantly clear that no one except the Father and the Son knows the precise time of Christ's coming.

THE OPENING OF THE SEVENTH SEAL

When we speak of the Millennium, we know not only that it will occupy the last thousand years of the world's history but also that it will be the most glorious and wonderful time the world has ever known. What makes that possible is that the Millennium begins with the Second Coming of Christ, which will cleanse the earth by fire and usher in a millennium of peace and righteousness. Numerous scriptures attest to this linkage, and a moment or two of reflection suggests why. Without the destruction of all that is wicked and the cleansing of the earth, how could there be a thousand years of faith and righteousness? Christ's return to earth as King of kings and Lord of lords provides the enabling power that makes the Millennium possible.

However, with that said, there is an interesting concept introduced in another question that Joseph put to the Lord.

> Q. When are the things to be accomplished, which are written in the 9th chapter of Revelation?
> A. They are to be accomplished after the opening of the seventh seal [i.e., after the last thousand years begins], before the coming of Christ (D&C 77:13).

And there it is, a concept not specifically taught anywhere else in scripture. The Lord very clearly states that there will be a time—with no enlightenment on the duration of that time—between the beginning of the last thousand years—or the millennium, lowercase *m*—and the time Christ actually comes and ushers in the Millennium, uppercase *M*.

That raises all kinds of questions.

- The first and most obvious is, how long will that time be? We are not told.
- Is it possible that we have already entered into that interim time period? Since we do not know when it begins or ends, we can't say for sure, but it could be possible.
- Does that mean that the Millennium—uppercase *M*—will be less than a thousand years? Possibly. As we just discussed, the Lord's language may be approximate here, even though there are numerous scriptures that specifically talk about the Millennium as being a thousand years (see, for example, D&C 29:11, 22; 88:101).

With that, let's deal with some additional questions and issues that D&C 77 brings to mind.

(1) *Can we really say that John's revelation gives us precise information on the timing of Christ's coming and other things of the last days?*

No, not if by "precise" we mean that we can calculate the time of His coming. We cannot do that, as we have shown above.

(2) *But with that said, isn't it possible that we could be so far off on our time*

calculations that the Millennium could still be five, six, or seven hundred years in the future?

When there are so many unknown variables, one can make only tentative statements. But as noted above, while 4000 B.C. is an estimate rather than a precise number, it is widely accepted as a good approximation of when the Fall occurred. Thus, to authoritatively say that we are five or six hundred years off from that mark would require more than just hope and supposition.

Many signs of the times have been or are being fulfilled. That suggests the time is drawing nigh. But remember, by the Lord's own declaration, no one—not even the angels in heaven—knows the timing of His coming except the Father and the Son. Nor shall they know until He comes (see D&C 49:7).

(3) *Has the Lord given us any more specific and perhaps even more precise time markers?*

If we are asking whether there is something such as precise calendar dates, the answer again is no. That doesn't seem to be the Lord's way. But that doesn't mean that He totally leaves us in the dark about what is coming. While we don't have precise time markers, there is another kind of marker that can be quite precise and very helpful to us. We could call these "event markers." The scriptural name for these events is "the signs of the times." Many of these are quite specific.

Before we look at these, let us examine the structure that we find in the book of Revelation, especially as it relates to the seven seals. There is a pattern in how John presents them to us that is enlightening.

- One of the first things we notice is that the seven seals do not get equal attention. In fact, the disparity between them is quite dramatic.
- The first four seals get two verses each, and the first verse in each case is an introductory verse, so in actuality, they get one verse each.
- The fifth seal gets three verses. So the first five seals, or first five thousand years, are summarized in a total of just eleven verses.
- The sixth seal changes that pattern significantly. It has a total of twenty-three verses (see Revelation 6:12–17; 7:1–17). So, the sixth seal gets more than twice as much page space as the first five seals combined. This is of interest to us because the sixth seal seems to cover c. A.D. 1000 to A.D. 2000, or modern times. But even then, all of the first six seals together only get two chapters, or a total of thirty-four verses.
- How much time does the seventh seal get? The next dozen chapters! That's right. The opening of the seventh seal begins in chapter 8, but

John does not see the actual Second Coming until chapter 19 and the Millennium until chapters 19–22. So even though the last seal is only one seventh of the total time span, it gets about seven times the page space of the other six seals combined. That certainly confirms what Nephi saw—that the Apostle John had the stewardship to write about the last days.

SUMMARY AND CONCLUSIONS

How soon the end? That is the question that is on many minds around the world today. And we're not just talking about members of The Church of Jesus Christ. There seems to be a growing anxiousness, a growing concern of urgency, as the world grows darker and more dangerous and more chaotic all around us. And the effects of the COVID-19 pandemic on the entire world is one more dramatic example of that.

The Lord has chosen not to give us precise information on the timing of future events. But this doesn't mean that He hasn't given us some specific markers to help us. These are called the signs of the times. We could also call them event markers, and these can be remarkably specific.

We shall discuss the concept of the signs of the times in the next chapter. And much of the rest of the book will discuss specific signs of the times in greater detail. God wants us to know what is coming so that we can appropriately prepare ourselves and our families.

We are living in a time when great things are happening. The Lord chooses when we come to earth, and part of that is so we can help fulfill His purposes. We live in a time of great wickedness, turmoil, war, and tribulation. That is the time the Lord chose for us to come to earth.

In a recent devotional at Brigham Young University, President Russell M. Nelson raised a startling and stimulating possibility concerning our generation:

> You are the children whom God chose to be part of His battalion during this great climax in the longstanding battle between good and evil—between truth and error. I would not be surprised if, when the veil is lifted in the next life, we learn that you actually pled with our Heavenly Father to be reserved for now. I would not be surprised to learn that premortally, you loved the Lord so much that you promised to defend His name and gospel during this world's tumultuous winding-up scenes. One thing is certain: You are of the house of Israel and you have been sent here to help

father God's elect (Nelson, "The Love and Laws of God," BYU devotional, September 17, 2019).

Perhaps this is why President Nelson feels such an urgency for us to prepare ourselves for what is coming. In an interview given while he and Elder Gary E. Stevenson were in South America, President Nelson said this: "There is much more to come. Wait until next year and then the next year. *Eat your vitamin pills. Get your rest. It's going to be exciting*" (published in Newsroom, October 30, 2018).

CHAPTER 9

THE ANGELS OF JUDGMENT

The world will increase in confusion, doubt, and horrible strife.... So will the Spirit of God also be withdrawn from them. The darkness upon their minds in relation to eternal things will become blacker, nations will engage in frightful and bloody warfare, the crimes which are now becoming so frequent will be of continual occurrence, the ties that bind together families and kindred will be disregarded and violated, the passions of human nature will be put to the vilest uses, the very elements around will seem to be affected by the national and social convulsions that will agitate the world, and storms, earthquakes, and appalling disasters by sea and land will cause terror and dismay among the people; ... the earth ... will begin to withhold her fruits in their season; the waves of the sea will heave themselves beyond their bounds, and all things will be in commotion; and in the midst of all these calamities, the master-minds among nations will be taken away, and fear will take hold of the hearts of all men. (Charles W. Penrose, *Millennial Star*, 21:582, September 19, 1859)

MINISTERING OF ANGELS

In section 43 of the Doctrine and Covenants, the Lord tells us that He speaks to the world through different "voices," such as earthquakes, lightning, and thunder (v. 22). But in this same passage, the Lord also says that He speaks to us through the voice of the "ministering of angels" (v. 25). When we think of ministering angels, we tend to think of examples like Gabriel coming to Mary and Joseph, the angels at the tomb of Jesus, or the angel who protected Daniel in the lion's den.

But the scriptures also speak of angels that carry out the Lord's will in other ways besides being ministering messengers. For example, in the book of Revelation, John often spoke of angels in terms of carrying out the judgments of God (see, for example, Revelation 7:1; 8:7–12; 9:15). We now turn to one of the signs of the times that is directly connected with angels in this second sense. These angels are first mentioned in one of the parables of Jesus given about two thousand years ago. It is called the parable of the wheat and the tares.

> The kingdom of heaven is likened unto a man which sowed good seed in his field: But while men slept, his enemy came and sowed tares among the wheat, and went his way. But when the blade was sprung up, and brought forth fruit, then appeared the tares also. So the servants of the householder came and said unto him, Sir, didst not thou sow good seed in thy field? from whence then hath it tares? He said unto them, An enemy hath done this. The servants said unto him, Wilt thou then that we go and gather them up? But he said, Nay; lest while ye gather up the tares, ye root up also the wheat with them. Let both grow together until the harvest: and in the time of harvest I will say to the reapers, Gather ye together first the tares, and bind them in bundles to burn them: but gather the wheat into my barn (Matthew 13:24–30).

"Tares" is a word that is no longer in common use today. The Greek word, *zizanion,* refers to a grass-like weed called "darnell," "bearded darnell," or "ryegrass." It is found virtually all over the world. In its early stages of growth, bearded darnell is almost indistinguishable from young wheat and thrives in the soil where wheat is sown.

In simple terms, tares, especially in their early growth, look so much like new wheat that it is difficult to distinguish one from the other. Though not specifically mentioned in the parable, there is another fact about ryegrass that adds to the power of the metaphor. The kernel-like seeds of the ryegrass look very much like kernels of wheat, but they are poisonous to both livestock and human beings, and can sometimes even be fatal. This, of course, gives more urgency to the need to separate out the wheat from the tares.

However, because they resemble each other so closely in the early stages of growth, in ancient times, farmers would let the wheat and the tares grow together until the harvest, then before the threshing process began, the tares would be carefully separated from the wheat, bound into separate bundles and then burned.

Matthew records that later that evening, after the multitude had gone away, the disciples came to Jesus and said: "Declare unto us the parable of the tares in the field" (Matthew 13:36). Jesus did so, going through the parable item by item and giving them the interpretation:

- He that soweth the good seed is the Son of man (v. 37).
- The field is the world (v. 38).
- The good seed are the children of the kingdom (v. 38).
- The tares are the children of the wicked one (v. 38).
- The enemy that sowed the tares is the devil (v. 39).
- The harvest is the end of the world (v. 39).
- The reapers are the *angels* (v. 39).

A few verses later, Jesus added, "The Son of man shall send forth his angels, and they shall *gather out of his kingdom* all things that offend, and them which do iniquity; and shall cast them into a furnace of fire: there shall be wailing and gnashing of teeth (Matthew 13:41–42).

Jesus warned that those in the kingdom who offend (i.e., live counter to the requirements of true discipleship), will, like the tares, be gathered out and burned in the fire.[1] This is an important point to remember. It is *how* we live, not whether we are members of the Church, that determines whether we are wheat or tares.

This reminds us of what we have said before. It is not being born into the house of Israel or holding membership in Christ's Church that determines who is wheat and who is tares, but the nature of a person's heart. We also need to remember the principle of accountability, which is that he who sins against the greater light has the greater condemnation (see D&C 82:3). In many cases, erring members of the Church would not be at the same level of wickedness as someone described as a child of the devil, but here Jesus says they will be considered one of the tares.

In chapter 1, we discussed how preparation and separation are often

> *Unless every member of this church gains for himself an unshakable testimony of the divinity of this church, he will be among those who will be deceived in this day when the "elect according to the covenant" are going to be tried and tested. Only those will survive who have gained for themselves that testimony.*
>
> HAROLD B. LEE,
> *TEACHINGS*, 133

---

1 The Book of Mormon teaches that this "burning" is not a literal fire but represents the mental, emotional, and spiritual torment that comes with knowing we have made foolish and terrible choices (see 2 Nephi 9:16; 28:23).

linked together in God's plan. We see this in the plan of happiness. It takes serious spiritual preparation if we do not wish to be separated from the presence of God after the Judgment. The parable of the wheat and the tares is another example of that. But in this chapter we are particularly interested in the angels of heaven who have a role to play in gathering out the tares to be burned. In modern scripture we are told more about them.

THE ANGELS OF JUDGMENT

In a revelation given to the Saints on January 2, 1831, when the Church was not yet a year old, the Lord again made reference to the parable of the wheat and the tares:

> All flesh is corrupted before me; and the powers of darkness prevail upon the earth, among the children of men, in the presence of all the hosts of heaven—Which causeth silence to reign, and all eternity is pained, and *the angels are waiting the great command to reap down the earth,* to gather the *tares* that they may be burned (D&C 38:11–12).

Though the structure and wording differs from Matthew's account, this passage reiterates the parable, but adds one insight. Here—in 1831—we are told that the *angels* are awaiting the command to reap down the earth. Before, they were described only as reapers.

About one year later, the Lord spoke once again of this parable in a revelation to Joseph Smith, only this time He added some new material, which updated the parable to modern times. The revelation begins with, "Verily, thus saith the Lord unto you my servants, concerning the parable of the wheat and of the tares" (D&C 86:1). The Lord does not repeat the parable, but expands on it significantly (see D&C 86:2–7). Here are the key elements:

- "*The apostles were the sowers*" (v. 2). In the New Testament version, Jesus was the sower of the seed. This change makes sense, for after His death, the Apostles took the gospel to the world. Also in our dispensation, the Apostles have that same responsibility. So this updates the parable to our time.
- "*After they have fallen asleep*" (v. 3). "They" seems to refer to the Apostles and possibly the first Christian converts. By A.D. 100, most of the Apostles had been martyred, and with the loss of the keys of the priesthood, the first signs of apostasy were beginning to appear.
- "*The great persecutor . . . the apostate, the whore, even Babylon, . . . even*

Satan" (v. 3). The whore and Babylon are the same thing and represent those who turn away from the Lord. They are called a "whore" because they were "married" to Jehovah when they covenanted to be faithful to Him but turned to other gods. Remember that in the parable of the ten virgins, Christ is the Bridegroom and the Church members are His bride. Babylon was renowned for its open wickedness and debauchery, so the Lord uses it as a grand type for all extreme wickedness (see Matthew 25:1–13; also 1 Nephi 13:5–6).

- "*He soweth the tares*" (v. 3). This is clearly Satan and his followers who entice the world into sin. Keep in mind that ryegrass looks very much like wheat, especially early in its growth, but if it is not rooted out, it can be like spiritual poison.

- "*Drive the church into the wilderness*" (v. 3). This imagery describes the Great Apostasy. The Christian Church went on to become the largest religion in the world, but the simple Church that Jesus initiated was eventually taken from the earth until the time of the Restoration (see also Revelation 12:6).

- "*Behold, in the last days, even now*" (v. 4). "Even now" confirms that the Lord is speaking for our day, the day when His Church is no longer in the wilderness.

- "*The blade is springing up and is yet tender*" (v. 4). The "blade" here refers to the wheat, that is, those who have accepted the covenant and are striving to be faithful. At this point, the Church was still in its infancy, like a tender seedling just beginning to sprout. In the beginning, its members were all first-generation converts, bringing with them their Christian traditions and limited knowledge of the fulness of the gospel. In its infancy, even some of the key leaders of the Church could be described as "tender." To try to root out the tares at that point could have ruined the Church.

- "*The angels are crying unto the Lord day and night*" (v. 5). Before, they were just waiting. Now they never stop pleading for permission to start their work, which is the reaping process. Note the progressive intensity in the three descriptions of the angels. In Matthew, the Savior said He would send forth His angels to be the reapers but makes no mention of timing. In D&C 38, given in January 1831, the angels were "waiting" for the command to start the reaping process. By December 1832, they were "crying unto the Lord day and night" for permission to begin their ministry, which conveys a sense of real urgency.

- "*But the Lord saith . . . , pluck not up the tares while the blade is yet tender. . . . Let the wheat and the tares grow together until the harvest* [the time of separation] *is fully ripe*" (vv. 6–7). Even in this latest revelation, and in spite of the angels' virtually begging to be released, they were held back. The Lord says that the wheat and the tares must grow together. It is not yet time for the process of separation.

This is a good place to pause and emphasize two points of importance.

First, we need to remember that the angels are servants of the Lord. They do not act independently of the will of the Father and the Son, but are instruments of Their will, working under Their direction.

In the second place, while the Lord speaks of the tares as being the unfaithful, the wicked, and the disobedient of the world—both in and out of the Church—we need to remember that this does not suggest that such judgments as natural disasters, social upheaval, and war fall exclusively on the wicked. In other words, we need to be careful that we don't find ourselves thinking, "Oh, those people must have been really terrible to have such a disaster strike them."

In August of 2005, Hurricane Katrina struck in the Gulf states of America, killing nearly two thousand people, flooding large portions of New Orleans, and causing $125 billion in damage. In general conference later that year, President Gordon B. Hinckley reminded us that these tragedies are part of the world in which we live and strike all levels of society:

> Now, I do not say, and I repeat emphatically that I do not say or infer, that what has happened is the punishment of the Lord. Many good people, including some of our faithful Latter-day Saints, are among those who have suffered. Having said this, I do not hesitate to say that this old world is no stranger to calamities and catastrophes. Those of us who read and believe the scriptures are aware of the warnings of prophets concerning catastrophes that have come to pass and are yet to come to pass (Hinckley, "If Ye Are Prepared Ye Shall Not Fear," *Ensign*, November 2005).

A question that comes immediately to mind is, "Why would the Lord tell His Church to let the wheat and tares grow together for a time, especially when tares can be poisonous and deadly to the wheat?" Let's express it in more modern language.

Why not have the Church set more stringent requirements before people can be baptized, such as making them undergo months of "trial membership"? Why not go after those members of the Church who are weak and faltering and demand that they either be all in or invite them to leave? Why should we put up with the complainers, the lukewarm and half-hearted members, the critical, the disobedient, or the doubters? Because, in the words of the parable, in trying to weed them out too soon, we could easily "pull up" some of the wheat with it.

The Church does take action against egregious violations of the commandments, but we do not excommunicate members for going inactive, for not paying tithing, for refusing to accept a calling, or for violating the Word of Wisdom. Part of the gospel covenant is to be longsuffering with the imperfect; to hold our temper when people are not quite the Saints we think they ought to be, or, as the Lord put it, to "succor the weak, lift up the hands which hang down, and strengthen the feeble knees" (D&C 81:5).

The parable of the wheat and the tares, which teaches this principle of not ripping out the tares too early, was first given to the Church in the time of Christ. It was given again in our dispensation in those first early days of The Church of Jesus Christ of Latter-day Saints. And it is still in effect today.

"THE ANGELS HAVE LEFT THE PORTALS OF HEAVEN"

With that foundation, let us examine more closely these angels who have been called to reap down the fields. Who are they? When did they live? What will they actually do in the reaping process? And perhaps most importantly, are they still being held back?

In A.D. 33, Jesus told His disciples that before He came again, He would send angels to gather in His elect (see JS—M 1:37). In January 1831, He told Joseph Smith that the angels were waiting for the signal to begin their mission. A year later, Joseph learned that the angels were crying day and night for permission to begin but were still being held back. That last revelation was given almost two centuries ago. So what is the Lord saying now? Do we know when that time will come? Or has it come already?

Though we don't have answers to all of those questions, happily we can say with confidence that, yes, we do know that the time has come and they have been released to do the work they have been called to do. We even know the date that this began. And, as is always the Lord's pattern, those answers come through His servants the prophets.

On April 6, 1893, exactly forty years after the cornerstone had been laid for the Salt Lake Temple, the building was formally dedicated. The prophet at the time was Wilford Woodruff, the fourth President of the Church. Since this was long before the days of television and satellite transmissions, under his direction, forty-one dedicatory sessions were held to accommodate those who desired to attend.

Somewhere during those services, perhaps in a meeting with the First Presidency and the Twelve, President Woodruff made a startling declaration. Though no extant record of what he said at the time has been found, Elder Joseph Fielding Smith, who would later become the tenth President of the Church, was present, and later recorded this witness:

> One theme that was on the mind of President Wilford Woodruff more than any other for a number of years before his death—in fact, from the time of the dedication of the [Salt Lake] Temple until his death—was this theme of the parable of the wheat and tares. . . . The first he said it, was at the time of the dedication of the Temple in 1893 (Smith, *Signs of the Times,* 112, 114).[2]

President Smith did not share many details of what President Woodruff said at the temple dedication, but fortunately, President Woodruff spoke of it often afterward, confirming what Joseph Fielding Smith had reported. One of those times was in 1894, when President Woodruff spoke to a group of temple workers:

> I want to bear testimony to you that God has held *the angels of destruction* for many years, lest they should reap down the wheat with the tares. But I want to tell you now, that *those angels have left the portals of heaven,* and they stand over this people and this nation now, *and are hovering over the earth waiting to pour out the judgments. And from this very day they shall be poured out.* Calamities and troubles are increasing in the earth. . . . If you do your duty, and I do my duty, we'll have protection, and shall pass through the afflictions in peace and safety (Woodruff, *Discourses,* 229–30).

Three months later in general conference, President Woodruff again spoke of the angels who had been held back by the Lord and explained what was happening:

> What is the matter with the world today? What has created this change that we see coming over the world? Why these terrible earthquakes, tornadoes, and judgments? What is the meaning of all these mighty events that are taking place? The meaning is, *these angels that have been held for many years in the temple of our God have got their liberty to go out and commence their mission and their*

---

2 There was no mention of this in the dedicatory prayer of the temple.

work in the earth, and they are here today in the earth (Woodruff, *Millennial Star*, Vol. 56, 643, October 8, 1894).

THE ANGELS OF DESTRUCTION

One of the surprising things about what President Woodruff said regarding these angels was that they were unleashing "calamities and troubles," "terrible earthquakes," "tornadoes," and "judgments." When the Savior spoke of the separation of the wheat and the tares, it seems like He was talking about a separation of individuals based on their wickedness or righteousness.

The terms President Woodruff used seem to suggest a more sweeping approach. But the idea of natural disasters and other types of calamities as part of the Lord's judgment had already been invoked by the Lord Himself in a passage of scripture quoted earlier, when He said that He would speak to the nations of the earth "by the mouth of my servants, and *by the ministering of angels,* and by mine own voice, and by the voice of thunderings, and by the voice of lightnings, and by the voice of tempests, and by the voice of earthquakes, and great hailstorms, and by the voice of famines and pestilences of every kind" (D&C 43:25).

President Woodruff didn't specifically say that these natural and manmade calamities were going to be the only way God separates the wheat from the tares, but it is certainly going to be part of the work of these angels, which would explain why President Woodruff referred to them as "angels of destruction," not just angels of judgment.

In 2004, President Dallin H. Oaks spoke of the signs of the times in the last days. After listing nine signs of the times related to the Second Coming, the majority of which were either natural or manmade disasters, he spoke of a study he had undertaken, with these findings:

> These signs of the Second Coming are all around us and *seem to be increasing in frequency and intensity.* For example, the list of major earthquakes in *The World Almanac and Book of Facts, 2004* shows twice as many earthquakes in the decades of the 1980s and 1990s as in the two preceding decades. It also shows further sharp increases in the first several years of this century. The list of notable floods and tidal waves and the list of hurricanes, typhoons, and blizzards worldwide show similar increases in recent years. Increases by comparison with 50 years ago can be dismissed as changes in reporting criteria, *but the accelerating pattern of natural disasters in the last few decades is ominous* (Oaks, "Preparing for the Second Coming," *Ensign*, May 2004).

As I began writing this book, I decided that I might undertake a more careful study of what has been happening from the time of Wilford Woodruff up to the present time. This turned out to be a daunting task. Detailed records containing this data back to the time of Wilford Woodruff are not readily available. Fortunately, more modern data is available on the Internet. I also relied on the *World Almanac and Book of Facts, 2019*. Here are some of the interesting trends and results that I discovered:

- Since the late 1890s, the Richter scale has been the world's standard for measuring the strength of earthquakes. A quake of 7.0+ is considered a major earthquake, and 8.0+ is deemed to be a catastrophic quake. From 1900 to 1949, only about one in five (22%) of all earthquakes were ranked at 8.0 or higher. There were none in the 9.0 range during that time period. From 1950 to 1999, only 10% were in the catastrophic range, but we saw our first two examples of 9.0+ quakes. (Remember, each point on the Richter scale is ten times more powerful than the previous level.) There have been only four 9.0+ quakes recorded since Richter scale records began, and two of them have occurred in the last fifteen years (see *The World Almanac*, 330–31). Of the sixteen strongest earthquakes in the world since 1900, five of them—nearly a third—have happened in the last seven years (United States Geological Survey Earthquake Information Center, see earthquake.usgs.gov/earthquakes/world).
- The earthquake in the Indian Ocean on the day after Christmas, 2004, is still the third largest earthquake ever recorded. The tsunami it triggered ranks as the most powerful and deadly tsunami on record.
- On March 11, 2011, an 8.9 earthquake, the fourth strongest in recorded history, struck near the east coast of Japan's Honshu Island, causing widespread damage, sending a tsunami smashing its way inland for several miles, and rupturing a nuclear power plant.
- Hurricane Maria ripped through Puerto Rico in September 2017. Though the government listed only 64 official deaths, Harvard researchers later catalogued 4,645 deaths, making Maria the second deadliest hurricane in the United States.
- Hurricane Katrina, which came out of the Gulf of Mexico in September 2005 and emptied the entire city of New Orleans of half a million people, flooded a large majority of the city and was the costliest natural disaster in the history of the United States to that point. Katrina is now ranked as the second most intense hurricane ever recorded.

- In 2010 and 2011, Australia recorded their second and third highest rainfalls since records have been kept. As a result, Australia experienced extensive flooding over an area *the size of France and Germany* combined. This became Australia's costliest natural disaster in recorded history.
- Up until June 1, 2011, the most tornadoes ever recorded in one year in the U.S. occurred in 2003, when 1,376 tornadoes were reported. But in the first five months of 2011, there were 1,448 tornadoes reported in the United States. In one four-day period of 2011 (April 25–28), there were 332 confirmed tornadoes—an average of 83 tornadoes per day. A few weeks later, on May 22, 2011, a tornado struck Joplin, Missouri, killing 158 people and injuring more than a thousand.
- In November 2018, the Camp Fire in northern California became the worst fire in California history, destroying some 18,000 structures and killing 89 people.
- Though wildfires are common in Australia, from September 2019 to February 2020, hundreds of major fires burned more than 46,000,000 acres, killing more than a billion animals.

SUMMARY AND CONCLUSIONS

It has been about two thousand years since Christ said there were angels waiting to reap down the fields but were being held back. A little over a hundred years ago, at the dedication of the Salt Lake Temple, President Woodruff declared that the time had come for those angels to be released, and indicated that part of this gathering process would involve natural disasters and other calamities. We should not conclude that these disastrous events are the only way these angels are able to carry out the preparations for Christ's return. If they are gathering the tares, then they are also working to gather the wheat.

This is sobering when we see the consequences of a world turning more and more from their Creator and Redeemer. But it is also thrilling to be witnesses to major events that are an integral part of the prophesied signs of our times. They testify of the validity of the prophetic voice. They testify of God's mercy and His justice. Perhaps most importantly for our day, these signs we see all around us testify that the coming of the Lord draws ever closer.

We shall close with one other thought. We have not been told who the angels of judgment would be. But we know that even in our day, there will be tares growing among the wheat. So, as the Savior said, the reaping process will include those in His kingdom, therefore involving some members of

The Church of Jesus Christ of Latter-day Saints. Knowing that our day has many more challenges and obstacles than earlier generations, we are going to more and more need a "sin-resistant" strain of "wheat" to cope with what is coming.

President Ezra Taft Benson didn't refer specifically to the parable of the wheat and the tares, but he spoke of youth being reserved for this time:

> You have been born at this time for a sacred and glorious purpose. It is not by chance that you have been reserved to come to earth in this last dispensation of the fulness of times. Your birth at this particular time was foreordained in the eternities. You are to be the royal army of the Lord in the last days. You are "youth of the noble birthright" (Benson, *Teachings,* 221).

> *If the afflictions which have been predicted do come upon us, they will come upon us because we have not kept the faith and because we have been disobedient and have thrown away the opportunities that our Heavenly Father has given us to prepare for the day of calamity which He foretold, over one hundred years ago, would come in this generation.*
>
> Harold B. Lee,
> "Living in the Bonds of Brotherhood," *Improvement Era 49*, May 1946, 322

These promises are wonderful and highly encouraging, but we must also remember that the Lord described some of the tares as coming from His kingdom. President Harold B. Lee gave a similar reminder that being the elect does not guarantee that we will remain faithful to our covenants:

> The history of the Lord's dealings with His children is filled with incidents that indicate that many of those who are the "elect according to the covenant," or that are of the "chosen" of God to be born through the chosen lineage of the house of Israel or the Lord's "portion" in the pre-existent world, will fail of their callings because of their sins (Lee, *Teachings,* 25–26).

This too is part of the lesson of the parable of the wheat and the tares and helps us better understand the work of the angels of judgment now going on in the world.

CHAPTER 10

THE TIMES OF THE GENTILES

The gospel is now restored to us Gentiles, for we are all Gentiles in a national capacity, and it will continue with us if we are faithful, until the law is bound, and the testimony sealed, and the times of the Gentiles are fulfilled. . . . When this time arrives, which is nigh, even at our doors, let the Gentile nations who reject the gospel which is now sent to them, prepare to meet the judgments of an offended God! (Wilford Woodruff, *Discourses*, 115)

THE GENTILES AND THE HOUSE OF ISRAEL

We have spoken of the Gentiles, noting that the term as used in the scriptures refers to anyone not of the house of Israel. It is found in various scriptural phrases. For example, on the first night that the angel Moroni came to Joseph Smith, he cited different prophetic scriptural passages from the Old and New Testament and said that they were about to be fulfilled. He stated "that *the fulness of the Gentiles* was soon to come in" (JS—H 1:41).

Gentiles is often found in other phrases such as "the *nations* of the Gentiles, "the *multitude* of the Gentiles," "the *times* of the Gentiles," "the *hand* of the Gentiles," or "the *fulfilling* of the times of the Gentiles."

This frequent use of the word *Gentiles* indicates that it is a term of importance in the scriptures. Three of those phrases—the times of the Gentiles, the fulness of the Gentiles, and the fulfilling of the times of the Gentiles— are directly linked to an important sign of the times that has to do with the house of Israel in the last days. They describe what we earlier have called "event markers."

This section of the book addresses the question, "How soon the end?" We have looked at specific signs of the times, at the angels of judgment, and at time indicators given in the seven seals of the book of Revelation. In this chapter we shall examine another sign of the times that is very specific in its links to the Second Coming. It also shows that we are in the last days, and it is not likely that the Second Coming is still hundreds of years away. To help understand that, we need to define the three phrases above.

THE TIMES OF THE GENTILES

Let's begin by defining the word "times" and the phrase "the times of." Both are found frequently in the scriptures. In modern vernacular, if we say, "It is *time* to go," or "Let's set a *time* to meet next week," generally we are referring to a specified moment in time. But when we use the plural form of the word, e.g., "*times* of war" or "*times* of stress," this generally refers to an extended *period* of time, usually of undefined duration.

To better understand the meaning of "times of the Gentiles," we need to place that phrase alongside another: "the times of Israel." This specific phrase is not found in the scriptures but describes the time when the Lord chose to make a covenant with His chosen people that He would be their God if they would be His people. This was an exclusive covenant that started with the Abrahamic Covenant and was extended to the house of Jacob. During that time, Israelites were the only people of the covenant, except for the Jaredites who had gone to America.

> *The Lord has designated these days in which we live as "the times of the Gentiles." The Gentile nations are essentially the so-called Christian nations—North and South America and the European nations from which we came.*
>
> Ezra Taft Benson,
> *Come unto Christ*, 110

Others could come into the covenant through what we would call conversion, meaning they had to embrace the covenant and its requirements. The times of Israel lasted about two thousand years, from the time of Abraham to the time of Jesus Christ.

When Jesus started His mortal ministry, He offered a new covenant to the house of Israel. It was called the gospel of Jesus Christ and was administered under a new organization called the Church of Jesus Christ (I'll add "of Former-day Saints" to distinguish it from the Church of our day). This new covenant would fulfill the law of Moses. Jesus and His followers had much success, and many people were baptized and became His disciples. But a large majority of the Jews (so named at this point because their homeland is Judea) rejected their Messiah. Their leaders eventually condemned Him before Pilate, and He was crucified.

After Christ's death, the Apostles continued the work, but a short time later, Peter was told to take the gospel to the Gentiles (see Acts 10). The Roman Empire at that time provided a rich seed ground for the work of the gospel, and tens of thousands of Gentiles who had previously worshipped only pagan Gods flocked to a religion that taught them about life after death and eternal joy in the life to come. Early on, the covenant people took upon themselves a new name. They were called Christians (see Acts 11:26), a title that was applied equally to both Jewish and Gentile converts.

When Judea was destroyed by the Romans in A.D. 66–70, and the few surviving Jews were scattered across the empire, this signified the end of the times of Israel and the coming in of the times of the Gentiles. The phrase "times of the Gentiles" is found five times in the scriptures (see D&C 45:25, 28, 30; Luke 21:24; JST Luke 21:25).

Even though many of the new converts were Christians and in the covenant, they were still called Gentiles because they came from Gentile nations.

THE FULNESS OF THE GENTILES

This phrase is found only once in the Bible but several times in modern scripture. Appropriately, it was given by the Apostle Paul, who after his conversion from Judaism became, by his own description, the "apostle of the Gentiles" (Roman 11:13; see also 1 Timothy 2:7). Writing to the Church in Rome, which almost certainly had more Gentile converts than Jews, Paul gave a short lesson on the house of Israel. He told the Church members that Israel was foreordained to be God's elect and chosen people, but when they hardened their hearts against the covenant, they lost that privilege. This opened up the way for the Gentiles to be "grafted in," or to become a part of covenant Israel as members of The

> *In the Dispensation of the Meridian of Time, the gospel was first preached to the Jews, and when they rejected it, then it was carried to the Gentiles. In this Dispensation of the Fulness of Times, the gospel is first to the Gentiles and then is to go to the Jews. The first have become last and the last first in this dispensation in fulfilment of the teachings of our Lord.*
>
> JOSEPH FIELDING SMITH,
> ANSWERS TO GOSPEL QUESTIONS, 1:140

Church of Jesus Christ of Former-day Saints. Paul then declared that this preference for the Gentiles to receive the gospel first would continue "until the *fulness* of the Gentiles be come in" (Romans 11:25).

Though Paul did not explain what that fulness was, nor when it would come, modern scripture clearly defines what this means. Note the language in these passages:

- "And after the house of Israel should be scattered they should be gathered together again; or, in fine, *after the Gentiles had received the fulness of the Gospel,* the natural branches of the olive tree, or the remnants of the house of Israel, should be grafted in, or come to the knowledge of the true Messiah, their Lord and their Redeemer" (1 Nephi 10:14).
- "And now, the thing which our father meaneth concerning the grafting in of the natural branches *through the fulness of the Gentiles,* is, that in the latter days, when our seed [the Lamanites] shall have dwindled in unbelief, yea, for the space of many years, . . . after the Messiah shall be manifested in body unto the children of men, then shall *the fulness of the gospel* of the Messiah come unto the Gentiles, and from the Gentiles unto the remnant of our seed" (1 Nephi 15:13).
- "I must bring forth *the fulness of my gospel* from the Gentiles unto the house of Israel" (D&C 14:10).
- "When the times of the Gentiles is come in, *a light shall break forth among them that sit in darkness,* and it shall be *the fulness of my gospel*" (D&C 45:28).

These references make it very clear that the "fulness" in the phrase the "fulness of the Gentiles" does not refer to something the Gentiles will *do*, but rather something they will *receive*, and this was the *fulness* of the gospel.

What does that mean? It is related to the fact that the Restoration of the priesthood and the Church in the last days opens up a new dispensation of the gospel. It is called the dispensation of the *fulness* of times. Our generation has the fulness of the gospel covenant including *all* that has been revealed in earlier dispensations and things that have not *ever* been revealed to any previous dispensation (see chapter 5 for more on the dispensation of the fulness of times).

In 2018, President Russell M. Nelson indicated that even though our dispensation opened almost two hundred years prior, there are yet many things to come. "We are witnesses to a *process* of restoration. If you think the Church has been fully restored, you are just seeing the beginning. There is much more to come" ("President Nelson Dedicates Concepción Chile Temple, *Church News,* 30 October 2018).

THE TIMES OF THE GENTILES FULFILLED

This background helps us better understand a phrase used by the Savior in that same Olivet Discourse. This phrase is of great interest to us because when Jesus used it, He gave us a time marker that links it to the prophecies of the last days. He told His disciples that "Jerusalem shall be trodden down *of the Gentiles,* until *the times of the Gentiles be fulfilled* (Luke 21:24).

Obviously, His first use of the word *Gentiles* clearly referred to the Romans, and those brutal Gentile empires that would rule the land thereafter, and that would continue until the times of the Gentiles were fulfilled. Has that time come? Yes! The last Gentile empires to rule over Jerusalem were the Ottoman Empire, which lost control of the Middle East at the end of World War I, and the British Empire, who ruled in their place. In 1947, the United Nations voted to partition Palestine between the Palestinians and the Jews. One year later, when the Palestinians refused to accept the partition and war broke out, the Jews created the state of Israel with Jerusalem as its capital.

Why is this so significant for our discussion? Note what Jesus said next:

> Then his disciples asked him, saying, Master, tell us concerning thy coming? And he answered them, and said, In the generation in which *the times of the Gentiles shall be fulfilled,* there shall be signs in the sun, and in the moon, and in the stars; and upon the earth distress of nations with perplexity (JST Luke 21:24–25; see also D&C 45:28–31).

So here we have another event marker that is directly tied to the last days and the judgments that precede the coming of Christ. The Lord said that these signs would come in the same generation when the times of the Gentiles would be fulfilled. That's quite specific.

HOW LONG IS A GENERATION?

To answer questions about how specific this sign of the times really is, we have to define the word *generation.* The Lord is very clear in saying it will be in the same generation as when the times of the Gentiles are fulfilled. But how long is a generation?

In the New Testament, the root word for *generation* is *genesis*, and its derivative, *gennema*. Its general meaning is "beginning," and it refers to offspring or progeny. In Webster's 1828 dictionary, two definitions are helpful. The first is "a single succession in natural descent" (*Webster*, s.v. "generation"). So a parent would be one generation, a child the second generation, and so on. This is why demographers say there are an average of five generations per century, or a new generation about every twenty years.

But a second definition is "the people of the same period, or living at the same time" (ibid.). Many families have four generations living at the same time, and occasionally we find one with five generations. This would extend a generation to more like eighty to a hundred years.

In our day, we also use the term to describe a time period in which a group of people with similar traits are born; e.g., the "baby-boomer" generation or the "millennial" generation. These vary in length but usually are twenty years or less. Finally, in the Book of Mormon, two places suggest they considered a generation to be about a hundred years (see Helaman 13:9–10; 4 Nephi 1:14, 22).

In some cases, a "generation" seems to be used in the same way we use "dispensation," i.e., an undefined period of time (see D&C 45:31). Joseph Fielding Smith saw it as a marker sufficiently specific to draw a conclusion that provides a tremendously important time window on what is coming:

> We all know that from the time of the destruction of Jerusalem in the year A.D. 70 until near the close of World War I, Jerusalem was trodden down of the Gentiles, and during all of that time the Jews were scattered and almost without privileges in the Holy Land. The Lord said they should remain scattered among the nations until the times of the Gentiles were fulfilled. Moroni said the times of the Gentiles were about to be fulfilled. . . . The day of the Gentiles has come in, and the day of Judah and the remnant of downtrodden Israel is now at hand. *The sign for the fulfilment of this prophecy has been given* (Smith, *Doctrines of Salvation*, 3:258).

What we can say from all of this is that the long centuries when the descendants of ancient Israel have been without the gospel covenant are now over. In other words, the times of Israel have come back and joined in partnership with the fulness of the times of the Gentiles. And the evidence of that fulfillment is quite remarkable.

THE GENTILES AND THE SEED OF JOSEPH

In chapter 5, we discussed at some length a seminal talk on the gathering of Israel that was given by Elder Bruce R. McConkie while traveling in South America doing regional conferences with President Spencer W. Kimball. He described the growth of the Church in three phases:

> **Phase I**—From the First Vision, the setting up of the kingdom on April 6, 1830, and the coming of Moses on April 3, 1836, to the secure establishment of the Church in the United States and Canada, a period of about 125 years. In the terms we are using here, this began the fulness of the Gentiles.
>
> **Phase II**—From the creation of stakes of Zion in overseas areas, beginning in the 1950s, to the Second Coming of the Son of Man, a period of unknown duration. This time up to the present time was also part of the fulfilling of the times of the Gentiles and the return of the times of Israel.
>
> **Phase III**—Still future to us and will include the Millennium.

Our purpose here is to illustrate with actual data how truly this prophecy has been and is being fulfilled.

THE CHURCH OF JESUS CHRIST: PHASE I

One of the last charges given to the Twelve by the resurrected Christ before His ascension was, "Go ye therefore, and teach all nations, baptizing them in the name of the Father, and of the Son, and of the Holy Ghost" (Matthew 28:19). It was a charge that would be given again 1,800 years later.

On April 6, 1830, under the direction of the Prophet Joseph Smith, The Church of Jesus Christ of Latter-day Saints was organized as a legal religious organization in the State of New York. Six members signed the official document, as required by law. However, there were others present that day, many of whom were baptized after the services. It was still a very small group—probably around twenty-five or thirty—for such an auspicious occasion. Not long after that day, the Savior gave the same command to His fledgling Church as He had given in His day: "Go ye into all the world, preach the gospel to every creature" (D&C 68:8). It was a command repeated twice more (see D&C 84:62; 112:28). The members took that charge, and though their beginnings were humble, their efforts brought immediate success and the Church began to grow.

In those first years and the years to come thereafter, virtually all members of the Church would be considered Gentiles since they came from Gentile nations and had no recognizable ties to the house of Israel.

Through a vigorous missionary effort, the Church grew rapidly. By 1835, there were about 9,000 members. Five years later that had nearly doubled again. The Lord's promise that the field was white and ready to harvest was fulfilled. By the year the Prophet was martyred, there were more than 26,000 members, many of those recently arrived in the United States from the British Isles.

Considering the Church's size, their limited resources, and the constant persecution they faced, the members' effort to go into the world and find the remnants of lost and scattered Israel was highly successful, especially considering that our modern means of transportation and communication were still many years away. Here is just a sampling of their efforts to go into all the world.[1]

1830–1859: Canada, 1830; England, 1837; Scotland, 1839; Germany, Australia, Wales, Ireland, 1840; Austria, Romania, the Netherlands, Tonga, 1841; Norway, 1842; Russia, Sweden, Pacific Islands, 1843; Guatemala, 1847; France, 1848; Denmark, 1849; Switzerland, Italy, 1850; Chile, 1851; India, Malta, Laos, 1852; Nicaragua, Barbados, South Africa, Hong Kong, 1853; New Zealand, Malaysia, Thailand, 1854.

1860–1889: Belgium, Finland, 1861; American Samoa, Samoa, 1863; Iceland, 1873; Mexico, 1874; Czechoslovakia, 1884; Armenia, Hungary, Turkey, 1885.

1890–1919: The Philippines, 1898; Greece, 1899; Bulgaria, 1900; Japan, 1901.

1920–1950: Latvia, 1923; Argentina, Fiji, 1924; Zimbabwe, 1925; Brazil, 1927; Poland, 1929; Spain, 1932; Uruguay, 1940; Panama, 1941; Costa Rica, 1947; El Salvador, 1949.

Several things are worthy of note from this data:

- No one can say that Church leadership and members did not take their charge to go to all the world seriously. In the first thirty years of the

---

1 Primary source is the *Deseret News 2012 Church Almanac*, "World Wide Church," country histories. The dates given in most cases represent the first official Church-sponsored contact. In many cases those were missionaries, but not always. Only in a very few cases were formal missions established in these countries. Many would wait decades before missionaries returned.

- Church's existence, missionaries were sent to over three dozen countries, only two of which shared borders with the United States.
- What is especially impressive is that most of these missionaries were adult men who left wives and families behind, often for three and four years. They were also, for the most part, from lower economic classes—farmers, storekeepers, etc.—and received virtually no monetary help from the Church. They went without purse or scrip, and depended on the goodness of people they met, often pausing in their journeys to find work and earn enough cash money to continue their travels.
- These nations, with very few exceptions, were Gentile nations, meaning they didn't have large populations of those we call Jews or descendants of Lehi. This confirms that this was a major part of the fulfillment of the "fulness of the Gentiles."
- Those countries where the field was truly white and ready to harvest—especially the British Isles, Scandinavia, Germany, and Switzerland—brought tens of thousands of converts into the Church. However, these new members were strongly encouraged to come to America and help build up Zion, leaving only small congregations in their native countries for a long time.
- In this early stage of missionary efforts, work among the countries with large populations of descendants of Lehi's colony (found throughout North and South America, particularly in many native tribes, and some of the Polynesians in the Pacific Islands), did not see a lot of success other than in the Pacific Islands. For example, the Church sent seven missionaries to Mexico in 1875. They were not well received, so they split up. Five went among the native population and were well received but had no baptisms. The other two missionaries had only five converts.

All of this was in Phase I of the gathering of Israel in the last days, and lasted 125 years. Then things began to change beginning about 1955.

THE CHURCH OF JESUS CHRIST: PHASE II

Phase II, which Elder McConkie described as the time when Church members began to gather to the stakes of Zion throughout the world, began about 1955. The transition didn't happen overnight, of course. Things had been moving in this direction but now began to change at an accelerated pace.

There had been stakes of Zion before 1955, of course, even before the

Saints came to Utah. Stakes were created in Ohio, Missouri, Illinois, and Iowa, all of which were disbanded when the Saints went west. The first stake in Utah was organized in 1848 in Salt Lake City, the year after they arrived in the Salt Lake Valley. Other stakes were added steadily, but at the onset of the twentieth century, seventy years into the Church's history, there was still only a total of forty stakes.

By the end of 1955, there were 224 stakes in the Church. All but six of those were in the United States. Five were in Canada (all in the province of Alberta), and the sixth was at Colonia Juárez, which was created to serve members from the United States who left to escape persecution for plural marriage. Hawaii had a large population of ethnic native Hawaiians, considered to be Polynesians. But Hawaii had several U.S. military installations and so there were also a significant number of Caucasians there as well. Other Polynesian congregations had been in place since missionaries arrived in the 1840s, such as in Samoa and Tonga, but they had not grown to the point of having any stakes at this time.

So while there were a significant number of members who came from Book of Mormon peoples in 1955, of the 224 stakes in the Church at that time, not one could be described as a stake made up mostly of known descendants of the house of Israel. This was about to undergo a dramatic change.

One of the first indicators that the Church was maturing and rolling forth to fill all the earth (see D&C 65:2) was the growth in the number of stakes in the years after 1955. Here is a sample of when various countries got their first organized stakes. We will also take note of where those stakes were, particularly in regards to indigenous peoples that may include descendants of the children of Lehi.

Why do we care about this? Because we are trying to show that early on, the Church largely came from Gentile countries. But the Lord had spoken of a time when there would be a *fulfilling of the times of the Gentiles*. Therefore, having the gospel go to peoples who are descendants of known members of the house of Israel would be evidence that the time of Israel was coming back in. This did not, and still does not, mean that the Church would stop going to the Gentiles, but rather that *both* efforts would move together in tandem now. Remember, we are told that in the last days "it shall come to pass that the righteous shall be gathered out from among all nations" (D&C 45:71).

Since stakes are the basic building blocks of a strong Church organization, we shall use the stakes of Zion as our measuring stick for when the gospel began to go to the house of Israel again. (For simplicity, we shall hereafter designate those stakes with significant populations of the remnants of Israel as "indigenous stakes" and the others as "Gentile stakes," though we recognize that all members of the Church are now considered to be modern Israel because they are covenant Israel and not just blood Israel.)

As we begin this study, let us remember what Nephi tried to teach to his recalcitrant brothers when they were confused about the gathering of Israel in the last days:

> In the latter days, *when our seed shall have dwindled in unbelief* [which was complete by about A.D. 400], yea, for the space of many years, and many generations after the Messiah shall be manifested in body unto the children of men, *then shall the fulness of the gospel of the Messiah come unto the Gentiles* [the first generations of converts to the Church], and *from the Gentiles unto the remnant of our seed* [descendants of Lehi] (1 Nephi 15:13).

The Lord taught the same principle in modern revelation: "Wherefore, I must bring forth the fulness of my gospel *from the Gentiles unto the house of Israel*" (D&C 14:10). Therefore, to highlight the difference, in the chart below,[2] which examines when stakes were first organized in other countries, we shall mark with an asterisk those that are the indigenous stakes.

New Zealand*: 1958
England, Australia, Tonga*: 1960
Germany, Mexico,*[3] Switzerland: 1961
Samoa,* Scotland: 1962
Argentina,* Brazil*: 1966
Guatemala*: 1967
American Samoa*: 1969
Peru,* Japan: 1970
Chile,* Tahiti*: 1972
Korea, Philippines: 1973
Sweden, Wales: 1975

That is astonishing! We went 125 years with only one stake outside of the U.S. and Canada, and none of them primarily served the descendants of Lehi. Then in the next twenty years, eleven countries had indigenous stakes created for the first time. But that counts only the first stake in a country.

---

2 Data reported in *Deseret News 2012 Church Almanac*.
3 This was the first Spanish-speaking stake in the Church.

During that same time period, most of those countries had other stakes created as well. In some cases, the increase in numbers was quite remarkable. For example:

- England didn't get its first stake until 1960, but in the next fifteen years added twelve more.
- New Zealand, a relatively small country, got its first stake in 1958, and added eight more over the next seventeen years.
- Mexico saw stunning growth. It didn't get its first Spanish-speaking stake until 1961, but by 1975 it had added twenty-four more. In 1975 alone, fifteen new stakes were created! Currently, there are over 200 stakes in Mexico.
- Though the growth of indigenous stakes was higher than that of the Gentile stakes, it is clear that rapid growth was happening in both sectors of the Church. In that period of twenty years, the indigenous stakes saw a remarkable 58% growth. But the Gentile stakes were up 42%. Most business corporations would be delighted with a 42% growth in two decades.

That suggests that the work among the Gentile nations is not going to go away when the times of the Gentiles are fulfilled and the times of Israel come back in. Both are here to stay, but the domination in terms of numbers of Gentile stakes in Phase I gave way to a much more balanced situation as we entered Phase II.

SIGNS OF THE TIMES BEING FULFILLED

We include several statistical tables here as supporting evidence that what was prophesied by Nephi centuries ago is now in the process of being fulfilled. The times that were prophesied about many years ago are now being fulfilled in our lifetime. The following tables (from information reported in *Deseret News 2012 Church Almanac*) give evidence that this is now happening in a remarkable way. Just as the examination of trends in natural disasters supports Wilford Woodruff's prophecies that the angels of destruction are now released to do their work, so this provides another kind of supporting evidence. And once again, knowing that the Lord has all things in hand, this fulfillment of another of the important signs of the times is further evidence that we can trust in the Savior's admonition to "be not troubled."

Growth of the Church: 1955–2018

Four key points in time have been selected to represent pivotal dates.

- **1955** The year we began Phase II of the gathering of Israel.
- **1971** This year the Church reached three million members.
- **2010** The 180th anniversary of the Church.
- **2018** Latest statistics on the worldwide Church.

	Total Members	Stakes	Missions	Converts	Operating Temples	Languages
1955	1,357,224	224	44	21,669	9	NA
1971	3,090,353	562	94	83,514	13	12[4]
2010	14,131,467	2,896	340	272,814	134	NA
2018	16,313,467	3,383	407	234,332	161	182

Growth of the Church: 1971–2018 by Geographic Areas as Measured by Stakes[5]

Area	Stakes 1971	Stakes 2018	Total Growth %	Annual % Growth: 1971–2018
U.S./Canada	515	1679	326%	4.8%
Europe	12	128	1066%	22.7%
South America	7	669	9557%	203.7%
Central America	4	383	9575%	203.3%
Pacific	23	141	613%	13.0%
Asia	1	186	18,600%	395.7%
Africa	1	165	16,500%	351.1% (611.1% from 1991)

---

[4] No specific data available. Estimate based on stakes in those language areas.

[5] Growth rates of large populations are naturally smaller than in small populations.

Church Membership by Geographic Areas: 2018 with Stakes and Percent of Total Membership

This is a breakdown of current Church membership by general areas of the world. Note that these are not the same as current designated priesthood areas.

Total Membership: 16,313,735	Total Members in Area	Percent of Total Church Members
U.S./Canada	6,879,539	42.2%
Europe	493,970	3.0%
Central America	2,811,830	17.2%
South America	4,093,363	25.1%
Pacific	562,341	3.4%
Asia	1,296,148	7.4%
Africa	621,448	3.8%

OBSERVATIONS

Here are some things to note from the data above and also observations we can draw from this data:

- The growth of the Church has been steady throughout its history. There has never been a year since 1830 that the Church has declined in the number of its members.
- It took until 1947 (117 years) for the Church to reach its first million members, yet just twenty-five years later, the Church had tripled that. They added another 3 million in the next fifteen years.
- In the forty-seven years from 1971 to 2018, the U.S. and Canada—both of which are Gentile nations—had a robust growth of 226% in total, or about 5% annually.
- In the early years of the Church, the nations of Europe—all of which are considered to be nations of the Gentiles—sent tens of thousands of converts to America. For example, the emigration of German members of the Church to America up to 1930 totaled 15,416 (see Scharffs, *Mormonism in Germany*, 68). Approximately 65,000 Saints emigrated from the British Isles to America up to around 1880 (Bloxham, *Truth Will Prevail*, 165). Many of those came to Nauvoo before the Saints moved west. A historian described this migration in this way: "Of the

60,000 to 70,000 Saints who emigrated to the Salt Lake Valley in the late 1800s [i.e., after Brigham Young's arrival in the Valley], more than 98 percent of the survivors were from Europe, and 75 percent were from Great Britain" (/history.lds.org/article/pioneer-story-the-convert-immigrants).

- Yet even with that loss due to out-migration, since 1971, Europe's Church membership has grown at about four times the rate of that of the U.S. and Canada, with new European countries—including some from the former Communist Bloc—being opened to missionary work since 1971.
- The amazing rates of growth in Asia and Africa are evidence that the *fulfilling* of the times of the Gentiles does not mean that the Gentiles are going to fade away. We are gathering out the seed of Abraham who have been scattered among all nations, and that is happening in a marvelous way all over the world.
- The first missionary work among the Pacific Islands (Hawaii, Samoa, Tonga, etc.) began back in the 1840s. This area and Western Europe were the only places outside of the United States where early missionary work had significant success in those early years.
- Another thing to keep in mind as we look at the Polynesians as a group is that the population of the various islands was much smaller than that of countries like England, Germany, or Mexico.
- Also, the Polynesians did not experience a large-scale emigration to America as Europe did in those early years, but that has changed in more recent times. There are now significant numbers of Polynesian members in the United States. But even with those unique circumstances, including out-migration, their growth rate from 1971 to 2018 was more than double that of the U.S. and Canada.
- Once the Church began opening missionary work among the descendants of Lehi in what we call Latin America (Central and South America), the growth has been continuous and astonishing. Remember that early efforts to establish missionary work in those countries failed. But once the "Day of the Lamanite" came in, the growth was explosive.
- In the sixteen years from 1955 to 1971, things began to change, but Central and South America added only eleven more stakes in that time. Then in the next fifteen years, they added just over three hundred more, an average of twenty-one stakes every year.

In summary, currently there are over one thousand stakes in Latin

America, compared to 1,679 stakes in the U.S. and Canada. Their annual growth rate over nearly fifty years has been an astonishing 200% annually. That is remarkable evidence that the times of Israel have returned.

Africa's situation is much different from the other areas because the policy on the priesthood kept the Church from sending missionaries to the native peoples of Africa until the Church was almost 150 years old. The first stake on the African continent was organized in 1970 in the white neighborhoods of Johannesburg, South Africa. In 1978, soon after President Spencer W. Kimball announced that all worthy males could hold the priesthood, vigorous missionary work began among the black African nations, and with great success. The first stake in countries where native African peoples were in the majority was organized in Ghana in 1991.

With that unique situation in mind, we have given two annual growth rates for Africa in the chart on the previous page. The first goes back to 1971 and includes the South African stakes in the computation. That is a period of forty-one years. The second computation begins at 1991 and spans just twenty-seven years, up to 2018. It too includes the South African stakes but starts twenty years later, when the first stake outside of South Africa was organized, in Ghana. As we can see, either way, the annual growth rate is stunning. But if we look at only the annual growth rate among native Africans, we see that it has far and away the fastest growth rate of any area in the world.

Asia is another area that has shown a remarkable annual growth since 1971. It is almost double the rate of the Latin American countries.

One additional evidence of the wide ethnic diversity in the Church was noted by President Dallin H. Oaks following a sustaining of the general officers of the Church:

> With the sustaining that has just taken place, we now have 116 General Authorities. Nearly 40 percent of them were born outside the United States—in Germany, Brazil, Mexico, New Zealand, Scotland, Canada, South Korea, Guatemala, Argentina, Italy, Zimbabwe, Uruguay, Peru, South Africa, American Samoa, England, Puerto Rico, Australia, Venezuela, Kenya, the Philippines, Portugal, Fiji, China, Japan, Chile, Colombia, and France (Oaks, "The Sustaining of Church Officers," *Ensign,* May 2018).

SUMMARY AND CONCLUSIONS

The Lord has tasked His Church with gathering in the seed of Abraham—both those that are recognizable remnants of the covenant people, such as the Jews and the Lamanites, and those who have bloodlines tracing back to the twelve tribes of Israel, though they do not know that. But what we do know with certainty is that we are gathering in the seed of Abraham from every corner of the world, as the prophets of old have prophesied again and again.

The Savior gave a charge to His Twelve Apostles that they should take the gospel to the world. They took that commandment seriously and spent their lives—and gave their lives—fulfilling that charge. When the Church was restored to the earth again, that same task was given to Joseph Smith and the prophets that followed him. Now, as we approach the 200th anniversary of the organization of the Church, we are providing Church materials in 187 languages and have more than 400 missions with tens of thousands of missionaries teaching the gospel both in the nations of the Gentiles and in countries that have recognizable remnants of the house of Israel.

And let us not forget the gathering of Israel going on beyond the veil. Since the beginning of the Restoration, we have performed untold millions upon millions of ordinances for the dead, and those who have gone before are preaching the gospel to all who will listen.

All of that has been done in an attempt to fully merit this promise by the Lord given in 1832: "Blessed are ye if ye continue in my goodness, a light unto the Gentiles, and through this priesthood, a savior unto my people Israel. The Lord hath said it" (D&C 86:11).

In closing, let us note that these statistics are a wonderful verification of what the Lord taught Samuel the Lamanite. This was given just five years before the birth of Christ, and about forty years before Christ appeared and ministered to the Nephites. Samuel had spoken about the steadfastness of several generations of Lamanites since they had been converted, starting with the work of Ammon and the sons of Mosiah.

> And now, because of their steadfastness, . . . because of their firmness when they are once enlightened, behold, the Lord shall bless them and prolong their days, *notwithstanding their iniquity—* Yea, *even if they should dwindle in unbelief the Lord shall prolong their days,* until the time shall come which hath been spoken of by our fathers, . . . concerning the restoration of our brethren, the Lamanites, again to the knowledge of the truth—Yea, I say unto you, that in the latter times the promises of the Lord have been extended to our brethren, the Lamanites; and notwithstanding the many afflictions which they shall have, . . . *they shall again*

be brought to the true knowledge, which is the knowledge of their Redeemer. . . . Therefore, saith the Lord: I will not utterly destroy them, but I will cause that *in the day of my wisdom they shall return again unto me,* saith the Lord (Helaman 15:10–13, 16).

Part III

The Dreadful Day

CHAPTER 11

"THE GREAT AND DREADFUL DAY OF THE LORD"

We are living in the prophesied time "when peace shall be taken from the earth," when "all things shall be in commotion" and "men's hearts shall fail them." There are many temporal causes of commotion, including wars and natural disasters, but an even greater cause of current "commotion" is spiritual. Viewing our surroundings through the lens of faith and with an eternal perspective, we see all around us a fulfillment of the prophecy that "the devil shall have power over his own dominion." . . . Evil that used to be localized and covered like a boil is now legalized and paraded like a banner. The most fundamental roots and bulwarks of civilization are questioned or attacked. Nations disavow their religious heritage. Marriage and family responsibilities are discarded as impediments to personal indulgence. . . . The good, the true, and the beautiful are being replaced by the no-good, the "whatever," and the valueless fodder of personal whim. (Dallin H. Oaks, "Preparation for the Second Coming," *Ensign*, May 2004)

A DUAL SCENARIO

Since writing *The Coming of the Lord* so many years ago, I cannot count the number of times I have had active, faithful members of the Church, especially youth and young adults, come up after a class or a lecture and say things like, "I hope I die before all this happens," or, "How bad is it really going to get?" or, "How good do you have to be to survive?" That last question is an interesting one. If people are asking how good they have to be to see things through, in a way they're asking how far can they stray without it pushing them off the track.

I have tried to answer their questions, but I always conclude with this:

The Second Coming of the Lord

"It makes me sad that you feel that way. Me? *I hope I live long enough* to see some of this come to pass. This is the greatest time in the history of the world." Their response usually varies from incredulity to open skepticism. But this is a deeply held belief for me, and part of that conviction comes from an experience I had many years ago that gave me a different perspective about the future.

> *Experienced pilots understand that they can't always control the things that happen around them. They can't just turn off the turbulence. They can't make the rain or snow vanish. They can't cause the wind to stop blowing or change its direction. But they also understand that it's a mistake to fear turbulence or strong winds—and especially to be paralyzed by them. The way to land safely when conditions are less than ideal is to stay on the correct track and glide path as perfectly as possible.*
>
> Dieter F. Uchtdorf,
> "Landing Safely in Turbulence,"
> *Ensign*, February 2016

As part of my position as an administrator in the Church Educational System, I had the responsibility to oversee training for our teachers throughout the world. From time to time, I would travel to other areas of the world to meet with our teachers.

One of those trips was to South America, where I visited the seminary and institute programs in ten major countries. As we neared the end of our trip, we were scheduled to fly from Buenos Aires, Argentina, to Asunción, Paraguay, a flight of about an hour and a half. When we were called to board, I was dismayed to see that our plane was not a large jet aircraft. It was a much smaller, four-prop plane, originally designed as a military cargo plane. It seated only about thirty people. To my further dismay, I saw that the sky was now dark with towering black clouds and occasional flashes of lightning. As we walked across the tarmac to the plane, it started to rain, and I knew that this was not going to be the best flight I had ever taken.

To be clear, I am not nor have I ever been afraid of flying. And in all the travel I have done over the years, though I have been on some wildly turbulent flights, I have never once been airsick. But I hate turbulence. So my only hope for that flight was that we could get high enough to be above the storm.

As the area director and I got buckled into our seats, the pilot came on the intercom and instantly dashed any hopes I had. "Ladies and gentleman," he said, "please be sure your seat belts are securely fastened. Unfortunately, as you can see, we have a bit of weather today, and that will be the case all the way to Asunción. Our plane is not allowed to go above an altitude of 21,000 feet, so we'll be going right through the heart of the storm. But we assure you the plane is a good one and that we will get you to your destination safely."

"A lot of turbulence" was a vast understatement. For the entire flight we bounced all over the sky—sliding sideways, dropping two or three hundred feet, then shooting back up again. I still am inclined to believe that what was supposed to be a ninety-minute flight took at least nine hours, but I gritted my teeth and hung on as we bucked our way toward our destination.

About halfway through the flight, the area director, who was a long-time friend and who seemed completely unperturbed by what was going on, leaned over and said, "Jerry, it's going to be all right."

I shot him a dirty look and said, "I know that, but that doesn't mean I have to like it."

And then he said this: "Look, I know it's rough. There's a lot of turbulence up here, but just keep two things in mind. First, this is a sturdy aircraft that has flown through many storms. Second, the pilots have much experience and know how to get us there safely. Sometimes we just have to endure the turbulence."

It was an analogy that has brought me comfort many times. There is a lot of prophesied turbulence ahead, and the Lord hasn't promised us that all will be smooth-as-silk air and bright sunshine on this journey of ours. But the craft in which we are traveling is called The Church of Jesus Christ of Latter-day Saints, and that craft is not going down. And, as President Nelson so aptly put it that day in the lunchroom, "God is at the helm." If we let Him, He will take us through the storms to our destination.

I will prophesy that the signs of the coming of the Son of Man are already commenced. One pestilence will desolate after another. We shall soon have war and bloodshed. The moon will be turned into blood. I testify of these things, and that the coming of the Son of Man is nigh, even at your doors. If our souls and our bodies are not looking forth for the coming of the Son of Man; and after we are dead, if we are not looking forth, we shall be among those who are calling for the rocks to fall upon them.

JOSEPH SMITH,
TEACHINGS, 251

GREAT OR TERRIBLE?

On Sunday, March 27, 1836, Joseph Smith dedicated the first temple in the dispensation of the fulness of times. One week later, on April 3, Joseph and Oliver Cowdery had a vision of Jesus Christ in all of His glory, followed by visitations from Moses, Elias, and

Elijah. Elijah's final words were: "Know *that the great and dreadful day* of the Lord is near, even at the doors" (D&C 110:16). At first, that phrase sounds like a contradiction. How can something be both great and dreadful at the same time? Note that it does not say great *or* dreadful, but great *and* dreadful.

The Hebrew word that is translated as "great" basically carries the same meaning it typically has for us, meaning something large in size or of high importance or value.

The word "dreadful" is more complicated. In the Old Testament, it is sometimes used to describe the nature of God. "Dreadful" comes from a Hebrew word that means "to fear, to be feared, or fearful." But it can also convey the idea of awe and great respect (see Wilson, *Old Testament Studies*, 134).

It would be more comfortable if all Elijah meant by "dreadful" was that it would be "a great and awesome day," because we are uncomfortable with the idea of a loving God being responsible for dreadful things. But as we shall see, there are truly dreadful things outlined in the prophetic view of the future. And knowing that we are now living in that prophesied day doesn't add to our comfort. This is the reality, however, as we discussed earlier.

As we noted earlier, in the scriptures we find both a voice of promise and a voice of warning. That is so because both voices are proof of a loving Heavenly Father. The Lord warns us because, due to the consequences of growing wickedness in the last days, there are some truly dreadful things coming. Charles W. Penrose, who was a Counselor in the First Presidency to both Joseph F. Smith and Heber J. Grant, gave this vivid description of the dreadful side of the vision of the future:

> The world will increase in confusion, doubt, and horrible strife. As the upright in heart, the meek of the earth, withdraw from their midst, so will the Spirit of God also be withdrawn from them. The darkness upon their minds in relation to eternal things will become blacker, nations will engage in frightful and bloody warfare, the crimes which are now becoming so frequent will be of continual occurrence, the ties that bind together families and kindred will be disregarded and violated, the passions of human nature will be put to the vilest uses, the very elements around will seem to be affected by the national and social convulsions that will agitate the world, and storms, earthquakes, and appalling disasters by sea and land will cause terror and dismay among the people; new diseases will silently eat their ghastly way through the ranks of the wicked; the earth, soaked with gore and defiled with the filthiness of her

inhabitants, will begin to withhold her fruits in their season; the waves of the sea will heave themselves beyond their bounds, and all things will be in commotion; and in the midst of all these calamities, the master-minds among nations will be taken away, and fear will take hold of the hearts of all men (Penrose, "The Second Advent," *Improvement Era*, March 1924).

That certainly qualifies as being dreadful. But if these things are to be part of the grim reality of what is coming, then we need to know that. The point is, as we saw in the example of President Nelson's counsel on "God is at the helm," if we let the dreadful side of what is coming dominate our thoughts and actions, things may turn out to be truly dreadful.

However, that is only one part of what lies ahead. And just because those things are happening all around us doesn't mean that every person in the world will be affected by them. We see that in our lives right now. There are terrible things going on in the world, and yet most of us are not directly affected by them. Many are blessed to live in enclaves of peace and stability and safety.

And while the Lord has not promised that the faithful will be totally shielded from these dreadful things, He has given us many promises of protection and refuge and safety. We need to constantly remind ourselves that the terrible things are only one side of the equation. As President Nelson put it: "Saints can be happy under every circumstance. We can feel joy even while having a bad day, a bad week, or even a bad year!" (Nelson, "Joy and Spiritual Survival," *Ensign*, November 2016).

Scoffers often say that evil and violence have always been part of the human scene and always will be. And that's all right. As the Lord said to Moroni, "Fools mock, but they shall mourn" (Ether 12:26). Sister Julie B. Beck, then serving as the Relief Society General President, indicated that some of that mocking is especially aimed at the sisters of the Church:

> *Wonderful as this time is, it is fraught with peril. Evil is all about us. . . . We live in a season when fierce men do terrible and despicable things [this was two months after 9/11]. I do not know what the future holds. I do not wish to sound negative, but I wish to remind you of the warnings of scripture and the teachings of the prophets. . . . The time will come when the earth will be cleansed and there will be indescribable distress.*
>
> Gordon B. Hinckley,
> "Living in the Fulness of Times,"
> *Ensign*, November 2001

Because we are living in the last days of this earth, there are signs of a great struggle everywhere. Myths and misperceptions regarding the strength, purpose, and position of Latter-day Saint women abound. Prevailing myths imply that we are of lower importance than men, that we are generally sweet but uninformed, and that no matter what we do, we will never be enough to be accepted by our Heavenly Father. As the Apostle Peter said, there are "false teachers among you, who privily shall bring in damnable heresies, even denying the Lord that bought them" (Beck, "Daughters in My Kingdom': The History and Work of Relief Society," *Ensign*, November 2010).

SUMMARY AND CONCLUSIONS

The next two sections of this book are based on the words of Malachi, which Elijah quoted to Joseph Smith and Oliver Cowdery. We shall first examine a series of prophecies that are terrible and dreadful. So, as President Nelson counseled, we need to buckle our seat belts. Some parts of the "ride" are going to be rough. If you wish, you can always skip over these chapters and come back to this section later. But although this section will be unpleasant in many ways, it can also be awesome as we realize what a blessing it is to have the Lord warn us in advance of what is coming.

We should take particular comfort and joy from the words of Joseph Smith, who saw both sides of what is coming:

> Prophets, priests and kings . . . have looked forward with joyful anticipation to the day in which we live; and fired with heavenly and joyful anticipations they have sung and written and prophesied of this our day; but they died without the sight; *we are the favored people that God has made choice of to bring about the Latter-day glory;* it is left for us to see, participate in and help to roll forward (Smith, *Teachings*, 186).

CHAPTER 12

"The Devil Shall Have Power over His Own Dominion"

I [prophesy] in the name of the Lord God anguish & wrath . . . & tribulation and the withdrawing of the spirit of God await this [generation]. Until they are visited with utter desolation. This generation is as corrupt as the [generation] of the Jews that crucified Christ. And if he were here today & should preach the same doctrine he did then they would [crucify] him. ("Journal, December 1842–June 1844; Book 3, 15 July 1843–29 February 1844," p. [131], *The Joseph Smith Papers*; https://www.josephsmithpapers.org/paper-summary/journal-december-1842-june-1844-book-3-15-july-1843-29-february-1844/137)

A PROPHET'S LAST LAMENT

As we begin our examination of the terrible things that are coming, remember that we are still discussing what the Lord calls the signs of the times. As already noted, these signs are given by a merciful God so that we can be aware of what is coming. With that understanding, we can better prepare ourselves and those we love for whatever the future might hold and can secure for ourselves the promise of the Savior when He said, "Be not troubled" (D&C 45:35).

In this chapter we shall look at one of the most oft-repeated warnings about our time. It is also one of the depressing and discouraging aspects of the last days. This is not just because we are seeing its fulfillment all around us, but because we know that it will continue to increase right up to the final winding-up scenes.

The name of this sign of the times comes from a statement in the preface to the Doctrine and Covenants: *"The devil shall have power over his own dominion"* (D&C 1:35).

The implications of that simple statement are enormous and deeply disturbing, but it is supported by numerous other references, each of which describes our day. We do not desire to dwell long on such awful prophecies, but neither can we simply step around them because they are so unpleasant. The prophets certainly felt compelled to warn us of what they were shown.

Here is what our prophets, ancient and modern, have been inspired to share with us. Note how often these are not just sweeping generalities but very specific descriptions of our days.

- "This know also, that in the last days perilous times shall come. For men shall be lovers of their own selves, covetous, boasters, proud, blasphemers, disobedient to parents, unthankful, unholy, without natural affection, trucebreakers, false accusers, incontinent [without self-control], fierce, despisers of those that are good, traitors, heady [rash, reckless], highminded [puffed up with pride], lovers of pleasures more than lovers of God; having a form of godliness, but denying the power thereof: from such turn away" (2 Timothy 3:1–5).
- "And it came to pass that Enoch saw the day of the coming of the Son of Man. . . . But before that day he saw great tribulations among the wicked" (Moses 7:65–66).
- "In the last days, . . . those who shall come upon this land and those who shall be upon other lands, . . . will be drunken with iniquity and all manner of abominations" (2 Nephi 27:1).
- "In that day shall be heard of wars and rumors of wars, and the whole earth shall be in commotion. . . . And the love of men shall wax cold, and iniquity shall abound" (D&C 45:26–27).
- After watching his people go down to utter destruction, Moroni was shown in vision our day and described what it would be like: "It shall come in a day when the blood of saints shall cry unto the Lord, because of secret combinations and the works of darkness. Yea, it shall come in a day when the power of God shall be denied, and churches become defiled and be lifted up in the pride of their hearts; . . . Yea, it shall come in a day when there shall be great pollutions upon the face of the earth; there shall be murders, and robbing, and lying, and deceivings, and whoredoms, and all manner of abominations" (Mormon 8:27–28, 31).

In our day, those we sustain as prophets, seers, and revelators have also warned of the pervasive influence of Satan in our time. Here are just a few examples:

Russell M. Nelson: "I am optimistic about the future. It will be filled with opportunities for each of us to progress, contribute, and take the gospel to every corner of the earth. But I am also not naive about the days ahead. We live in a world that is complex and increasingly contentious. The constant availability of social media and a 24-hour news cycle bombard us with relentless messages. If we are to have any hope of sifting through the myriad of voices and the philosophies of men that attack truth, we must learn to receive revelation" ("As We Go Forward Together," *Ensign*, May 2018).

Boyd K. Packer: "These are days of great spiritual danger for this people. The world is spiraling downward at an ever-quickening pace. I am sorry to tell you that it will not get better. I know of nothing in the history of the Church or in the history of the world to compare with our present circumstances. Nothing happened in Sodom and Gomorrah which exceeds the wickedness and depravity which surrounds us now. Satan uses every intrigue to disrupt the family. The sacred relationship between man and woman, husband and wife, through which mortal bodies are conceived and life is passed from one generation to the next generation, is being showered with filth. Profanity, vulgarity, blasphemy, and pornography are broadcast into the homes and minds of the innocent. Unspeakable wickedness, perversion, and abuse—not even exempting little children—once hidden in dark places, now seeks protection from courts and judges. . . . The sins of Sodom and Gomorrah were localized. They are now spread across the world, wherever the Church is. The first line of defense—the home—is crumbling. Surely you can see what the adversary is about. We are now exactly where the prophets warned we would be" ("On the Shoulders of Giants," BYU J. Reuben Clark Law Society devotional, 28 February 2004, 7–8).

M. Russell Ballard: "The conditions in the world are uncertain and dangerous, and the economies of the world are unstable and unpredictable.

> *Why do we need such resilient faith? Because difficult days are ahead. Rarely in the future will it be easy or popular to be a faithful Latter-day Saint. Each of us will be tested. The Apostle Paul warned that in the latter days, those who diligently follow the Lord "shall suffer persecution." That very persecution can either crush you into silent weakness or motivate you to be more exemplary and courageous in your daily lives.*
>
> Russell M. Nelson,
> "Face the Future with Faith,"
> *Ensign*, May 2011

The cherished values of life, liberty, and the pursuit of happiness are under attack by those who want to restrict agency and make us dependent rather than encourage us to use our skills and talents to create new and exciting ways of doing things. Standards of morality are failing. The family is under attack and is crumbling. Love in the hearts of men and women has waxed cold and is unnatural. There is a continuing breakdown in the integrity, honesty, and righteousness of political, business, and other leaders. Wars and rumors of wars among nations and creeds abound. And even more destructive than any armed conflict is the war raging between good and evil—between the Savior with His army of light and Satan with his evil minions of darkness—for the very souls of the children of God" ("Face the Future with Faith and Hope," *Ensign*, January 2014).

Russell M. Nelson: "These are the latter days, so none of us should be surprised when we see prophecy fulfilled. A host of prophets, including Isaiah, Paul, Nephi, and Mormon, foresaw that perilous times would come, that in our day the whole world would be in commotion, that men would 'be lovers of their own selves, . . . without natural affection, . . . lovers of pleasures more than lovers of God,' and that many would become servants of Satan who uphold the adversary's work. Indeed, you and I 'wrestle . . . against the rulers of the darkness of this world, [and] against spiritual wickedness in high places.' . . . Conflicts between nations escalate, . . . cowardly terrorists prey on the innocent, and . . . corruption in everything from business to government becomes increasingly commonplace" ("Joy and Spiritual Survival," *Ensign*, November 2016).

THE SCOPE OF SATAN'S EFFORTS TO HINDER GOD'S WORK

This is a gloomy and depressing thing to contemplate. But some may say, "Hasn't this always been the case? Satan has been around since the Garden of Eden, wreaking havoc and bringing sorrow and misery. Is our day really any different, other than perhaps in the size of the problem?"

Of course Satan has always been around. Of course his purposes have always been the same. Humanity needed opposition and choices between good and evil to make the plan of salvation work. It has ever been so. But to downplay the seriousness of our situation seems to be an example of spiritual myopia. Let's use a simple analogy.

Let's suppose that one day a mother is in her home preparing dinner. Suddenly, the grease in the frying pan bursts into flame. That is a serious and dangerous thing. But this family keeps a fire extinguisher in the home. She snatches it up and puts the fire out. Her heart is beating faster, but she doesn't call the fire department, because the crisis is over. But suppose this family lives in a heavily wooded area and one summer afternoon the mother smells smoke. At first she pays little attention. But as it grows stronger, she goes out on her porch and sees a towering pillar of smoke off to the east. It's still several miles away, but her reaction is equally swift. She calls the fire department. They say it is a major forest fire a few miles away but the wind is blowing the fire in her direction. They strongly recommend that all citizens in the projected path of the fire evacuate immediately.

Suppose the woman says to herself, "Oh, I've dealt with fires before. I can handle this." She gets her fire extinguisher and goes out on her back porch to wait for the fire. Not many would commend her for being prepared. When it comes to evil, size matters. Intensity matters. Frequency matters.

The Lord has said that the "devil has power over his dominion." The definition of "dominion" can either be "domain" or "sovereign or supreme authority." So we should not be surprised that we now see major conflagrations of evil spreading rapidly all across the world.

In a vision shown to Enoch, we get a vivid and chilling insight into the nature of Satan and those who follow him. This was given at a time before the flood when "the power of Satan was upon all the face of the earth" (Moses 7:24). As he mourned for what he saw all around him, Enoch was enveloped in vision, and he "beheld Satan; and he had a great chain in his hand, and it veiled the whole face of the earth with darkness; and *he looked up and laughed, and his angels rejoiced*" (Moses 7:26).

To appreciate the full horror of that vision, let us look at what we might label as seven of Satan's primary strategic goals and his success in achieving those goals.

1. *Collapse of societal morals and values.* As the decline of a civilization progresses, more and more the overall society begins to abandon the moral and social values that made them a strong people. This includes things like the erosion of traditional family values and the ensuing weakening of families.

2. *Obsession with wealth and material things.* Often this begins through an overall rise in the prosperity and stability of a society. This is a theme we see over and over in the Book of Mormon (see, for example, 1 Nephi 4:14; 2 Nephi 1:20; Mosiah 27:7). The Apostle Paul said that "the *love* of money is the root of all evil" (1 Timothy 6:10). It's not really the money that we love; it's what money can do for us. And that is more than just acquiring

physical things. With wealth comes fame, prestige, influence, opportunities, companionship, etc.

3. *Oppression, neglect, and exploitation of the poor, the needy, the sick, and the afflicted.* This is another thing that has always permeated humanity's relationships with their neighbors. The Lord often speaks of those we think of as less fortunate than ourselves. He describes them as the poor, the needy, the sick, the afflicted, the halt and the lame, the weak, the aged, widows and orphans. But how we view them and how we treat them is also spoken of often in the scriptures. Here are verbs that the Lord has used to describe how mankind has treated this group of people: despise, smite, rend, turn our backs on, oppress, consider them to be evil, believe their plight is just reward, forsake, kill, cause them to cry out for relief, persecute, cast down, mock, stop our ears from their cries, rob, devise ways to destroy, and secretly devour. All of these offend the Lord.

4. *Deep and pervasive corruption in government and the ruling classes.* A given of the human experience is that people tend to gather together in groups. This requires some kind of social contract to meet their needs and let them live peaceably together. Civil governments of various forms have been organized throughout history. They range from a single village leader up to vast nations with millions of government workers in their employ. Those in positions of leadership carry the ability to tax, to make and enforce laws, to fine, to police the populace, to incarcerate, and even to execute. Larger governments can raise armies and wage war. And since moral agency is key to the plan of salvation, Satan has used governments to entice people to become corrupt rulers because of the immense wealth, prestige, power, and self-gratification this can bring.

5. *Deep and pervasive corruption of religious institutions.* Religion was given to us to be a blessing and a comfort. But Satan is well aware of its potential as well and works hard to corrupt religions in general—often by sharing government power with them—and to demean and ridicule the humble and faithful believers of any or all religions. King Noah and his priests are only one example of this combination of civic and religious power (see Mosiah 11).

6. *Widespread and pervasive war and social upheaval.* War seems to be another "given" that follows wherever humans go. We have records of war that go back to the dawn of history. It may be spontaneous clashes between neighboring communities over land or water rights, or empires slugging it out over vast dominions and wealth. Surely one of the things that makes Satan lean back and laugh is that he entices individuals to war in order to

gain power and wealth and create a strong empire, then as succeeding generations become more and more corrupt, he brings in other empires to destroy them and starts the cycle anew. With war comes unrestrained violence, cruelty, savagery, destruction of property and natural resources, famine, disease, starvation, rape, murder, the death of children, subjugation, torture, savagery, and widespread suffering at virtually every level of society.

7. Teachings of false philosophies from the intellectual and secular elite. One of the more unusual chapters in the Book of Mormon is Alma 30. Alma records an interchange with a person whose name was Korihor, whom Alma calls an "Anti-Christ." This was a man who was going about teaching doctrines contrary to the gospel and having great success in doing so. What makes this chapter unusual is that Alma records in great detail what it was that Korihor taught, then how Alma refuted those false teachings. Here are some of the key false doctrines Korihor taught, which we still see all around us today dressed up as various philosophical or social or religious systems.

- There is no Christ and, by extension, no Atonement, no Church, no gospel, no doctrine, no goodness nor badness, no Second Coming, no Final Judgment.
- No person can know of things that are to come, which "proves" that those who claim to be prophets are a fraud.
- Believers in God and religion are bound down with a foolish and a vain hope. "Bound" suggests slavery. Korihor's argument was that such hope is foolish because no one can know of things to come—we can know only what we learn through our five senses, which means that one cannot prove there is a God.
- Your hope is therefore vain, because no one is coming to save you from your sins.
- What you say are prophecies are the foolish traditions of your parents. They are foolish because this has always been how the older generations try to control and hold back the rising generations.
- From all of this, we can conclude that your hope for a remission of sins (through the Atonement) is not based on any empirical evidence, and therefore is not true.
- This means that your hope for redemption is totally illogical and is the result of a frenzied and deranged mind, i.e., you are mentally unbalanced.
- The real truth is that people in this life fare according to their own abilities, gifts, and ingenuity—what Darwin called the survival of the

fittest. If there is no God, then human beings are the supreme creatures of the universe and can determine what is right or wrong for themselves.
- An extension of that philosophy is that the poor and weak are inferior by nature and therefore do not deserve any compassion or pity.
- By logical extension, this also means that whatever a person does cannot be not a crime because there is no ultimate truth or Divine Being giving us eternal laws.
- This also means there is no life after death, no continuance of our existence, no Final Judgment hovering over our heads, no accounting of what we do in this life. After death, there is nothing, so there is nothing to fear from some imagined punishment waiting for us at "the Judgment."

This philosophy, in one form or another, has enticed people to turn away from God and justify themselves in whatever kind of life they choose to live. For the natural man, that is a very enticing and helpful philosophy to live by. Is it any wonder that people flock to such teachers, often making them rich and famous? Korihor, and others like him, not only remove the guilt for sin, but they provide a sophisticated justification for doing whatever you choose to do.

Alma describes the reaction of the people to this philosophy in these words: "And thus he did preach unto them, leading away *the hearts* [not just the minds] of many, *causing them to lift up their heads in their wickedness*" (Alma 30:18). Note that last phrase. To "lift up their heads" is another way to say that they were proud, that they actually gloried in their wickedness.

Elder Quentin L. Cook described false philosophies as one of the most pernicious of Satan's strategies that bring us under spiritual subjugation:

> The most universal subjugation in our day, as it has been throughout history, is ideology or political beliefs that are inconsistent with the gospel of Jesus Christ. Substituting the philosophies of men for gospel truth can lead us away from the simplicity of the Savior's message. . . . This is emblematic of our own day, where gospel truths are often rejected or distorted to make them intellectually more appealing or compatible with current cultural trends and intellectual philosophies. If we are not careful, we can be captured by these trends and place ourselves in intellectual bondage (Cook, "Lamentations of Jeremiah: Beware of Bondage," *Ensign*, November 2013).

So we shouldn't be surprised that from ancient times, we have been warned against Satan's sophistries:

- During His mortal ministry, Christ warned His disciples about "false prophets, which come to you in sheep's clothing, but inwardly they are ravening wolves" (Matthew 7:15).
- Speaking of the churches that would become corrupted in the last days, Nephi said, "Because of pride, and because of false teachers, and false doctrine, their churches have become corrupted" (2 Nephi 28:12).
- In another place, after describing the 200 years of a "Zion-like" peace and righteousness that prevailed among the Nephites, Mormon described how they slipped back into apostasy: "The people did harden their hearts, for they were led by many priests and false prophets to build up many churches, and to do all manner of iniquity" (4 Nephi 1:34).

SUMMARY AND CONCLUSIONS

So, here's a practical question for us to ponder. The Lord has chosen to warn us about Satan's rise in influence, power, and dominion in the last days. It is one of the prevalent signs of the times given to us so that we can "be not troubled." So what is the Lord's expectation for us?

We are to push back against the influences of Satan and his followers *wherever* we meet them, *whatever* form they come in, and *however* enticing they may be. It is not easy, but it is that simple.

Elder Neil L. Andersen spoke of a "compensatory power" that can help protect us and our families from the powers of darkness:

> As evil increases in the world, there is a compensatory spiritual power for the righteous. As the world slides from its spiritual moorings, the Lord prepares the way for those who seek Him, offering them greater assurance, greater confirmation, and greater confidence in the spiritual direction they are traveling. The gift of the Holy Ghost becomes a brighter light in the emerging twilight. . . . But as with all spiritual gifts, it requires our desiring it, pursuing it, and living worthy of receiving it. . . . I emphasize once again: As evil increases in the world, the Lord does not leave us on the same footing. In a world that would diminish or discard or impair belief, there is an added spiritual power for those who are willing to set their course on increasing their faith in Jesus Christ" (Andersen, "A Compensatory Spiritual Power for the Righteous," BYU Education Week devotional, August 18, 2015, 4–6).

CHAPTER 13

"There Shall Be Wars and Rumors of Wars"

> *I have just been handed a note that says that a U.S. missile attack is under way. I need not remind you that we live in perilous times. I desire to speak concerning these times and our circumstances as members of this Church. You are acutely aware of the events of September 11, less than a month ago. Out of that vicious and ugly attack we are plunged into a state of war. It is the first war of the 21st century. The last century has been described as the most war-torn in human history. Now we are off on another dangerous undertaking, the unfolding of which and the end thereof we do not know. For the first time since we became a nation, the United States has been seriously attacked on its mainland soil. But this was not an attack on the United States alone. It was an attack on men and nations of goodwill everywhere. It was well planned, boldly executed, and the results were disastrous. . . . It was cruel and cunning, an act of consummate evil.* (Gordon B. Hinckley, "The Times in Which We Live," *Ensign*, November 2001)

AN AGE OF WAR

On Christmas Day, 1832, the Prophet Joseph Smith described conditions that were existent in the world at that time. Cholera was prevalent in many large cities. India was experiencing an epidemic of the plague. America had just weathered a serious crisis with the state of South Carolina threatening to secede from the nation. On that day, Joseph wrote this simple sentence: "On Christmas day, I received the following [revelation and prophecy on war]" (Joseph Smith, "History, 1838–1856, volume A-1 [23 December 1805–30 August 1834]," p. 244, *The Joseph Smith Papers*; https://www

.josephsmithpapers.org/paper-summary/history-1838–1856-volume-a-1-23-december-1805–30-august-1834/250):

> Verily, thus saith the Lord concerning the wars that will shortly come to pass, beginning at the rebellion of South Carolina, which will eventually terminate in the death and misery of many souls; *And the time will come that war will be poured out upon all nations, beginning at this place* (D&C 87:1–2).

There, in a few words, is another of the prominent signs of the times the Lord has chosen to give us in the latter days. War! Worldwide, global war. Our day has already seen much war. This revelation makes it clear that it is not over yet. It is interesting that this revelation came a little less than three weeks following section 86, which was the revelation on the wheat and the tares and releasing the "angels of judgments" to gather in the tares (see chapter 9). Then two days after receiving section 87, the Prophet received section 88, which he described as the "'olive leaf' . . . plucked from the Tree of Paradise, *the Lord's message of peace to us*" (see heading, D&C 88).

The three revelations form an interesting set:

- **D&C 86.** The time has come for the reaping of the fields and separating the righteous from the wicked.
- **D&C 87.** A revelation on war. War will be one of the ways that the reaping of the fields will take place.
- **D&C 88.** Joseph receives "the Lord's message of peace to us."

Joseph's revelation was not the first time war had been prophesied in the scriptures. Before His death, Jesus told His disciples that our day would be a time of "wars and rumors of wars" (see JS—M 1:23, 28; D&C 45:26). Nephi also saw worldwide war in his vision and used the same phrase: "I beheld that the wrath of God was poured out upon that great and abominable church, insomuch that there were wars and rumors of wars among *all the nations and kindreds of the earth*" (1 Nephi 14:15). In another section of the Doctrine and Covenants the Lord reveals that He has a direct hand in those wars: "I have . . . decreed wars upon the face of the earth, and the wicked shall slay the wicked, and fear shall come upon every man; And the saints also shall hardly escape" (D&C 63:33–34). In the book of Revelation, John saw warfare and was told that "the number of the army of the horsemen [was] two hundred thousand thousand" (Revelation 9:16). If that is a literal number, that's *two hundred million soldiers!* For comparison, in World War II there were 58 combatant nations involved, with an estimated total military personnel of 65 to 70 million men and women. John saw a future army vastly larger than that!

In a way, these prophecies should not surprise us. An article in the *New York Times* discussed the history of war, defined by the author as "an active conflict that has claimed more than 1,000 lives." The author asked: "Has the world ever been at peace?" His answer follows:

> Of the past 3,400 years [going back to about 1400 B.C.], humans have been entirely at peace for 268 of them, or just 8 percent of recorded history. How many people have died in war? At least 108 million people were killed in wars in the twentieth century. Estimates for the total number killed in wars throughout all of human history range from 150 million to 1 billion. War has several other effects on population, including decreasing the birthrate by taking men away from their wives. The reduced birthrate during World War II is estimated to have caused a population deficit of more than 20 million people (Chris Hedges, "What Every Person Should Know about War," nytimes.com/2003/07/06/books).

In his study of the prophecies of the latter days, President Joseph Fielding Smith cited a much earlier study on war that is also enlightening:

> Does war tend to decline as nations become more civilized? Many philosophers have said so, but now two sociologists of Harvard University have turned the cold and dispassionate eye of science upon the question. . . . Far from declining, wars increase in number and intensity as nations progress, and the worst flare-up since the dawn of history has occurred in our own century. . . . They have reached their conclusion through a study of all the wars known to have taken place in Europe, ancient Greece and the Western Roman Empire over a period of more than 2,400 years—from 500 B.C. to A.D. 1925. . . . These scientists say . . . they have learned that in these countries war grew from [an index number of] 2.678 in the twelfth century to 13,735.98 in the first twenty-five years of the twentieth century. . . . These men conclude that "all commendable hopes that war will disappear in the near future are based on nothing more substantial than hope and a belief in miracles" (Smith, *The Progress of Man*, 402–3).

Note that they came to this conclusion before World War II, the Korean War, the Vietnam War, two wars in Iraq, and the Afghanistan wars. And those are only wars in which the United States was involved.

About eighty-five years before the outbreak of World War I, and more than a hundred years before World War II began, Joseph Smith prophesied that war would eventually be poured out on all nations.

Years after Joseph's death, two Apostles spoke of the prophecy on war and added some additional warnings. Elder Orson F. Whitney had been serving in England for a time. As he prepared to return home in 1856, he issued an apostolic "prophetic warning" to Great Britain. Among other things he said:

> *The world will present a scene of conflict such as has never been experienced before. Still, men's hearts will be hardened to the revelations from heaven. Even greater signs shall then be given to manifest the approaching great day of the Lord.*
>
> Ezra Taft Benson,
> "Prepare Yourselves for the Great Day of the Lord,"
> New Era, May 1982

The days are near at hand, woe unto you when that day shall come! For it shall be a day of vengeance upon the British nation; and your armies shall perish; your maritime forces shall cease; *your cities shall be ravaged, burned, and made desolate,* and your strongholds shall be thrown down (Whitney, *Saturday Night Thoughts*, 68–69).

Images of the London blitz and the devastation that the German Luftwaffe rained down upon England come to mind. In World War II, the United Kingdom lost approximately 450,000 of their citizens, counting military and civilian deaths, with 43,000 Londoners killed in the nine months of the London blitz alone.

Orson Hyde, another of the early members of the Twelve, wrote this about Europe in 1862, just as the Civil War in America was in full swing: "After many days, when the demon of war shall have exhausted his strength and madness upon American soil, . . . he will *remove his headquarters to the banks of the Rhine*" (Hyde, *Millennial Star*, 24:274).

The Rhine River, one of Europe's major rivers, has its longest expanse within Germany's borders and is Germany's largest river. The "banks of the Rhine" almost certainly signifies Germany. That the two greatest conflicts in the history of the world had Germany as one of the major combatants is a dramatic validation of his prophecy.

Though cities had been put to the torch by conquering enemies for centuries, beginning with World War I, something new and terrible began. Firebombing of major cities became a strategic way to demoralize the enemy. In World War I, German Zeppelin balloons firebombed London. In World War II, the Germans firebombed several British cities, leaving behind massive destruction. Later, the Allies retaliated. In Hamburg, Germany, British bombers killed an estimated 44,600 and left a million homeless. In Dresden, 500 American bombers dropped incendiary bombs and started a firestorm that reached over 1500 degrees Fahrenheit. About 28,000 houses were destroyed. The exact number of deaths is unknown, but ranges between 35,000 and as many as 100,000.

President Boyd K. Packer, who was a pilot in World War II, listed some of the horrors of that second global war:

> In the Second World War every bond between man and man was to perish. Crimes were committed by the Germans under the Hitlerite domination . . . which find no equal in scale and wickedness with any that have darkened the human record. The wholesale massacre by systemized processes of six or seven millions of men, women, and children in the German execution camps exceeds in horror the rough-and-ready butcheries of Genghis Khan, and in scale reduces them to pigmy proportions. . . . The hideous process of bombarding open cities from the air, once started by the Germans, was repaid twenty fold by the ever-mounting power of the Allies, and found its culmination in the use of the atomic bombs which obliterated Hiroshima and Nagasaki. . . . We have at length emerged from a scene of material ruin and moral havoc the like of which had never darkened the imagination of former centuries. After all that we suffered and achieved, we find ourselves still confronted with problems and perils not less, but far more formidable than those through which we have so narrowly made our way (Packer, *Let Not Your Heart Be Troubled*, 165).

What makes descriptions such as this so chilling is knowing that the signs of the times that speak of war *are not yet fulfilled*.

A PROPHECY ON WAR

There are many prophecies on war in the scriptures, but section 87, which Joseph called a "revelation and prophecy on war," is one of the most remarkable and most detailed. Though it contains only eight verses, the revelation's scope is such that we shall analyze it verse by verse.

First, let us briefly review the historical circumstances at the time Joseph received the revelation. South Carolina and other Southern states were angry over tariffs that were harming their economy, as well as attempts to block slavery from being legalized in new states and territories. South Carolina threatened to secede from the Union, which would have created a major constitutional crisis. When Congress nullified the tariffs and made other concessions, the crisis was averted.

But twenty-nine years later, some seventeen years after Joseph was martyred, the Southern states formed a confederacy, and on April 12, 1861, South Carolina fired on federal troops at Fort Sumter and America went to war. As we examine the revelation verse by verse, note that the majority of the revelation has nothing to do with the Civil War.

"*Verily, thus saith the Lord concerning the wars that will shortly come to pass, beginning at the rebellion of South Carolina, which will eventually terminate in the death and misery of many souls*" (D&C 87:1). Note that it is "wars," and not "war." The Civil War began with the rebellion of South Carolina, but what are these other wars? There were no other wars spawned by the Civil War. This suggests these other wars were separate from and would occur after the Civil War.

The phrase "terminate in the death and misery of many souls" could refer to either the Civil War, or to the later wars, or to both. The Civil War certainly fulfills that description. Of all the wars the United States has ever been engaged in, the Civil War is still the deadliest war. Total deaths (from combat, accidents, sickness, suicide, or murder) totaled 665,000. The next closest is World War II, with 405,000 deaths. As we shall see, the wars that followed the Civil War also resulted in the death and misery of many souls. Death and misery are appropriate terms, for they are the ubiquitous companions of warfare.

"*And the time will come that war will be poured out upon all nations, beginning at this place*" (v. 2). "This place" refers to South Carolina, but that cannot mean that the Civil War would

> *This tremendous forecast, relating not only to the fierce internecine struggle between the Northern and Southern States of the American Union, but to other and mightier upheavals as well, some past and some yet future, was launched at Kirtland, Ohio, on the 25th of December, 1832. It may be said, therefore, that it came as a solemn Christmas gift to the inhabitants of the world, warning them to prepare for terrible events.*
>
> Orson F. Whitney, *Saturday Night Thoughts*, 48–49

eventually spread to become a global conflict, for no such thing came of it. It was strictly an American war, vast and terrible as it was. Note also that it doesn't say "at *that* time," but rather "the time will come." This suggests that this prediction would occur sometime in the future. Nor can "this place" be interpreted to mean that wars to follow would begin in the South, or even in the United States. The meaning is clear: beginning at this place *in time*, or at this point *in history* when the Civil War began in South Carolina, from that point on, eventually war would be poured out upon all nations.

"For behold, the Southern States shall be divided against the Northern States, and the Southern States will call on other nations, even the nation of Great Britain, as it is called, and they shall also call upon other nations, in order to defend themselves against other nations; and then war shall be poured out upon all nations" (v. 3). This verse is critical to our understanding of the prophecy, but is not immediately clear because the antecedents for words like "they," "themselves," and "then" need to be carefully sorted out. The Confederacy did call on Great Britain and France for help, and those countries did provide some support, mostly because they relied heavily on cotton from the South. But neither nation dared to send troops to aid the Confederacy because President Lincoln had warned Europe that any country joining the South would be at war with the United States. The other problem for Great Britain was that, years before, they had stopped the slave trade coming into their provinces, and many of their citizens were disgusted by the fact that the South was trying to perpetuate slavery. So, while the South did call on Great Britain, their response was cautious and limited.

So to whom does "they" in "*they* shall also call upon other nations" refer? The Southern states or Great Britain? Both are used in the lead-up in that sentence, but Great Britain is the closer noun. It also perfectly fits what actually happened in history, whereas the Southern states interpretation does not. In the first place, war was not poured out upon all nations when the Southern states called on Great Britain. But in both World War I and World War II, Great Britain did call on other nations for help, including those in their commonwealth, such as Canada, India, and Australia, as well as other nations in Europe and the United States. And it was when they—Great Britain—called on those other nations that war was truly poured out upon all nations.

"And it shall come to pass, after many days, slaves shall rise up against their masters, who shall be marshaled and disciplined for war" (v. 4). Here too we have several points of ambiguity. What is meant by "many days"? Who are the slaves? And who are the masters? Since the Civil War was fought mainly over slavery, many automatically assume it referred to the slaves in America. But history suggests a broader interpretation of this passage. First, though fear of slave uprisings was common among the Southern enslavers, they never materialized on a large scale. Many slaves escaped and went north to

join the Union, but there was no widespread uprising against their enslavers. Even after Abraham Lincoln issued the Emancipation Proclamation, there was not a general uprising of formerly enslaved people in the South. Also, the text here tells us that the slave uprising doesn't happen until "after many days," which would seem to eliminate any ties to the Civil War period.

How long is "many days"? This phrase was common among the people of earlier days, who lived when time was not measured in hours and minutes. It suggests a passage of time such as "after a time," or "a long while." In some cases, "many days" referred to hundreds of years.

So who are the slaves the prophecy is referring to? The description of their "masters" is helpful here. First, we are told that they are "marshaled and disciplined for war." In Webster's 1828 dictionary of the American language, "marshal" is a verb that means "to arrange in a suitable manner, as to *marshal* an army; to *marshal* troops." It is interesting that the two illustrations Webster used both involve military imagery. Webster's definition of the very "disciplined" also uses a military example: "to instruct and govern, to teach rules and practices, . . . as in discipline troops."

This helps us not so much to identify *who* they are, but *what* they are. These are not individual slave owners but more like what we would call political or military leaders of states or countries. And if that is the case, then their "slaves" are most likely the citizens of those states or countries. We spoke of totalitarian states earlier and saw that many countries today are such states, and their citizens are in virtual slavery, even though they don't wear shackles or live behind bars.

A nonpartisan organization called Freedom House evaluates various countries' political systems and places them in one of three categories: free, partly free, and not free. In 2018, they gave eighty-eight nations a ranking of free, and placed forty-nine in the not-free category, noting that democracy is in decline in many nations (See Gavin Haines, "Mapped: The world's most (and least) free countries," www.telegraph.co.uk).

There is another kind of slavery that could be included in this prophecy—the slavery of crushing poverty. We have all seen the images of refugee camps, slums, or inner-city neighborhoods where people scavenge for food in the garbage, where crime rules, where raw sewage runs in the streets, where youth die violently and younger children die of malnutrition. Many of these situations involve multigenerational slavery. Whichever kind of slavery is meant here, it is no surprise if it breeds perpetual anger, deep rage, and violent revolution.

"And it shall come to pass also that the remnants who are left of the land

will marshal themselves, and shall become exceedingly angry, and shall vex the Gentiles with a sore vexation" (v. 5). A key word in this verse is "remnants," which is plural. The context suggests this is a remnant of those "slaves" mentioned in the previous verse. But it could also refer to remnants of the house of Israel, for *remnants* is a word the Lord often uses to describe what is left of His covenant people today. Whichever it is, the fact that they too will "marshal themselves" and "vex the Gentiles" supports the idea of violent revolution. That they are exceedingly angry should not surprise us, for these have known great tribulation and discrimination for years, often even decades. Synonyms for *vex* include verbs like *irritate, make angry, plague, torment, harass*, and *afflict* (*American Dictionary*, s.v. "vex").

With that in mind, we are taught two key things about these "remnants" in the last days. The first is that they are those who "are left of the land." Note that it doesn't say "*this* land," but "*the* land," a more general reference. We are not sure who that includes or what they are "left" from.

Second, we learn that these remnants are going to be actively engaged in fighting against the Gentile nations and cause them much vexation. This sounds like it is going to be much more than an occasional, isolated uprising of the citizens of a country.

"*And thus, with the sword and by bloodshed the inhabitants of the earth shall mourn; and with famine, and plague, and earthquake, and the thunder of heaven, and the fierce and vivid lightning also, shall the inhabitants of the earth be made to feel the wrath, and indignation, and chastening hand of an Almighty God, until the consumption decreed hath made a full end of all nations; That the cry of the saints, and of the blood of the saints, shall cease to come up into the ears of the Lord of Sabaoth, from the earth, to be avenged of their enemies*" (vv. 6–7). All of the peace conferences, all of the efforts of the United Nations and other political and governmental organizations around the world are not going to bring us to world peace. The prophecies are crystal

---

I [prophesy] that that man who tarries after he has an opportunity of going, will be afflicted by the Devil. Wars are at hand. . . . When wars come we shall have to flee to Zion— The cry is to make haste. . . . Ye shall not have time to have gone over the Earth until these things come. It will come as did the Cholera, War, and Fires burning, Earthquakes one pestilence after another &c until the Ancient of Days come then judgment will be given to the saints.

Joseph Smith,
"History, 1838–1856, volume C-1 [2 November 1838–31 July 1842] [addenda]," pp. 12–13 [addenda],
The Joseph Smith Papers

clear on this. War is the inevitable result of the wickedness of men. As wickedness increases in the world, so will war.

"Wherefore, stand ye in holy places, and be not moved, until the day of the Lord come; for behold, it cometh quickly, saith the Lord" (v. 8). How simple and yet how profound is this closing verse. As we shall see in later chapters, the Lord has promised us that He will protect and preserve His people. He has promised that there will be places of peace, safety, and refuge in the terrible times that are coming. He has promised that if we are faithful we shall not be left alone to face the wickedness of the world.

In the last section of this book, we shall focus on those wonderful promises. We shall also discuss where those holy places are in which we can stand fast during the tribulation that is to come.

SOME QUESTIONS RELATED TO WAR

Before leaving the signs of the times that have to do with wars and rumors of war, let us address five questions related to this subject and the Second Coming:

- How does the revelation and prophecy on war (D&C 87) relate to the final war before Christ comes, which is commonly known as the battle of Armageddon?
- Can we say that there will be a World War III or a World War IV before Christ comes?
- Do the prophets foretell what we call a nuclear holocaust, or worldwide nuclear war?
- Some prophecies describe what could be called "widespread collapse of social order," in circumstances similar to but possibly outside of full-scale war. What do we learn from this?
- Will faithful members of the Church be directly involved in these wars?

WARS AND RUMORS OF WAR AND THE BATTLE OF ARMAGEDDON

Since Armageddon is one of the last things to happen before Christ comes, we are going to save our discussion of it until that point, even though it clearly is one of the dreadful signs of the times. But we will note a few things here. First, the term "battle of Armageddon" is not found in the scriptures. Only the word "Armageddon" is used. In Hebrew, the word means "Valley of Megiddo." This is another name for what is now called the Jezreel

Valley in modern Israel. It is a broad and fertile plain that has been a natural staging area for armies for centuries and evidently will be again.

WILL THERE BE A WORLD WAR III?

Yes, absolutely. But who knows if it will be called by that name. The real question is not whether there will be a war *called* World War III but whether there will be another global conflict like World War II. Considering what we just said about Armageddon, the answer to the question is a definite yes. There may be more than one global war, but we know for certain that there will be *at least* one more, for Armageddon will be a world war on a scope never before seen. Remember, the "prophecy on war" closed with these words: "War will be poured out upon all nations" (D&C 87:2).

WILL THERE BE A NUCLEAR HOLOCAUST?

This question usually brings much anxiety. It is also a question that is more complicated than it may seem. Nuclear *holocaust* typically means nuclear warfare on a global scale, with missiles carrying nuclear warheads raining down from the sky and massive mushroom clouds spreading radiation poisoning across the globe. What makes this subject so sobering is that while only a very small number of nations have access to nuclear weapons (under ten at current count), the total number of nuclear weapons is estimated to be somewhere between 13,000 and 15,000. And these are only those that have been acknowledged. That is certainly enough to cause a worldwide holocaust.

The prophets have often spoken of the earth being cleansed by fire at Christ's coming. The best known scripture on this topic is found in Malachi: "For, behold, the day cometh, that shall burn as an oven; and all the proud, yea, and all that do wickedly, shall

> *Now, all of us know that war, contention, hatred, suffering of the worst kind are not new. The conflict we see today is but another expression of the conflict that began with the War in Heaven. . . . That must have been a terrible conflict. . . . From the day of Cain to the present, the adversary has been the great mastermind of the terrible conflicts that have brought so much suffering. Treachery and terrorism began with him. And they will continue until the Son of God returns to rule and reign with peace and righteousness among the sons and daughters of God.*
>
> GORDON B. HINCKLEY, "THE TIMES IN WHICH WE LIVE," *ENSIGN*, NOVEMBER 2001

be stubble: and the day that cometh shall burn them up, saith the Lord of hosts" (Malachi 4:1). Stubble, of course, refers to the stalks of grain left after the reapers have harvested.

Could this be fulfilled through nuclear holocaust? The answer is not certain, but it is highly unlikely. First, the cleansing of the earth by fire seems to be the direct result of Christ's Second Coming. He is a celestial Being of unimaginable glory, and the scriptures directly tie the cleansing fire to His coming in glory (see D&C 133:41–44). Here are other scriptural examples:

- "In the last days, . . . behold all the nations of the Gentiles and also the Jews, . . . yea, even upon all the lands of the earth, behold, they will be drunken with iniquity and all manner of abominations—And when that day shall come they shall be visited of the Lord of Hosts, . . . with the flame of devouring fire" (2 Nephi 27:1–2).
- "And the world shall be burned with fire" (Jacob 6:3).
- "I, the Lord . . . will come down in heaven from the presence of my Father and consume the wicked with unquenchable fire" (D&C 63:34).

Secondly, a nuclear holocaust would leave vast areas of the world uninhabitable for many generations and would have enormous implications for the world's environment. How could an era of peace, righteousness, and progress take place on a ravaged planet? We do not find any hint of that kind of vast, total, global destruction in the prophecies.

Thirdly, unquenchable fire is often used in the scriptures as a metaphor for the intense guilt and suffering the wicked will feel when they are brought into the presence of the Father and the Son for judgment (see Jacob 6:10; Mosiah 2:38; Alma 12:14). How these three possibilities will interact and what will actually take place is not clear, but a worldwide nuclear holocaust seems unlikely.

With that said, however, it does not exclude the possibility of limited use of nuclear weapons sometime in the future. We know, for example, that there are several fanatical extremist groups who would not hesitate to use tactical nuclear weapons on large cities if they could get their hands on them. We also have nations who either now have or are rapidly developing nuclear capability, and some of these are led by radical leadership that would likely use them. One passage in Isaiah certainly sounds like it is describing the result of a nuclear detonation:

> The Lord hath a sacrifice . . . a great slaughter in the land of Idumea [land of the Edomites, a bitter enemy of ancient Israel]. . . . And the streams thereof shall be turned into pitch [tar or other flammable materials], and the dust thereof into brimstone [bitumen, a flammable substance, such as tar, sulfur, etc.], and the land thereof shall become burning pitch. *It shall not be quenched night nor day; the smoke thereof shall go up for ever: from generation to generation it shall lie waste; none shall pass through it for ever and ever* (Isaiah 34:6, 9–10).

John the Revelator described something similar that he saw in vision using these words: "And the fourth angel poured out his vial upon the sun; and power was given unto him to scorch men with fire. And men were scorched with great heat, and blasphemed the name of God" (Revelation 16:8–9). Also, several scriptures refer to "pillars of smoke" or "vapors of smoke." The towering mushroom cloud of a nuclear weapon would certainly qualify for those descriptions. This is not to say there *will* be cases where nuclear weapons are used, only that it is a *possibility* sometime in the future.

One other thing to consider is whether the visions of Isaiah and John have already been fulfilled. Is what they saw the bombing of Hiroshima and Nagasaki near the end of World War II? Anyone who has seen photos of the utter desolation that resulted from those attacks knows that it fits what the prophets describe.

WILL THERE BE WIDESPREAD COLLAPSE OF SOCIAL ORDER?

The answer to that is a strong affirmative. Though we may not think of it as war in the usual sense of the word, it is very much another form of warfare. We use different names for this phenomenon—civil unrest, rioting, rampage in the streets, protests—but these can be, and often are, another form of warfare. This may accompany war when large civilian populations are displaced or get caught up in what the experts blandly call "collateral damage." Think of the effect on the greater population when war destroys community services such as water, power, and sewage, or leads to severe shortages of food, lack of safe shelter, limited medical treatment, and other necessary commodities on which we all rely. This often brings another form of war, though on a more limited scale.

A phrase that captures all of these different scenarios is the collapse of social order. One of the things that defines civilization is what sociologists call "social contracts." A social contract is defined as an implicit agreement between individuals and groups—i.e., it is typically not a formal document. It is an agreement to comply with certain basic rules of social interaction so as to maintain order and harmony. Members of a society cooperate with each other and respect one another's rights, often without consciously thinking about them. This brings some degree of order, cooperation, and mutual social benefits to all involved.

When normal conditions no longer exist, for whatever reason, the social contracts break down, social order collapses, and chaos and anarchy result. This can rapidly escalate into widespread violence, destruction of private property, the breakdown of law and order, arson, looting, separating into rival "tribal" groups or gangs, and living in a perpetual state of violence and anarchy. This situation can even be worse than formal warfare because there are no rules or norms to rely on.

The breakdown of social order can be triggered by something that on the surface may seem quite trivial and that has been tolerated for years. Here are just a few things that have led to widespread rioting and destruction down through the ages:

- Crime-infested and violent neighborhoods where citizens daily fear for their lives.
- Shortages of the basic necessities of life caused by drought, corrupt governments, natural disasters, famine, war, or other reasons.
- Runaway inflation, like the hyper-inflation in Germany where it took wheelbarrows full of money to buy a single loaf of bread.
- Economic collapse, such as in the Great Depression of the 1930s.
- Riots among a disaffected segment of society that can quickly engulf whole communities.
- Natural disasters that do widespread damage to a society's infrastructures.
- Racial, ethnic, religious, political, or other forms of discrimination and persecution.
- The rise of crime syndicates that create great wealth for their members through violence, intimidation, and widespread murder.
- Harsh, totalitarian, and despotic governments. Usually these are on a national or state basis, but sometimes can occur at a regional or even local level.
- War of all kinds.

It has been proven throughout history that when social order breaks down, life is so disrupted that people will choose a dictatorship over anarchy because even under a harsh and despotic government, order is maintained that people can depend on as they go about their daily lives with some degree of normalcy.

Gratefully, a large majority of our Church members today live in societies where the rule of law is clearly established, and where governments, even with their many flaws, provide order and stability and basic freedoms for their citizens. Therefore, the incidents of a collapse in social order may be the exception for our members, not the rule. But the prophets have clearly foretold of times when social collapse could affect greater numbers of people, including members of the Church.

- "And it shall come to pass in that day, that a great tumult from the Lord shall be among them; and they shall lay hold every one on the hand of his neighbour, and his hand shall rise up against the hand of his neighbour" (Zechariah 14:13).
- There will be a "great hailstorm sent forth to destroy the crops of the earth" (D&C 29:16). Consider the implications of a worldwide food shortage for a moment. Almost overnight, order would begin to collapse as people desperately struggled for food.
- Mormon was an eyewitness to social collapse on a national scale, and his descriptions of the suffering that followed are horrible (see Mormon 5:8–9; Moroni 9:9–11, 14).
- Another example from the Book of Mormon shows how extensive the collapse of social order can become and how quickly it can occur. After years of unsuccessful efforts to put down the Gadianton robbers—a people who rejected all social contracts but their own—the situation had become so dangerous that the Nephites gathered all of their citizens to one place where they underwent a long siege in order to survive (see 3 Nephi 3:21–26).

A scripture in the Doctrine and Covenants describes what is still in the future but will likely occur in the United States—note the reference to New Jerusalem—as well as other places.

> And they will take up the sword, one against another, and they will kill one another. . . . And it shall come to pass among the wicked, that *every man that will not take his sword against his neighbor* must needs flee unto Zion for safety. And there shall be gathered unto it out of every nation under heaven; and it shall be the only people that shall not be at war one with another (D&C 45:33, 68–69).

Elder Orson Pratt, who was told in the Doctrine and Covenants that he should lift up his voice and prophesy (see D&C 34:10), said this of such times:

> What then will be the condition of that people, when this great and terrible war shall come? It will be very different from the war between the North and the South. . . . It will be a war of neighborhood against neighborhood, city against city, county against county, state against state, and they will go forth destroying and being destroyed, and manufacturing will, in a great measure, cease, for a time, among the American nation. Why? Because in these terrible wars, they will not be privileged to manufacture; there will be too much blood-shed—too much mobocracy—too much going forth in bands and destroying and pillaging the land to suffer people to pursue any local vocation with any degree of safety. What will become of millions of the farmers upon that land? They will leave their farms and they will flee before the ravaging armies from place to place; and thus will they go forth burning and pillaging the whole country (Pratt, in *Journal of Discourses,* 20:151).

WILL FAITHFUL MEMBERS OF THE CHURCH BE DIRECTLY INVOLVED IN THESE WARS?

Speaking through Joseph Smith in our day, the Lord warned:

> I, the Lord, am angry with the wicked; I am holding my Spirit from the inhabitants of the earth. I have sworn in my wrath, and decreed wars upon the face of the earth, and the wicked shall slay the wicked, and fear shall come upon every man (D&C 63:32–33).

Many of us do not like to think of our Heavenly Father as bringing these dreadful things down upon the world. But let us remember that just because a person warns us of danger doesn't mean that person is responsible for causing the danger. The horrible things that are coming are the natural consequences of millions upon millions of people deliberately, systematically, and consistently turning from the light toward the darkness. This is what creates the awful situations we have been discussing.

Fortunately, in His great mercy and grace, our Father also shows us how to prepare for such times. "And the saints also shall *hardly escape;* nevertheless, I, the Lord, am with them, and will come down in heaven from the presence of my Father and consume the wicked with unquenchable fire"

(D&C 63:34). In several other places, He promises us protection and says that we do not need to fear (see 1 Nephi 22:16–22).

That doesn't mean that we can expect to move through these times all sunshine and smiles. In the first place, we have to recognize that faithfulness is not something that we either have or don't have. We have different levels of faith and therefore different abilities to call down the powers of heaven in behalf of ourselves and our families. The compensatory power that Elder Andersen spoke of is directly influenced by our faith and our faithfulness.

In the second place, the scriptures are very clear that even the strongest of the faithful are not exempt from life's trials and challenges. If that were so then Jesus would not have died on the cross, Abinadi would not have been burned at the stake, Peter would not have been crucified upside down in Rome, and Joseph and Hyrum Smith would not have died in Carthage Jail. Joseph himself taught:

> I . . . explained concerning the coming of the Son of Man &c also that it is a false idea that the Saints will escape all the judgments whilst the wicked suffer—for all flesh is subject to suffer, and "the righteous shall hardly escape"—still many of the Saints will escape, for the just shall live by faith—yet many of the righteous shall fall a prey to disease, to pestilence, &c by reason of the weakness of the flesh, and yet be saved in the Kingdom of God (Joseph Smith, "History, 1838–1856, volume C-1 [2 November 1838–31 July 1842]," pp. 967–68, *The Joseph Smith Papers*; https://www.josephsmithpapers.org/paper-summary/history-1838-1856-volume-c-1-2-november-1838-31-july-1842/150).

But this much is clear. Though not all will escape some of the trials and tribulations, the faithful will always be better off than the wicked when the judgments come.

SUMMARY AND CONCLUSIONS

War and widespread social collapse—these are two signs of the times that are truly dreadful. We are living in a day when D&C 87 is in the process of being fulfilled. The American Civil War did take place, but it had a minimal effect on the Church and its members because by that time they had moved west, and it passed over them with few negative consequences. Global war followed, not once but twice, and we have been living in an age of war ever since.

The scriptures are very clear. There will be more war, more social upheaval, more sorrow, more death, more suffering. This is the prophetic picture. And in the next few chapters we will see other dreadful things that accompany this age of war.

But we need to remember not to lose sight of what Nephi saw in his vision of the last days. He saw that the number of the Saints would be few in comparison to the world's population. But he was also shown that the Church of the Lamb would be "armed with righteousness and with the power of God in great glory" (1 Nephi 14:14).

And in His preface to the Doctrine and Covenants, though the Lord did say that Satan would have power over his own dominion, He also made this promise: "The Lord shall have power over his saints, and shall reign in their midst, and shall come down in judgment upon Idumea, or the world" (D&C 1:36).

That is where the prophetic view of the future can help us to "be not troubled."

CHAPTER 14

NATURAL DISASTERS, FAMINE, PLAGUE, PESTILENCE

The Latter-day Saints . . . believe that great judgments are coming upon the world because of iniquity; they firmly believe in the statements of the Holy Scriptures, that calamities will befall the nations as signs of the coming of Christ to judgment. They believe that God rules in the fire, the earthquake, the tidal wave, the volcanic eruption, and the storm. Him they recognize as the Master and Ruler of nature and her laws, and freely acknowledge his hand in all things. We believe that his judgments are poured out to bring mankind to a sense of his power and his purposes, that they may repent of their sins and prepare themselves for the second coming of Christ to reign in righteousness upon the earth. . . . We believe that these severe, natural calamities are visited upon men by the Lord for the good of his children, to quicken their devotion to others, and to bring out their better natures, that they may love and serve him. We believe, further, that they are the heralds and tokens of his final judgment, and the schoolmasters to teach the people to prepare themselves by righteous living for the coming of the Savior to reign upon the earth, when every knee shall bow and every tongue confess that Jesus is the Christ. (Joseph F. Smith, *Gospel Doctrine: Selections from the Sermons and Writings of Joseph F. Smith*, 55)

THE SEAS HEAVING THEMSELVES BEYOND THEIR BOUNDS

In the law codes of many countries they are designated as "acts of God." Which is ironic, for many of the world's jurists and lawyers openly reject the concept of a Supreme Being. Others prefer a less divisive title for these phenomena. They prefer to call them "natural disasters," putting the blame on the more neutral concept of Mother Nature.

While I was serving as a General Authority Seventy, my wife and I were assigned to serve in the Europe West Area Presidency, with headquarters in Solihull, England, a suburb of Birmingham. Our area included nearly two dozen countries, including all of the British Isles and the countries that occupy the western part of the continent of Europe.

Much of northern Europe has winters that are dreary and prolonged, with short days, long nights, and heavy, overcast skies much of the time. For that reason, it is a very popular thing in northern Europe for people to use the Christmas and New Year holiday season to head for warmer climes.

Sites along the Mediterranean Sea are popular spots, but with modern air travel, large numbers of tourists travel to the southern hemisphere, where full summer is underway. Thailand, Indonesia, Malaysia, and the islands of the South Pacific, along with other countries, have also become popular tourist destinations for Europeans.

On Sunday, the day after Christmas, 2004, at 7:59 a.m. local time, a massive underwater earthquake struck off the coast of the Indonesian island of Sumatra. It registered 9.1 on the Richter scale, making it the third strongest earthquake in modern times. World Vision, an international humanitarian service organization, describes what immediately followed:

> The quake caused the ocean floor to suddenly rise by as much as 40 meters [about the height of a thirteen-story building], triggering a massive tsunami. Within 20 minutes of the earthquake, the first of several 100-foot waves hit the shoreline of Banda Aceh [the largest city on the island of Sumatra], killing more than 100,000 people [eventually the death toll for the city reached 170,000, more than half of the city's total population] and pounding the city into rubble. Then, in succession, tsunami waves rolled over coastlines in Thailand, India, and Sri Lanka, killing tens of thousands more. Eight hours later and 5,000 miles from its Asian epicenter, the tsunami claimed its final casualties on the coast of South Africa. In all, nearly 230,000 people were killed, making it one of the deadliest disasters in modern history (worldvision.org/disaster-relief-news-stories/2004-indian-ocean-tsunami-facts).

Within hours, the news hit western Europe. As the casualty figures came in over the next few days, we learned that almost 2,000 people from western Europe, including about 150 from the British Isles, were among the victims. As images began appearing almost nonstop in newspapers and on television, people all across Europe went into mourning. In England, large bottles, tubs, and boxes began appearing in stores and businesses labeled with "Tsunami Fund" or "Help for the Tsunami Victims." In a few weeks almost £1,000,000 (about $2.25 million) had been collected. It was refreshing evidence that many people want to do something to help others in need.

Not long after that positive indicator, religious skeptics started in as well. "How can you believe in a God like this?" shouted one poster with a picture of the vast devastation. Major news outlets made it a topic of discussion. Even a prominent cleric in the U.K. admitted that he was struggling to reconcile this disaster with his belief in a loving and benevolent God.

As we watched and listened, I can remember being struck by the irony of it. Every day millions of people around the world are blessed with peace, prosperity, employment, families, good health, sunshine, bounteous crops, freedom, and hundreds of other blessings. And they never think to give God credit for any of it. But let a tragedy strike, and immediately some start wondering how God could ever do such a terrible thing.

THE LORD'S VOICES AND TESTIMONIES

One hundred and seventy-two years before the Indonesian tsunami struck in the Indian Ocean, Joseph Smith received a revelation. In it, the Lord made reference to various "voices" through which He speaks to His children:

> For after your testimony cometh the *testimony* of earthquakes, that shall cause groanings in the midst of her, and men shall fall upon the ground and shall not be able to stand. And also cometh the *testimony* of the *voice* of thunderings, and the *voice* of lightnings, and the *voice* of tempests, and the *voice* of the *waves of the sea heaving themselves beyond their bounds*. And all things shall be in commotion; and surely, men's hearts shall fail them; for fear shall come upon all people (D&C 88:89–91).

Nearly two thousand years before that, Jesus also warned His disciples of coming disasters, promising that there would be "upon the earth distress of nations, with perplexity; *the sea and the waves roaring*" (Luke 21:25; see also JST Luke 21:24–25). In Matthew's account of that time, other forms of natural disaster were mentioned:

> Immediately after the tribulation of those days [the time just preceding the Second Coming] shall the sun be darkened, and the moon shall not give her light, and the stars shall fall from heaven,

and the powers of the heavens shall be shaken: And then shall appear the sign of the Son of man in heaven: and then shall all the tribes of the earth mourn, and they shall see the Son of man coming in the clouds of heaven with power and great glory (Matthew 24:30–31; see also JS—M 1:33, 36).

These "signs in the heavens" are also mentioned throughout modern scripture:

- "The Lord God surely shall visit all the house of Israel at that day, some with his *voice*, because of their righteousness, unto their great joy and salvation, and others with the thunderings and the lightnings of his power, by tempest, *by fire, and by smoke, and vapor of darkness*, and by the opening of the earth, and by mountains which shall be carried up" (1 Nephi 19:11).
- "For *the stars of heaven and the constellations thereof shall not give their light; the sun shall be darkened in his going forth, and the moon shall not cause her light to shine.* . . . Therefore, *I will shake the heavens, and the earth shall remove out of her place*, in the wrath of the Lord of Hosts, and in the day of his fierce anger" (2 Nephi 23:10, 13; from Isaiah 13).
- "Before that great day shall come, *the sun shall be darkened, and the moon be turned into blood; and the stars shall refuse their shining, and some shall fall*, and great destructions await the wicked" (D&C 34:9; see also D&C 45:39–42).
- "And they shall see signs and wonders, for *they shall be shown forth in the heavens above*, and in the earth beneath. And they shall behold *blood, and fire, and vapors of smoke. And before the day of the Lord shall come, the sun shall be darkened, and the moon be turned into blood, and the stars fall from heaven*" (D&C 45:39–42).
- "For not many days hence and the earth shall tremble and reel to and fro as a drunken man; and *the sun shall hide his face, and shall refuse to give light; and the moon shall be bathed in blood; and the stars shall become exceedingly angry, and shall cast themselves down as a fig that falleth from off a fig-tree*" (D&C 88:87).

It is clear from these and many other prophecies that the Lord can use the natural forces of Mother Earth to teach and correct, and yes, even punish His children. This is taught often enough that clear doctrine and principles can be drawn from what we are taught.

DOCTRINES AND PRINCIPLES ASSOCIATED WITH NATURAL DISASTERS AND OTHER CALAMITIES

In the opening quotation, President Joseph F. Smith taught several principles that actually define what we could call gospel principles used by Heavenly Father. We don't usually put doctrines of the gospel in the same sentence with natural disasters, but that is what we have in President Smith's writings (see Joseph F. Smith, *Gospel Doctrine*, 55) and tie them to a doctrinal principle.

1. "[Latter-day Saints] *believe that God rules in the fire, the earthquake, the tidal wave, the volcanic eruption, and the storm. Him [we] recognize as the Master and Ruler of nature and her laws, and freely acknowledge his hand in all things.*"

Some people use the term Mother Nature as a nice way of describing the natural forces that created the world and all that is in it. These people, many of whom are highly intelligent, totally reject the idea of a Supreme Being who watches over and judges us.

Others who accept God disassociate Him from the natural phenomena we see around us. They are known as Deists. They deeply believe that there is a God and that He is the Creator of all things. But they see Him as remaining aloof from His creations, allowing the earth to run through natural laws without further support from Him.

Our concept of God is profoundly different. To members of The Church of Jesus Christ of Latter-day Saints, and many other believers, God is not only the Creator and a Divine Judge, but He is literally our Heavenly Father, Creator of our spirits and our physical bodies. This profoundly changes what we know about His character and attributes, the most important of which is His infinite love for His children. But this does not lessen His perfection in other areas, such as being omnipotent, or having all power. And a key part of that power was used to create the universe and put in place the natural laws that keep it running.

This is what President Smith tells us in this first statement. Since God created the fire, the earth, and all things in and on and around the earth, they are all under His control. Though to our mortal, finite minds natural disasters seem like random, unpredictable events that "just happen," we strongly believe that the Father and the Son have direct control and influence over all of creation, including natural laws and natural disasters.

That is not to say that They sit at some great master control panel manipulating all aspects of our environment and our experience. The Creation carries both many wonderful things and many destructive things, and the Lord puts all of His children where they can experience both. Remember what the Savior taught: the Father "maketh his sun to rise on the evil and on the good, and sendeth rain on the just and on the unjust" (Matthew 5:45). That means all of His children will experience the challenges of mortality, including natural disasters.

2. *"We believe that his judgments are poured out to bring mankind to a sense of his power and his purposes, that they may repent of their sins and prepare themselves for the second coming of Christ to reign in righteousness upon the earth. . . . We believe that these severe, natural calamities are visited upon men by the Lord for the good of his children, to quicken their devotion to others, and to bring out their better natures, that they may love and serve him."* This is a unique perspective about the nature of God. President Smith was very clear that we don't believe natural disasters are only random events. President Smith taught that they can also remind us of God's great power, which then can bring us to humility and repentance.

President Smith also noted a positive side of these events. Though we often read of those who selfishly think only of themselves in a crisis, in virtually every major disaster we also read accounts of how the tragedy "brings out the best in people." We read of people who risk their own lives, or share their own meager goods, or who are so moved with compassion that they send money and materials.

3. *"We believe, further, that they are the heralds and tokens of his final judgment, and the schoolmasters to teach the people to prepare themselves by righteous living for the coming of the Savior to reign upon the earth."* Here is another important doctrine related to natural disasters. These events can be a form of God's judgment on His children. Some of His children are so stubborn and intransigent that it takes something drastic to get their attention and soften their hearts. Some who are caught in these events see it as a personal warning and undertake serious changes in their lives thereafter. If nothing else, they

> *God is speaking through the elements in the midst of the nations of the earth. He will manifest his power as never before. This Church will have the opportunity to demonstrate its power and its influence in the world. If only we will adhere to these principles, we shall rise and shine, and no power on earth or in hell shall stop the progress and growth and development of this work. The power to make it succeed is in our hands.*
>
> MELVIN J. BALLARD,
> IN CONFERENCE REPORT,
> APRIL 1928, 117

are determined to be better prepared if a disaster strikes again. Thus, not all of the consequences of natural disasters are disastrous.

Elder Bruce R. McConkie also drew similar doctrinal principles from natural disasters:

> The disasters of earth—*controlled as they are in the infinite wisdom of that Lord who knoweth all things*—are used by him to temper and train us. He uses natural disasters to bring to us the conscious realization that we are dependent upon a Supreme Being for all things. He uses them as a means of judgment to punish us for evil deeds done in the flesh. He uses them to humble us so that perchance we will repent and live as he would have us live. . . . And all of this has particular application in this day of wickedness when the world is being prepared to receive its rightful King (McConkie, *Millennial Messiah*, 374).

THE LORD'S SERMONS

The Lord speaks of the various "voices" and "testimonies" He uses to help people prepare themselves for what is coming. We could liken those to God's sermons that call on us to hear His voice and return to Him, and He specifically links those to natural disasters.

- "What will ye say when the day cometh when the *thunders shall utter their voices* from the ends of the earth, speaking to the ears of all that live, saying . . . Yea, and again, *when the lightnings shall streak forth from the east unto the west, and shall utter forth their voices unto all that live,* and make the ears of all tingle that hear, saying these words—Repent ye, for the great day of the Lord is come? . . . O, ye nations of the earth, . . . how oft have I called upon you by the mouth of my servants, and by the ministering of angels, and by mine own voice, *and by the voice of thunderings, and by the voice of lightnings, and by the voice of tempests, and by the voice of earthquakes, and great hailstorms, and by the voice of famines and pestilences of every kind,* . . . but ye would not!" (D&C 43:21–23, 25).

- "And thus, with the sword and by bloodshed the inhabitants of the earth shall mourn; and with famine, and plague, and earthquake, and the thunder of heaven, and the fierce and vivid lightning also, shall the inhabitants of the earth be made to feel the *wrath, and indignation, and chastening hand of an Almighty God,* until the consumption decreed hath made a full end of all nations" (D&C 87:6).

Natural Disasters, Famine, Plague, Pestilence

Let us now briefly explore those natural phenomena that we call natural disasters. We shall see that God Himself teaches us that these are used as a means to get His children to turn back to Him, as opposed to manmade disasters such as war or the collapse of social order. We shall group them into four categories:

- *Geologic disasters:* Earthquakes, tsunamis, volcanos, landslides, etc.
- *Weather-related disasters:* Tempests, tornados, hurricanes, dust storms, severe lightning and thunderstorms; severe heat waves; hailstorms, torrential rains, drought, blizzards, ice storms, etc.
- *Signs in the heavens:* The sun darkened, the moon turned to blood, stars falling from heaven, pillars of fires and vapors of smoke, etc.
- *Famine, pestilence, sickness, disease, plagues:* Famine is often linked with drought; pestilence would include locusts, grasshoppers, worms, insects, rodents, etc.

GEOLOGIC DISASTERS

From historical records—both scriptural and secular—we know that catastrophic disasters have always been part of life on earth. Here are just a few examples:

- In A.D. 526, an earthquake in Syria killed 250,000 people. In 1556, an earthquake in Shaanxi, China, killed 830,000 (see *World Almanac*, 2019, 330).
- In the fourteenth century, bubonic plague spread across Europe, eventually taking about 60% of its population (see www.historytoday.com/archive/black-death-greatest-catastrophe-ever).
- In A.D. 536, incessant volcanic eruptions in Iceland produced millions of tons of ash and plunged the northern hemisphere into semidarkness for eighteen months. One Harvard scholar said this was the worst year in history to be alive. In addition to the darkness, it caused continental crop failure and extreme drought and famine with economic effects that lasted for a century (see www.dailymail.co.uk/sciencetech/article-6397621/Why-536-AD-worst-year-alive).
- Flooding in China in August 1831, killed an estimated 3,600,000 (see *World Almanac*, 2019, 330).
- The eruption of a volcano in Tambora in Indonesia in April 1815 is still considered to be the largest volcanic eruption in history. It blew off approximately 4,000 feet of the mountaintop, instantly killing

10,000 people in nearby towns and villages. (For comparison, Mount St. Helens, which exploded on May 18, 1980, lost about 1,000 feet of its peak.) Here too, millions of tons of ash were spewed into the atmosphere, which affected the world's climate for a time. Ironically, the event in Indonesia had an interesting effect in the history of the Church. In Vermont, the year 1815 is still known as the "year without a summer." With the filtering out of the sunlight, they had hard frost and snow in July and August and the crops failed. Joseph Smith Sr. and his wife Lucy Mack Smith had already been struggling to survive financially. This was the final blow. Joseph Smith Sr. traveled to upstate New York after hearing of rich wheat harvests there. Eventually, he moved his family west, settling near Palmyra, New York. By happy "coincidence," their farm was a short distance from a hill in the area known as the Hill Cumorah (see *Saints: The Standard of Truth*, 3–5).

These natural phenomena are, and always have been, part of the world that is our home.

SIGNS IN THE HEAVENS

Note that the Lord frequently links signs on earth to signs in the heavens. It seems safe to assume that the signs on earth include the ones we have been discussing, such as earthquakes, storms, tsunamis, and so on. But He also specifically mentions signs in the heavens. These include:

1. *The heavens will be darkened so that the sun, moon, and stars do not give their light to the earth* (see Matthew 24:29; 2 Nephi 15:30; Moses 7:61). This does not imply that these heavenly bodies will be destroyed, only that their light is diminished here on earth. This could be caused by several things happening on the earth such as widespread fires, massive dust storms, volcanic eruptions, nuclear explosions, or even severe air pollution.

2. *The moon shall be turned to blood* (see D&C 29:14; 34:9; 45:42; 88:87). This is not likely literal, but it will appear as if the moon were made of blood. Though not a common occurrence, neither is it unusual for the moon to turn a blood red. It happens naturally from time to time. For example, astronomers speak of a "blood moon," a phenomenon that occurs during an eclipse or when there is heavy air pollution.

3. *The stars shall fall from the heavens* (see D&C 34:9; 45:42; 88:87; Acts 2:20). Modern science speaks of meteor showers in the skies at night, or asteroids passing by us out in space. Though we know they are meteors entering the earth's atmosphere and burning up, we frequently call them

"falling stars." These are part of the natural phenomena of our world and the heavens around us. However, some scriptures make it clear that the Lord is talking about something more than what we normally experience now. Note the language in D&C 88:87: *"The stars shall become exceedingly angry, and shall cast themselves down."*

4. *The powers of heaven shall be shaken* (see 2 Nephi 23:13; D&C 21:6; 43:18; 45:48). This is mentioned in several places. We speak often about earthquakes, but "heaven-quakes"? Here again, the Lord chooses not to give us more detail, but the implication is that when it actually comes, we will recognize it as one of the signs He has foretold.

5. *Fires and vapors of smoke* (see Mormon 8:29; D&C 45:41). If these are widespread from war, volcanic eruptions, storms, major wildfires, or other causes, that would explain the darkening of the heavens.

6. *The earth will reel to and fro and will be moved out of its place* (see D&C 45:48; 49:23; 88:87; Isaiah 24:20). We have already discussed earthquakes, especially those of a high magnitude, that strike with incredible power, shifting the massive tectonic plates beneath the earth to a measurable degree. Here too the Lord chooses not to give us more detail, but it does appear that He is speaking of something beyond what we normally experience.

As Elder Melvin J. Ballard put it:

> I bear witness to you that God is speaking through the elements in the midst of the nations of the earth. He will manifest his power as never before. This Church will have the opportunity to demonstrate its power and its influence in the world. If only we will adhere to these principles, we shall rise and shine, and no power on earth or in hell shall stop the progress and growth and development of this work (Ballard, in Conference Report, April 1928, 117).

A DESOLATING SCOURGE: SICKNESS, DISEASE, FAMINE, PESTILENCE

Though it is not mentioned as frequently as the ones above, there is another sign of the times on this "dreadful" side of the ledger that deserves a discussion here. Several things are included under this heading as well, but the Lord seems to use the word "scourge" as a general term for something that brings great suffering.

In Webster's 1828 dictionary, "scourge" is both a noun and a verb. The noun is defined as "a whip, or a lash, an instrument of punishment." Therefore, a scourge is a person or a thing "that greatly afflicts, harasses or destroys."

Though Webster does not include this concept in his definition, in the scriptures the idea of a scourge suggests conditions that last for a prolonged period of time. This is in contrast to other natural disasters that, while potentially catastrophic, are typically brief in duration. For example, Nephi talks about a scourge that lasts many generations (see 2 Nephi 25:16), and the prophet Helaman, despairing over the people's lack of repentance, pleaded with the Lord: "O Lord, do not suffer that this people shall be destroyed by the sword; but O Lord, rather let there be a famine in the land, to stir them up in remembrance of the Lord their God, and perhaps they will repent and turn unto thee" (Helaman 11:4). The Lord heard his prayer, and after three years of famine, the people turned back to the Lord (see vv. 5–9).

A prolonged time of suffering is generally found in these warnings about scourges:

- "For whom the Lord loveth he chasteneth, and scourgeth every son whom he receiveth" (Hebrews 12:6).
- "*A desolating scourge* shall go forth among the inhabitants of the earth, and shall *continue to be poured out from time to time,* if they repent not, until the earth is empty, and the inhabitants thereof are consumed away and utterly destroyed by the brightness of my coming" (D&C 5:19).
- "And there shall be men standing in that generation, that shall not pass until they shall see an *overflowing scourge; for a desolating sickness* shall cover the land" (D&C 45:31).
- "I, the Almighty, have laid my hands upon the nations, *to scourge them for their wickedness.* And *plagues* shall go forth, and they shall not be taken from the earth [i.e., they shall continue for a prolonged period of time] until I have completed my work, which shall be cut short in righteousness" (D&C 84:96–97).

Note how famine, plague, sickness, and pestilence are often mentioned together as part of the Lord's warning voice (see, for example, JS—M 1:29; 2 Nephi 6:15; Mosiah 12:4; D&C 45:31). This could be because very often these things are naturally linked to each other. As one example, drought brings on famine; famine weakens the human body; weakened bodies are more susceptible to disease. Food shortages often lead to the collapse of social stability.

Here are just a few modern examples showing that particular signs of the times seem to be increasing in our time:

- Due to warming climate, drought, and human overuse, some of the world's largest lakes are drying up. Bolivia's second largest lake is now a dry lake bed. Africa's Lake Chad is a sliver of its former self. Iran's Lake Urmia, the second largest lake in the Middle East, has shrunk by 80% in the last thirty years. The carcasses of abandoned ships can be seen locked into the silt that was once lake bottom (see www.nationalgeographic.com/magazine/2018/03/drying-lakes-climate-change-global-warming-drought/).
- In the thirty-eight years between 1980 and 2018, the United States experienced twenty-five major droughts, which caused about 3,000 deaths and created losses of $241 billion (*World Almanac*, 322).
- As mentioned, the bubonic plague in Europe killed about half the population of Europe during the dark ages. What is less known is that in modern times an estimated 50 to 100 million people were killed in the great flu epidemic of 1918–19, more commonly known as the Spanish flu epidemic. It is still considered the most deadly outbreak of a disease in history. In Utah, The Church of Jesus Christ of Latter-day Saints canceled General Conference to help contain the spread of the disease.
- The HIV/AIDS epidemic, or pandemic, which began in the 1980s, has now killed 25 million worldwide (see www.healthcarebusinesstech.com/the-ten-deadliest-epidemics-in-history). For a time it was one of the leading causes of death in the 25–44 age group in the U.S.
- The 1957 Asian flu pandemic killed about 2,000,000 worldwide.
- First discovered in 1976 in Central Africa, the Ebola virus has now taken thousands of lives. Though the numbers are not catastrophic as yet, the rate of death for those infected is over fifty percent, according to the World Health Organization.
- About 575,000 died worldwide from the swine flu pandemic of 2009–10, which was first detected in the U.S.
- Centers for Disease Control experts estimate there are 19,000,000 people in the U.S. alone who are infected with sexually transmitted diseases. That is about 17% of the population. If that were to hold true worldwide, then about 1.3 billion people are infected, and many of these are innocent victims.
- We have already discussed the COVID-19 pandemic and the tremendous upheaval and suffering it has caused. Just as we refer back to catastrophic examples from the past, future generations will look back on our time as another major turning point in history.

SUMMARY AND CONCLUSIONS

From Biblical times, the Lord has warned His people and the world that in the last days there would be much commotion and upheaval in both nature and society. Those warnings are also found throughout modern scripture and the words of modern prophets. They make for sobering and even depressing reading. Occasionally we hear of some who say, "I don't watch the news anymore. It is too depressing." While those feelings are understandable, the Lord has warned us in advance of these things so that we can prepare. He wants us to be informed of the world around us (see, for example, D&C 88:78–79) so that we can, as stated before, "be not troubled."

Our study of the dreadful side of the last days can, strangely enough, bring us comfort and hope in the midst of the dread. These signs provide powerful evidence that our Father is all-knowing and that in spite of His anger and wrath at the wickedness of the world, His love for us has led Him to give us so much detail about the darker side of what is coming. And His invitation is always there, even for the most wicked of the world: "Come unto me, and I will give you rest" (see Matthew 11:28–30), and, "Be not troubled" (D&C 45:35).

Each individual will make his or her way in a constantly changing world—a world of competing ideologies. The forces of evil will ever be in opposition to the forces of good. Satan constantly strives to influence us to follow his ways and make us miserable, even as he is. And the normal risks of life, such as illness, injury, and accident, will ever be present. We live in a time of turmoil. Earthquakes and tsunamis wreak devastation, governments collapse, economic stresses are severe, the family is under attack, and divorce rates are rising. We have great cause for concern. But we do not need to let our fears displace our faith. We can combat those fears by strengthening our faith.

RUSSELL M. NELSON,
"FACE THE FUTURE WITH FAITH,"
ENSIGN, MAY 2011

CHAPTER 15

BY A THREAD: THE UNITED STATES IN PROPHECY

The founding of this nation paved the way for the Restoration. In no other nation under heaven could the Church have been organized and gone forward as we have in this nation. The founding of the United States was not an accident. The giving to us of the Constitution of the United States was not an accident. Our Heavenly Father knew what would be needed, and so he paved the way to give us the Constitution. It came under the influence of prayer, and he guided those who framed that wonderful document. (George Albert Smith, *Teachings*, 167)

THE CHURCH OF JESUS CHRIST AND THE GOVERNMENT OF THE UNITED STATES OF AMERICA

If the Restoration was to happen so that the kingdom of God could spread across the world like a stone cut from the mountain without hands, as Daniel foresaw (see Daniel 2:34), then something had to happen first. Absolutely essential to the Restoration was a nation that guaranteed the right of its citizens to free speech, the rights of property, and especially, freedom of religion. Had the Church been restored even in the more enlightened countries of Europe at that time, it would have been quickly crushed by state-sponsored religions, which vigorously opposed the rights of other religions.

When the founding fathers created the Constitution in 1787 and added the Bill of Rights in 1789, the separation of church and state was firmly established in the land. Though the founding fathers did not realize what would come of their vision, Heavenly Father did. The Constitution, with its first ten amendments, was put in place about thirty years before the young

Joseph Smith went into a grove of trees and took the first step in opening a new dispensation.

The darker side of the irony lies in the fact that in spite of the Constitution and the Bill of Rights, religious persecution began immediately after Joseph Smith came out of the Sacred Grove.[1] In those first early years, the persecution came mostly from violent individuals who ignored the law of the land, with some cooperation from government officials. By 1833, things changed. A significant number of Latter-day Saints had moved to Independence, Jackson County, Missouri, which the Lord had declared was the center place of Zion. This was a settlement on the western border of the United States and, at that time, was far from the law and order that prevailed elsewhere in the country. The clash between Saints and local residents was almost inevitable and quickly turned violent. A group of men took the law into their own hands, with the support of local judges and constables, and set out to drive the "Mormons" from their county. Private property was looted or destroyed. Leaders were tarred and feathered. Livestock were killed. Men were savagely beaten, and some were killed. Women and children were driven from their homes in the middle of the night in their nightclothes and without shoes.

> *The American Constitution is, as far as I can see, the most wonderful work ever struck off at a given time by the brain and purpose of man.*
>
> THOMAS S. MONSON,
> FAVORITE QUOTATIONS, 193

In a revelation given to the Prophet, the Lord instructed the Saints to appeal to the laws of the land, reminding them that He had established the Constitution for this very purpose:

> And again I say unto you, those who have been scattered by their enemies, it is my will that they should continue to importune for redress, and redemption, by the hands of those who are placed as rulers and are in authority over you—*According to the laws and constitution of the people,* which I have suffered to be established, and should be maintained for the rights and protection of all flesh, according to just and holy principles; . . . And for this purpose [the

---

[1] In this chapter we will discuss only the injustices leveled against the Latter-day Saints, but the Church is not the only group whose rights of freedom of religion have been ignored. We know that down through our history, many other religious and ethnic minorities have had their rights heavily restricted or taken away completely.

protection of individual rights] have I established the Constitution of this land, by the hands of wise men whom I raised up unto this very purpose, and redeemed the land by the shedding of blood (D&C 101:76–77, 80).

The Lord reminded them of a parable from the New Testament, sometimes called the parable of the importunate woman (see Luke 18:1–6). To importune means to press one's cause with unwearying zeal until redress is granted. The Lord then continued:

> Thus will I liken the children of Zion. Let them importune at the feet of the judge; And if he heed them not, let them importune at the feet of the governor; And if the governor heed them not, let them importune at the feet of the president; And if the president heed them not, *then will the Lord arise and come forth out of his hiding place, and in his fury vex the nation;* And in his hot displeasure, and in his fierce anger, in his time, will cut off those wicked, unfaithful, and unjust stewards, and appoint them their portion among hypocrites, and unbelievers (D&C 101:85–90).

When the state and county officials, including judges, refused to defend the rights of the Saints, the members of the Church eventually moved to northern Missouri, where there were very few towns and only scattered residents. They quickly created towns and villages, plowed the prairie, and turned it into rich farmland. The number of Saints grew rapidly as conversions to the Church continued and as problems in Kirtland caused many members to leave Ohio and come to the land of Zion.

In 1838, the persecution began again, this time with the full support of the governor and the state militia, as well as local constables, judges, and city and county officials. When the governor issued an edict that the Saints were to be driven from the state or exterminated, the floodgates were thrown wide open. Seventeen members of the Church, including an aged Revolutionary War veteran and a ten-year-old boy, were brutally murdered in a raid on Hawn's Mill. Livestock were shot.

> *This nation will . . . endure. It is God-ordained for a glorious purpose. We must never forget that the gospel message we bear to the world is to go forth to the world from this nation. And that gospel message can prosper only in an atmosphere of freedom. We must maintain and strengthen our freedom in this blessed land.*
>
> Ezra Taft Benson, "This Nation Shall Endure," BYU devotional, December 4, 1973

Homes and barns were burned. Again men were savagely whipped and beaten. Women were ravished by the militia. Dozens of men were marched off to prison, including Joseph Smith and other key leaders. The commanding general gave his troops license to loot and destroy a city of over 5,000 people, then drive them from the state in the dead of winter.

While Joseph and other leaders were languishing in Liberty Jail—what an ironic name!—Joseph received instruction to begin "gathering up a knowledge of all the facts, and sufferings and abuses put upon them by the people of this State; . . . *that the whole nation may be left without excuse*" (D&C 123:1–6).

They did so and eventually took that evidence to the Supreme Court of Missouri. They were turned away. They next appealed to the Congress of the United States. They were given a chance to plead their cause but were told that this was not a federal matter; they had to take their appeal to the state of Missouri. This was said knowing that Missouri had already rejected their petitions. Finally they appealed directly to the president of the United States, Martin Van Buren. Joseph met with him face to face. After reading some of the petitions, Van Buren agreed that their cause was just, but he made it clear that his political position took precedent over justice. "I can do nothing for you," Van Buren said, playing the part of a consummate politician. "If I were for you, I should go against the whole state of Missouri, and that state would go against me in the next election" (*Saints: The Standard of Truth*, 408).

Greatly discouraged, Joseph submitted a petition to Congress, asking that they at least compensate the Saints for their losses. The results were basically the same. There was a lot of political posturing, and though Congress acknowledged the distress of the Saints, in the end they said they had no power to intervene in what were state affairs. Henry Clay, one of the most powerful senators at that time, coldly suggested they move to the Oregon Territory—in other words, leave the United States so as to avoid further conflict (ibid., 413–14). Thus the duly elected officials of the United States of America refused to extend to them the guarantees the Constitution offered to all of its citizens.

Nor was the persecution over. Driven to the state of Illinois, the Saints once again transformed empty and useless land into homes, farms, businesses, and a thriving, prosperous city. Nauvoo and other settlements quickly grew along both banks of the Mississippi River. Then, just six years following their expulsion from Missouri, Joseph and Hyrum Smith were murdered in the Carthage, Illinois, jail by a mob with painted faces. This was after the governor of the state of Illinois had promised that he would protect them from the mobs, then abandoned them. Soon, once again with the support of the governor of the state, the Saints were given another ultimatum. Leave the state or be destroyed. To further deepen the irony, this time the governor threatened to call in federal troops to force law-abiding citizens from their homes yet again. Their only recourse at this point was to leave the United States and start a new home "far away in the West . . . where none shall come to hurt or make afraid" (*Hymns*, no. 30).

A BANNER OF LIBERTY IN A LAND OF PROMISE

We still reap the blessings of the U.S. Constitution more than two hundred years later. But other prophets gave warning about the land of promise (all of North and South America), which would also be applicable to the United States. For example, as the brother of Jared was being prepared to take his people to a new land, the Lord promised him that it would be "*a land of promise; and whatsoever nation shall possess it shall serve God, or they shall be swept off when the fulness of his wrath shall come upon them. And the fulness of his wrath cometh upon them when they are ripened in iniquity. . . . This is a choice land, and whatsoever nation shall possess it shall be free from bondage, and from captivity, and from all other nations under heaven, if they will but serve the God of the land, who is Jesus Christ*" (Ether 2:9, 12).

Much later, Lehi's colony was also taken to the promised land and given the same warning and promise. The promise was that if the people kept the Lord's commandments, they would prosper in the land (see 1 Nephi 4:14). The warning was, "Inasmuch as ye will not keep my commandments ye shall not prosper in the land" (Omni 1:6).

In light of what we see in our nation today—and other nations all around the world—there is one

I believe the reformers played an important role in preparing the world for the Restoration. So did the early explorers and colonizers of America and the framers of the Constitution of the United States. God needed a philosophical climate that allowed for theological restoration and a political arena where people could share ideas and talk about their beliefs openly without fear of persecution or death. He created such a place on the American continent. . . . Never in the history of the world did the sincere seeker of truth have more ecclesiastical options from which to choose.

M. RUSSELL BALLARD,
OUR SEARCH FOR HAPPINESS, 32

prophetic warning given by King Mosiah that has great relevance for our day. This is especially significant because after Mosiah's sons refused to accept the kingdom, Mosiah created a new form of government for his people. He changed a monarchy system into a government run by "judges," who were elected by the voice of the people, not chosen by the head of the state. Though Mosiah doesn't specifically say that he created a written document to formalize this remarkable change, that seems to be the case, and the form of government was changed for the remainder of the Book of Mormon times. It was so significant that they began to mark the passage of the years starting with the first year of the judges (see Mosiah 29:44).

But King Mosiah also left a sobering warning about the responsibilities that this put on the Nephite citizenry, which has great relevance for our day:

> Now it is not common that the voice of the people desireth anything contrary to that which is right; but it is common for the lesser part of the people to desire that which is not right; therefore this shall ye observe and make it your law—to do your business by the voice of the people. And if the time comes that the voice of the people doth choose iniquity, *then is the time that the judgments of God will come upon you; yea, then is the time he will visit you with great destruction even as he has hitherto visited this land* (Mosiah 29:26–27).

As we know from the Book of Mormon, when the Nephites implemented this new form of government they prospered greatly. But, as it often does, prosperity led to pride, and the righteousness of the people began to decline. This eventually brought them into various political crises as well as creating serious problems for the Church. Think of the king-men versus the freemen, the Gadianton robbers versus the elected government, and finally the total collapse of the government when the Gadianton robbers seized full power. These examples may serve as types or shadows of things that are to happen in our day.

THE UNITED STATES IN PROPHECY

Disillusioned and bitterly disappointed after getting no help from Washington, Joseph Smith returned to Nauvoo. But out of that bitter experience, something else came. He was the Lord's prophet, chosen to open the final dispensation before Christ's coming. He had translated the Book of Mormon and learned that America was a promised land, a gathering place for the scattered remnants of the house of Israel. He also knew that two of the nations that inhabited this land in earlier times had ended when they were utterly destroyed by their own wickedness.

Through revelation, he also knew that the Constitution of the United States was a divinely inspired document given by God. Then, barely fifty years after the ratification of the Constitution, the highest levels of constitutional government had refused to uphold the Constitution. As Joseph pondered over what had happened, the visions of heaven were opened, and he saw the ultimate consequences for this country if it did not change its ways.

Before he went to Washington, Joseph prophesied what would come if the government leaders rejected the petitions of the Saints. Pay particular attention to the language he uses, which bears a powerful witness to this being more than just his own frustrations boiling over:

> While discussing the Petition to Congress I prophesied by virtue of the Holy Priesthood vested in me, and in the name of the Lord Jesus Christ, that if Congress will not hear our petition, and grant us protection, they shall be broken up as a Government (Joseph Smith, "History, 1838–1856, volume E-1 [1 July 1843–30 April 1844]," p. 1805, *The Joseph Smith Papers;* https://www.josephsmithpapers.org/paper-summary/history-1838–1856-volume-e-1-1-july-1843–30-april-1844/177).

In May 1843, in the midst of his frustration with Congress and the president, Joseph met with Judge Stephen A. Douglas, a prominent judge in Illinois. William Clayton, who served as a scribe for Joseph, was present and recorded the meeting. Joseph laid out the sufferings the Saints had experienced in Missouri, and Douglas agreed that Missouri needed to be punished. William Clayton then recorded what followed. Again, note Joseph's definitive wording:

> *I [prophesy] in the name of the Lord God of Israel,* unless the United States redress the wrongs committed upon the Saints in the State of Missouri and punish the crimes committed by her officers, that in a few years *the Government will be utterly overthrown and wasted,* and *there will not be so much as a [potsherd]* (a small piece of broken pottery) *left,* for their wickedness in permitting the murder of men, women, and children, and the wholesale plunder and extermination of thousands of her citizens to go unpunished (Joseph Smith, "History, 1838–1856, volume D-1 [1 August 1842–1 July 1843]," pp. 1552–53, *The Joseph Smith Papers;* https://

www.josephsmithpapers.org/paper-summary/history-1838–1856-volume-d-1-1-august-1842–1-july-1843/196).

Earlier, in the midst of the persecution, Joseph indicated that he had been shown in vision what would come of such injustice. "I discovered that popular clamor, and personal [aggrandizement] were the ruling principles of those in authority, and *my heart faints within me, when I see by the visions of the Almighty, the end of this nation,* if she continues to disregard the cries and petitions of her virtuous citizens, as she has done, and is now doing" ("History, 1838–1856, volume C-1 [2 November 1838–31 July 1842]," p. 1023, *The Joseph Smith Papers;* https://www.josephsmithpapers.org/paper-summary/history-1838–1856-volume-c-1-2-november-1838–31-july-1842/195).

Do we have any more details of what he was shown in these visions? Yes. Several years earlier, on July 2, 1839, shortly after he had escaped from Liberty Jail and made his way to Nauvoo, Joseph met with the Twelve and some of the Seventy. The Twelve were preparing to leave for a second mission to the British Isles. Joseph spent much time instructing them and spoke of the Second Coming and the signs of the times. He then described in grim detail what he had been shown in a vision:

> I saw men hunting the lives of their own Sons and brother murdering brother, women killing their own Daughters, and Daughters seeking the lives of their Mothers. I saw Armies arrayed against Armies, I saw Blood, Desolation, Fires, &c. The son of man has said that the mother shall be against the Daughter, and the Daughter against the Mother &c. These things are at our Doors. They will follow the Saints of God from City to City Satan will rage, and the Spirit of the Devil is now enraged I know not how soon these things will take place and with a view of them shall I cry peace? No! I will lift up my voice and testify of them. How long you will have good Crops and the famine be kept off I do not know. when the Fig tree leaves, know then that the summer is nigh at hand (Joseph Smith, ibid., p. 13 [addenda]).

Elder Jedediah M. Grant was present when Joseph described what he had seen to some of the brethren. He said that Joseph told them he had "gazed upon the scene his vision presented, until his heart sickened, and he besought the Lord to close it up again" (Grant, *Improvement Era,* February 1915, 287).

THE CONSTITUTION SHALL HANG BY A THREAD

Joseph must have spoken on these threats to the national government more than once, for several of those who were closest to him later recalled his teachings. And one phrase that is recalled again and again had to do with a threat to the Constitution itself. By this time, Brigham Young had become the President of the Quorum of the Twelve. Much later in his life, when he was President of the Church, he said that Joseph had once said: "When the Constitution of the United States hangs, as it were, *upon a single thread*, they will have to call on the 'Mormon' Elders to save it from utter destruction; and they will step forward and do it" (Young, *Discourses*, 361). On another occasion Brigham asked a question:

> Will the Constitution be destroyed? No: it will be held inviolate by this people; and, as Joseph Smith said, "*The time will come when the destiny of the nation will hang upon a single thread*. At that critical juncture, this people will step forth and save it from the threatened destruction." It will be so (*Discourses*, 469).

John Taylor, who was second in seniority in the Twelve at the time of Joseph's death, also spoke of a time when the Constitution would be in danger:

> When the *people shall have torn to shreds the Constitution* of the United States, the elders of Israel will be found holding it up to the nations of the earth and proclaiming liberty and equal rights to all men, and extending the hand of fellowship to the oppressed of all nations. This is part of the program, and as long as we do what is right and fear God, he will help us and stand by us under all circumstances (Taylor, *Gospel Kingdom*, 219).

Jedediah M. Grant, who later served in the Presidency with Brigham Young, gave this short account: "What did the Prophet Joseph say? When the Constitution shall be tottering we shall be the people to save it from the hand of the foe" (Grant, *Deseret News Weekly*, January 19, 1870).

We also have testimony from one of the prominent women of that time. Eliza R. Snow was a sister to Lorenzo Snow. She was also very close to both Joseph and Emma and was one of the prominent leaders in the Church. She shared what she remembered of Joseph speaking on this subject. Note the details she gives about the government turning away from the Constitution:

> I heard the prophet Joseph Smith say if the people rose up and mobbed us, and the authorities countenanced it, they would have

mobs to their hearts content. I heard him say that the time would come when this nation would so far depart from its original purity, its glory and its love for freedom, and its protection of civil rights and religious rights that the Constitution of our country would hang as it were by a thread. He said also that this people, the Sons of Zion, would rise up and save the Constitution and bear it off triumphantly (Snow, *Deseret News Weekly*, January 19, 1870, 556).

When I first wrote *The Coming of the Lord* many years ago, I was impressed with the number of witnesses who shared what they had heard Joseph teach. But I remember thinking how nice it would be to have a firsthand account from Joseph himself. Even one account would be significant.

Then, to my surprise and great delight, President Ezra Taft Benson prepared a small booklet on the Constitution. This was about 1986. In it, he cited a quote on the Constitution that was an original source directly from the Prophet Joseph. This was given July 19, 1840, while the Church was collecting evidence on the wrongs they had endured. The source came from a document in the Church Historian's archives. Here is what Joseph said at that time:

> Even this Nation will be on *the very verge of crumbling to pieces and tumbling to the ground* and when *the constitution is upon the brink of ruin* this people will be the staff upon which the Nation shall lean and they shall bear the constitution away from the very verge of destruction (as cited in Benson, *The Constitution: A Heavenly Banner*, 28).

Later, I was able to find a version that had additional lines not quoted by President Benson:

> Then shall the Lord say: Go tell all my servants who are the strength of mine house, my young men and middle aged &c., Come to the land of my vineyard and fight the battle of the Lord [America]—Then the Kings and Queens shall come, then the rulers of the earth shall come, then shall all Saints come, yea the foreign Saints shall come to fight for the land of my vineyard, for in this thing shall be their safety and they will have no power to choose but will come as a man fleeth from a sudden destruction. . . . I know these things by the visions of the Almighty ("Discourse, circa 19 July 1840, as Reported by Unknown Scribe–A," p. 2, *The Joseph Smith Papers*; https://www.josephsmithpapers.org/paper-summary/discourse-circa-19-july-1840-as-reported-by-unknown-scribe-a/2).

This adds a very important expansion of who it is that will come to save the Church. It is not just the elders of the Church, or the Church leaders, but all the Saints, including those from foreign lands. What Joseph said is so broad in scope that it provides a compelling look into the future for our nations.

THE CONSTITUTION: A HEAVENLY BANNER

Writing from his cell in Liberty Jail in March of 1839, Joseph Smith praised the Constitution, calling it "a glorious standard," and "a heavenly banner," even though the nation's leaders had failed to protect the rights guaranteed to the Saints by the Constitution. It was not long after this that Joseph spoke of the long-term consequences that would come if we, as a nation, turned away not just from righteousness but from the principles of the Constitution. Modern prophets have issued the same warning.

Before being called to the Quorum of the Twelve, President Dallin H. Oaks was a professor at the law school at the University of Chicago, and eventually served on the Supreme Court of the State of Utah. In an article he wrote on the Constitution, he cited a colleague—not a member of the Church—who made an observation about Latter-day Saint law students. "They all seemed to believe that the Constitution was divinely inspired," he said, "but none of them could ever tell me what this meant, or how it affected their interpretation of the Constitution." President Oaks then indicated that he took that as a personal challenge and became a student of the Constitution throughout his career (Oaks, "The Divinely Inspired Constitution," *Ensign*, February 1992).

One of the points that President Oaks said is critical to understanding the Constitution is to understand the "rule of law":

> All the blessings enjoyed under the United States Constitution are dependent upon the rule of law. That is why President J. Reuben Clark said, "Our allegiance run[s] to the Constitution and to the principles which it embodies, and not to individuals." *The rule of law is the basis of liberty.* It is part of our civic duty to be moral in our conduct toward all people. There is no place in responsible citizenship for dishonesty or deceit or for willful law breaking of any kind. We believe with the author of Proverbs that "righteousness exalteth a nation: but sin is a reproach to any people." *The personal righteousness of citizens will strengthen a nation more than the force of its arms* (ibid.).

President Oaks quoted J. Reuben Clark Jr. He was a brilliant attorney, a civil servant in the U.S. State Department, a member of the Twelve, and a Counselor in the First Presidency under two different Presidents. (Also, the law school at Brigham Young University is named for him.) While serving in the First Presidency, President Clark spoke about the dangers of drifting away from the principles of the Constitution. He then gave a very specific and very sobering prophecy:

> If we are to have an amendment [to the Constitution] by the will of one man, or of a small group of men, . . . then we shall lose the Constitution; because each succeeding person or group who come into a position of place and power where they can "amend" the charter, will want to amend it again, and so on until no vestige of our liberties shall remain. Thus it comes that an amendment of our Constitution by one person or by a group is a violation of the revealed will of the Lord to the Church, as that will is embodied in that inspired Constitution. Brethren, let us think about that, because I say unto you with all the soberness I can, that *we stand in danger of losing our liberties,* and that once lost, *only blood will bring them back;* and once lost, *we of this Church will, in order to keep the Church going forward, have more sacrifices to make and more persecutions to endure than we have yet known,* heavy as our sacrifices and grievous as our persecutions of the past have been (Clark, in Conference Report, April 1944, 116).

President Benson expressed his assessment of the coming challenges to the Constitution:

> To all who have discerning eyes, it is apparent that the republican form of government established by our noble forefathers cannot long endure once fundamental principles are abandoned. *Momentum is gathering for another conflict*—a repetition of the crisis of two hundred years ago. This collision of ideas is worldwide. The issue is the same that precipitated the great premortal conflict—will men be free to determine their own course of action or must they be coerced? (Benson, *A Heavenly Banner,* 26–27).

THE BOOK OF MORMON AS A TYPE AND SHADOW OF AMERICA AND THE WORLD

We are told that the Book of Mormon is the keystone of our religion. A keystone is the block in an arch that holds everything else together. And as we shall see, it is a keystone in our understanding of what constitutes good government and good citizenship.

After noting that the Book of Mormon writers saw our day and wrote for our day, President Ezra Taft Benson made this observation about how the Book of Mormon can be a keystone in our lives:

> If they saw our day, and chose those things which would be of greatest worth to us, is not that how we should study the Book of Mormon? We should constantly ask ourselves, "Why did the Lord inspire Mormon or Moroni or Alma to include that in their records? What lesson can I learn from that to help me live in this day and age?" And there is example after example of how that question will be answered. For example, *in the Book of Mormon we find a pattern for preparing for the Second Coming.* A major portion of the book centers on the few decades just prior to Christ's coming to America. *By careful study of that time period we can determine why some were destroyed in the terrible judgments that preceded His coming and what brought others to stand at the temple in the land of Bountiful* and thrust their hands into the wounds of His hands and feet (Benson, *Teachings,* 59).

With that counsel, let us examine the pattern we find in the Book of Mormon in the time leading up to Christ's appearance, especially as it has to do with the Nephite system of government. Once they arrived in the promised land, Nephi's people loved and honored him so much that they wanted to make him their king. Nephi refused but continued to serve as their leader and protector (see 2 Nephi 5:18). But before he died, Nephi anointed Jacob to be their king and ruler as well as the head of the Church. That pattern of leadership combined ecclesiastical authority and civil authority—a prophet-king—continued, as near as we can tell, until the time of King Benjamin and his son, Mosiah.

When King Mosiah's sons refused to be king, Mosiah set up a democratic government. This took place in 92 B.C. Since that is within the time frame President Benson used above, let us look at those last few decades to see if we can discern a pattern in how the Nephites were governed during that time.

- Alma the Younger was sustained by the voice of the people to be both the new chief judge and the head of the Church (see Mosiah 29:42).
- A few years later, Alma determined that he needed to focus on the spiritual needs of the Church and resigned that position. A new chief

judge was elected, and the two functions were officially separated (see Alma 4:15–19).
- Though problems crept into the Church from time to time and the Lamanites began a prolonged war with the Nephites, this dual system of government seemed to work very well, with civic leaders and chief captains of the army frequently turning to the prophet for guidance and help. Sadly, war became almost a constant fact of life.
- By 67 B.C., a new problem arose. Some of the wealthy and aristocratic classes decided that "a few particular parts of the law should be altered" (Alma 51:2). They wanted to be led by a king, not an elected chief judge. When the chief judge refused to change the laws, the king-men, as they were called, demanded a vote. When the voice of the people elected to stay with the current system, the king-men were so angry they took up arms and went to war with their own people. This was a major turning point. A significant number of people refused to acknowledge the law of the land. This led to the first full-scale civil war among the Nephites, with the king-men making an alliance with the Lamanites (see Alma 51). This became a pattern for years to come.
- With peace finally established once again, prosperity followed. Many turned to the Church in gratitude. But pride began to creep into the Church. Pride led to class distinctions and more division among the people. There was a great disparity between the rich and the poor (see Helaman 3:36; 4:12).
- With pride and class distinctions (see 3 Nephi 6:12), "they who chose evil were more numerous than they who chose good," and "the laws had become corrupted" (Helaman 5:2–3). Many citizens decided they would not be governed by the laws of the land.
- The secret combinations became so powerful that they "usurped the power and authority of the land," and took over the government, using that organization to sustain them in their wickedness. They became so powerful they eventually defied the armies of the Nephites (see Helaman 7:4–5).
- Over and over, the record mentions corruption in the government, with people enriching themselves through the corruptness of the laws or by changing the laws (see Helaman 4:22; 6:23–24).
- The wicked became so powerful in the government that they threatened to kill all believers if the signs of Christ's birth didn't come as predicted by Samuel the Lamanite (see 3 Nephi 1).
- The rising generation (the Nephite youth) began to turn to wickedness.

- The power of the Gadianton robbers became so great that all the Nephites gathered together and went into siege mode in order to survive (see 3 Nephi 3:22–26).
- Persecution of the faithful became commonplace, and some of the prophets were murdered secretly by the lawyers and the judges—governmental officials (see 3 Nephi 7:6).
- Eventually the head of state was assassinated, the entire government collapsed, people reverted to tribal rule, and "the regulations of the government were destroyed" (3 Nephi 7:1–6). This was the condition of the Nephite nation when the signs of Christ's death were given.

We are not suggesting that this is a detailed outline of what we can expect in America. Though we can find examples of modern countries that have followed that path—or are on that path now—this is only a pattern, not a blueprint.

But there is a lesson for our day. It was nicely put by John Adams, one of the founding fathers: "Our Constitution was made only for a moral and religious people. It is wholly inadequate to the government of any other" (as cited in Benson, *A Heavenly Banner*, 23).

SUMMARY AND CONCLUSIONS

We began this discussion on the future of the United States by examining the source of its greatness—the Constitution of the United States of America. We also reviewed prophecies about the future of our government and our nation. These are part of the "dreadful" side of the signs of the times, but along with those terrible things there are marvelous promises for the faithful.

This chapter concludes our study of the dreadful signs of the times. (Feel free to breathe a great sigh of relief.) They have been troubling chapters in some ways. But as noted time and again, we need to study these signs of the times so that we can "be not troubled" (D&C 45:35). This is possible because of what we know about the Lord's plan and His promises for His people.

Some years ago, President Boyd K. Packer published a book entitled *Let Not Your Heart Be Troubled*. In one of the chapters in that book he made reference to Joseph Smith's prophecies about the Constitution. He then added some great counsel for those of us who are living in the days when his prophecies are being fulfilled:

It has been prophesied that the Constitution of the United States will hang by a thread and that the elders of Israel will step forth to save it. In my mind that does not require a few heroes in public office steering some saving legislation through the halls of Congress, neither some brilliant military leaders rallying our defense against an invading army. In my mind, it could well be brought about by the rank and file of men and women of faith who revere the Constitution and believe that the strength of democracy rests in the ordinary family and in each member of it (Packer, *Let Not Your Heart Be Troubled*, 68).

Part IV

The Great Day

CHAPTER 16

AN AMERICAN ZION

The building up of Zion is a cause that has interested the people of God in every age; it is a theme upon which prophets, priests and kings have dwelt with peculiar delight; they have looked forward with joyful anticipation to the day in which we live; and fired with heavenly and joyful anticipations they have sung and written and prophesied of this our day; but they died without the sight; we are the favored people that God has made choice of to bring about the Latter-day glory; it is left for us to see, participate in and help to roll forward. (Joseph Smith, *Teachings*, 514–15)

ZION: THE PURE IN HEART

The statement above was given May 2, 1842, a time when the Saints were well established in Nauvoo and the horrors of Missouri were behind them. Work on a new temple had begun, and new converts—many from the British Isles—were coming in with gratifying swiftness. In spite of the severe persecutions the Saints had experienced in Missouri, the membership of the Church had doubled in the previous six years, from 13,000 to 26,000. Nauvoo was larger than Chicago at that time, and missionaries had gone to Europe and the Pacific Islands to spread the gospel further. There was much to be grateful for.

There was also much cause to mourn. One great disappointment expressed by the Prophet was that not only had the Saints endured severe persecution in Missouri, including the killing of numerous members of the Church, but they also had been driven out of the land of Zion.

Their hopes to be the ones chosen to establish a new Zion had been dashed. To further add to their sorrow, the Lord revoked the commandment to redeem the land of Zion at that time, saying that the Saints were not yet ready, i.e., not yet faithful enough. The Lord didn't say that they had lost Zion forever, but the time for its redemption was not yet.

The redemption of Zion and all that accompanies it is one of "great" signs of the time the Lord has given us. As dreadful as the "dreadful" signs are, the promises of the Lord far outshine the dreary side of the future. And the concept of Zion in the last days is proof of that. So, as we begin our study, let us remember: *Zion is first and foremost a people, who in their desire to qualify themselves as God's chosen people are diligently striving to become pure of heart. But Zion is also the place where the pure in heart live.*

ZION: A CONCEPT, A PLACE, A PEOPLE

While the core meaning of the word *Zion* describes the spiritual nature of a people—the pure in heart—the word is also attached to places where those people live. It will be helpful to briefly examine each of these places to provide context for the Zion that is yet to come.

- The city of Enoch
- Old Jerusalem under King David
- Ancient Jerusalem under Melchizedek
- Jackson County, Missouri, and surrounding areas
- The stakes of Zion
- The city of New Jerusalem
- The Heavenly, Eternal Zion, also known as the Celestial Kingdom

THE CITY OF ENOCH

In the Old Testament, the name of Enoch is included in the genealogies (see Genesis 5), but with that mention comes these words:

And Enoch *walked with God* after he begat Methuselah three hundred years, and begat sons and daughters: And all the days of Enoch were three hundred sixty and five years: And *Enoch walked with God: and he was not; for God took him* (Genesis 5:22–24).

The phrase "God took him" could just mean that he eventually died and went to heaven. However, the Apostle Paul clearly defined what that meant: "By faith Enoch was *translated* that he should not see death; and was not found, because God had translated him: for before his translation he had this testimony, that he pleased God" (Hebrews 11:5).

We get more detail from the book of Moses, which is part of Joseph Smith's work on the Joseph Smith Translation. This gives us the clearest picture of Enoch and why he is part of our discussion on Zion. We are told that when Enoch was called by the Lord to be His prophet, he demurred, saying that he was too young and was "slow of speech." The Lord promised him that if he went forth, he would be blessed with what to say and also with great power (see Moses 6:31–32). Enoch went on to lead his people in battle against their enemies and demonstrated great faith and power in battle (see Moses 7:13).

Eventually Enoch was so successful in bringing his people to a state of righteousness that "he built a city that was called the City of Holiness, even Zion," which, after a time, "was taken up into heaven" (Moses 7:19, 23). The wording there is important, for we often speak as though the City of Zion was in heaven all along. But here it is clear that it was a city on the earth, and only after many years did that change:

> *Zion has been established many times among men. From the day of Adam to the present moment—whenever the Lord has had a people of his own; whenever there have been those who have hearkened to his voice and kept his commandments; whenever his saints have served him with full purpose of heart—there has been Zion.*
>
> Bruce R. McConkie,
> "Come: Let Israel Be Gathered,"
> *Ensign*, May 1977

> And all the days of Zion, in the days of Enoch, were three hundred and sixty-five years. And Enoch and all his people walked with God, and he dwelt in the midst of Zion; and it came to pass that Zion was not, for God received it up into his own bosom; and from thence went forth the saying, Zion is fled (Moses 7:68–69).

Enoch was sixty-five years of age when he founded the City of Zion and 430 years old when he and his city were taken up (see D&C 107:48; Moses 8:1), so the city was on earth for 365 years. To give us some perspective on that, if we were to go back that far from our time (A.D. 2020), it would be A.D. 1655, just thirty-five years after the pilgrims came in the Mayflower. Though we commonly say that the City of Zion was taken up to heaven, Elder McConkie reminds us that it was not the city itself, but its citizens:

> Zion is people; Zion is the saints of God; Zion is those who have been baptized; Zion is those who have received the Holy Ghost; Zion is those who keep the commandments; Zion is the righteous. . . . *It was people who were caught up into heaven, not brick and mortar and stone.* . . . After these righteous saints went to dwell beyond the veil, others, being converted . . . "were caught

up by the powers of heaven into Zion" (Moses 7:27). (McConkie, "Come: Let Israel Build Zion," *Ensign*, May 2007).[1]

While this is interesting information, why are we discussing something that happened that long ago as part of the signs of the times? Because it has very much to do with our day. From another prophecy of Enoch, we know that the city of Enoch—or to be more precise, the people of the city of Enoch—will return to earth at some future time, its citizens coming down from heaven to meet the citizens of a New Jerusalem. This will be discussed more fully in chapter 18.

OLD JERUSALEM UNDER KING DAVID

The first use of the word *Zion* in the King James Version of the Bible occurred at the time of King David. In the writings of Samuel we find, "Nevertheless David took the strong hold of Zion: the same is the city of David" (2 Samuel 5:7). The City of David was another name for Jerusalem that became popular after the conquest. At that time, the city of Jerusalem was held by the Jebusites, one of the Canaanite tribes still left in the land. Scholars, not knowing of the numerous references to Zion found in modern scriptures that precede King David by centuries, assumed that the name derived from Mount Zion, one of the hills on which the city was built. Mount Zion is frequently mentioned in the Old Testament thereafter. That was because after the conquest, David built his palace and government buildings on Mount Zion, and the title of Zion was used for the whole city.

The name is still used to this day. For example, in modern times, Mount Zion is still there, and Jews who are determined to return to their promised land call it the land of Zion, and are called Zionists.

ANCIENT JERUSALEM UNDER MELCHIZEDEK

From modern scripture, we know that Jerusalem was a holy city long before King David came along. Though there is nothing in the record indicating that it was called Zion at that time, the language clearly describes it as a city of holiness. This would have preceded King David by about a thousand years. And it could provide an explanation as to how Mount Zion got its

---

[1] This refutes a rumor that was popular many years ago. An early member of the Church was purported to claim that he heard Joseph Smith say that the Gulf of Mexico was once the site of the City of Zion and the gulf was created when that whole land mass was taken up to heaven.

name when it was controlled by Canaanites. Perhaps that name goes back to the time of Melchizedek.

The Old Testament briefly mentions a "king of Salem" named Melchizedek who ruled at the time of Abraham. He was also called a "priest of the most high God" (Genesis 14:18). In the Old Testament that is all we are told about him. Note that the city was called Salem, not Jerusalem. However, *Salem* is derived from the Hebrew word *shalom*, which means peace. Jerusalem means "teaching of peace," so it is clear that Melchizedek was the king of ancient Jerusalem, though that's about all we know of him from the Old Testament.

The Apostle Paul spoke of this king at some length in his writings to the Hebrews (see Hebrews 7). Paul specifically called him the "King of Righteousness, . . . King of Salem, which is, King of peace" (Hebrews 7:2). He was such a model of holiness and righteousness that the Lord named the higher priesthood after him (see D&C 107:4). Alma also his taught his people about Melchizedek:

> Now this Melchizedek was a king over the land of Salem; and his people had waxed strong in iniquity and abomination; yea, they had all gone astray; they were full of all manner of wickedness; But Melchizedek having exercised mighty faith, and received the office of the high priesthood according to the holy order of God, did preach repentance unto his people. And behold, they did repent; and Melchizedek did establish peace [*shalom*] in the land in his days; therefore he was called the prince of peace, for he was the king of Salem; and he did reign under his father (Alma 13:17–18).

This is important information, for it shows that Melchizedek followed the same model as Enoch. Enoch successfully preached to a wicked people (see Moses 6:37–38) to the point that they became pure in heart and moved to a city of righteousness, which was eventually translated and taken to heaven. In Alma, we see that Melchizedek also brought his people, who had been wicked, to a point where they called their city the City of Peace, or Salem. Thus we see that Melchizedek, like Enoch, was a man of great righteous and faith. But the parallels between these two men and their cities of holiness go deeper than that. Note what we learn from the Joseph Smith Translation:

> Now Melchizedek was a man of faith, who wrought righteousness; and when a child he feared God, and stopped the mouths of lions, and quenched the violence of fire. And thus, having been

approved of God, he was ordained an high priest after the order of the covenant *which God made with Enoch,* it being after the order of the son of God. . . . And men having this faith, *coming up unto this order of God, were translated and taken up into heaven.* And now, Melchizedek was a priest of this order; therefore he obtained peace in Salem, and was called the Prince of peace. And his people *wrought righteousness, and obtained heaven, and sought for the city of Enoch* which God had before taken, separating it from the earth, having reserved it unto the latter days, or the end of the world. . . . And this Melchizedek, *having thus established righteousness, was called the king of heaven* by his people, or, in other words, the King of peace (JST—Genesis 14:26–36).

This tells us that even though the city of Enoch had been taken to heaven hundreds of years before the time of Melchizedek, Melchizedek brought his people to such a state of holiness that some of them were taken up to join the city of Enoch, or were translated. So in that sense, Jerusalem, under Melchizedek, had also become a holy city, and therefore had achieved to at least some degree the status of Zion. Whether Melchizedek and his people ever referred to their city as Zion or a place of Zion, we are not told. But this could account for why a thousand years later, David found a mount there named Zion and why Jerusalem also came to be called a City of Zion. In David's time, they had not come anywhere close to achieving a Zion state, but that was their hope.

THE CENTER PLACE OF ZION

On March 26, 1830, Egbert B. Grandin's print shop in Palmyra, New York, announced that the first copies of the Book of Mormon were now for sale. Eleven days later, a small group of people crowded into the Peter Whitmer cabin in Fayette, New York, and officially organized The Church of Jesus Christ of Latter-day Saints. The timing of those two seminal events was not accidental.

Historians often speak of "core documents" that set the course and define the boundaries for civilization for years to come. These include documents like the Holy Bible, the Magna Carta, the Mayflower Compact, the Declaration of Independence, the U.S. Constitution, and the Bill of Rights. These documents have become pivotal influences in the development of civilizations.

So it was with the newly formed Church. Along with the Holy Bible, the Book of Mormon would become the core document of the Church, the "keystone of our religion" (see Introduction, Book of Mormon). But it was only the first in a flood of new scripture that would enrich the doctrinal foundations of the fledgling Church. Even before the Church was formally organized, Joseph began receiving revelations that would eventually become the Doctrine and Covenants. In late June 1830, before the Church was even four months old, Joseph was instructed to begin an extensive revision of the first few chapters of Genesis. This was the beginning of the Joseph Smith Translation. He made so many changes in those early chapters of Genesis that they were published separately as the book of Moses in the Pearl of Great Price. One of the things he restored was an extensive amount of material about Enoch—both the man and the city he founded. This new treasure trove of revelation was eagerly received by the Saints, and of particular impact were references to a future Zion and the city of New Jerusalem in both the Book of Mormon and the book of Moses:

> *The Lord loveth the gates of Zion more than all the dwellings of Jacob. Glorious things are spoken of thee, O city of God.*
>
> PSALM 87:2–3
> THESE VERSES WERE READ WHEN JOSEPH LAID THE CORNERSTONE FOR THE JACKSON COUNTY TEMPLE (SEE *SAINTS: THE STANDARD OF TRUTH*, 132)

- "So great was the glory of the Lord, which was upon his people . . . they were blessed upon the mountains, and upon the high places, and did flourish. And the Lord called his people ZION, because they were of one heart and one mind, and dwelt in righteousness; and there was no poor among them. And Enoch continued his preaching. . . . And it came to pass in his days, that *he built a city that was called the City of Holiness, even ZION*" (Moses 7:17–19).
- "And behold, this people will I establish in this land, . . . and it shall be a New Jerusalem" (3 Nephi 20:22).
- "And they [the Gentiles] shall assist my people, the remnant of Jacob, and also as many of the house of Israel as shall come, that *they may build a city, which shall be called the New Jerusalem. And then shall they assist my people that they may be gathered in*, who are scattered upon all the face of the land, *in unto the New Jerusalem*" (3 Nephi 21:23–24).
- "This land . . . *became a choice land above all other lands, a chosen land of the Lord*; . . . that *it was the place of the New Jerusalem*, which should come down out of heaven, and the holy sanctuary of the Lord. Behold,

Ether saw the days of Christ, and he spake concerning a *New Jerusalem upon this land*" (Ether 13:2–4).

There is no ambiguity here. In the latter days, there will be another Zion established, a *New* Jerusalem, and it will not be thousands of miles away in the Old World. When the early Saints read these and other revelations, is it any wonder that they were thrilled to be the generation chosen to see it become reality?

In 1831, as directed by the Lord, Joseph Smith and other Church members traveled to Missouri, where the Lord had promised that He would reveal to them the location of Zion. There in the city of Independence, Joseph asked in a yearning prayer: "When will Zion be built up in her glory, and where will thy Temple stand . . . ?" (heading, D&C 57). The Lord's answer was also very specific:

> *We accept the fact that the center place where the City New Jerusalem is to be built, is in Jackson County, Missouri. It was never the intention to substitute Utah or any other place for Jackson County. But we do hold that Zion, when reference is made to the land, is as broad as America, both North and South—all of it is Zion.*
>
> Joseph Fielding Smith,
> *Doctrines of Salvation*, 3:72

Hearken, O ye elders of my church, saith the Lord your God, who have assembled yourselves together, . . . in this land, . . . which I have appointed and consecrated for the gathering of the saints. Wherefore, this is the land of promise, and *the place for the city of Zion*. . . . Behold, the place which is now called Independence is the *center place* (D&C 57:1–3).

This defined with perfect clarity a second place of Zion, a latter-day Zion in the new world. With those revelations, Joseph Smith could emphatically declare that "the city of Zion spoken of by David, in the one hundred and second Psalm [102:13, 16, 21], will be built upon the land of America" (Joseph Smith, *Teachings*, 188). In other early revelations, the Lord spoke often of His Second Coming and the judgments that would precede it (see, for example, D&C 29; 34; 43; 45). He also made mention of Enoch and the City of Zion (see D&C 38:4). So interest among the Saints in this whole topic of Zion was very high.

As we know, in response to the Lord's command, many members of the Church moved to Missouri to start new lives there. Eventually, Kirtland was abandoned and Church headquarters moved to Far West. What a shock it would turn out to be when the Saints were met with mobs and muskets rather than angels and heavenly choirs. Before 1838 had come to an end, seventeen people living in the settlement of Hawn's Mill would be dead at the hands of a mob. Joseph and other leaders would be in jail. Far West would be a smoking ruins, and there would be an order of extermination that carried the governor's signature for any Mormons left in the state. And that was not the final blow. A short time later, Joseph received another revelation stating that the redemption of Zion would have to wait for "a little season" (D&C 105:9–13).

It is now about 180 years since the expulsion from Missouri, yet the Lord has not yet called His people to return to Zion. From the beginning, the Lord warned the Saints that living in Zion came with special obligations of faithfulness. When many of them failed in that, they were expelled by the Missourians. Yet that was only to allow them (and future generations) to become a Zion people.

> Let your hearts be comforted; for all things shall work together for good to them that walk uprightly, and to the sanctification of the church. For I will raise up unto myself a pure people, that will serve me in righteousness (D&C 100:15–16).

So why did the Lord demand so much of them when they were still so young in their faith?

Many years ago, I experienced a wonderful teaching moment given by a wise and inspired teacher. This was in a Church history class at BYU. We had just finished our study of the persecutions in Missouri and the eventual expulsion of the Saints from the state. As the teacher finished, one student raised his hand. "I know all of this is true, and I love learning about the faith of our forefathers in the face of their suffering, but what I don't understand is why the way was so hard. Okay, so they weren't perfect, but they were certainly better people than the Missourians who drove them out."

The professor sat back, thoughtful for a moment, and then had us turn to section 100, where we read the two verses cited above. Then he said something like the following: "What we have to understand is this. Going to Utah and colonizing a desolate land still lay ahead for these early Saints. They didn't know that, but the Lord did. So, consider this reality. By the time the Saints reached the Salt Lake Valley and began to spread out to colonize the West, in terms of the people Brigham Young had to work with, most of the physically weak had died or stayed behind, and most of the spiritually weak had left the Church, becoming what we might call 'drop-out pioneers.'"

The instructor grew even more somber as he concluded: "So what Brigham had when the Saints reached the Valley was *pure steel*. Which was exactly what was needed to build up a new Zion in the West."

Isaiah was taught a similar principle when the Lord said, "Behold, I have created the smith that bloweth the coals in the fire, and that *bringeth forth an instrument for his work*" (Isaiah 54:16).

Here we are, seven or eight generations later, and how many of us today are still being influenced by the rock-hard faith of those early pioneers? President Gordon B. Hinckley spoke of the debt our generation still owes to them:

> It is good to look to the past to gain appreciation for the present and perspective for the future. It is good to look upon the virtues of those who have gone before, *to gain strength for whatever lies ahead*. It is good to reflect upon the work of those who labored so hard and gained so little in this world, but out of whose dreams and early plans, so well nurtured, has come a great harvest of which we are the beneficiaries. *Their tremendous example can become a compelling motivation for us all,* for each of us is a pioneer in his own life, often in his own family, and many pioneer daily in trying to establish a gospel foothold in distant parts of the world (Hinckley, "The Faith of the Pioneers," *Ensign,* July 1984).

THE STAKES OF ZION

As we saw in chapter 5, a major turning point in the gathering of Israel began to unfold in the late 1950s and early 1960s. After years of asking the Saints to come to wherever the main body of the Saints happened to be at that point, the call went out for members to stay in their homelands and gather to the stakes of Zion. That has been the policy ever since and will continue to be until the First Presidency directs otherwise.

With over three thousand stakes around the world now, we see the continuing fulfillment of that call. Therefore, it will be instructive to better understand why the Lord uses the imagery of tents and tent pegs, or stakes, to describe a key element in the organization of the Church. The imagery is drawn from the prophet Isaiah, as he was shown the latter days: "Look upon Zion, the city of our solemnities: thine eyes shall see Jerusalem a quiet [peaceful, secure] habitation, a tabernacle that shall not be taken down; not *one of the stakes thereof shall ever be removed,* neither shall any of *the cords thereof be broken*" (Isaiah 33:20).

In a later chapter, Isaiah expands on the metaphor: "*Enlarge the place of thy tent,* and *let them stretch forth the curtains* of thine habitations: spare not, *lengthen thy cords,* and *strengthen thy stakes*" (Isaiah 54:2).

Moroni, drawing on Isaiah's imagery said;

> Awake, and arise from the dust, O Jerusalem; yea, and put on thy beautiful garments, O daughter of Zion; and *strengthen thy stakes* and enlarge thy borders forever, *that thou mayest no more be confounded,* that the covenants of the Eternal Father which he hath made unto thee, O house of Israel, may be fulfilled" (Moroni 10:31).

Clearly, the imagery here is that of a tent. That would be an appropriate symbol of the covenant people because it is the Abrahamic covenant, and it is very likely that Abraham and his family lived in these tents for most if not all of their lives. Thus, the tent becomes a wonderful metaphor for the Lord's kingdom on earth. Isaiah doesn't give us any interpretations, so we shall suggest some possibilities:

- *The desert.* The typical Bedouin tent in the Middle East is found in what most would consider to be a desolate and very harsh place to live. Forage is often sparse and quickly grazed off. This is why their tents are portable. They have to move with the available food for their stock. This is a wonderful metaphor for our mortal experience here on earth. Though the *earth* itself has many places of exquisite beauty, spiritually it can be a harsh, desolate, and sometimes very dangerous place.
- *The tent.* These tents were very different from modern tents. They were likely what we think of today as Bedouin tents. A tent provides both shelter and a place for social interaction with families and others. These tents had to be both portable and stable. They had to withstand violent desert sandstorms and other weather. The design of these tents made it easy to "enlarge the tent," by attaching additional sections of fabric, or to take it down when it was time to move on. The tent is a wonderful metaphor for places of shelter and safety in a hostile and dangerous landscape. So, for the purpose of our analogy, let us liken the tent to the Church and kingdom of God. This is what provides us with spiritual shelter in a difficult world. It can be set up wherever it is needed

and can be enlarged to accommodate as many who wish to be part of the family.

- *The fabric.* Even a tent for one family requires many yards of fabric. The Bedouin tent is usually made of woven goat's hair, which is very tough but also water resistant. To accommodate a multigenerational family, which was a common thing back then, the fabric had to be both extensive and come in numerous separate sections that could be easily transported, and, when the tent was put up, hang free to provide inner compartments, as well as being attached together to form the outer walls of the "home." As a family size increases, more fabric must be added. Let us liken the fabric to the members of the Church. We enlarge the tent of Zion by bringing in more members, either through birth or conversion. That is how we "enlarge" the place of our tents.
- *The tent poles.* The poles must be long enough to hold the tent up so that people can move about inside. In ancient times, tent poles were made from the hardest wood available. This provides the strength to withstand the fiercest storms. If the poles break, the tent collapses. Except in the smallest of tents, there would be literally dozens of poles. To what shall we liken the poles, then? What is it that, if it were taken away, would cause the tent (the Church) to collapse? The doctrines and principles of the gospel fit that metaphor perfectly. Take away the doctrines and gospel principles and everything unravels. That's what happened during the Great Apostasy. Once the doctrine changed, the Christian Church drastically changed as well.
- *The stakes.* Today these are often made of metal, but in ancient times they were made from the very hardest of woods. They were sharpened on one end so they could be driven into the ground, with a notch of some kind carved in the other end so the cords could be attached in way that they would not slip off the stakes. The stakes had to be strong enough to be driven deep into the ground without breaking. In this case, we don't have to wonder what the stakes represent, for we use that word all the time. The stakes are the key *organizational unit* in the Church. A church with 16 million members is by nature a very large tent, a very complex organization, with many facets to it. These include things such as administrative divisions (priesthood quorums, children and youth programs, a women's organization, welfare, humanitarian services, etc.). There are also geographical units such as branches, districts, missions, and wards set up so members do not have to travel long distances. In the Church today, a stake is formed when

there is a sufficient number of faithful Latter-day Saints in a geographic area to form a new Church unit. It is a primary anchoring structure in the Church and kingdom of God that greatly strengthens the Church and its members. This could be why Isaiah stresses that the stakes must be strengthened.

- *The cords, or ropes.* This final item is used to attach the fabric to the stakes so that the whole structure is anchored firmly when the wind blows. Here too the material used to make up the cords had to be strong and durable. What shall we liken the cords to? Since they fasten the fabric (Church members) to the stakes (the organization), we could liken the cords to the power of the priesthood and the organization of the priesthood, which would include not just ordained priesthood quorums but all organizations in the Church.

It is a wonderfully rich metaphor and one that has many nuances of meaning and application. If the work of gathering Israel is to help people get on the covenant path and stay on that path, then every part of the tent must fulfill its assigned function, and do so with strength and consistency. As President M. Russell Ballard put so succinctly a few years ago:

> New converts . . . gather to their local congregations, where the Saints worship our Heavenly Father in the name of Jesus Christ. With more than 30,000 congregations established around the world [the majority of which are found within stakes], all are gathered to their own Zion. As the scriptures note, "For this is Zion—the pure in heart" (Ballard, "The Trek Continues!," *Ensign*, November 2017).

SUMMARY AND CONCLUSIONS

As Joseph Smith said, the subject of Zion is of great interest to people of faith. We have now laid some foundations to help us as we continue our study of this subject in the next chapters. We close here with another wonderful summary by President Nelson:

> The choice to come unto Christ is not a matter of physical location; it is a matter of individual commitment. People can be "brought to the knowledge of the Lord" without leaving their homelands. True, in the early days of the Church, conversion often meant emigration as well. But now the gathering takes place in each nation. The Lord has decreed the establishment of Zion in each realm where He has given His Saints their birth and

nationality. . . . Every nation is the gathering place for its own people. . . . Zion is wherever righteous Saints are. . . . Spiritual security will always depend upon how one lives, not where one lives. Saints in every land have equal claim upon the blessings of the Lord (Nelson, *Hope in Our Hearts*, 72–73).

CHAPTER 17

THE LAW OF CONSECRATION AND STEWARDSHIP

By grave and solemn proclamation, the members of the Church were commanded to observe all these laws [given in D&C 42] and others which were yet future, but would be given for the establishment of the City of Zion—New Jerusalem—which was to be built by the law of consecration and obedience to the fulness of the Gospel. . . . In this revelation the Law of Consecration is stated definitely as the law on which the New Jerusalem is to be built. This law is given for the benefit of the poor, for the building of Zion and the work of the ministry. . . . Through this celestial law (Consecration) the Saints are to become the covenant people of the Lord. . . . Those who cannot abide the law of tithing cannot partake of this law of consecration, or the higher law, and they will be deprived of an inheritance when the inheritances are divided. (Joseph Fielding Smith, *Church History and Modern Revelation*, 1:169–70, 183–84)

ALL THINGS IN COMMON

One of the things that has characterized the Lord's covenant people through the ages is a responsibility to care for the poor and those in need. The city of Enoch was described as a people who "were of one heart and one mind, and dwelt in righteousness; and *there was no poor among them*" (Moses 7:18). Mormon described the Nephites following Christ's visit as having "all things common among them; therefore *there were not rich and poor, bond and free,* but they were all made free, and partakers of the heavenly gift" (4 Nephi 1:3). Shortly after Christ's death, the Christian Church in Jerusalem undertook a similar program:

And the multitude of them that believed were of one heart and of one soul: neither said any of them that ought [any] of the things which he possessed was his own; but they had *all things common*. . . . Neither was there *any among them that lacked:* for as many as were possessors of lands or houses sold them, and brought the prices of the things that were sold" (Acts 4:32, 34).

This is one of the highest expressions of the golden rule: "Therefore all things whatsoever ye would that men should do to you, do ye even so to them" (Matthew 7:12). It is also a sentiment that the natural man openly sneers at, seeing very few things that would be more foolish than worrying about other people (see 1 Corinthians 2:14).

Early in the beginning of this dispensation, the Lord made it clear that a model for our day would be the city of Enoch. Even before the Church was organized, the Lord gave a signal that purity of heart was expected of His Saints. "Seek to bring forth and establish the cause of Zion" was the counsel given as early as 1829 (see D&C 6:6; 11:6; 12:6; 14:66).

That challenge to become a new Zion was formalized when those early members were called to establish Zion in America. When Joseph arrived in Kirtland, Ohio, in early February 1831, he found that some members had formed a communal society based on the New Testament model. They called themselves "the family" and said that all their possessions were jointly owned. However, the group was having all kinds of relationship problems and much contention, so Joseph asked them to disband. A short time later, Joseph received a revelation that the Lord declared to be the "law of the Church" (see D&C 42). Part of that section directed them to "remember the poor, and consecrate of thy properties for their support" (v. 30). Some basic principles were laid down for how to do that, then as further revelations came, a program was developed that came to be known as the law of consecration and

> *Those who dwell in the perfect Zion must be qualified to live the law of consecration, and obedience to that law is the very way in which the New Jerusalem will be built. As is well known, the early saints attempted to live the Law of consecration as it operated through a United Order, but they failed. And up to this point in time we are living only the lesser law of tithing, though some of the principles of consecration are found in the Church Welfare Program.*
>
> BRUCE R. MCCONKIE,
> NEW WITNESS FOR THE
> ARTICLES OF FAITH, 618

stewardship. John A. Widtsoe, of the Twelve, outlined the four basic principles on which this law operated:

> First, *the earth is the Lord's*. Men are stewards of their possessions. All that man has should be used therefore in accordance with the Lord's expressed will.
>
> Second, *all men are children of God*—of a divine family. Therefore, the Lord requires that they must help one another as needs arise, provided that he who will not work shall have no claim upon his brother [see D&C 42:42].
>
> Third, *every man must be respected as a free agent.* He may enter the order at his pleasure. Once in the order, he must be allowed to use, fully, and as he pleases, any properties placed in his hands. He may leave the order at his pleasure.
>
> Fourth, *the government of the order is vested in a central agency,* sustained by the members of the order, presided over by the bishop, his counselors, and such helpers as may be needed. This central agency would have power to adjust the disputes normally arising among strongly individualized human beings (Widtsoe, *Joseph Smith—Seeker after Truth, Prophet of God,* 192).

THE LAW OF CONSECRATION

To begin with, we need to distinguish between a doctrinal principle called the "law of consecration" and the formal program known as the law of consecration and stewardship. The first is a formal covenant that members of the kingdom make with God. In that covenant we acknowledge that all things come to us from God and, therefore, what we "own" will be used to further His work (see D&C 104:18). This is a celestial law designed to help us become a celestial people, also known as a Zion people.

THE LAW OF CONSECRATION AND STEWARDSHIP

Something quite different from the covenant of consecration is the law of consecration and stewardship. This was an economic system set up within the Church based on both revealed principles of consecration and the concept of stewardship. This was entered voluntarily by Church members, also through covenant. But in this case the covenant was to abide by the policies and practices of the order. We introduce it here because, as we shall see, this law and economic organization, in some form or another, will be practiced in New Jerusalem.

After the Saints were expelled from Missouri in 1838, the Lord revoked the law of consecration and stewardship, replacing it with the law of tithing (see D&C 119). That is still the law of the Church today and will continue as such until the First Presidency directs otherwise.

Church members are still encouraged to live the doctrinal principles behind the law of consecration and stewardship, even though the formal program was discontinued. They are also encouraged to make other contributions to the Church through fast offerings and donations to humanitarian services, the missionary fund, etc., as well as helping the poor and needy wherever possible.

THE UNITED ORDER

There is one other thing that needs clarification. Some people think that the "United Order" and the law of consecration and stewardship were the same thing in the early Church. It is a little confusing, for the Lord referred to His law as a "united order" (D&C 92:1), and some early Church leaders referred to it by that name. However, after the law of consecration and stewardship was rescinded, especially once the Saints came to Utah, there were a few economic groups formed that practiced some principles of the formal law. They sometimes referred to these organizations as a united order. But these were more like what we today call a "cooperative," an organization where people band together for economic benefits. These were never a part of the formal organization instituted by Joseph Smith (see Ludlow, *Encyclopedia of Mormonism*, 4:1493).

KEY WORDS AND KEY CONCEPTS

To better understand the law of consecration and stewardship, we need to more closely examine the two key words found in its title.

Consecration: To consecrate means to make holy or to fully dedicate yourself to something holy, such as a principle, a cause, or a task. In this economic order, individuals consecrated themselves to God by living in harmony with His will. They dedicated their lives and everything in them to the Lord as a mark of their gratitude for all He had given them.

Stewardship: A steward is a person employed by someone of wealth and means to manage and supervise that person's properties and financial affairs. A steward is entrusted with a great deal of responsibility, but the true steward never forgets that the properties belong to the master. The Lord teaches this principle of stewardship very clearly:

It is expedient that I, the Lord, should make every man accountable, as a *steward over earthly blessings,* which *I have made* and prepared for my creatures. I, the Lord, stretched out the heavens, and built the earth, my very handiwork; and *all things therein are mine.* And it is my purpose to provide for my saints, for all things are mine. But it must needs be done *in mine own way;* and behold this is the way that I, the Lord, have decreed to provide for my saints, that *the poor shall be exalted, in that the rich are made low.* . . . Therefore, if any man shall take of the abundance which I have made, and impart not his portion, according to the law of my gospel, unto the poor and the needy, he shall, with the wicked, lift up his eyes in hell, being in torment. . . . Behold, *all these properties are mine,* or else your faith is vain, and ye are found hypocrites, and the covenants which ye have made unto me are broken; and *if the properties are mine, then ye are stewards"* (D&C 104:13–18, 55–56).

Though the phrase "the rich are made low" might at first sound like they are forced to do so, we know that agency is a core concept of the gospel and that God does not force us to do anything. But if wealthy persons see their possessions as not their own property—that they too are stewards over those properties—then they can be "made low" by voluntarily consecrating their properties to the order.

Can we see how the two concepts are inextricably linked together? People are willing to consecrate all that they have *only* when they truly believe that all we have comes from God and therefore we are only stewards over those possessions. People cling to things when they believe that they "own" them. They think this entitles them to use them for their own purposes, selfish or otherwise.

> *The test of putting others' interests ahead of self-interest is a rigorous one. It is inherent in the practice of consecration, which the Lord described as "every man seeking the interest of his neighbor, and doing all things with an eye single to the glory of God." It is the essence of the example of our Lord and Savior, Jesus Christ, who gave himself as a sacrifice for all of us.*
>
> Dallin H. Oaks,
> The Lord's Way, 184

HOW DID THE LAW OF CONSECRATION AND STEWARDSHIP WORK?

Here too Elder Widtsoe gives a very simple and clear explanation of how the program worked in the lives of the members who joined the order.

The operation of the order under these four heads [the principles listed earlier] is extremely simple. Those who join the order would place all their possessions,[1] irrevocably, in a common treasury—the rich man, his wealth; the poor man, his penny. Then each member would receive a sufficient portion, called "an inheritance," from the common treasury, to enable him to continue in his trade, business, or profession as he may desire. The farmer would receive land and implements; the tradesman, tools and materials; the merchant, the necessary capital; the professional man, instruments, books, etc. Members who work for others would receive proportionate interests in the enterprises they serve. No one would be without property—all would have an inheritance.

A person's inheritance would be his personal property, to operate permanently and freely for his benefit and that of his family. Should he withdraw from the order, his inheritance would go with him, but he would have no claim upon that which he had placed in the common treasury. At the end of the year, or a set period, the member who had earned more than his business and family needs required would place the surplus in the common treasury. Thus, for example, large fortunes would be administered by the order as a whole rather than by one individual. The member who, despite intelligent diligence, had lost from his operations would have his loss made up by the general treasury for another start, or he might with his consent be placed in some activity better fitting his gifts.

In short, the general treasury would set up every man in his preferred field and would care for and help those unable to profit from their inheritance. The general treasury, holding the surpluses of the members, would also finance the erection of public buildings and make possible all community enterprises decided upon by the order (Widtsoe, *Joseph Smith—Seeker after Truth, Prophet of God*, 193).

Since this program was directly supervised by the bishop, that would suggest that each community would be about the same size as a ward today. It appears that each ward worked independently of each other, though cooperation between wards would be likely. However, the program was never fully established long enough to say for sure how it would have worked on a large scale.

To see how it might work, let's take the example of a case of a natural

---

[1] Typically this was only their land, buildings, and other major items such as livestock, farm equipment, and such. Clothing and other smaller personal items were not required.

disaster—e.g., a town being devastated by a powerful tornado. It would be likely that the bishop's storehouse in that town would also be destroyed. But surplus food and other necessities from the bishop's storehouses in surrounding towns and cities would be immediately distributed without cost to those in need.

SUMMARY AND CONCLUSIONS

As we mentioned at the beginning of this chapter, we have included this discussion on the economic order the Lord gave to the Church shortly after it was organized for a specific reason. Although the Lord rescinded the law of consecration and stewardship for a time, we know that it will be introduced again as part of the establishment of a new Zion society that will exist in the New Jerusalem. It is one of the signs of the times of the last days. It may have some differences in the details of how it works, but the principles, which are designed to make sure that there are no poor among the people, are based on the law of consecration. And that will be part of the great future day that lies ahead.

It doesn't take a lot of pondering to realize that this system only works if there is a very remarkable group of people committed to the system. This is why the only places we know of where it actually worked were places of Zion, places whose citizens were of pure hearts.

> *If you think about it clearly, when you think about our storehouses where we are putting in all the surpluses we can, when we are paying a full tithing, when we are giving assistance in the health services, when we are giving assistance in the programs by which we reach out to those who are far afield, teaching them how to take care of themselves, we will not be far from living the united order.*
>
> J. REUBEN CLARK,
> ADDRESS AT WELFARE SERVICES
> MEETING, OCTOBER 1973

President Spencer W. Kimball taught how we live so as to achieve that commitment in life:

> May I suggest three fundamental things we must do if we are to "bring again Zion," three things for which we who labor for Zion must commit ourselves. First, we must eliminate the individual tendency to selfishness that snares the soul, shrinks the heart, and darkens the mind. . . . It is incumbent upon us to put away selfishness in our families, our business and professional pursuits, and our Church affairs. . . . Second, we must cooperate completely and

work in harmony one with the other. There must be unanimity in our decisions and unity in our actions. After pleading with the Saints to "let every man esteem his brother as himself," the Lord concludes his instructions on cooperation to a conference of the membership in these powerful words: "Behold, . . . if ye are not one ye are not mine." . . . If the Spirit of the Lord is to magnify our labors, then this spirit of oneness and cooperation must be the prevailing spirit in all that we do. Third, we must lay on the altar and sacrifice whatever is required by the Lord. We begin by offering a "broken heart and a contrite spirit." We follow this by giving our best effort in our assigned fields of labor and callings. We learn our duty and execute it fully. Finally we consecrate our time, talents, and means as called upon by our file leaders and as prompted by the whisperings of the Spirit. In the Church, . . . we can give expression to every ability, every righteous desire, every thoughtful impulse, and in the end, we learn it was no sacrifice at all (Kimball, "Becoming the Pure in Heart," *Ensign*, May 1978).

And with that, let us remember what the Lord promised to those who were driven out of Jackson County almost two hundred years ago: "Zion shall not be moved out of her place, notwithstanding her children are scattered. They that remain, and are pure in heart, shall return, and come to their inheritances, they and their children, with songs of everlasting joy, to build up the waste places of Zion" (D&C 101:17–18).

CHAPTER 18

THE NEW JERUSALEM: LAND OF PEACE, CITY OF REFUGE, PLACE OF SAFETY

And with one heart and with one mind, gather up your riches that ye may purchase an inheritance which shall hereafter be appointed unto you. And it shall be called the New Jerusalem, a land of peace, a city of refuge, a place of safety for the saints of the Most High God; And the glory of the Lord shall be there, and the terror of the Lord also shall be there, insomuch that the wicked will not come unto it, and it shall be called Zion. (D&C 45:65–67)

ZION SHALL NOT BE REDEEMED

When the residents of Independence, Missouri, drove the Latter-day Saints out of Jackson County, the Lord told Joseph Smith to raise an army to go and rescue Zion. The Lord asked for five hundred men but said He would accept as few as a hundred. The army was called Zion's Camp, and their 800-mile march to Missouri provided a marvelous training experience for future Church leadership. But it was not to accomplish the purpose it had set out to do.

When the army was within ten or fifteen miles of Independence, word reached them that several Missouri counties were raising militia to stop the hated Mormons from helping their people. A major battle seemed inevitable. Then, on June 22, 1834, while camped at Fishing River, Joseph received a revelation addressed to Zion's Camp that would revoke the commandment to redeem "mine afflicted people" (D&C 105:1). This came as a bitter blow to many, but a huge relief to others. In the revelation, the Lord explained why He was revoking the command to fight for the land of Zion.

- The Lord said that He would have redeemed the exiles already if it weren't for the transgressions of the people. They were "full of all manner of evil, and do not impart of their substance, as becometh saints [especially Saints under covenant to live the law of consecration and stewardship] . . . to the poor and afflicted among them" (D&C 105:2–3).
- They were not united according to the law of the celestial kingdom, and Zion cannot be built up except on those laws (vv. 4–5).
- His people had to be chastened until they learned obedience through what they suffered (v. 6).
- The churches abroad held back their moneys, asking why God wasn't delivering those that were suffering persecution (v. 8).

> *We must prepare to redeem Zion. It was essentially the sin of pride that kept us from establishing Zion in the days of the Prophet Joseph Smith. It was the same sin of pride that brought consecration to an end among the Nephites.*
>
> Ezra Taft Benson,
> Sermons and Writings of President
> Ezra Taft Benson, 337

The Lord concluded with what must have come as a bitter blow, not only to the men in Zion's Camp but to all the Saints: "Therefore, in consequence of the transgressions of my people, it is expedient in me that mine elders *should wait for a little season for the redemption of Zion*" (v. 9). The Lord then gave them five reasons why Zion would not be redeemed at this time:

1. The leaders needed to be prepared.
2. His people needed to be taught more perfectly.
3. The people needed to have more experience.
4. They needed to know more perfectly their duty and what the Lord required of them.
5. They must be endowed with power from on high (see D&C 105:9–13).

Though the Lord mentioned that this would be "for a little season," any hopes that this meant the redemption would be very soon were dashed when He promised, "Inasmuch as they follow the counsel they receive, they shall have power *after many days* to accomplish all things pertaining to Zion" (D&C 105:37). Then He reminded them of the promise that He had given them before: "All things shall work together for your good" (D&C 105:40, see also 100:15).

Since it has now been almost two hundred years since the Jackson

County experience, clearly "a little season" was speaking in the Lord's perception of time, for the "many days" statement has now been verified.

RETURN TO THE LAND OF ZION

Though the Saints had lost the center place of Zion, the Lord made it clear that Zion would not be moved out of her place and that His people would someday return there. Four months earlier, as the Lord chastised the Saints for their lack of faithfulness, He gave them this comforting promise: "Behold, this is the blessing which I have promised after your tribulations, and the tribulations of your brethren—*your redemption,* and *the redemption of your brethren,* even *their restoration to the land of Zion, to be established, no more to be thrown down*" (D&C 103:13). What followed was another remarkable promise. The Lord described in some detail how that return would take place:

> Behold, I say unto you, the redemption of Zion *must needs come by power;* Therefore, I will raise up unto my people a man, who shall lead them like as Moses led the children of Israel. For ye are the children of Israel, and of the seed of Abraham, and ye must needs be led *out of bondage* by power, and with a stretched-out arm. And *as your fathers were led at the first, even so shall the redemption of Zion be.* Therefore, let not your hearts faint, for I say not unto you as I said unto your fathers: Mine angel shall go up before you, but not my presence. But I say unto you: *Mine angels shall go up before you, and also my presence,* and in time *ye shall possess the goodly land* (D&C 103:15–20).

To have their return compared to Moses and ancient Israel must have been to them—and still is to us—an amazing statement. To fully understand the implications of what the Lord said, we need to explain some of the language used here:

The redemption of Zion must needs come by power. . . . Ye must needs be led out of bondage by power. The Lord made it clear in the Old Testament that it was only under His power that Israel had escaped from Egypt, made their way through the wilderness, and conquered the Canaanites. Moses declared: "By strength of hand the Lord brought us out from Egypt, from the house of bondage" (Exodus 13:14). "We were Pharaoh's bondmen in Egypt; and the Lord brought us out of Egypt with a mighty hand" (Deuteronomy 6:21). Here, the Lord confirms that His power will be required in the return to a new promised land.

I will raise up unto my people a man, who shall lead them like as Moses led the children of Israel. In Deuteronomy 18:17–19, the Lord told Moses of a "prophet" who would be raised up "like unto thee." This is a clear reference to the Messiah, which Nephi confirms in 1 Nephi 22:21. The mortal Jesus Christ fulfilled that prophecy.

But in modern revelation there are additional references to a prophet like unto Moses. Two different revelations make it clear that this title can also be applied to Presidents of the Church. "Verily, verily, I say unto thee, no one shall be appointed to receive commandments and revelations in this church excepting *my servant Joseph Smith*, Jun., for *he receiveth them even as Moses*" (D&C 28:2). "And again, the duty of the *President of the office of the High Priesthood* is to *preside over the whole church*, and *to be like unto Moses*—behold, here is wisdom; yea, *to be a seer, a revelator, a translator*, and *a prophet, having all the gifts of God which he bestows upon the head of the church*" (D&C 107:91–92). These two passages are strong indicators that this return to Zion will be under the direction of, and perhaps even led personally by, the President of the Church at that time.

And as your fathers were led at the first, even so shall the redemption of Zion be. The term "fathers" refers to the people of Israel under Moses. But this statement clearly affirms that sometime in the future, another "Moses" will lead the covenant people back to their own promised land, which this time will be Jackson County, Missouri.

We accept the story of Moses and the Exodus as a literal record of an actual historic event. Yet like so many other events in the Old Testament, historical realities had symbolic parallels. For example, in mortality, all who reach the age of accountability make choices that alienate them from God and bring them under the power of sin, which is likened to bondage (see D&C 84:49–51). Moses, whose name in Hebrew

---

> *I also beheld the redemption of Zion, and many things which the tongue of man cannot describe in full. Many of my brethren who received this ordinance with me saw glorious visions also, angels ministered unto them, as well as myself, and the power of the highest rested upon us; the house was filled with the glory of God, and we shouted hosanna to God and the Lamb. My scribe also received his anointing with us, and saw in a vision the armies of heaven protecting the saints in their return to Zion—and many things which I saw.*
>
> Joseph Smith, "History, 1838–1856, volume B-1 [1 September 1834–2 November 1838]," p. 696, *The Joseph Smith Papers*

means to "draw out," is, as we have just seen, a type of Jesus Christ, for he drew out Israel from their bondage.

In the Passover, it was the blood of the lamb put on the doorposts of the houses that protected the house of Israel from the angel of death. The blood of the Lamb of God, shed in the Garden of Gethsemane, is what protects us from the angel of both spiritual and physical death. The lamb chosen had to be a firstborn male without any spot or blemish. Jesus Christ is the Firstborn of the Father, and it was the death of God's Firstborn Son, who was perfect in every way, that delivers us from our captivity. As the Israelites went into the wilderness, they passed through water (the Red Sea) and were overshadowed by a pillar of fire. These two events are likened unto the baptism of water and of fire (the Holy Ghost).

They were nourished in the wilderness with "bread from heaven" (what the Israelites called manna—see Exodus 16:4) and water from a rock (see Numbers 20:8), both of which are emblems of the Savior, which we partake of each Sabbath in remembrance of His sacrifice for us.

Lest some think we are stretching these similitudes too far, note Paul's declaration:

> Moreover, brethren, I would not that ye should be ignorant, how that all our fathers were *under the cloud,* and all *passed through the sea;* And *were all baptized unto Moses* in the cloud and in the sea; And did *all eat the same spiritual meat;* And did *all drink the same spiritual drink:* for they drank of that spiritual Rock that followed them: and *that Rock was Christ*" (1 Corinthians 10:1–4).

That imagery seems to be part of what is meant by the phrase "as your fathers were led at first." Once again, the children of Israel will be led by a new Moses back to the promised land where their ancestors had once lived, and we have reason to believe that they will see their own spiritual parallels in their journey.

I say not unto you as I said unto your fathers: Mine angel shall go up before you, but not my presence. But I say unto you: Mine angels shall go up before you, and also *my presence, and in time ye shall possess the goodly land.* The context for "mine angels" is key to understanding who those angels are. When the Lord first called Moses to deliver Israel from bondage, He said, "I am come down to deliver them out of the hand of the Egyptians, and to bring them up out of that land unto a good land" (Exodus 3:8). That was a direct promise that Jehovah would personally accompany Israel on their journey.

As they traveled in the wilderness, Jehovah created a pillar of smoke by day and a pillar of fire by night that rested over the Tabernacle. This was a visible—and dramatic!—token of Jehovah's guiding and guarding presence. The pillar of fire is not just a symbol. It was real enough that it kept Pharaoh and his chariots at bay all that night before the Israelites passed through the Red Sea the next day (see Exodus 14:19–20). There are numerous references to this amazing phenomenon: "And the *Lord went before them* by day in a pillar of a cloud, to lead them the way; and by night in a pillar of fire, to give them light; to go by day and night" (Exodus 13:21–22; see also 14:24; Numbers 9:15–16; 10:34; Deuteronomy 1:33).

But after the golden calf incident and the debauchery that accompanied it, the Lord was angry with Israel and made it very clear that this changed His former promise. "I will send *an angel before thee;* . . . unto a land flowing with milk and honey: for *I will not go up in the midst of thee;* for thou art a stiffnecked people" (Exodus 33:2–3; see also 14:19). He didn't remove the pillar of fire and smoke. It still continued, but now it was only His angels that it symbolized.

Once we understand that detail in the account of the Exodus, then the promise here is quite remarkable. By His own word, Jehovah promised that these future Saints, who will return to the New Jerusalem, will have *both the angels of God and the presence of Jehovah Himself to lead them.* That not only is the promise of a wonderful miracle but a firm indicator that, unlike how it was for ancient Israel, this return of modern Israel will be righteous enough that they will be worthy to be led by Jehovah, also known as our Savior and King.

Will there actually be a pillar of smoke and fire this time? Will those Saints see miracles like the parting of the Red Sea, manna from heaven, water from the rocks, or the myriad of other miracles ancient Israel experienced? We are not told that specifically. But does that matter? What we do know is this: Jesus, speaking in the first person, promised without equivocation that *"my presence"* would lead them on, and that "in time, ye shall possess the goodly land" (D&C 103:20).

President Joseph F. Smith once spoke of that return to Zion in descriptive detail:

> When God leads the people back to Jackson County, how will he do it? Let me picture to you how some of us may be gathered

and led to Jackson County. I think I see[1] two or three hundred thousand people wending their way across the great plain, enduring the nameless hardships of the journey, herding and guarding their cattle by day and by night, and defending themselves and little ones from foes on the right hand and on the left, as when they came here. They will find the journey back to Jackson County will be real as when they came out here. Now, mark it. And though you may be led by the power of God "with a stretched-out arm," it will not be more manifest than leading the people out here to those that participate in it. They will think there are a great many hardships to endure in the manifestation of the power of God, and it will be left, perhaps to their children to see the glory of their deliverance, just as it is left for us to see the glory of our former deliverance, from the hands of those that sought to destroy us. This is one way to look at it. It is certainly a practical view. Some might ask, what will become of the railroads? (I fear that the sifting process would be insufficient were we to travel by railroads.) We are apt to overlook the manifestations of the power of God to us because we are participators in them, and regard them as commonplace events. But when it is written in history—as it will be written—it will be shown forth to future generations as one of the most marvelous, unexampled and unprecedented accomplishments that has ever been known to history (Joseph F. Smith, in *Journal of Discourses*, 24:156–57).

The practical implication of what the Lord taught those early Saints who had lost their chance to build up Zion was that all was not lost. They were being driven from the center place of Zion, but there would be a future generation, almost certainly containing some of their descendants, who would return to Zion and establish another Holy City. This is an astonishing promise given in this detail nowhere else in scripture. It is so amazing that it raises numerous questions.

We don't have all the answers, but based on this and other scriptures, we do know more than one might think.

THE ARMY OF THE LORD

Historians agree that war is a "given" of human history. Every known civilization has experienced war. Many empires were born through war and

---

[1] His choice of wording here is ambiguous. Some would like to assume that what he describes is what he saw in vision. Or it could easily be his way of saying, "This is how I picture it in my mind." We cannot say for sure either way.

later died in war. Villages have attacked and raided nearby villages from time immemorial. Cities have warred against cities, states against states, nations against nations. In our day, we have seen vast alliances choose sides and engage in prolonged, devastating wars. How many children of our Heavenly Father have lost their lives in war? How much human suffering has come from war? If it were possible to tally the economic costs of every war in history, the figure would be astronomical.

The Lord's people have not been exempted from this scourge of humanity. One indicator of that is how many prophets have also had to lead their people in battle. Enoch was a powerful general, leading his people in war before he taught them how to become a Zion people (see Moses 7:13–15). Melchizedek, Abraham, Moses, Joshua, Nephi, King Benjamin, Alma, Helaman, Mormon, and Moroni were all both prophets and warriors. War was frequent and prolonged among ancient Israel. The history of the Nephite/Lamanite civilization is rife with accounts of their wars. An indication of how pervasive war was in the Americas over the centuries is the fact that words closely associated with war, armies, and battles are found in the Book of Mormon 429 times!

Does that mean that those who will return to Zion to build the city of New Jerusalem will face armed conflict? The answer to that seems to be yes, though we are not given a lot of specific details of what that war will look like. It was the Lord who commanded Joseph Smith to gather an army to redeem Zion, and they went to Zion with the full intent to do battle. In a parable concerning the redemption of Zion, the Lord said, "And inasmuch as *they gather together against you,* avenge me of mine enemies, that by and by I may come with the residue of mine house and possess the land" (D&C 101:58). That suggests that they will face conflict along the way.

In the same revelation we cited above, where the Lord described the return to Zion, He made this promise: "And my presence shall be with you *even in avenging me of mine enemies, . . . Let no man be afraid to lay down his life for my sake*" (D&C 103:26–27).

In the revelation where the Lord said that the redemption of Zion would have to wait for a season, the Lord went on to say: "Behold, I have commanded my servant Joseph Smith, Jun., to say unto the strength of my house, *even my warriors,* my young men, and middle-aged, to gather together for the redemption of my people, and *throw down the towers of mine enemies,* and scatter their watchmen" (D&C 105:16). The Lord went on, counseling them to continue to buy land in Jackson County, until the time when:

> Mine elders, whom I have appointed, shall have time to gather up the strength of my house. . . . And after these lands are purchased, I will hold the *armies of Israel* guiltless in taking possession of their own lands, . . . and of *throwing down the towers of mine enemies* that may be upon them, and *scattering* their watchmen, . . . But first let *my army* become very great, and let it be sanctified before me, that it may become fair as the sun, and clear as the moon, and that *her banners may be terrible* unto all nations; that the kingdoms of this world may be constrained to acknowledge that the kingdom of Zion is in very deed the kingdom of our God and his Christ (D&C 105:27, 30–32).

We also need to remember, as we saw in chapter 13, that beginning with the Civil War, we entered an "age of war" that will continue right up until Christ comes. This was also prophesied by the Savior before His death (see Matthew 24:6–7).

In the chapter on the United States in prophecy (chapter 15), we cited a little-known prophecy by Joseph Smith concerning our country at a time when the Constitution would be in grave danger. In that same prophecy, the Prophet foresaw the Saints engaged in warfare to save the country from destruction. We cite it again here because of its relevance to our questions.

> Then shall the Lord say: Go tell all my servants who are the strength of mine house, my young men and middle aged &c., *Come to the land of my vineyard and fight the battle of the Lord* [America]—Then the Kings and Queens shall come, then the rulers of the earth shall come, then shall all Saints come, yea the foreign Saints shall come to fight for the land of my vineyard, for in this thing shall be their safety and they will have no power to choose but will come as a man fleeth from a sudden destruction ("Discourse, circa 19 July 1840, as Reported by Unknown Scribe–A," p. 2, *The Joseph Smith Papers;* https://www.josephsmithpapers.org/paper-summary/discourse-circa-19-july-1840-as-reported-by-unknown-scribe-a/2).

Could this upheaval be happening at the same time we are returning to Zion? We can't tell for sure, but in referring to the call for the Saints to come, they are to come "to the land of my vineyard." In the revelation given after the Saints had been driven out of Jackson County, the Savior gave a parable in which He likened the land of Zion to His vineyard (see D&C 101:43–62).

On the other hand, it was the Lord who declared that the Saints would be "the only people that shall not be at war one with another" (D&C 45:69).

PEACE, REFUGE, SAFETY

But all is not dark and grim. It will be for the world. We have seen that over and over. But there are promises related to the New Jerusalem and God's chosen that give us hope and some degree of peace. In one revelation, sandwiched between descriptions of war and civil unrest, we find a passage that shines like a light in the darkness. First the Lord says, "Ye hear of wars in foreign lands; but, behold, I say unto you, they are nigh, even at your doors, and not many years hence ye shall hear of wars in your own lands" (D&C 45:63).

"In your own lands" is very likely a reference to the Civil War, which would begin just thirty years later. A few verses later, the Lord picks up the idea of war again, only this time perhaps it is war of a different kind:

> *By and by the nations will be broken up on account of their wickedness, the Latter-day Saints are not going to move upon them with their little army, they will destroy themselves with their wickedness and immorality. They will contend and quarrel with one another, state after state and nation after nation, until they are broken up, and thousands, tens of thousands and hundreds of thousands will undoubtedly come and seek protection at the hands of the servants of God.*
>
> LORENZO SNOW,
> IN *JOURNAL OF DISCOURSES*, 14:309

And it shall come to pass among the wicked, that every man that will not take his sword against his neighbor must needs flee unto Zion for safety. And there shall be gathered unto it out of every nation under heaven; and it shall be the only people that shall not be at war one with another (D&C 45:68–69).

Let us look more closely at the wording in the last passage. The Lord speaks of man taking up his sword *"against his neighbor."* To take up the sword against your neighbor doesn't sound like a vast battle between hostile nations. When Americans fought Germans and Italians in World War II, we didn't think of that as fighting our neighbors. *Neighbor* strongly hints of a more localized kind of warfare, such as those described elsewhere during the collapse of social order (see chapter 13). This could be local conflicts such as civil unrest, neighborhood gang wars, or widespread rioting.

Though the scale is usually smaller in these situations, that doesn't make them any less devastating for those caught up in them. Sometimes violence erupts over something as trivial as a loss of some sports competition, but it can also include race riots, food riots, prison riots, religious violence, protests against the government, and so on.

For example, after the tragic assassination of Martin Luther King Jr., major riots broke out in more than 100 cities across the United States, including such major cities as New York, Chicago, Baltimore, and Washington, D.C. In those four cities alone, property damage approached half a billion dollars, and dozens of people were killed. In Washington, D.C., as rioting approached the White House, about 15,000 Federal and National Guard troops were called out to protect the city. This was the largest occupation of an American city by troops since the Civil War. That certainly qualifies as a real war.

The Lord plainly said that the return to Zion would be during a time of war and upheaval. However, as we said before, sandwiched between those descriptions of war and violence are three wonderful words and some marvelous promises:

> *We must acknowledge that the building up of Zion occurs in tumultuous times—"a day of wrath, a day of burning, a day of desolation, of weeping, of mourning, and of lamentation; and as a whirlwind it shall come upon all the face of the earth, saith the Lord." Thus, the gathering into stakes becomes "for a defense, and for a refuge from the storm, and from wrath when it shall be poured out without mixture upon the whole earth."*
>
> D. Todd Christofferson,
> "Preparing for the Lord's Return,"
> *Ensign,* May 2019

> With one heart and with one mind, gather up your riches that ye may purchase an inheritance which shall hereafter be appointed unto you. And it shall be called the New Jerusalem, a land of *peace,* a city of *refuge,* a place of *safety* for the saints of the Most High God; And the glory of the Lord shall be there, and the terror of the Lord also shall be there, *insomuch that the wicked will not come unto it,* and it shall be called Zion" (D&C 45:65–67).

SUMMARY AND CONCLUSIONS

What wonderful words those are: *peace, refuge,* and *safety.* They are supported by other promises that should also comfort us.

- "The time soon cometh that the fulness of the wrath of God shall be poured out upon all the children of men; for *he will not suffer that the wicked shall destroy the righteous*" (1 Nephi 22:16).

- "Wherefore, *he will preserve the righteous by his power,* even if it so be that the fulness of his wrath must come, and *the righteous be preserved, even unto the destruction of their enemies* by fire. Wherefore, *the righteous need not fear*" (v. 17).
- "Behold, *the righteous shall not perish;* for the time surely must come that all they who fight against Zion shall be cut off" (v. 19).
- "The Lord *will surely prepare a way for his people*" (v. 20).
- "For the time speedily cometh that the Lord God shall cause a great division among the people, and the wicked will he destroy; and *he will spare his people,* yea, even if it so be that he must destroy the wicked by fire" (2 Nephi 30:10).
- "The righteous need not fear, for they are those who shall not be confounded" (1 Nephi 22:22).
- "Great tribulations shall be among the children of men, but my people will I preserve" (Moses 7:61; see also D&C 38:31; 63:33–34; 101:11–12).
- "Ye that love the Lord, hate evil: *he preserveth the souls of his saints; he delivereth them out of the hand of the wicked*" (Psalm 97:10).
- "The Lord *preserveth all them that love him*" (Psalm 145:20).

With those promises lifting our hopes and gladdening our hearts, let us now look more closely at what a City of Zion will look like when it is fully established.

CHAPTER 19

LIFE IN THE CITY OF ZION

This great and last dispensation is building steadily to its climax—Zion on earth being joined with Zion from above at the Savior's glorious return. The Church of Jesus Christ is commissioned to prepare—and is preparing—the world for that day. And so, this Easter, let us truly celebrate the Resurrection of Jesus Christ and all that it portends: His return to reign for a thousand years of peace, a righteous judgment and perfect justice for all, the immortality of all who ever lived upon this earth, and the promise of eternal life. (D. Todd Christofferson, "Preparing for the Lord's Return," Ensign, May 2019)

A TEMPLE IN THE CENTER PLACE OF ZION

In John the Revelator's grand vision of the future, he saw the New Jerusalem and a temple that would be built there:

> Him that overcometh will I make a *pillar in the temple of my God,* and he shall go no more out: and I will write upon him the name of my God, and the name of the city of my God, which is *new Jerusalem,* which cometh down out of heaven from my God: and I will write upon him my new name (Revelation 3:12).

As we have discussed, not long after the organization of the Church, the Lord revealed that the center place of Zion was in Jackson County, Missouri. When Joseph and others went there, they were specifically told that a temple would be built there and were shown its exact location (see D&C 57:3). In a brief but solemn ceremony, Joseph laid a single cornerstone for the temple. Thrilled to be part of the fulfillment of prophecies thousands of years old, the Saints began to flock to Missouri. Just over a year later, the Lord gave Joseph further revelation about the temple:

> Yea, the word of the Lord concerning his church, established in the last days for the restoration of his people, . . . and *for the gathering of his saints to stand upon Mount Zion, which shall be the city of New Jerusalem.* Which city shall be built, beginning at the temple lot, which is appointed by the finger of the Lord, in the western boundaries of the State of Missouri, and dedicated by the hand of Joseph Smith, Jun., and others with whom the Lord was well pleased. Verily this is the word of the Lord, *that the city New Jerusalem shall be built by the gathering of the saints,* beginning at this place, *even the place of the temple,* which temple shall be reared *in this generation.*[1] For verily *this generation* shall not all pass away until an house shall be built unto the Lord, and a cloud shall rest upon it, which cloud shall be even the glory of the Lord, which shall fill the house (D&C 84:2–5).

> *Soon after the Latter-day Saints arrived in Missouri a temple site was selected, and this was dedicated at Independence, Jackson County, on August 3, 1831. The temple was never constructed. When the Saints were expelled from that area by the mobs in 1833 the site fell into other hands. Some day, however, in the Lord's own time, that site will be fully reclaimed and the house of the Lord built as we have been commanded to do it.*
>
> Boyd K. Packer,
> *The Holy Temple,* 172

The reaffirmation that the temple was to be built in Missouri was received with great excitement by the Saints. But when Zion's Camp was not able to restore the Saints to their lands in Jackson County, the Lord revealed that the return to Zion, and the building of the temple there, would have to wait for a time.

That did not stop temple building, however. The Kirtland Temple was dedicated in the spring of 1836. The Lord commanded the Saints to build a temple in Far West, and four cornerstones were laid there. When they were permanently driven out of the state of Missouri, they started again and built the Nauvoo Temple. Joseph didn't live to see that completed, but in it the Saints were endowed with power before they were expelled from the city.

Now, almost two hundred years later, with literally hundreds of temples dotting the world, we are still waiting for the command to construct a temple

---

[1] In an earlier chapter we learned that the word "generation" is used in several ways in the scriptures. Here, since it has now been almost two hundred years since this revelation was given, we can assume that "this generation" is used in the sense of an age or a dispensation.

in Jackson County, Missouri. Remember, though the Lord said it would be built in "this generation," one definition of "generation" is an "age," as in the Dark Ages, the Age of Enlightenment, or the Age of the Restoration.

A TEMPLE COMPLEX IN THE HOLY CITY

In the plat of Zion Joseph Smith drew up three larger plots right in the center. These would be an administrative complex, but the center plat was to be the site for a temple. Wilford Woodruff later saw this in a dream:

> I saw a short distance from the Missouri River, where I stood, twelve men dressed in the robes of the Temple. They stood in a square near by and I was given to understand that they represented the twelve gates of the new Jerusalem. Their hands were uplifted while they were consecrating the ground; and later they laid the corner-stones of the house of God. I saw myriads of angels hovering over them, and above their heads there was a pillar-like cloud. I heard the most beautiful singing in the words: "Now is established the Kingdom of our God and His Christ, and He shall reign forever and forever, and the Kingdom shall never be thrown down, for the Saints have overcome." . . . I saw people coming from the river and from distant places to help build the Temple. It seemed as though there were hosts of angels helping to bring material for the construction of that building. Some were in Temple robes, and the pillar-like cloud continued to hover over the spot (in Matthias F. Cowley, *Wilford Woodruff: History of His Life and Labors*, 505).

Other modern prophets, seers, and revelators have spoken about the city and its temple, enlightening us with a marvelous richness of detail. In a proclamation to the world, issued on the fifteenth anniversary of the Church, April 6, 1845, the Twelve Apostles declared:

> We further testify that the Lord *has appointed a holy city and temple to be built on this continent* for the endowment and ordinances pertaining to the priesthood; and for the Gentiles, and the remnant of Israel to resort unto, in order to worship the Lord; and to be taught in his ways and walk in his paths: in short, to finish their preparations for the coming of the Lord (in James R. Clark, *Messages of the First Presidency of The Church of Jesus Christ of Latter-day Saints*, 1:254).

Charles W. Penrose, of the First Presidency, used language that contains a wonderful promise for the faithful:

> They [the Saints] will come to the Temple prepared for him, and *his faithful people will behold his face, hear his voice, and gaze upon his glory.* From his own lips they will receive further instructions for the development and beautifying of Zion and for the extension and sure stability of his Kingdom (Penrose, *Millennial Star*, 21:582–83).

Contemplate that thought for a moment. Can we not also hope that sometime during His visit to the temple that we, like those who were at the temple in the land of Bountiful, will have the privilege of being invited to come forward and feel for ourselves the wounds in His body and in His hands and feet? Does that seem so incredibly impossible that we think it could never happen to us? Wasn't that exactly how the Nephites must have felt when they were the ones to fulfill the prophecies? Or the women at the tomb in Jerusalem? Or Thomas, who doubted? Or the five hundred who saw Him taken up to heaven? These marvelous experiences did happen to some who have been faithful to their covenants in times past. Why would they not happen in times future?

> *One appearance will be to the righteous Saints who have gathered to the New Jerusalem here in America. In this place of refuge they will be safe from the wrath of the Lord which will be poured out without measure on all nations.*
>
> Ezra Taft Benson,
> "Prepare Yourselves for the Great Day of the Lord," *New Era*, May 1982

We are told that the New Jerusalem will be built prior to the Millennium, but we do not know if this visit from the Master will take place before or after His Second Coming. But that He will come is sure.

We have been told that a major work of the Millennium will be doing the ordinance work for the dead. President Joseph Fielding Smith described another experience that lies in the future, though he didn't tie it directly to the temple in New Jerusalem, but possibly to all temples at that time:

> During this time of peace, when the righteous shall come forth from their graves, they shall mingle with mortal men on the earth and instruct them. The veil which separates the living from the dead will be withdrawn and mortal men and the ancient saints shall converse together. Moreover, in perfect harmony shall they labor for the salvation and exaltation of the worthy who have died without the privileges of the gospel. The great work of the millennium shall be performed in the temples which shall cover all parts

of the land and into which the children shall go to complete the work for their fathers, which they could not do when in this mortal life for themselves. In this manner those who have passed through the resurrection, and who know all about people and conditions on the other side, will place in the hands of those who are in mortality, the necessary information by and through which the great work of salvation for every worthy soul shall be performed, and thus the purposes of the Lord, as determined before the foundation of the world, will be fully consummated (Smith, *Doctrines of Salvation*, 2:251–52).

LIFE IN THE CITY OF ZION

What we have shared would be ranked as miraculous events. And so they are. But much of what will go on in the New Jerusalem, and the other cities of Zion that will dot the earth, will be more down-to-earth, more part of our everyday lives. There are those who will be privileged to live during this time if they are pure in heart. Note that it doesn't require us to be perfect, but pure in heart. What will everyday life be like for them? Again we aren't given much detail, but the prophets have shared a few choice insights.

President John Taylor described life in the New Jerusalem in the most glowing of terms.

> We believe that we shall rear splendid edifices, magnificent temples and beautiful cities that shall become the pride, praise and glory of the whole earth. We believe that this people will excel in literature, in science and the arts and in manufacture. In fact, there will be a concentration of wisdom, not only of the combined wisdom of the world as it now exists, but men will be inspired in regard to all these matters in a manner and to an extent that they have never been before, and we shall have eventually, when the Lord's purposes are carried out, the most magnificent buildings, the most pleasant and beautiful gardens, . . . and be the most healthy and the most intellectual people that will reside upon the earth. This is part and parcel of our faith (Taylor, *Gospel Kingdom*, 216).

Brigham Young was another prophet who tried to describe how life will be in such a setting of purity and holiness:

> Are we prepared now to establish the Zion that the Lord designs to build up? I have many times asked the questions, "Where is the man that knows how to lay the first rock for the wall that is

to surround the New Jerusalem, or the Zion of God on the earth? Where is the man who knows how to construct the first gate of the city? Where is the man who understands how to build up the kingdom of God in its purity and to prepare for Zion to come down to meet it? . . . He will not send His angels to gather the rock to build up the New Jerusalem. He will not send His angels from the heavens to go to the mountains to cut the timber and make it into lumber to adorn the city of Zion. He has called upon us to do this work; and if we will let Him work by, through, and with us, He can accomplish it; otherwise we shall fall short, and shall never have the honor of building up Zion on the earth (Brigham Young, in *Journal of Discourses*, 13:313).

Another Apostle, who would go on to become a President of the Church, tried to describe in common terms what life in Zion would really be like. This statement was made during the Great Depression, long before the days of high technology we now enjoy, which makes his views all the more interesting:

If we have in mind the physical Zion, then we must strive for more fertile acres; bring from the mountains gold and silver in abundance; found factories to furnish more employment; extend in length and width our concrete public highways; build banks to protect . . . the wealth we accumulate; transform our vast coal fields into electricity that will furnish light, heat and power to every family; improve the means of communication until *with radios in our pockets we may communicate with friends and loved ones from any point at any given moment* [the first mobile phones were not invented until 1973]. Is it these physical phrases of Zion which we are to build? Certainly it is difficult to picture the City of Zion without at least some—if not all—such modern necessities and luxuries (David O. McKay, *Improvement Era*, April 1935, 229).

Some might assume that with such comforts and innovations that life would be easy for us. President Woodruff thought otherwise:

We can't build up Zion sitting on a hemlock slab singing ourselves away to everlasting bliss; we have to cultivate the earth, to take the rocks and elements out of the mountains and rear temples to the Most High God; and this temporal work is demanded at our hands by the God of heaven. . . . This is the great dispensation in which the Zion of God must be built up, and we as Latter-day Saints have it to build. We are obliged to build cities, towns and villages, and we are obliged to gather the people from every nation under heaven to the Zion of God, that they may be taught in the ways of the Lord. We have only just begun to prepare for the celestial law when we are baptized into the Church of Jesus Christ of Latter-day Saints (Wilford Woodruff, *Discourses*, 164).

And finally, Hyrum Mack Smith, a son of Joseph F. Smith and a member of the Quorum of the Twelve, made this interesting observation:

> One great purpose of God in establishing Zion is to save the world, through its laws and institutions, from the curse of poverty and destitution. The object is to give to the world an entirely new social order, to establish a community in which even the poor would share the "fat things" with "the rich and the learned, the wise and the noble." Zion is to be a place for the "supper of the house of the Lord"—a banquet hall—"unto which all nations shall be invited." . . . It is the New Jerusalem, consisting of the City of Zion and the "Jerusalem which is above," that is, "the Bride of the Lamb." The two will be united when our Savior comes in His glory. "Blessed are they who are called unto the marriage supper of the Lamb." Yea, blessed are they who will be called to become citizens in the City of Zion (Hyrum M. Smith and Janne M. Sjodahl, *Doctrine and Covenants Commentary*, 336–37).

SUMMARY AND CONCLUSIONS

Most of my childhood years were spent in Murray, Utah, a suburb of Salt Lake City. Now fully developed with housing everywhere, back then it was a mostly rural area with lots of open land and only a few scattered houses. My father was a smelter worker and so, by today's standards, we would be considered to have lived near the poverty level, though we never saw it that way.

I began elementary school while America was still heavily engaged in World War II. On the surface, that might not seem like an auspicious time to live, but as I look back on it now and compare it to our current times, it seems pretty idyllic.

As just one example of how things have changed, our elementary school was about two miles from my home, which back then was not quite far enough to qualify us to ride the school bus. We had only one car, which my father took to work each day, so my friend and I, from the time we were in first grade and on, walked to and from school every day. I remember quite clearly that the only thing my mother ever warned me about when I left for school was to "watch out for cars."

In our day now, virtually every elementary school experiences a serious traffic jam before and after school because parents do not dare let their younger children walk to or from school, even if they live only a block or two away. Why? Because the threat of danger is almost ever present. Even in public restrooms with crowds of people around, adults dare not let their younger children go in unaccompanied for the same reasons. We could multiply those examples by the hundreds.

How the world has changed in the last seventy to eighty years! Child abuse, sexual assault, gang activity, inner-city neighborhoods so dangerous that even going out in broad daylight is a risk—these are the realities of our day.

> *In the last days a new Zion will receive the Lord at His return. Zion is the pure in heart, a people of one heart and one mind, dwelling in righteousness with no poor among them.*
>
> D. TODD CHRISTOFFERSON,
> "PREPARING FOR THE LORD'S RETURN,"
> *ENSIGN*, MAY 2019

I don't remember ever hearing the word "pornography" until I was in my high school years, and when my friends and I were told about it, I had no idea what they were talking about. Now it is a multibillion dollar industry. Even the highest levels of vigilance may not be sufficient to keep this scourge out of our homes or off the electronic devices that are virtually ubiquitous in our day, even with elementary and junior high school students.

The point is, how long can this moral decline go on? For it continues to spread and deepen today. Will we ever see things come back to some degree of normalcy? The prophets answer that with a resounding and astounding, "Yes!" It is called Zion.

Notice Mormon's detailed description of what followed Christ's visit to the Nephites. Knowing the life of war and conflict that Mormon experienced from his youth, and knowing that he was an eyewitness of the total annihilation of his people, this description must have been particularly poignant to him. And it is stunning to us as well.

> And it came to pass in the thirty and sixth year, the people were all converted unto the Lord . . . and there were *no contentions and disputations* among them, and *every man did deal justly* one with another. And *they had all things common* among them; therefore there were *not rich and poor, bond and free, but they were all made free,* and partakers of the heavenly gift. . . . And the Lord did *prosper*

Life in the City of Zion

them exceedingly in the land; yea, insomuch that they did build cities again. . . . And now, behold, it came to pass that the people of Nephi *did wax strong,* and *did multiply exceedingly fast,* and *became an exceedingly fair and delightsome people.* And they were married, and given in marriage, and *were blessed according to the multitude of the promises which the Lord had made* unto them. . . . And it came to pass that there was *no contention* in the land, because of the love of God which did dwell in the hearts of the people. And there were *no envyings, nor strifes, nor tumults, nor whoredoms, nor lyings, nor murders,* nor any manner of *lasciviousness* [to be lustful, lewd, filled with unnatural sexual desire]; and surely *there could not be a happier people among all the people who had been created by the hand of God* (4 Nephi 1:2–3, 7, 10–11, 15–16).

And that is what life is like for the pure in heart.

CHAPTER 20

THE CITY OF ZION

The kings and the potentates of the nations will come up to Zion to inquire after the ways of the Lord, and to see great knowledge, wisdom and understanding manifested through the Saints of the most high. . . . They will be drawn to Zion by the great wisdom displayed there. . . . [They will be asked by the Saints], "What do you want to do, ye strangers from afar?" "We want to live our own religion." . . . They will ask, "If I bow the knee and confess that he is that Saviour, the Christ, to the glory of the Father, will you let me go home and be a Presbyterian?" "Yes." "And not persecute me?" "Never." "Won't you let me go home and belong to the Greek Church?" . . . "O yes, anything you wish to be, but remember that you must not persecute your neighbors, but must mind your own business, and let your neighbors alone." . . . When you have paid this tribute to the Most High, who created you and preserves you, you may then go and worship what you please, or do what you please, if you do not infringe upon your neighbors. (Brigham Young, in Journal of Discourses, 2:317)

A PLAN FOR THE CITY OF ZION

When reports kept filtering back about problems in Jackson County, Missouri, Joseph and the other leaders of the Church were gravely concerned. There was petty jealousy, covetousness, and light-mindedness, and some were disregarding the requirements to obtain an "inheritance in Zion." Joseph wrote to them, sending an "olive leaf" given by the Lord (see D&C 88). Joseph encouraged them to repent, warning that "if Zion will not purify herself, He will seek another people. . . . Repent, repent, is the voice of the Lord to Zion" (*Church History in the Fulness of Times*, 128).

The leaders in Missouri wrote back, calling for a "day of confession and repentance," and wrote a letter to Kirtland in behalf of the Saints in Zion expressing their desire to keep the commandments henceforth. The Lord then gave Joseph a revelation, saying that "the angels rejoice" over the Saints in Missouri (D&C 90:34).

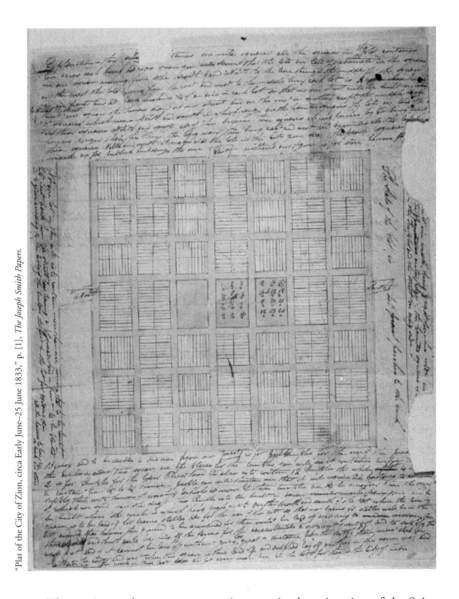

"Plat of the City of Zion, circa Early June–25 June 1833," p. [1], *The Joseph Smith Papers*.

That spring and summer saw an increase in the migration of the Saints to Zion that exceeded the previous year. On June 25, 1833, the Prophet sent a plat (a map of a parcel of land proposed for development) to the Saints in

Missouri. The plat was drawn to scale, and included an explanation written in the margins. Here is a brief description of what the plat contained:

- The plat was one mile square. All the squares in the plat were ten acres each, except for the seven center ones, which were twenty acres each.
- The lots were laid out so every other square faced the opposite direction, which avoided having long streets of homes all facing the same way.
- The plat was designed to house from 15,000 to 20,000 people.
- Each lot was half an acre in size, giving everyone the same amount of land. Homes were to be set back from the street and have gardens in the backyard.
- Only one house per lot was allowed, and they were to be built of brick and stone.
- The streets were to be eight rods (128 feet) wide, making them pleasant thoroughfares and not narrow alleys.
- Each house had to be set back at least 25 feet from the street and have a pleasant front yard.
- The central, double-sized squares were reserved for twenty-four "temples," twelve for the Melchizedek Priesthood and twelve for the Aaronic Priesthood. Though he called them temples, Joseph later indicated that some of these would be used for what we would call Church administrative offices, including schools, houses of worship, a building for the presidency, and bishops' storehouses. This suggests something that we might call a headquarters or administrative complex. But, as we shall see, there was to be a temple built in the city as well. This was to be in the center square. This brings to mind the camp of ancient Israel where the tabernacle, which was the house of the Lord, was always at the center of the camp, just as God should be the center of our lives.
- The land to the north and south of the city plan was to be used for agricultural purposes. This allowed farmers and ranchers to live in the

> *The plan which [Joseph Smith] presented was given to him by vision, and the future will prove that the visions of Joseph concerning Jackson County, all the various stakes of Zion and the redemption of Israel will be fulfilled in the time appointed of the Lord.*
>
> WILFORD WOODRUFF,
> JOURNAL HISTORY, APRIL 6, 1837

city and not have to travel too far to work their land. As necessary, the same could happen on the east and the west.

Joseph finished his notes with this comment: "Where this square is thus laid off and supplied [i.e., fully occupied] lay off another [square] in the same way and so *fill up the world* in these last days and let every man live in the City for this is the City of Zion" (see "Plat of the City of Zion, circa Early June–25 June 1833," p. [1], *The Joseph Smith Papers;* https://www.josephsmithpapers.org/paper-summary/plat-of-the-city-of-zion-circa-early-june-25-june-1833/1).

THE CITY OF ZION

Ancient prophets have often spoken of the New Jerusalem. Though we have no record of Jesus speaking of it during His earthly ministry, the resurrected Christ spoke of it more than once during His visit to the Nephites. "Behold, this people will I establish in this land, . . . and *it shall be a New Jerusalem.* And the powers of heaven shall be in the midst of this people; yea, even I will be in the midst of you" (3 Nephi 20:22). A short time later, Jesus spoke of it again: "And they [those of Gentile nations who are Church members] shall assist my people, . . . and also as many of the house of Israel as shall come, *that they may build a city, which shall be called the New Jerusalem.* And then shall they assist my people that they may be gathered in, . . . unto the New Jerusalem" (3 Nephi 21:23–24).

Ether also taught "that a *New Jerusalem should be built up upon this land,* unto the remnant of the seed of Joseph, . . . *This land* . . . shall be a land of their inheritance; and *they shall build up a holy city unto the Lord"* (Ether 13:6, 8). And, as we discussed earlier, through revelations given to Joseph Smith, we know that the city of New Jerusalem is to be built in Jackson County, Missouri, the center place of Zion.

This great and last dispensation is building steadily to its climax—Zion on earth being joined with Zion from above at the Savior's glorious return. The Church of Jesus Christ is commissioned to prepare—and is preparing—the world for that day.

D. TODD CHRISTOFFERSON, "PREPARING FOR THE LORD'S RETURN," ENSIGN, May 2019

This is truly one of the "great" signs of the times that Elijah promised. And the implications it has for members of the Church sometime in the future is so incredible that at times it may seem to be more of a dream than a reality. But seeing Joseph's plat of the city and reading his vision of what the city will be like helps us grasp that at some point the vision and dream will become a reality.

Before exploring what that means, we need to remind ourselves that the city of New Jerusalem will not be the only place of gathering. Currently there are about sixteen million members of the Church. There is no way they could fit into one city plat a mile square—or even into all of Jackson County. And as we see from Joseph's plat plan, this will not be just one city, but many.

We also know that New Jerusalem will be one of two capital cities during the Millennium, Old Jerusalem being the other. And that is not just because it will be the worldwide headquarters for the Church. It will also be the world capital for the kingdom of God when Christ comes again as King of kings (see chapter 29).

Earlier we read the Lord's fascinating description of how modern Israel will return to Jackson County in much the same manner as Israel of old. While that is a marvelous concept, it reveals very few details of how it will actually happen, to say nothing of when it will happen. There are also many questions we have about what life will be like once there. We shall choose only six, and these shall be questions about which we have enough information to answer definitively, or to engage in some "informed speculation."

Do we know who will lead the return to Jackson County?

Yes. As noted, the Lord clearly said that the group going back to Jackson County to restore Zion at some future day would be led by a man "like unto Moses." As we saw, that title was first given to Jesus Christ, then later was also applied to the prophet and President of The Church of Jesus Christ of Latter-day Saints. He is like unto Moses in that he has an assignment from the Lord to preside over the house of Israel and eventually lead them to the promised land. Moses came personally to Joseph Smith and Oliver Cowdery in the Kirtland Temple and gave them the keys of (1) gathering of Israel from the four parts of the earth; and (2) leading the ten tribes from the land of the north (see D&C 110:11), which makes the comparison to Moses all the more pertinent.

Knowing what a momentous day that will be, it would not be surprising if the prophet were to be the one to actually lead that first group back. But "lead" could also mean that it is his responsibility to oversee this enormously complex assignment and that he might wait and go with a later group. Another thing that seems to be a fairly certain assumption is that this return will not be a one-group, one-time-only experience. Though we have modern transportation, we don't know if that will be available or not. But even with that, the sheer numbers of faithful members at that time would suggest that it won't be just a single large group that goes. Even with the highly organized system that Brigham Young led, it took about thirty years to get the 70,000 to 80,000 members of the Church to Utah.

Will all faithful members be called to return to the New Jerusalem when the time comes?

In this case we have enough information to give a clear answer. And the answer is no, they will not. Here is why:

- In the first place, we have to take into consideration that if there are sixteen million members of the Church at the time this book was written, how many will there be when the command is given? And they will be scattered all over the earth. Imagine the logistical and financial resources it would take to move even half of them across the distances required, feeding them on the way and providing housing for them when they arrive.
- We know for sure that the ten lost tribes will come separate from this group. So there's another reason why we can say no. Not all of Israel will come at the same time.
- When Joseph Smith sent the plat of the city to the Saints, he told them that there will be many, many smaller cities of Zion eventually. So not everyone will be coming to the New Jerusalem.
- Directly related to that is the concept of stakes of Zion. As we have seen, the stakes of Zion are an integral part of Zion. President Russell M. Nelson and others of the Brethren have reminded us that it is not where we live that determines our salvation.
- The Church has administrative facilities and temples all around the world. If everyone were to go to Jackson County, we would have to abandon a lot of property. It is very possible that some faithful members will be called to stay where they are.

There are very few indicators of how some things will be determined for the return to Zion—who will go or not go, when they will go, even where they will go. Obviously existing circumstances, such as whether it is a time of war, would have an impact on that decision. Here again, the experience of the early pioneers offers some possibilities. A lead pioneer company was formed by invitation only—the leaders chose those with skills that would be important not only on the trek itself but also to get basic needs in the Valley met quickly for when the main body began to arrive. At the same time, there were some who were asked by Church leadership to stay behind or stop along the way to provide needed services along the route. It seems reasonable that similar "assignments" would be made in this case as well. But as a general principle, all were eventually invited to go, and support was provided to help them make the trip. It seems logical that we would see similar arrangements taking place in this case too.

Will we have any access to means of modern transportation as we make this journey?

In the quote describing the return of the Saints to Jackson County (see chapter 18), President Joseph F. Smith spoke of herding cattle along the way and said that railroads would not be available because of widespread social collapse. This suggests that we may not be able to charter planes or caravan in our SUVs to Jackson County.

Some don't agree with that conclusion. They note that at the time President Smith made this statement, railroads were the fastest means of transportation. He had no concept of automobiles, national freeway systems, bullet trains, or airplanes, so it was natural for him to describe what he did. But, they ask, why would we send thousands of people on foot for such an arduous journey when we have modern means of mass transportation widely available?

It is a valid question. Why not use what is available, especially when there could eventually be millions going there? Here are some things to consider.

The pioneers coming to the Mountain West provide a good model. The first groups came by sailing ships, wagons, handcarts, and on foot, because those were the only options they had. But when sailing ships were replaced by steamships, which cut the journey from months to days, the pioneers took advantage of that. When the transcontinental railroad was finished, the time of long wagon caravans came to an end. We can assume that Church leaders will encourage people to take the best means of transportation available at the time. That's the first thing to keep in mind.

The second thing is that, as we have seen, the prophecies strongly suggest that at the time we are talking about, there may be widespread social chaos through war, riots, civil uprising, mobocracy, etc. In those circumstances, even the most modern of transportation options could very likely not be available. Think, for example, how the COVID-19 pandemic affected global transportation systems, including airlines, railroads, and ships. That doesn't mean that we will permanently revert to a pioneer way of life—only that for a time there is a strong probability that modern means of transportation would not be available.

The third thing to consider is that saying that one or more of the groups returning to Zion will go on foot, as armies have done for centuries, doesn't mean that everyone will go that same way. As the Church gets established in Missouri, things will likely eventually stabilize, which could restore more efficient ways for people to travel to Zion. But until then, there may be no choice but to make our way back as best we can.

Zion is a place where the pure in heart gather, so does this mean that the New Jerusalem will be exclusively for righteous members of The Church of Jesus Christ of Latter-day Saints?

This is an important question, for if the answer is yes, that suggests we will become a church of exclusion, not inclusion. We talked about preparation for coming separation earlier. By "separation" we mean to separate ourselves from worldliness, not to separate ourselves into exclusive communities. There are scriptures that make it clear that gathering "His people" or "the righteous" to places of safety is a major part of God's plan (see, for example, 3 Nephi 21:28; D&C 45:71). But we must keep in mind that the invitation to come to the covenant is open to all except for a very few individuals who have done things in their lives that hold them out of the Church. Note how inclusive this gathering is in another passage where Nephi quotes Isaiah:

> The Lord shall set his hand again the second time to recover the remnant of his people which shall be left, from Assyria, and from Egypt, and from Pathros, and from Cush, and from Elam, and from Shinar, and from Hamath [all Gentile nations], and from the islands of the sea. And he shall set up an ensign for the nations, and *shall assemble the outcasts of Israel,* and gather together the *dispersed of Judah* from the four corners of the earth (2 Nephi 21:11–12).

And note what the Lord Himself said in the context of gathering to Zion and the New Jerusalem: "And it shall come to pass among the wicked, that every man that will not take his sword against his neighbor *must needs flee unto Zion for safety*" (D&C 45:68). A careful reading of that passage shows that the Lord is not saying that the wicked will flee to Zion, but that good people of the earth, those who will not join in the violence and mayhem around them, will come to the Church, not to be baptized but to find haven from the storm. Two verses later, we are told that the wicked will not dare go up to Zion, because Zion is "terrible," i.e., it fills them with terror (D&C 45:70). Also note the following statements from Church leaders:

> The day is not far distant when this nation will be shaken from centre to circumference. . . . And then will be fulfilled that prediction to be found in one of the revelations [that] . . . those who will not take up their sword to fight against their neighbor must needs flee to Zion for safety. And they will come, saying, we do not know anything of the principles of your religion, but we perceive that you are an honest community; you administer justice and righteousness, and we want to live with you and receive the protection of your laws, but as for your religion we will talk about that some other time. Will we protect such people? Yes, all honorable men (John Taylor, in *Journal of Discourses*, 21:8).

> By and by the nations will be broken up on account of their wickedness, the Latter-day Saints are not going to move upon them with their little army, they will destroy themselves with their wickedness and immorality. They will contend and quarrel with one another, state after state and nation after nation, until they are broken up, and *thousands, tens of thousands and hundreds of thousands will undoubtedly come and seek protection at the hands of the servants of God* (Lorenzo Snow, in *Journal of Discourses*, 14:309).

These declarations are supported by what two Old Testament prophets taught many centuries ago. Both suggest that there will be people *not* of the covenant who come to Zion to learn about our God. Zechariah prophesied: "And it shall come to pass, that every one that is left of all the nations which came against Jerusalem *shall even go up from year to year to worship the King,* the Lord of hosts, and to keep the feast of tabernacles" (Zechariah 14:16; see also Psalm 86:9).

Isaiah spoke in more detail in a chapter focused on the time of the Second Coming, even suggesting that missionary work will continue after that time:

> I will gather all nations and tongues; and *they shall come, and see my glory*. And I will set a sign among them, and *I will send those that escape* of them unto the nations [he then lists several Gentile nations of that day], . . . to the isles afar off, that have not heard my fame, neither have seen my glory; and they shall declare my glory among the Gentiles. And *they shall bring all your brethren for an offering unto the Lord out of all nations* upon horses, and in chariots, and in litters, and upon mules, and upon swift beasts, to my holy mountain Jerusalem, saith the Lord (Isaiah 66:18–20).

The City of Zion

Remember how the City of Zion is described: "a land of peace, a city of refuge, a place of safety." Latter-day Saints won't be the only ones who are seeking those three conditions.

What about the people who are living in that area of Missouri now? What happens to them?

We have no known prophetic commentary on that question. We do know that the Kansas City metropolitan area includes both Kansas and Missouri and covers fourteen counties with a population of millions. It is hard to conceive how that area might be totally desolate when we return, but we are not told how that will be resolved. Large metropolitan areas are more susceptible to the collapse of social order, so that could be a factor. But even then, to assume that there will be no one left there when we come seems very unlikely.

(Note: *The Coming of the Lord* includes a quote from the *Deseret News* that was attributed to Heber C. Kimball. He supposedly said that when the Saints returned to Jackson County to redeem Zion, there wouldn't be so much as a yellow dog left there to wag its tail in greeting. Later it was discovered that although the statement had been quoted in Church sources, its reliability could not be verified. I mention that here only because it is still quoted from time to time by people who assume it is a valid statement.)

What does this mean for Salt Lake City? Will we abandon the current headquarters of the Church and all that we have built up in the Mountain West?

As we have seen, New Jerusalem will become one of the two world headquarters for the kingdom of God (the other being Old Jerusalem). But that doesn't mean that the Church will abandon the considerable resources and infrastructure that it now has in Utah or other places in the world. We know that in the Millennium, the Church and kingdom will be a truly global organization. That means there will be regional administrative and worship facilities all around the world. And temples. Knowing that temple work will be a major work of the Millennium, we can safely assume that the temple in New Jerusalem will not be the only operating temple. Can't we assume that many of the existing temples we now enjoy will continue into the Millennium?

President Joseph Fielding Smith stated: "We accept the fact that the center place where the City New Jerusalem is to be built, is in Jackson County, Missouri. It was never the intention to substitute Utah or any other place for Jackson County" (Smith, *Doctrines of Salvation*, 3:72). This confirms that while Salt Lake City will not be the permanent center place of the Church, neither does President Smith say that it will be abandoned.

SUMMARY AND CONCLUSIONS

When we speak of the New Jerusalem and who will live there, we are speaking of one phase of the gathering of the house of Israel in the last days. It is a unique and wonderful part of the gathering, and those privileged to go there will have marvelous experiences. Ultimately, New Jerusalem is only one of many places where the pure in heart will dwell. It is to Zion that we are called to gather, not just one City of Zion or one particular stake of Zion.

Some people are growing anxious about where they should live as they see the world spiraling ever rapidly downward, but again and again, our prophets have counseled that we do not have to seek out some safe haven in order to ride out the storm. Some even assume that refuge should be found in places away from the cities and towns, where people can hole up and defend themselves if necessary. Others feel that their only safety lies in a bomb shelter stocked with food and ammunition. But Church leaders have said over and over that it's not *where* we live that makes the big difference, but *how* we live. That is not to say that individual families may not be prompted to move to places where the Church is strong and their families can become part of communities of faith. But the principle is simple. If the Lord wants us to gather to places of safety other that what we have just described, that counsel will come from the leadership of the Church. President Harold B. Lee spoke quite forcefully on this subject:

> The Lord has placed the responsibility for directing the work of gathering in the hands of the leaders of the Church, to whom He will reveal His will where and when such gatherings would take place in the future. It would be well, before the frightening events concerning the fulfillment of all God's promises and predictions are upon us, that the Saints in every land prepare themselves and look forward to the instruction that shall come to them from the First Presidency of this church as to where they shall be gathered. *They should not be disturbed in their feelings until such instruction is given to them as it is revealed by the Lord to the proper authority* (Lee, *Ye Are the Light of the World*, 166–67).

I heard a group of anxious people asking, "Is now the day for us to come up to Zion, where we can come to the mountain of the Lord, where we can be protected from our enemies?" I pondered that question, I prayed about it. What should we say to those people who were in their anxiety? . . . *I know now that the place of safety in this world is not in any given place; it doesn't make so much difference where we live; but the all-important thing is how we live* (Lee, "Hearing the Voice," *Improvement Era*, July 1943, 445).

As one studies the commandments of God, it seems crystal clear that the all-important thing is not where we live, but whether or not our hearts are pure. . . . There is only one place of safety and that is within the realm of the power of Almighty God that He gives to those who keep His commandments and listen to His voice, as He speaks through the channels that He has ordained for that purpose (Lee, *Stand Ye in Holy Places*, 24, 383).

CHAPTER 21

THE LOST TRIBES OF ISRAEL

Behold, the days come, saith the Lord, that it shall no more be said, The Lord liveth, that brought up the children of Israel out of the land of Egypt; But, The Lord liveth, that brought up the children of Israel from the land of the north, and from all the lands whither he had driven them: and I will bring them again into their land that I gave unto their fathers. (Jeremiah 16:14–15)

THE TEN LOST TRIBES OF ISRAEL

The prophet Jeremiah, who lived around 600 B.C., was a contemporary of Lehi and his family. It was a time when Babylon's armies were hovering over the Southern Kingdom, threatening to strike if the kingdom didn't break off its alliance with Egypt. This was an especially sobering threat, for it had been just over a hundred years earlier that the Assyrians had swept in, conquering the Northern Kingdom and taking them back to Assyria as slaves. That was the worst national tragedy Israel had experienced since their bondage in Egypt about five hundred years before.

Jeremiah's prophecy (in the epigraph above) must have come as a tremendous shock to his listeners. By this point, most were assuming the ten tribes had been so thoroughly assimilated into Assyrian society that they were no longer Israelites at all. Isaiah, who lived at the time of the Assyrian capture, had made a few comments about the north countries giving up their captives, but these were very general promises. Jeremiah, on the other hand, not only said they would be restored sometime in the future but that it would be done in such a miraculous manner that it would even overshadow their delivery from Egypt. That must have been an electrifying pronouncement back then, because all Israel looked back on the exodus from Egypt as one of the seminal events in their history.

Several Old Testament prophets—Isaiah, Jeremiah, Amos, Zechariah—spoke of the return of the lost tribes. Nephi, a contemporary of Jeremiah's, spoke of their return. When Jesus came to the Nephites after His death, He specifically said that those lost tribes were still out there and that He would visit them. Ether also spoke of them. After the Restoration, modern revelation spoke of the tribes in the north countries several times (see Topical Guide, "Israel, Ten Lost Tribes of"). With all of that, it shouldn't surprise us that the lost ten tribes is a topic of much interest, not just to Latter-day Saints but to Christians and Jews as well. There has been much speculation about their whereabouts and when they will return. Many theories have been put forth about where they are now. Several of the proposed answers could be described as exotic theories. For example, a very popular idea in the nineteenth century was the "hollow earth" theory. Adherents postulated that they were living in a large hollow area beneath the polar ice cap, heated by deep volcanic thermal energy. With the thorough exploration of the polar regions, that has proved to be pure fantasy.

Others believe that they are still together, living as some remote, undiscovered tribe in deepest Africa or the Amazon rainforest. This ignores the fact that while there are remote tribes, they are not unknown, and they are usually small in number. It also ignores the fact that neither Brazil nor Africa would be considered as "north countries."

There are also "off-the-earth" theories that propose they were taken to another planet to await Christ's coming and their return. They cite Moses as proof of this. He said that Israel would be gathered "from all the nations, whither the Lord thy God hath scattered thee," then added, "if any of thine *be driven out unto the outermost parts of heaven,* from thence will the Lord thy God gather thee" (Deuteronomy 30:3–4). Mark's gospel shows the Lord used similar language in His great Olivet Discourse (see Mark 13:27). Though at first that sounds pretty definitive, it does raise the question of how they would make the return journey to earth. More importantly, we have a scriptural passage that speaks in detail of their return, and nothing extraterrestrial is even hinted at. We shall look at that passage in the next chapter, but Joseph Smith once made reference to the verse in Deuteronomy and emphatically indicated that the language Moses used "must mean *the [breadth] of the earth*" ("History, 1838–1856, volume B-1 [1 September 1834–2 November 1838]," p. 624, *The Joseph Smith Papers;* https://www.josephsmithpapers.org/paper-summary/history-1838-1856-volume-b-1-1-september-1834-2-november-1838/78).

All of this interest and speculation has led to many questions. Here are just a few: Do we have any idea where the lost ten tribes might be? Do we know when they are coming back? How do you "lose" that many people? Why were only ten of the twelve tribes lost? Will all twelve tribes come back together again sometime? Do they know who they are? Are they all in one place? Will they come back before or after the Second Coming? How will they know when it's time for them to return? It says they're in the "north countries"—what does that mean? Where will they be coming to? What will they do when they get there? Will they use modern transportation? Will they be Christians? Will the Jews be part of that return? Will there be members of The Church of Jesus Christ of Latter-day Saints among them? Since they live in the north countries, do they live in a land of ice and snow? Will they have their own prophets?

Clearly, we do not have enough details—not to mention space in this book—to answers many of these questions, but through ancient and latter-day scripture and ancient and latter-day prophets, we know much more about the lost ten tribes than some people might think. And from that we can say that the return of the lost tribes is one of the leaves on the fig tree the Lord has given us in the latter days to help us know what is coming so we can "be not troubled." And this particular sign is definitely on the "great" side of the ledger.

For that reason we shall try to answer several of the more important of these questions.

IS THE RETURN OF THE LOST TEN TRIBES THE SAME AS THE GATHERING OF ISRAEL?

The answer to that is no, but it is a qualified no. And understanding how they are different provides important insights for our study of the lost tribes of Israel.

Of course the return of the lost tribes is part of the overall gathering of scattered Israel. However, just because there are two parts to a whole doesn't mean that the two parts are the same. Some people, including a few members of the Church, believe that the return of the lost tribes will not be some grand, dramatic, and miraculous event known to all the world. They say it has been happening for decades in a very natural way as our missionaries go out to all the world, including the north countries, and bring people into the covenant. They agree that it is a miracle because of its scope, not because it is a one-time event. It is a persuasive argument. However, the scriptures suggest otherwise.

Several passages of scripture very specifically and emphatically delineate between the gathering of Israel and the return of the lost tribes from the north countries. Note the specificity of Jeremiah 16:15: "The Lord liveth, that *brought up the children of Israel from the land of the north,* AND *from all the lands whither he had driven them.*" If they are the same thing, why list them separately?

On April 3, 1836, Joseph Smith and Oliver Cowdery had a remarkable series of heavenly visitations in the Kirtland Temple. After a personal visit from the Savior, three ancient prophets—Moses, Elias, and Elijah—appeared and conferred upon them priesthood keys, which allowed them to undertake important aspects of the Restoration. The first was Moses, and this is what Joseph recorded: "Moses appeared before us, and committed unto us the keys of *the gathering of Israel from the four parts of the earth,* AND the *leading of the ten tribes from the land of the north*" (D&C 110:11). This clearly implies that they are two separate things.

The prophet Ether also spoke of these as related but separate things: "They are they who were scattered and *gathered in from the four quarters of the earth,* AND *from the north countries,* and are partakers of the fulfilling of the covenant which God made with their father" (Ether 13:11). With such clear and forceful declarations, we can surmise that the Lord is trying to teach us something.

Elder Bruce R. McConkie, who wrote extensively on the ten lost tribes, explained why this difference is important for us:

> The gathering of Israel is one thing, the return of the Ten Tribes to a specified place is another; and Moses gave to men in our day the keys and power to perform both labors. This means that Israel is gathered at the direction and pursuant to the power and authority vested in the legal administrators who preside over The Church of Jesus Christ of Latter-day Saints. And it also means that the Ten Tribes—scattered, lost, unknown, and now in all the nations of the earth—these Ten Tribes, with their prophets, with their scriptures, in faith and desiring righteousness, shall return. . . . The President of the Church is the only person on earth at any given time who does or can exercise these or any other priesthood keys in their eternal fulness. He will direct the return of the Ten Tribes. It will not come to pass in any other way. . . . The gathering of Israel is one thing, the return of the Ten Tribes to a specified place is another; and Moses gave to men in our day the keys and power to perform both labors (McConkie, *Millennial Messiah,* 322).

Though these two aspects of the Restoration are obviously closely related, the differences are significant. The gathering of Israel in the latter days is a *process* that has spanned almost 200 years now, whereas the return of the ten lost tribes is a specific *event*. But how do we explain the separation of two things that seem so closely related? Here's another: Many members of the Church have been told in their patriarchal blessings that they are of the tribe of Ephraim. Many others of Lamanite ancestry are told that they are of the tribe of Manasseh, which was Father Lehi's tribal line.

In recent years, we are seeing more members being told their lineage is through one of the lesser-known tribes, such as Asher or Gad. But with the exception of Judah and Benjamin, all of those tribes constituted the ten tribes of Israel that formed in the Northern Kingdom. So aren't the ten tribes to at least some degree already being gathered? How can they be lost if they are already part of the modern kingdom of God? It is a valid question, and an important one to understand. To do so, we need to carefully analyze the language of the scriptures. A famous saying, attributed to numerous people, is "God is in the details." That is the case here too, so we shall more carefully examine the details.

In the Church, because of our patriarchal blessings, we are much more keenly aware of the tribes of Israel than most other people. And, with our focus on family history and genealogical research, we may be more inclined to think of the tribes of Israel as mostly a genealogical designation. In other words, if we are told that we come from the tribe of Ephraim, we may assume that means we are a direct descendant of Ephraim.

Here's the problem with that. By the time of the Assyrian captivity, the tribes of Israel had been living together for several hundred years in a land about the size of the state of Utah. By then, there had been so much intermarriage between the tribes that virtually every Israelite could likely trace their lineage to all twelve of the tribes. And that bloodline diversity has been multiplied millions of times over in the 2,700 years since.

So it is not incorrect to say that we are of the tribe of Ephraim, but we need to remember that most if not all of us can also say we are from Judah, Asher, Levi, Zebulon, Dan, and so on. Remember, a patriarch declares our "lineage of blessing," not necessarily our dominant genealogical bloodline.

And with that complex definition of Israel, the idea of "lost" Israel also became somewhat confusing, for it too took on diverse meanings. For example, after Solomon's death, two political kingdoms were created, the Northern Kingdom of Israel (Israel now becoming a political term) and the Southern Kingdom of Judah, or the Jews (also now a political term as well as a tribal lineage). But we have to keep in mind that these were no longer just tribal divisions, but political ones as well.

So when we speak of "the ten lost tribes," we need to keep in mind that some from all twelve bloodline tribes were almost certainly included in that loss. We also need to keep in mind that we are talking about the political entity of the nation of Israel that was lost. They were taken away, never to return.

If that is not confusing enough, there is one more sense in which the term "lost" was used to refer to the ten tribes. When they were taken to Assyria, except for one small group that we shall discuss in a moment, the Israelites were melded into Assyrian culture—as slaves at first, but eventually as Assyrian citizens. So in that captivity, the ten tribes (by political designation) lost their freedom, lost their land, lost their faith, and eventually lost their very identity as Israelites. Thus, the "lost" tribes of Israel carries multiple levels of meaning, which we need to keep in mind as we talk about where they are now and how they will come back.

But let us emphasize again, as we close this section, this key concept: The Lord has told us that there will be two great aspects of the gathering of Israel in the last days. First there is the *gathering* of all the tribes of Israel from among all the nations of the world, a process that has been going on for almost two hundred years now. Second there is the *return* of the ten lost tribes from the north countries, which seems to be one major event still in the future.

With that in mind, let's see why they are associated with the north countries. This will help us better understand why these two subsets of the gathering are emphasized by the Lord.

DO WE KNOW WHERE THE TEN TRIBES WENT AND WHAT EVENTUALLY HAPPENED TO THEM?

Yes, we do, though only in more general terms. First, let us reiterate this key point: Members of all the tribes of Israel (by bloodline), not just the ten lost ones, were eventually lost and are now everywhere in the world. Our task is to find them and invite them to the covenant to become true Israel. It is an error to think that only ten tribes—Ephraim, Manasseh, Reuben, Levi, Zebulon, etc.—were lost, while two tribes—Judah and Benjamin— were not. Eventually all of Israel was scattered and lost their identity as the covenant people. The Jews were scattered too, but surprisingly many kept their identity as Jews over the centuries.

Apocrypha is a Greek word meaning "things that are hidden." It is a name attached to several scriptural books that have not always been included in the canonized editions of the Bible. These are books that don't have the same provenance or authenticity as the books that make up the Bible today.

The King James Bible that Joseph Smith used when he started his work on the Joseph Smith Translation contained the books of the Apocrypha. Not sure if he was expected to include these books in his translation work, Joseph asked the Lord for further direction. The Lord's answer provides an interesting insight into the Apocrypha:

> Verily, thus saith the Lord unto you concerning the *Apocrypha*— *There are many things contained therein that are true,* and it is mostly translated correctly; *There are many things contained therein that are not true,* which are interpolations by the hands of men. Verily, I say unto you, that it is not needful that the Apocrypha should be translated. Therefore, whoso readeth it, let him understand, for the Spirit manifesteth truth; And *whoso is enlightened by the Spirit shall obtain benefit therefrom*; And whoso receiveth not by the Spirit, cannot be benefited; Therefore it is not needful that it should be translated (D&C 91:1–6).

So the Lord did not condemn the Apocrypha outright, noting there were good things in it, but He told Joseph he was not required to translate it.

With that in mind, we shall examine a short excerpt from one of the books in the Apocrypha known as 2 Esdras, for it has direct application to our study of the lost tribes of Israel. Because of the significance of this passage, we share the full text here, with a brief, point-by-point analysis.

> Those are the ten tribes which were carried away prisoners out of their own land in the time of Osea [Hoshea] the king, whom Salmanasar the king of Assyria led away captive. . . .

The author of Esdras breaks his narrative on another topic to use the ten tribes to make a point. This explains the rather abrupt start, but he makes it clear that these were the ten tribes from the Northern Kingdom of Israel.

> . . . and he carried them over the waters and so came they into another land (2 Esdras 13:40).

"He" is a reference to the king of Assyria. "Them" refers to the Israelites. "Waters" most likely refers to the great Euphrates River system, which ran through the heart of the Assyrian Empire. This is a logical conclusion because there are no large bodies of water such as lakes or seas on the route between Israel and Assyria. "Another land" is clearly Assyria.

Do we know exactly, or even approximately, where they were taken once they arrived in Assyria? The Old Testament writer said that the captives were taken by the Assyrians to an area called "Halah and in Habor by the river of Gozan, and in the cities of the Medes" (2 Kings 17:6; 2 Kings 18:11). While place names have changed over the centuries, according to an atlas of the ancient world, Hara was near the modern city of Haran, which is located in the general area where Turkey, Syria, and Iraq now share common borders. Back then, this area was part of the Assyrian Empire. Haran is about 800 miles from the land of Israel (see Wright, *Westminster Historical Atlas*, 31, 79, 124).

This northern placement makes sense because it means that if the Israelites tried to escape and return to their homeland, they would have to pass through hundreds of miles of territory occupied by the Assyrians. We also know that this was typical of where the Assyrians placed captive populations so they would not attempt to escape.

> But they took this counsel among themselves, that they would leave the multitude of the heathen, and go forth into a further country, where never mankind dwelt, that they might there keep their statutes, which they never kept in their own land (2 Esdras 13:41–42).

This part of the narrative is of special interest for our discussion because it introduces a new element into the equation. "They" is not defined, but from the context we see that it refers to a subgroup of the exiles from Israel. It was likely a relatively small group, for a large body on the move would have attracted the attention of Assyrians citizens, who would then report it to the authorities. Their intent was to escape from Assyria and bondage. They chose to head into areas that were not known to be inhabited, again surely to avoid detection and pursuit.

What is most interesting for our purposes here is the phrase "*that they might keep their statutes, which they never kept in their own land.*" We can make some likely assumptions from that brief statement:

- It appears that this small band recognized that the catastrophic disaster that had befallen their nation was due to the wickedness of the people, themselves included. They decided to return to the covenant, but could only do that if they got away from the pagan Assyrians.
- They had no intention of returning to the Holy Land. There could be two reasons for that. First, the distance they would have to travel

through enemy territory would put them at great risk. Second, they had seen their nation destroyed and would likely assume there was nothing left to go back to.
- They were likely planning to go as families, just as the Jaredites and Lehi's colony did when they were looking for a new home (see Ether 1:33–43; 1 Nephi 7).
- They would take their flocks and herds with them so they would have food along the way and also a means for sustaining themselves en route.
- They planned to leave secretly so they would not be detected. This would help explain why they chose to go "where never mankind dwelt." This doesn't necessarily imply that no humans had ever been there before—only that it was not an area with established populations. We have examples of captive peoples doing the same thing in the Book of Mormon (see Mosiah 22; 24).

And they entered into Euphrates by the narrow places of the river. For the most High then shewed signs for them, and held still the flood, till they were passed over (2 Esdras 13:43–44).

This passage is of special interest, for it speaks of specific geographical features that can be linked with some confidence to known locations today. The meaning of the phrase "they entered into Euphrates" is not clear. One possibility is that if they lived on the upper reaches of the Habor River, a tributary to the Euphrates, and if they went straight west, through less inhabited country, they would have reached the main river in a hundred miles or so.

The phrase "the narrow places of the river" is especially helpful, first because it describes a specific location, and second because it describes an identifiable geological feature. That far north, the Taurus Mountains form a great wall across Turkey that stretches from the Mediterranean Sea to the Caucasus Mountains on the border of present-day Turkey and Armenia. The Taurus Mountains have a limited number of places that allow easy passage. This means that the group either had to find a way through or detour for many miles. But if they followed the river gorge, that would take them through.

In the region where the Euphrates comes out of the Taurus Mountains, there is a geologic feature that closely fits our author's brief description of "narrow places" and "floods." In an article titled "The Valley of the Upper Euphrates River and Its People," a member of a prestigious geographical society described that very area in these terms: "[Where] the two main branches of the Euphrates unite . . . [the river] enters at once into a cañon, . . . only to plunge into the deepest and wildest of all the cañons. This deep gorge through the mountains is, in certain places, almost as deep and grand as that of the Colorado [River, which runs through the Grand Canyon in America]" (Huntington, *Bulletin of the American Geographical Society* 34, no. 4, 304).

Because the tenth article of faith mentions the "restoration of the Ten Tribes," Elder James E. Talmage in his classic work on the articles of faith discussed this passage from the Apocrypha. He cites the writings of Elder George W. Reynolds, a Seventy and secretary to the First Presidency for many years. In his book *Are We of Israel?*, Elder Reynolds discussed at some length the same passage from 2 Esdras that we have been studying here. Elder Talmage summarizes Brother Reynolds's conclusions:

> The upper course of the Euphrates lies among lofty mountains; near the village of Pastash, it plunges through a gorge formed by precipices more than a thousand feet in height, and so narrow that it is bridged at the top; it shortly afterward enters the plain of Mesopotamia. How accurately this portion of the river answers to the description of Esdras of the "Narrows" where the Israelites crossed! (Talmage, *The Articles of Faith*, 460).

The writer of Esdras spoke of "signs" the people experienced. Often in the scriptures that is another word for miracles. "[Holding] still the flood" certainly fits that description. It would have had special significance for this group because twice before the house of Israel had miraculously had waters held back by the Lord so that the people could pass through to safety (see Exodus 14:22; Joshua 3:17). Could there be a more dramatic way for the Lord to show that He was guiding this little band who had repented and come back to the covenant?

The author of 2 Esdras shares this final comment about this group:

> For through that country there was a great way to go, namely, of a year and a half: and the same region is called Arsareth [Hebrew for "another land"]. Then dwelt they there until the latter time; and now when they shall begin to come, the Highest shall stay the springs of the stream again that they may go through: therefore sawest thou the multitude with peace (2 Esdras 13:47–48).

Though the writer of Esdras gives us no further details of their travels, from a study of current topography and geography we can theorize a likely route they would have taken. If they came through the Taurus Mountains to the headwaters of the Euphrates River, the vast expanse of the Black Sea blocked their route to the north. If they went east, they would quickly encounter the Caucasus Mountains, another major natural barrier with peaks towering up to 18,000 feet, the highest in Europe. But between the sea and the mountains is a broad fertile plain about 200 miles wide. If they continued north, traveling through that natural corridor, in a few hundred miles they would come to what is present-day Russia and her neighboring countries. There the land opens up into a vast area of inhabitable lands extending west into the continent of Europe and east into central Asia and the Far East.

> They [ten tribes] were still a distinct people many hundreds of years later, for the resurrected Lord visited and ministered among them following his ministry on this continent among the Nephites. Obviously he taught them in the same way and gave them the same truths which he gave his followers in Jerusalem and on the American continent; and obviously they recorded his teachings, thus creating volumes of scripture comparable to the Bible and Book of Mormon.
>
> Bruce R. McConkie,
> *Millennial Messiah*, 458

If they traveled for a year and a half to the north, even assuming they were moving slowly with their herds, in eighteen months they could easily cover a thousand miles or more. This would definitely put them into the "north countries," a term often associated with the ten tribes.

So this is a possible answer to our second question. Do we know where the ten tribes went? Not exactly. But from the Bible and the Apocrypha, we can say with some confidence that the ten tribes of Israel were carried to Assyria and for the most part were assimilated into that society. But a small group of them escaped and went into the north countries and, as our source in Esdras tells us, "they dwelt there until the latter time." Scholars believe that Esdras was a Palestinian Jew who wrote his book around A.D. 100, which could define what he means by "the latter time." That is of interest for us because if that timing is correct, it would confirm the existence of a group from the lost tribes that the Savior said He was going to visit (see 3 Nephi 16:1–3).

DO WE KNOW WHERE THE LOST TEN TRIBES ARE NOW?

Yes, but only in general terms. The scriptures discussed above tell us that they are in two places: the nations of the world, and also in the north countries, which means that we can postulate three things. First, the ten tribes who were captured by Assyria eventually lost their identity and became

Gentiles. Through the centuries, their seed, along with the seed of all the tribes of Israel, is now found among all nations. Second, the descendants of that small group that settled what we now call the north countries[1] also have many descendants, some of whom still live in those countries. This could include, but is not limited to, northern Europe, Scandinavia, Russia and its neighbors, and central Asia and the Far East.

Isaiah supported this when he prophesied: "They shall not hunger nor thirst; neither shall the heat nor sun smite them: for he that hath mercy on them shall lead them, even by the springs of water shall he guide them. And I will make all my mountains a way, and my highways shall be exalted. Behold, these shall come from far: and, lo, *these from the north and from the west; and these from the land of Sinim*" (Isaiah 49:10–12). Notice he doesn't say from the south, the direction of Assyria. If they migrated east, once they came past the Black Sea, they would eventually come to the land of Sinim. Sinim is very likely the ancient name for modern China. Ptolemy, the ancient Greek historian who lived before Christ, defined the Greek word *Seenai* as "southern China." We still find that root in phrases like the Sino-Soviet bloc, which describes the political alliance between Russia and Red China.

Is it possible that a small group could spread so far and become so numerous even over centuries of time? Let's use the Book of Mormon as a model. Lehi's group probably numbered around thirty to forty when they arrived in America, but in 600 years, they grew into two major societies who covered large areas of both North and South America.

Here's another way to look at it. Population experts say that a new generation comes forth about every twenty years on average. So very quickly, a community of 100 could swell to a thousand or more. Villages would become towns, towns would become cities, and nascent nations would begin to form.

That little band of Israelites arrived in the north countries somewhere around 700 B.C. That's 2,700 years ago, or about 135 generations! To appreciate what that means, consider these demographics. Let's assume we have a family consisting of a father, a mother, and four children. If each of their four children marry and have four children, and that pattern continues to the fifth generation—or one century—that single multigenerational family would have over 1,700 members!

---

[1] We need to keep in mind that "north" was defined by those living in the Middle East, not the New World, so Canada and Alaska would not be included, while Russia, Europe, and Asia could be included.

Not all families would increase that quickly, of course, but some would increase at a faster rate. Remember, in agrarian societies, children were an economic necessity, and families with eight, ten, or even twelve children were common. But even an average of four per family gives us an idea of how rapidly a population can expand. Thus, it is not unreasonable to say that even a small group from the lost ten tribes could have grown exponentially over the centuries and spread across vast expanses of territories.

DO THE MEMBERS OF THE LOST TRIBES KNOW WHO THEY ARE?

For the vast majority of those who are descendants of the lost tribes, the answer is no. Millions of them wouldn't know what we were talking about if we spoke of the tribes of Israel. Though Christianity has the largest number of believers of any religion in the world, they still constitute only about a third of the world's population. That means there are literally billions of people in the world who don't know who Jesus Christ is, let alone anything about the ten tribes. Even many believing Christians know little or nothing about the house of Israel. So saying that a vast majority do not know who they are is not an exaggeration.

On the other hand, there are many people around the world who not only know about the covenant, the house of Israel, and the lost ten tribes, but also believe that they are descendants of those tribes. They have written proof of that in their patriarchal blessings. One of the things an ordained patriarch is required to do when giving a patriarchal blessing is to declare the person's lineage through one of the twelve tribes. It is a personal revelation that is officially included in the records of the Church.

For generations, the vast majority of those blessings have indicated that a person was linked to the tribe of Ephraim. But in recent years, with the expansion of the Church globally, more and more members are being told they come from one of the other tribes. And they are proud of that heritage. So, yes, there are people who know they are members of the house of Israel, and some know they are from the tribes that were lost.

With that extensive background, let us now turn to the key aspect of our study of the lost tribes: What about their return?

CHAPTER 22

THE RETURN OF THE LOST TEN TRIBES

Art thou not it which hath dried the [Red] sea, the waters of the great deep; that hath made the depths of the sea a way for the ransomed to pass over? Therefore the redeemed of the Lord shall return, and come with singing unto Zion; and everlasting joy shall be upon their head: they shall obtain gladness and joy; and sorrow and mourning shall flee away. I, even I, am he that comforteth you. (Isaiah 51:10–12)

DO WE KNOW THE DESTINATION OF THE LOST TRIBES WHEN THEY RETURN?

In the last chapter we answered questions regarding where the ten tribes went and what eventually happened to them. In this chapter we will discuss in depth the return of the lost tribes. The first question is whether we know the destination of the ten tribes when they return.

Once again we can answer that in the affirmative, but it requires further discussion. To answer the question, we first need to remember what President Spencer W. Kimball clearly taught:

> The *gathering of Israel consists of joining the true church and their coming to a knowledge of the true God.* Any person, therefore, who has accepted the restored gospel, and who now seeks to worship the Lord in his own tongue and with the Saints in the nations where he lives, has complied with the law of the gathering of Israel and is heir to all of the blessings promised the Saints in these last days (Kimball, *Teachings*, 438).

This is a key point because, as we have emphasized several times thus far, our task is not to gather every possible blood descendant of the house of

Israel. That would include most of the world's population. We have the task to gather *covenant* Israel, not all of Israel.

The next thing to remember is that we have two distinct aspects of the gathering, as we saw in the previous chapter. First we are gathering the house of Israel out from among all nations, through our missionary program and other outreach efforts. Second, one subset of that greater group is those who are living in the "north countries" when that time comes. So that is a limited gathering, where the first is a general one. Another difference between these two gatherings is that in the first group, we have members seeking out those who would like to join the covenant. In the second, as we shall see in a moment, the group that will return will, for the most part, already be members of the Church. It is likely that others seeking safety and refuge will come with them, but the main body will be active, faithful Latter-day Saints who live in the north countries. Why? Because the gathering is of covenant Israel, and the Church is where the covenant is. That covenant is extended to all, but it is found within the Church.

The scriptures tell us of two different places that will be their destination: Old Jerusalem (see Jeremiah 16:15; Isaiah 27:12–13; Ether 13:11) and the City of Zion, also known as Mount Zion and New Jerusalem (see Moses 7:62; D&C 133:18).

There is some evidence that suggests that the lost ten tribes may come to both sites, first to get their blessings from the hands of Ephraim, i.e., the Church, and then to go on to their ancestral promised land, which is their inheritance—Old Jerusalem in the land of Israel. Another possible reason for coming to the New Jerusalem could be so they are present at the great priesthood conference to be held in Adam-ondi-Ahman (see chapter 23).

WHAT DO WE KNOW ABOUT THEIR JOURNEY?

Happily, the answer to that is, we know more than many would expect. Once again, this comes through a combination of scriptures—ancient and modern—and teachings from prophets—ancient and modern. As we have seen, both Isaiah and Jeremiah spoke often of the gathering of Israel, and also of the return of the lost tribes from the north. Both lived at a time when the house of Israel was conquered by invading armies and carried into captivity.

Isaiah described the "highway"—i.e., the route—the ten tribes would take with some vivid imagery that testifies that they will be watched over by the tender care of the Lord:

> An highway shall be there, and a way, and it shall be called *The*

way of holiness; the unclean shall not pass over it; . . . No lion shall be there, nor any ravenous beast shall go up thereon, it shall not be found there; but *the redeemed shall walk there:* And the *ransomed of the Lord* shall return, and *come to Zion* with songs and everlasting joy upon their heads: *they shall obtain joy and gladness, and sorrow and sighing shall flee away* (Isaiah 35:8–10).

Here Isaiah stresses the power of God that will watch over and protect them from danger in their journey. It also suggests that this will not be part of some greater migration of other populations to escape danger. This highway is for the holy—another word for pure, as in pure of heart—and not the unclean. Though the journey may be difficult and long, they will be joyful as they come. Knowing that they are the ones who are literally fulfilling prophecies long foretold would explain a great deal of their joy. Isaiah doesn't indicate where that route will go.

Jeremiah described the event in equally joyful words:

Behold, I will bring them from the north country, and gather them from the coasts of the earth, and with *them the blind and the lame, the woman with child and her that travaileth with child together:* a *great company* shall return thither. They shall come with weeping, and with supplications will I lead them: I will cause them to walk by the rivers of waters in a straight way, wherein they shall not stumble: for I am a father to Israel, and Ephraim is my firstborn (Jeremiah 31:8–9).

From Jeremiah we learn that this will not be just an army of men but also of women, children, the disabled, and even the pregnant. It will be a mass migration, a "great company," as he calls it. Though he doesn't say this straight out, the feeling is not that of a convoy of trucks or a long chain of train cars. Coming on foot would partially explain the travail. But even so, they are weeping for joy. Because they are escaping social chaos and collapse? Because they know they are going to Zion to live with a Zion people? That could be part of it. The promise that they will not stumble seems to suggest that in spite of their hardships, they will come through triumphantly.

But it is in a latter-day revelation that we find the most detailed description of the return of the lost tribes. This is definitely part of the second part of the gathering as revealed by Moses, for here too we find the specific marker that was noted in earlier scriptures, a mention of "they who are in the north countries" (D&C 133:26). Doctrine and Covenants 133 was labeled as an appendix by Joseph Smith. Given when the Church was not yet two years old, Joseph wrote: "At this time there were many things which the Elders desired to know relative to preaching the Gospel to the inhabitants of the earth, and concerning the *gathering*. . . . I inquired of the Lord and received the following important revelation" (heading, Doctrine and Covenants 133). It is a revelation filled with prophecies of the last days, and in it, the Lord gives us one of the most detailed revelations on the return of the lost ten tribes that we find anywhere in scripture. Because of its significance, we shall analyze it carefully.

> And they who are in the north countries shall come in remembrance before the Lord; and their prophets shall hear his voice, and shall no longer stay themselves (D&C 133:26).

Several things are of interest here. As already noted, "They who are in the north countries" tells us that the Lord is not talking about the *general process* of gathering Israel, but the *specific return* of one segment of that gathering. "Shall come in remembrance before the Lord" could have a double meaning. First, the Lord is remembering the covenants He made with their fathers. Second, the people are remembering their commitments to the Lord when the missionaries taught them, or when they were baptized at eight years old, or in the temples of the Lord, or the covenants their ancient ancestors made with the Lord. "And their prophets shall hear his voice." Note the possessive pronoun here. "*Their* prophets," not just "the prophets." This might be a surprise to some. Does that mean they have had prophets among them all the time? It doesn't say that, only that they will have prophets at this time. But identifying them as "their" prophets suggest that these are members of The Church of Jesus Christ of Latter-day Saints. Elder McConkie commented on this phrase particularly and gave us an important insight:

> Let no one suppose that the Ten Tribes, having been gathered by the elders of Israel so as to return in a body; let no one suppose that because they bring their scriptures with them; let no one suppose that because prophets mingle among them—let no one suppose *that any of this shall happen independent of the senior apostle of God on earth who holds the keys of gathering and who is authorized to use them as the Spirit directs. There is one God and one Shepherd over all the earth, and there is one prophet and one presiding officer of the earthly kingdom, and he has rule over all of the Lord's affairs in all the earth* (McConkie, *Millennial Messiah*, 203).

This is an important point that is often overlooked. Moses restored "the keys of the gathering of Israel from the four parts of the earth, *and* the leading of the ten tribes from the land of the north" to Joseph Smith and Oliver Cowdery in the Kirtland Temple (D&C 110:11). In a great revelation on priesthood organization and authority, we are told that "the power and authority of the higher, or Melchizedek Priesthood, is to hold the keys of all the of all the spiritual blessings of the church" (D&C 107:18). Those keys are now held by the President of The Church of Jesus Christ of Latter-day Saints. To have other prophets, seers, and revelators somewhere on the earth that are totally independent of the keys held by the President of the Church would be contrary to the order of priesthood authority.

We are not suggesting that every one of the lost tribes who returns from the north countries will be members of the Church. We expect that many good people will join them in order to find peace and safety. But the ten tribes will come under the direction of the First Presidency of the Church, for they are, "of necessity, . . . [the] presiding officers" (D&C 107:21).

As we have seen, we now have members of the Church all around the world, including in those northern countries. So when the call comes for them to return, it will come from the same source that has the keys to gather Israel from the four parts of the earth.

Another scripture greatly expands our understanding of what the word *prophet* means. John the Revelator taught us an important concept about the spirit of prophecy. In John's great vision, an angel stood before him, and John was so overcome with awe that he fell at his feet to worship him. But the angel said: "See thou do it not: I am thy fellowservant, and of thy brethren *that have the testimony of Jesus:* worship God: *for the testimony of Jesus is the spirit of prophecy*" (Revelation 19:10). That is an interesting definition of a testimony of Jesus. But as we think on that, having a true testimony of Christ is the essence of prophecy.

Speaking of Alma, Mormon said that he spoke "according to the spirit of prophecy which was in him, according to the *testimony of Jesus*" (Alma 6:8). This tells us that those who have a testimony of Jesus are considered to be prophets—not necessarily ordained, set-apart prophets, but prophets nevertheless. Joseph Smith confirmed this when he said, "No man is a minister of Jesus Christ without being a Prophet. No man can be a minister of Jesus Christ except he has the testimony of Jesus; and this is the spirit of prophecy" (Joseph Smith, *Teachings*, 384). By "man" here, Joseph seems to mean any person, for surely women in the Church have the testimony of Jesus and are therefore prophets in their homes and in their callings. With that principle in mind, and in reference to this very passage, Elder McConkie went on to say:

Their prophets! Who are they? Are they to be holy men called from some unknown place and people? Are they prophets unbeknown to the presiding officers of "the only true and living church upon the face of the whole earth"? Perish the thought! The President of the Church, who holds the keys to lead the Ten Tribes from the nations of the north wherein they now reside, holds also the keys of salvation for all men. There are not two true churches on earth, only one; there are not two gospels or two plans of salvation, only one; there are not two competing organizations, both having divine approval, only one. . . . *Their prophets are members of The Church of Jesus Christ of Latter-day Saints.* They are stake presidents and bishops and quorum presidents who are appointed to guide and direct the destinies of their stakes and wards and quorums (McConkie, *Millennial Messiah,* 325).

And knowing what we know about how the Church works, we can safely assume that along with those stake presidents and bishops, there will be stake and ward Relief Society presidencies, Young Women presidencies, and Primary presidencies helping to keep the group moving forward.

Once again, we are not given a lot of specific information, such as how many it will be or if there will be more than one group. But knowing that there are thousands upon thousands of faithful members in those northern areas strongly suggests that this is going to be a massive logistical undertaking.

And they shall smite the rocks, and the ice shall flow down at their presence (D&C 133:26).

This brings to mind Moses and the Exodus and the hardships and challenges ancient Israel faced in their journey through the wilderness. Moses never had to deal with ice that we know of, but he did smite a rock to get water for his people. Some wonder if the mention of ice suggests that they may travel through lands of perpetual ice and snow, such as lands above the Arctic Circle, but the text does not require that. If it is a time of winter when they travel, that could explain the phrase. It is of interest that the Lord speaks of the ice "flowing down," not shattering and crashing down. One wonders if that phenomenon with the ice is to make a passageway for them, or to provide pure water for them, or just the natural melting of ice because of warmer temperatures.

Though we are not given a lot of detail, it is fascinating to contemplate the possible ways in which these prophecies could be fulfilled. What is sure is that, like the small group from the lost ten tribes who saw "signs" along their way, this group too will have their miracles.

One practical implication that comes from this language is that their journey could potentially be a very long one. It appears that they will be coming to New Jerusalem, which means that if our assumptions about the general areas of the north countries are correct and they are somewhere on the continents of Europe and Asia, then unless they are flying by airplane, at some point they will have to contend with an ocean. Which brings us to our next verse:

> And an highway shall be cast up in the midst of the great deep (D&C 133:27).

This is an incredible statement. The "great deep" was the ancient Hebrew name for what we call the oceans (see 2 Nephi 8:10; Ether 7:27; Genesis 7:11). Is the Lord suggesting that just as He divided the waters of the Red Sea and the waters of the River Jordan at flood stage so that Israel might pass through, He will once again make a way for His people to pass through on dry land? If that is any part of an ocean, that is an incredible promise.

Though the Lord leaves us without any confirming details, we know that sometimes the Lord works great miracles through what we could call the forces of nature. For example, just a few verses earlier the Lord spoke of the great deep when He said: "He shall command the great deep, and it shall be driven back into the north countries, and the islands [the continents?] shall become one land; and the land of Jerusalem and the land of Zion shall be turned back into their own place, and the earth shall be like as it was in the days before it was divided" (D&C 133:23–24).[1]

We are not given any detail on what that means. One possibility is that this is tied to the great earthquake associated with the battle of Armageddon. One's first reaction to that statement might be, "How could dividing the great deep be possible when the water can be thousands of feet deep?" But we have to be careful about assuming that we know what is meant when the Lord speaks. Here is another possibility that would still be miraculous, but not so fantastic. (We are not suggesting that this is how it *will* happen, only how it *might happen*.)

---

1 The Old Testament has an enigmatic statement that in the days of Peleg, after Noah's time, the land was divided (see Genesis 10:25). These verses suggest that this division of the earth could be put back as it was before. We know very little about that, but we shall speak of it briefly in connection with the finals scenes that accompany the Second Coming of Christ.

There is one place in the world where two continents come within less than sixty miles of each other. It is called the Bering Strait, which borders the state of Alaska on the east and Russia on the west. So one possible "highway . . . in the midst of the great deep" could come if the temperature were cold enough to freeze the waters through that archipelago, something which happens regularly there. It would have to be frozen solid enough for a large group to pass over, but it would fit the description of a highway being cast up in the midst of the great deep.

We have taken the time with this little interlude to speculate on such possibilities only to make a point. When we are dealing with prophecies of the last days, we must be careful not to assume that our interpretation of what they mean is the correct one. We need to ponder the possibilities. We don't know exactly what it means when the Lord talks about *casting up* a highway in the midst of the great deep. But when it does finally happen, we should not be surprised if many of us say, "Ah, of course. Why didn't we think of that before?" With that said, we also remember the words of Jeremiah. The return of the ten tribes will be such an incredible event that it will be remembered with awe for many generations.

The next verses also provide much to consider:

> Their enemies shall become a prey unto them, and in the barren deserts there shall come forth pools of living water; and the parched ground shall no longer be a thirsty land (D&C 133:28–29).

As we noted in previous chapters, war and the collapse of social order could be very real concerns during this period. The reference to their enemies becoming prey to them could suggest that there will be upheaval in areas they are passing through, but this doesn't automatically imply open conflict. The Lord may turn them aside before they cause problems. That would fit that description too. It also reminds us of the promises of peace, refuge, and safety.

The mention of barren deserts in tandem with ice flowing down is an interesting pairing of contrasting landscapes. Does this suggest that the distance they have to travel will be extensive? Again, the Lord doesn't choose to explain.

> Pools of living water . . . no longer a thirsty land (D&C 133:29).

Here is yet another promise of Divine help. And in this case, it is not just a promise of water sources along the way; it is a promise of dramatic and lasting change in desert areas along their route.

This remarkable scripture is filled with intriguing revelations and provocative descriptions. Surely the accounts that will be recorded and shared by those privileged to take part will be shared in sacrament meetings, classrooms, firesides, general conferences, and family home evenings for generations to come, just as we now share stories of the wagon and handcart companies.

Continuing in D&C 133 we read:

> And they shall bring forth their rich treasures unto the children of Ephraim, my servants. And the boundaries of the everlasting hills shall tremble at their presence. And there shall they fall down and be crowned with glory, even in Zion, by the hands of the servants of the Lord, even the children of Ephraim. And they shall be filled with songs of everlasting joy. Behold, this is the blessing of the everlasting God upon the tribes of Israel, and the richer blessing upon the head of Ephraim and his fellows (D&C 133:30–34).

"*The children of Ephraim, my servants.*" As we saw in chapter 4, the tribe of Ephraim was not just one of the ten tribes in ancient days; it was the dominant, ruling tribe in the Northern Kingdom. Ephraim was also one of the tribes taken into captivity. So how could it be that "the children of Ephraim" will be waiting to bless the ten lost tribes when they return?

We have noted several times that in our day and age, the bloodlines of all twelve tribes are very likely found in most peoples of the world. President James E. Faust of the First Presidency taught this plainly:

> *Are you Jewish? That precious lineage may be claimed if your ancestors are from the loins of Judah. But most of us are of the lineage of Joseph through Ephraim or Manasseh. Joseph's was the lineage selected to pioneer the gathering of Israel, the seed to lead throughout the world in blessing all the nations of the earth.*
>
> RUSSELL M. NELSON,
> *PERFECTION PENDING*, 207

> Some might be disturbed because members of the same family have blessings declaring them to be of a different lineage. A few families are of a mixed lineage. We believe that the house of Israel today constitutes a large measure of the human family. Because the tribes have intermixed one with another, one child may be declared to be from the tribe of Ephraim, and another of the same family from Manasseh or one of the other tribes. The blessings of one tribe, therefore, may be dominant in one child, and the blessings of

another tribe dominant in yet another child. So, children from the same parents could receive the blessings of different tribes (Faust, *In the Strength of the Lord*, 385).

But in the last days, one of the blessings of Ephraim was that they would take the lead in the work of the Lord. President Joseph Fielding Smith explained this very clearly:

> It is Ephraim, today, who holds the Priesthood. It is with Ephraim that the Lord has made covenant and has revealed the fulness of the everlasting Gospel. It is Ephraim who is building temples and performing the ordinances in them for both the living and the dead. When the "lost tribes" come—and it will be a most wonderful sight and a marvelous thing when they do come to Zion—in fulfillment of the promises made through Isaiah and Jeremiah, they will have to receive the crowning blessings from their brother Ephraim, the "first-born" in Israel (Smith, *The Way to Perfection*, 125).

Ephraim was given the privilege and responsibility to lead out in the last days. The ten tribes will be blessed by the children of Ephraim and be crowned with glory—which may include all of the blessings of the temple ordinances—by the hands of Ephraim. The "richer blessing" has been bestowed "on the head of Ephraim." In each case, "Ephraim" is another way of saying the members of The Church of Jesus Christ of Latter-day Saints.

Elder John A. Widtsoe further explained this:

> In the great majority of cases, Latter-day Saints are of the tribe of Ephraim, *the tribe to which has been committed the leadership of Latter-day work.* Whether this lineage is of blood or adoption does not matter. This is very important, for it is through the lineage of Abraham alone that the mighty blessings of the Lord for His children on earth are to be consummated (Widtsoe, *Evidences and Reconciliations*, 322).

As we have mentioned, until recent decades when the Church became truly a global church, most members were told they were of the lineage of the tribe of Ephraim. Though Ephraim is still the most common tribal designation, we are seeing many more being told that their blessings come through one of the other eleven tribes.

Thus we see that The Church of Jesus Christ of Latter-day Saints will be intimately and extensively involved in the return of the lost ten tribes. The

Church was given the keys to gather Israel from Moses himself. And he also gave the Church the keys to bring the ten tribes out of the north countries.

WILL THEY HAVE THEIR OWN SCRIPTURES AND RECORDS WHEN THEY COME?

In the last verses of the passage on the return of the ten tribes, we are told that they will bring their rich treasures with them. Gold and silver and family heirlooms may come first to our minds, and there may be some of that, but the Lord speaks of a different treasure here. Whenever the Lord calls a people to do the work of His kingdom, He always requires that they keep records of the work. The prophets of earlier dispensations gave us the Old Testament. The Twelve and others in the days of Jesus gave us the New Testament. We have the Book of Mormon, which was collected over a thousand years.

What the scriptures have made clear is that we do not have all of the scriptures produced by earlier dispensations. But we are promised that at least some of them will be restored to us. These include the book of Enoch (see D&C 107:57) and the sealed portions of the Book of Mormon (see Ether 4:1–7). It seems strange to think of it in this way, but in the future we may have several more "standard works" to study in seminary and Sunday School.

We mention that here because we know of another sacred record that will come forth. We don't know what its formal name will be, but we do know it will be the record of the lost ten tribes. As the resurrected Christ told the Nephites that He was going to leave them for a time to visit the other sheep of His fold, He commanded them to write a record of what He had been teaching them. That became Third Nephi in the Book of Mormon. If that was His counsel to the Nephites, we can assume that He gave the other sheep the same instructions. We know from what our prophets have said that they did so and that one of the "rich treasures" they will bring with them will be those records—their scriptures. Nephi gives us one of the clearest statements on this:

> *The Ten Tribes of Israel . . . will return with their prophets, and their sacred records will be a third witness for Christ.*
>
> SPENCER W. KIMBALL,
> IN CONFERENCE REPORT,
> OCT. 1959, 61

And it shall come to pass that the Jews shall have the words of the Nephites, and the Nephites shall have the words of the Jews; *and the Nephites and the Jews shall have the words of the lost tribes of Israel;* and the lost tribes of Israel shall have the words of the Nephites and the Jews. . . . And my word also shall be gathered in one (2 Nephi 29:13–14).

Modern prophets have affirmed this again and again as well. In his work on the articles of faith, Elder James E. Talmage wrote:

> The tribes shall come, they are not lost unto the Lord; they shall be brought forth as hath been predicted; and I say unto you there are those now living[2]—aye some here present—who shall live to read the records of the Lost Tribes of Israel, which shall be made one with the record of the Jews, or the Holy Bible, and the record of the Nephites, or the Book of Mormon, even as the Lord hath predicted; and those records, which the tribes lost to man but yet to be found again shall bring, shall tell of the visit of the resurrected Christ to them, after he had manifested himself to the Nephites upon this continent (Talmage, *The Articles of Faith*, 513).

"But," some scoffers may decry, "those would be records that are at least two thousand years old. Most of the ancient records have now been discovered, and they are rare. To say that a whole new work of scripture will come forth seems very unlikely." The answer to that is simple. Moroni buried the record of his people in the earth, where it remained for about 1,600 years. The Qumran scrolls were left in an open cave in the Judean wilderness for almost 2,000 years. The Nag Hammadi Library, which dates back to early Christianity, was discovered in an ancient synagogue in 1945, and they were not metal plates. Just because we don't know of them now is not proof that they don't exist.

SUMMARY AND CONCLUSIONS

In a worldwide broadcast to the youth of the Church, Sister Wendy Nelson was asked to speak along with her husband, President Russell M. Nelson. The topic was on the gathering of Israel. She shared a most interesting experience as part of her remarks.

> Let me tell you of an experience that taught me firsthand about

---

[2] *The Articles of Faith* was first published in 1899. We are now far past the life span of those living when he spoke those words. But that doesn't mean that he was not inspired to say what he did. Remember what we have said several times in this book. Who of us will still be alive when Christ comes? All of us! That may not be true of our mortal bodies. But our physical bodies are not what defines who we are.

the historic days in which we live. We often talk about living in the latter days. We are, after all, Latter-day Saints. But perhaps these days are more "latter" than we have ever imagined. This truth became a reality for me because of what I experienced during one 24-hour period of time that commenced on June 15, 2013. My husband and I were in Moscow, Russia. While President Nelson met with priesthood leaders, I had the privilege of meeting with nearly 100 of our sisters. . . . When I stepped to the pulpit to speak, I found myself saying something I'd never anticipated. I said to the women: "I'd like to get to know you by lineage. Please stand as the tribe of Israel that represents the lineage declared in your patriarchal blessing is spoken." "Benjamin?" A couple of women stood. "Dan?" A couple more. "Reuben?" A few more stood. "Naphtali?" More stood. As the names of the Twelve Tribes of Israel were announced—from Asher to Zebulun—and as the women stood, we were all amazed with what we were witnessing, feeling, and learning. How many of the Twelve Tribes of Israel do you think were represented in that small gathering of fewer than 100 women on that Saturday in Moscow? Eleven! Eleven of the Twelve Tribes of Israel were represented in that one room! The only tribe missing was that of Levi. I was astonished. It was a spiritually moving moment for me.

Immediately after those meetings my husband and I went directly to Yerevan, Armenia. The first people we met as we got off the plane were the mission president and his wife. Somehow, she had heard about this experience in Moscow, and with great delight, she said, "I've got Levi!" Just imagine our thrill when my husband and I met their missionaries the next day, including an elder from the tribe of Levi who just happened to be from Gilbert, Arizona. . . . Imagine what it was like for me to be with members of all Twelve Tribes of Israel within one 24-hour period of time! (Wendy W. Nelson, "Hope of Israel," Worldwide Youth Devotional, June 3, 2018, 6–7).

We are reminded that ten of those tribes are considered to be the lost tribes of Israel. They are being gathered in with the rest of covenant Israel. But as part of that gathering, sometime in coming days, the Lord's anointed prophet will send out the word to the lost ten tribes, saying, "It is time to come home."

CHAPTER 23

ADAM-ONDI-AHMAN

We now come to the least known and least understood thing connected with the Second Coming. It might well be termed the best-kept secret set forth in the revealed word. It is something about which the world knows nothing; it is a doctrine that has scarcely dawned on most of the Latter-day Saints themselves; and yet it is set forth in holy writ and in the teachings of the Prophet Joseph Smith with substantially the same clarity as any of the doctrines of the kingdom.
(Bruce R. McConkie, *Millennial Messiah*, 578–79)

ADAM AND EVE—OUR FIRST PARENTS

For the most part, the traditional story of Adam and Eve is rejected by the world as imaginative fantasy used to explain evolutionary processes that early generations couldn't understand. Basically, the only religions whose adherents accept the story of Adam and Eve are called the Abrahamic religions—Judaism, Christianity, and Islam. Even within those religions, many believe that Adam and Eve are a "Creation myth," with no parallel to real life.

Members of The Church of Jesus Christ of Latter-day Saints have a much different concept of our first parents. Elder James E. Talmage summarized how we view the father and mother of all mankind:

> It has become a common practice with mankind to heap reproaches upon the progenitors of the family, and to picture the supposedly blessed state in which we would be living but for the fall; whereas our first parents are entitled to our deepest gratitude for their legacy to posterity—the means of winning title to glory, exaltation, and eternal lives. But for the opportunity thus given, the spirits of God's offspring would have remained forever in a state of innocent childhood, sinless through no effort of their own; negatively saved, not from sin, but from the opportunity of meeting sin;

incapable of winning the honors of victory because [they were] prevented from taking part in the conflict. As it is, they are heirs to the birthright of Adam's descendants—mortality, with its immeasurable possibilities and its God-given freedom of action. From Father Adam we have inherited all the ills to which flesh is heir; but such are necessarily incident to a knowledge of good and evil, by the proper use of which knowledge man may become even as the Gods (Talmage, *The Articles of Faith*, 63).

Knowing this about our first parents helps us better understand another of the "great" signs of the times given by the Lord. It is another of the marvelous signs that is unique to our faith.

As for Eve's place among all women, "Adam called his wife's name Eve, because she was the mother of all living; for thus have I, the Lord God, called the first of all women, which are many" (Moses 4:26). In Hebrew, Eve is *Hava*, which means "life," or "living," since from her womb sprang all of the human race.

Joseph Smith taught that Adam received the priesthood before coming to earth; that, as Michael in the premortal existence, he was second to Jesus Christ and helped create the earth; and that he was appointed to be the head of the human family. We also know that Michael led the forces of good in the War in Heaven (see Revelation 12:7) and will do so again at the Day of Judgment (see D&C 88:111–115).

From these very brief passages, we learn that Adam and Eve were given the fulness of the gospel and organized the Church of Jesus Christ on the earth, though we do not know if it was called by that name or not. But they did have the priesthood, the correct doctrine, the ordinances of salvation, and eventually the ordinances of exaltation found in our modern temples. This is a very different picture from what the world sees when they think of Adam and Eve.

A GREAT CONFERENCE OF THE FAITHFUL, CIRCA 3073 B.C.

The Old Testament account of Adam and Eve after their expulsion from the Garden of Eden is very brief. With additional details found in modern scriptures, we know that the Church was organized with a patriarch as its president. Adam was the first. Others included Enoch, Noah, Methusaleh—the oldest of all men—Melchizedek, and Abraham. Abraham's son, Isaac, and his grandson, Jacob, were also considered patriarchs. Thereafter, the house of Israel became the title for the covenant people, and the age of the patriarchs ended.

From the Bible and modern scriptures, we learn that those early patriarchs (and their wives too, we assume) had amazingly long life spans. That was probably part of the Lord's plan to quickly populate the earth. If Eve lived anywhere near as long as Adam, she could have had hundreds of children. We don't know exactly what year Adam and Eve left the garden, but most of the world accepts that it was around 4,000 B.C.

The age of each presiding patriarch was shown by a genealogical table of the patriarchal line from Adam down to Abraham (see Genesis 5; 10), a period of about 2,000 years. This period of history takes only eleven chapters in Genesis, a total of sixteen pages, which shows how very little we know about this age.

The long life spans meant that many generations overlapped. Enoch, who was the seventh generation from Adam, was born when Adam was 565 years old—still in his "middle age." It is a fascinating time, and we are told that a "book of remembrance was kept," in which things from Adam's day were recorded (see Moses 6:5). We also know that Enoch too wrote of things that will be "testified of in due time" (D&C 107:57).

In that same section, we learn of a meeting that took place three years before Adam's death:

> Three years previous to the death of Adam, he called Seth, Enos, Cainan, Mahalaleel, Jared, Enoch, and Methuselah, who were all high priests [and patriarchs], with the residue of his posterity *who were righteous, into the valley of Adam-ondi-Ahman,* and there bestowed upon them his last blessing (D&C 107:53).

Joseph Smith was privileged to see in vision this grand event. "I saw Adam in the valley of Adam-ondi-Ahman. He called together his children and blessed them with a patriarchal blessing. The Lord appeared in their midst, and he (Adam) blessed them all, and foretold what should befall them to the latest generation" (*Teachings of Presidents of the Church: Joseph Smith*, 105).

This is the forerunner of our patriarchal blessings today. But in this case, this was much more than Adam gathering some of his children, grandchildren, and great-grandchildren around him prior to his death. By this time there could have been as many as one hundred generations of posterity since the Fall. Even taking into account that many of Adam's posterity had turned away from the gospel by this point, this still could have been a very large gathering. Perhaps that is why he chose a valley as the meeting site. What happened next must have astounded those attending:

> And the Lord [Jehovah, the premortal Jesus Christ] appeared unto them, and they rose up and blessed Adam, and called him Michael, the prince, the archangel. And the Lord administered comfort unto Adam, and said unto him: I have set thee to be at the head; a multitude of nations shall come of thee, and thou art a prince over them forever. And Adam stood up in the midst of the congregation; and, notwithstanding he was bowed down with age, being full of the Holy Ghost, predicted whatsoever should befall his posterity unto the latest generation. These things were all written in the book of Enoch, and are to be testified of in due time (D&C 107:54–57).

Joseph explained what Adam's blessing entailed: "This is why Adam blessed his posterity; he wanted to bring them into the presence of God. They looked for a city, etc., ['whose builder and maker is God'—Heb. 11:10]" (Joseph Smith, *Teachings*, 105).

From the genealogical tables, we know that Enoch was sixty-five years old when the City of Zion began. That would have been around 3313 B.C. Adam lived 930 years, so he died in 3070 B.C. So this last conference was held about 3073 B.C. This means that by that time, the city of Enoch had been around for 240 years. We are also told that it remained on earth for 365 years before it was taken up. Again we remember that these dates are only approximate.

This gives new meaning to Joseph's statement that "they looked for a city whose builder and maker was God." That is almost certainly the city of Enoch. The implications of that are very exciting. We are not told where the city of Enoch was located, but we do know that the Garden of Eden was in Jackson County, Missouri (see Joseph Smith, *Encyclopedia of Joseph Smith's Teachings*, s.v. "Garden of Eden"). We also know that this conference was held in the valley of Adam-ondi-Ahman (see D&C 116), which is only about seventy miles northeast of Jackson County. This suggests that Adam had not moved very far from the garden after they were expelled. Would the city of Enoch also have been nearby? We are not told. But since Adam had only moved about seventy miles away, it is possible that Enoch and his city were not far away either.

We are told that Adam called only his righteous posterity to this last great conference. Surely that would have included those who were living in the City of Zion, for Zion is defined as the place where the pure in heart dwell. That is something we may overlook, but the residents of the city of Enoch could have been present at the council of Adam-ondi-Ahman.

Wouldn't we love to know more about that day? How many were in attendance? Were they of all ages? I like to think so. Did the Savior speak to the whole group or just to Adam? Did families pitch their tents with the doors facing the same direction, as the people of King Benjamin did? How long did the meeting last? All day? Several days? Did they sit around their campfires at night and talk about all they were experiencing? Did any of them record their experiences in their records?

The Lord said that all of this is recorded in the book of Enoch. Won't that be an exciting day, when we will have the Book of Enoch as promised?

THE VALLEY OF ADAM-ONDI-AHMAN

Latter-day Saints are very interested in visiting places where great events in our history have occurred—sites such as the Holy Land, the Sacred Grove, the Hill Cumorah, the Susquehanna River, the Peter Whitmer cabin where the Church was organized, the Kirtland Temple, the temple site in Independence, Far West, Hawn's Mill, Martin's Cove, and so many, many others. Visiting such sacred sites allows us to make spiritual connections to our heritage and to the Spirit.

That would surely be true of the valley of Adam-ondi-Ahman, where this incredible gathering took place more than 3,000 years ago. Gratefully, the Lord saw fit to tell Joseph Smith the location of the valley of Adam-ondi-Ahman, and that sacred site is now owned by The Church of Jesus Christ of Latter-day Saints. Sometime after the revelation that spoke of the council at Adam-ondi-Ahman, Joseph told some of the members there that the Garden of Eden had been located in Jackson County (see Dahl and Cannon, *Teachings of Joseph Smith*, 277). In an earlier revelation, Joseph had introduced the members to an unusual name:

> That you may come up unto the crown prepared for you, and be made rulers over many kingdoms, saith the Lord God, the Holy One of Zion, *who hath established the foundations of Adam-ondi-Ahman;* Who hath appointed Michael your prince, and established his feet, and set him upon high, and given unto him the keys of salvation under the counsel and direction of the Holy One, who is without beginning of days or end of life (D&C 78:15–16).

Note that this name was used in connection with Michael, the premortal name of Adam, saying that he held the keys of salvation under the direction of Jesus Christ. Here was another teaser that the country around Missouri had been home to Adam and Eve. Then things changed. By early 1834, the Saints had been driven out of Jackson County.

The Church petitioned the state of Missouri to create a new county in the unsettled northern parts of the state where the Latter-day Saints could settle. They did so, but created two counties—Caldwell and Daviess Counties. The Saints immediately began moving to Caldwell County, where they established the city of Far West. But as more and more members came to Missouri following the apostasy in Kirtland, some began moving farther north into Daviess County looking for land.

By this time, as noted in the *Encyclopedia of Mormonism,* several things had been firmly established:

- The Garden of Eden was in Jackson County, and when Adam and Eve were expelled, they went north and settled in the area of Adam-ondi-Ahman.
- "Ahman" is one of the titles of the Son of God (see D&C 78:20; 95:17).
- Three years before Adam died, he gathered his righteous posterity to Adam-ondi-Ahman and gave them his final blessing. The premortal Jesus Christ appeared during that meeting (see D&C 107:54–57).
- His name was connected to prophecies about the Ancient of Days given by the prophet Daniel (see Daniel 7:9–14, 21–27; 12:1–3) (*Encyclopedia of Mormonism*, 19–20).

A short time later, the Prophet took a survey team into Daviess County to scout for additional land for the Saints. When he reached a fertile valley along the Grand River, he found a few Latter-day Saints living there, including Lyman Wight, who had already built a ferry crossing and a cabin at a place called Spring Hill. While staying with Lyman, Joseph, with his usual gift for startling people with insights gained through revelation, made another bold declaration:

> In the afternoon I went up the river about half a mile to Wight's Ferry, accompanied by President Rigdon, and my clerk, George W. Robinson, for the purpose of selecting and laying claim to a city plat near said ferry in Daviess County . . . which the brethren called "Spring Hill," but by the mouth of the Lord it was named Adam-ondi-Ahman, because, said He, it is the place where Adam shall come to visit his people, or the Ancient of Days shall sit, as spoken of by Daniel the Prophet (see Joseph Smith, "History,

1838–1856, volume B-1 [1 September 1834–2 November 1838]," p. 798, *The Joseph Smith Papers;* https://www.josephsmithpapers.org/paper-summary/history-1838–1856-volume-b-1–1-september-1834–2-november-1838/252).

Though Joseph does not mention this, we know from others that during that visit something else quite remarkable happened. We know from the book of Moses that sometime after they had left the garden, Adam and Eve had offered sacrifices (see Moses 5:5–9). Here are eyewitness accounts from those who were with Joseph that day:

The world has not seen the last of Father Adam. He is coming again—coming as the Ancient of Days, to fulfill the prophecy of Daniel concerning him. And he will come to the very place where, bowed with the weight of his nine centuries . . . he blessed his posterity before the close of his earthly career. In the Valley of Adam-ondi-Ahman, now in Western Missouri, almost within hailing distance of the ancient site of the Garden of Eden, where the New Jerusalem is to rise, will sit the Ancient of Days, counseling his worthy children and preparing them for the second coming of the Son of God.

Orson F. Whitney,
in Conference Report,
April 1927, 99

Words of Orange L. Wight: "We moved to Daviess County, Missouri, and made our principal settlement at Adam-ondi-Ahman. The Prophet Joseph told us that it was the place where Adam offered his holy sacrifices. The altar was not far from our house" (in Joseph Smith, *Encyclopedia of Joseph Smith's Teachings,* 23).

Words of Edward Stevenson: "I stood with Joseph Smith and others when he pointed out the sacred spot of Adam's altar. Turning to the lovely valley below us, in a large bend of Grand River, he said, 'Here is the real valley where Father Adam called his posterity together and blessed them'" (in Joseph Smith, *Encyclopedia of Joseph Smith's Teachings,* 23).

Today, visitors can drive a few miles north of Cameron, Missouri, and there, in the midst of beautiful rolling hills covered with fields of corn, wheat, and other crops, they too can visit the site of Adam-ondi-Ahman. Unlike other Church history sites, at the time of this writing, there is no visitors' center there, no missionaries to greet visitors and escort them around. Much of the surrounding property is farmland owned by the Church and cared for by laboring missionaries rather than proselyting ones. It is a well-maintained site on a knoll covered with trees and spacious lawns, all of which overlooks the lush valley below. Paths lead down to the site of Spring Hill a short distance away.

On a personal note, our extended family visited various Church history sites from New York state to northern Missouri in the summer of 2016. Adam-ondi-Ahman was one of the last sites we visited before returning home. We read the various accounts included in this chapter, then separated to explore on our own or just sit and ponder. At a family gathering a few months later, I asked the family to think back to our trip and say which of all the sites had left the deepest impressions on them. Not surprisingly, the Sacred Grove was mentioned most frequently. They also spoke of other sites warmly—the Hill Cumorah, the baptismal site on the Susquehanna River, the Kirtland Temple, Nauvoo. But, to my surprise, over and over they spoke of how deeply our visit to Adam-ondi-Ahman had impressed them—including some of the younger teens. When I asked them to explain why, they fumbled for words. As one of my granddaughters put it, "I'm not sure. Part of it was knowing that I was walking where Adam and Eve had walked. Part of it was knowing what will happen here sometime in the future. But mostly, I was deeply moved by just being there."

I then shared with them a concept taught by President Boyd K. Packer many years ago when he was speaking of the importance of sacred sites. "Inspiration comes easier when you can set foot on the site related to the need for it" (in *BYU Magazine*, November 1995, 47).

A GREAT CONFERENCE YET TO COME

Let us examine the passage from Daniel's "night visions" mentioned earlier (see Daniel 7:7). The last chapters of Daniel (7–12) contain his apocalyptic visions of the last days. He uses much imagery and symbolism, and in many cases we have not been given the interpretation of what they mean. But in the case of his vision of the Ancient of Days cited above, modern revelation and the words of modern prophets help us interpret what he saw. Here is what he wrote:

> I beheld till the thrones were cast down, and the Ancient of days did sit, whose garment was white as snow, and the hair of his head like the pure wool: his throne was like the fiery flame, and his wheels as burning fire. A fiery stream issued and came forth from before him: thousand thousands ministered unto him, and ten thousand times ten thousand stood before him: the judgment was set, and the books were opened (Daniel 7:9–10).

"Thrones . . . cast down" is a clear reference to the destruction of worldly kingdoms, or, as the Doctrine and Covenants puts it, "a full end of all nations" (D&C 87:6). This then gives us a time context for what Daniel saw. We are talking about the last days when wickedness and war will eventually make an end to all nations. Daniel gives us two numbers to describe the assembly that he saw gathered before this person on the throne: A "thousand thousands" would be one million; and "ten thousand times ten thousand" would be one hundred million. It could be that those two figures were not meant to be precise numbers but to represent the vastness of the throng he saw before the throne.

This is an excellent illustration of how blessed we are to have modern revelation. Most Bible scholars assume that the title "Ancient of Days" refers to God, because He is eternal, and that this vast throng Daniel saw represents the final Judgment Day. But we know that what Daniel saw was what we could liken to a general conference. It will be a gathering that is very much like the meeting Adam called just three years before his death.

Starting with Joseph Smith, our modern prophets have confirmed this interpretation and given us much more detail. The Prophet Joseph taught:

> Daniel in his seventh chapter speaks of the Ancient of Days; he means the oldest man, our Father Adam, Michael; he will call his children together and hold a council with them to prepare them for the coming of the Son of Man. He (Adam) is the father of the human family, and presides over the spirits of all men, and all that have had the keys must stand before him in this grand council. The Son of Man stands before him, and there is given him glory and dominion. Adam delivers up his stewardship to Christ, that which was delivered to him as holding the keys of the universe, but retains his standing as head of the human family (Joseph Smith, *Teachings*, 104).

On another occasion Joseph gave more details:

> Adam . . . was the first man, who is spoken of in Daniel as being the "Ancient of Days." . . . Adam holds the keys of the dispensation of the fulness of times; i.e., the dispensation of all the times that have been and will be revealed through him from the beginning to Christ, and from Christ to the end of all the dispensations that are to be revealed (see Joseph Smith, *Teachings*, 107).

President Joseph Fielding Smith, one of the great gospel scholars of this dispensation, also wrote extensively on the subject. The detail he gives about this coming event is so helpful, we shall cite him extensively to take advantage of his knowledge:

> This gathering of the children of Adam, where the thousands, and the tens of thousands are assembled in the judgment, *will be one of the greatest events this troubled earth has ever seen.* At this conference, or council, all who have held keys of dispensations will render a report of their stewardship. Adam will do likewise, and then he will surrender to Christ all authority. Then Adam will be confirmed in his calling as the prince over his posterity and will be officially installed and crowned eternally in this presiding calling. Then Christ will be received as King of kings, and Lord of lords. We do not know how long a time this gathering will be in session, or how many sessions may be held at this grand council. It is sufficient to know that it is a gathering of the Priesthood of God from the beginning of this earth down to the present, in which reports will be made and all who have been given dispensations (talents) will declare their keys and ministry and make report of their stewardship according to the parable. Judgment will be rendered unto them for this is a gathering of the righteous, those who have held and who hold keys of authority in the Kingdom of God upon this earth. It is not to be the judgment of the wicked. When all things are prepared and every key and power set in order with a full and perfect report of each man's stewardship, then Christ will receive these reports and be installed as rightful Ruler of this earth. At this grand council he will take his place by the united voice of the thousands who by right of Priesthood are there assembled. This will precede the great day of destruction of the wicked and will be the preparation for the Millennial Reign (Joseph Fielding Smith, *The Progress of Man*, 483).

We can draw several conclusions from these explanations given by President Smith.

First, he makes it clear that this grand conference could last for several days and could include a series of meetings.

Second, in one place he speaks of the "gathering of the Priesthood of God." That sounds very much like a meeting for priesthood holders, just as we have priesthood sessions of conference. These, incidentally, are made available to all members of the Church. But later in that same paragraph he speaks of Christ being sustained to "take his place by the united voice of the thousands *who by right of Priesthood are there assembled.*" That could also mean all members of the Church who are invited to be there, not just priesthood holders. We know that women hold many positions of leadership under the authority of the priesthood—or another way to say that would be "by right of priesthood." Even in our general conferences we now have a women's session held under the direction of the priesthood, where only women are invited to attend. That could be possible in this gathering too.

Can we picture such a grand council with our Mother Eve being present? What about all of the righteous women who were part of Enoch's city? If the prophets of all dispensations will be there, surely many righteous women from across dispensations would be invited to some of the meetings as well.

Third, this "installing" of Jesus Christ as the rightful Ruler of this earth sounds very much like what we call a "solemn assembly," where a new President of the Church is sustained by all Church members in a very solemn and precise order. But in this case, we will be sustaining Jesus Christ as the King of kings and Lord of lords.

President Joseph F. Smith, who, incidentally, was President Joseph Fielding Smith's father, gave us this grand insight on the role of women in the kingdom and in future events:

> Among all the millions of spirits that have lived on the earth and have passed away, from generation to generation, since the beginning of the world, . . . you may count that at least one-half are women. Who is going to preach the gospel to the women? Who is going to carry the testimony of Jesus Christ to the hearts of the women who have passed away without a knowledge of the gospel? Well, to my mind, it is a simple thing. These good sisters who have been set apart, ordained to the work, called to it, authorized by the authority of the holy Priesthood to minister for their sex, in the House of God for the living and for the dead, will be fully authorized and empowered *to preach the gospel and minister to the women while the elders and prophets are preaching it to the men.* . . . Some of these good women who have passed beyond have actually been anointed queens and priestesses unto God and unto their husbands, to continue their work and to be the mothers of spirits in the world to come (Joseph F. Smith, *Gospel Doctrine*, 461).

The fourth thing to note is that "all who have held keys of dispensations will render a report of their stewardship" to Adam, who will then render his report to the Savior. That certainly suggests that people from former dispensations will be there to report their stewardships.

One can scarcely conceive of such a glorious experience.

There is one more thing we know about this conference. One of the meetings will be a sacrament service. We learn this from an early revelation. When Joseph was troubled by their enemies trying to sell them bad wine for the sacramental cup, he asked the Lord what to do. The Lord gave him counsel, but then spoke of a future sacrament meeting where He would be present: "I will drink of the fruit of the vine with you on the earth." Then He lists some of those who will be present, including Moroni, John the Baptist, Michael, and others. He closes with, "Also *with all those* whom my Father hath given me *out of the world*" (D&C 27:5–14).

Though this revelation did not specify when or where this sacrament meeting would take place, other sources confirm that this will be part of the Adam-ondi-Ahman experience.

> Before the Lord Jesus descends openly and publicly in the clouds of glory, attended by all the hosts of heaven; . . . before any of his appearances, which taken together comprise the second coming of the Son of God—before all these, there is to be a secret appearance to selected members of his Church. He will come in private to his prophet and to the apostles then living. Those who have held keys and powers and authorities in all ages from Adam to the present will also be present. And further, *all the faithful members of the Church then living and all the faithful saints of all the ages past will be present. It will be the greatest congregation of faithful saints ever assembled on planet earth.* It will be a sacrament meeting. It will be a day of judgment for the faithful of all the ages. *And it will take place in Daviess County, Missouri, at a place called Adam-ondi-Ahman* (Bruce R. McConkie, *Millennial Messiah*, 578, 587).

SUMMARY AND CONCLUSIONS

This chapter concludes Part IV, "The Great Day." Before moving on, we shall make a few observations about what we have studied here.

In chapter 3, "Voice of Warning, Voice of Promise," we talked about the two sides of what the Lord calls "My voice," and said that we find both voices throughout the scriptures. In chapter 11, "The Great and Dreadful Day of the Lord," we expanded on that concept, using the words of Elijah where he describes the last days with those two contrasting words—*great* and *dreadful*. That describes well what the future holds. There is much coming that is very dreadful. But that is more than balanced by what the Lord has given us on the "great" side.

We note this here as a reminder of what was said in the first chapter about "preparation for separation." When we spoke about the coming separation of the wicked from the righteous, we mostly emphasized that this is a threatening thing—which it is. Elijah's description is dreadful, and that is not an exaggeration. But in that separation, the faithful are not only going to avoid much of the effects of wickedness; they are going to be blessed with many wondrous events, such as the establishment of Zion, a temple in New Jerusalem, the return of the lost tribes, and a marvelous conference in Adam-ondi-Ahman. And that is to say nothing of a thousand years of peace and joy.

Fear and anxiety can be a powerful force for change. But the promises of such incredible experiences have even greater power to motivate us. Those who are not prepared often say, "I hope I die before all these things come to pass," whereas those who understand the great side find themselves saying, "Oh, how wonderful it would be if we were here on earth when these things took place."

Faithful members of the Church can and will survive spiritually, if we honor and keep our covenants made at the time of baptism and in the holy temples. We can be on the right side during the "great division," if we do not mirror the world. We can make an affirmative difference in the world for the better, if we are righteously different from the world. Happily, there are so very many decent and wonderful people of all creeds and cultures who likewise strive to do so!

ORSON F. WHITNEY,
IN CONFERENCE REPORT,
APRIL 1927, 99

Part V

The Winding-Up Scenes

CHAPTER 24

A WAR TO END ALL WARS

As we search the scriptures for prophetic statements about Armageddon, we must have the promised coming events in their true perspective. Armageddon is the final great battle in a war that covers the earth and involves all nations. . . . This coming conflict will be universal, and out of it will come the final day of destruction and burning. It will exceed in horror, intensity, and scope all prior wars. (Bruce R. McConkie, *Millennial Messiah*, 449–50)

A PERFECT STORM

In the year 2000, an American disaster movie based on an actual tragedy became a blockbuster hit. The tragedy occurred when a fishing boat in New England was caught between two storm systems, which created an unexpectedly powerful hurricane. The ship was lost at sea with all its crew. The title came from a comment made by an employee of the National Weather Service. He said that different weather conditions, usually not associated with each other, had all come together to create the "perfect storm."

Since then, the phrase has become a common metaphor. It conveys the idea that when various difficult conditions all come together at the same time, it can lead to disastrous results. It is a concept that describes our topic for the next few chapters: the battle of Armageddon.

In today's world, the word *Armageddon* is often used to describe the most unthinkable of catastrophic or apocalyptic events, such as a drastic change in our climate that will melt so much ice that coastal cities all over the world will be flooded, or a massive volcanic event.

Many years ago, I was teaching a class on the prophecies of the last days. I had announced in a previous class that on this night we would focus on the battle of Armageddon. As we were preparing to begin, a sister came up and pulled me aside. Her demeanor was grave and her voice fervent. "Brother Lund," she said, "I feel compelled to say that you should *not* talk about the battle of Armageddon tonight." A little taken aback both by her words and her gravity, I asked why she felt that way. Her answer came as a greater surprise: "If the Lord wanted us to know more about this awful, terrible thing," she said, "then He would have told us more about it. It is not wise to go beyond what the Lord has said."

I pondered that for a moment, touched by her concern. Then, after a moment's reflection, I gently said this to her: "Sister, I appreciate your concern. But did you know that if we did nothing else tonight but simply read through every scriptural passage on Armageddon, we would likely not get through them in the hour that we have?" She stared at me for a long moment, then, shaking her head, turned and left. She did not stay for class.

That may sound like a bit of an exaggeration, but here is a list of the most important scriptural passages on the last great war and the battle of Armageddon that ends that war. These will be the center of our discussion in these chapters.

> Isaiah 13:1–22; Isaiah 34:1–17; Jeremiah 25:15–38; Jeremiah 30:10–11; Ezekiel 38:1–23; Ezekiel 39:1–29; Ezekiel 47:1–12; Daniel 11:1–45; Daniel 12:1–13; Joel 1:1–20; 2:1–32; 3:1–21; Zechariah 13:7–9; 14:1–9; Revelation 9:1–16 (see also D&C 77:13); Revelation 11:1–19; Revelation 16:1–21; Revelation 19:11–21; Revelation 20:1–15; 2 Nephi 23:1–22 (which quotes Isaiah 13); D&C 29:16–20; D&C 45:51–53; D&C 87:1–7; D&C 88:104–110; D&C 133:40–56.

That is a total of over 400 verses! And these are just the major passages. Individual verses connected to this topic are also found throughout the scriptures.

Thinking back to our discussion of two voices—warning and promise—this certainly falls into the category of a warning voice. And yet, we have held it back to the section on the final winding-up scenes, which include some of the most remarkable of all the "great" signs of the times. This is because the scriptures make one thing clear: While the wars of Armageddon may go on intermittently for many years, the last great battle of that war, which will take place in the Holy Land and around the city of Jerusalem, will be one of the last things to occur before the Second Coming. And its magnitude will, in a way, represent all of the sorrow, suffering, evil, and wickedness that Mother Earth has known since the Fall of Adam. It will be a culminating coalition of the powers of evil unlike anything this world of ours has ever known.

Knowing that chills the soul. But it must be so, for this will also be a time of fulfillment of so many prophecies of the last days. For example, in chapter 9, we discussed at some length the parable of the wheat and the tares. The Lord taught that the wheat and the tares were to be left to grow together until the harvest. In the Savior's own words, then would come the time when "the tares are gathered and burned in the fire; so shall it be in the end of this world. The Son of man shall send forth his angels, and *they shall gather out of his kingdom all things that offend,* and them which do iniquity" (Matthew 13:40–41).

If this did not happen, then how could there possibly be a thousand years of peace and righteousness? Seeing how pervasive evil is in our day, and knowing that it is only going to get worse, how will the Lord fulfill His promises if the tares are not gathered for the harvest? This great war and its final battle will truly signal the end of the *world*—not the end of the earth, but the end of the worldly evil and suffering. It will also be a time of great separation of the righteous and the wicked, which requires careful preparation on the part of the Lord's people if we are to see it through. Here again we find the theme of preparation and separation connected.

So let us make this very clear as we begin: *The battle of Armageddon is a major part of that time of final gathering of the righteous and the wicked!* That is important to understand. It is not just the righteous being gathered to the covenant, but, as the parable of the wheat and the tares suggests, the wicked must be gathered too. It is the last major sign of the times to be fulfilled before the actual Second Coming of our Lord and Savior Jesus Christ.

Elder Neal A. Maxwell reminds us of what he calls the "polarization" that characterizes our day, and that there are solutions the Lord has and will put in place for those times:

> Yes, there will be wrenching polarization on this planet, but also the remarkable reunion with our colleagues in Christ from the city of Enoch. Yes, nation after nation will become a house divided, but more and more unifying Houses of the Lord will grace this planet. *Yes, Armageddon lies ahead—but so does Adam-ondi-Ahman!* (Maxwell, *Even as I Am*, 121).

With that in mind, let us now examine what is commonly called the battle of Armageddon.

WHY IS IT CALLED THE BATTLE OF ARMAGEDDON?

Many of those who refer to terrible calamities as an "Armageddon" might be surprised to learn that the original word, which comes from the Bible, does not convey some apocalyptic tragedy. The word itself is found only one time in the New Testament (Revelation 16:16) and once in the Old Testament in a cognate form, "Megiddon" (Zechariah 12:11). *Armageddon* is the Greek transliteration of two Hebrew words meaning a "mountain of troops."

One of the most important roads of the ancient world ran from Egypt along the eastern Mediterranean coastline. It went through a broad and fertile valley in central Israel known as the Jezreel Valley today. This valley was guarded by a fortress at the town of Megiddo. "Because of that strategic location, Megiddo and the valley of Esdraelon have seen some of history's bloodiest battles. Egyptian pharaohs, Roman legions, British troops, and Israeli tanks all have struggled in the valley of Megiddo" (*Ye Shall Be Witnesses unto Me,* 263).

Typically, Christians speak of the "*battle* of Armageddon." This is not a phrase found in the scriptures, but it is an accurate term. As we discussed earlier, our age is an age of war, and that war will eventually spread to all nations and will continue off and on until the Second Coming (see D&C 87:6). The "battle" of Armageddon technically describes just the last and final event in the age of war that began in South Carolina in 1861.

In a series of lectures given in Salt Lake City in the early months after America entered World War II, Joseph Fielding Smith, then a member of the Twelve, made this observation:

> We hear a great deal and we see a great deal in the prints today about this great second world war. I think in a previous talk I said I did not call it the second world war. This is the first world war. It is only a part, a continuation of the war of 1914 to 1918, and even that was not the beginning. *I have been asked a great many times if I thought this present war was the great last war before the coming of Christ, and I have said yes;* but I do not mean when I say that, that we will not have another spell, another armistice, when they may lay down their arms for a season only to get ready to take them up again, although I hope that will not be the case. I think the great world war commenced in April, 1861 (Joseph Fielding Smith, *Signs of the Times,* 118).

What is especially troubling, as we have seen, is that not only will the time preceding this last great battle be an age of war, but prophecy makes it very clear that it will also be an age of wickedness and depravity, an age of social upheaval and chaos, an age of natural disasters, famine, pestilence, and disease. This is also one of the reasons why President Nelson keeps reminding us that "in coming days, it will not be possible to survive spiritually without the guiding, directing, and comforting influence of the Holy Ghost. . . . I plead with you to increase your spiritual capacity to receive revelation" ("Revelation for the Church, Revelation for Our Lives," *Ensign*, May 2018).

But with all that said, it will be an age of great and marvelous events too, as we have also seen. It will be the age when a New Jerusalem and the Old Jerusalem become two world capitals. It will be an age of the return of the lost tribes of Israel, of a conference and sacrament meeting in the valley of Adam-ondi-Ahman, of the return of the city of Enoch from heaven, and, most important, the age when a millennium of peace, harmony, and safety will prevail on this old earth of ours. No wonder President Nelson also said: "Our Savior and Redeemer, Jesus Christ, will perform *some of His mightiest works between now and when He comes again.* We will see *miraculous indications* that God the Father and His Son, Jesus Christ, preside over this Church in majesty and glory" (ibid.).

WHO WILL LEAD THIS GREAT ARMY?

Often, prophecies of the last days are couched in more general terms, without many specifics. That is not the case with the battle of Armageddon. Several prophets—most notably Ezekiel, Jeremiah, Daniel, John the Revelator, and Joseph Smith—have provided us with significant details about this grand coalition of evil. Ezekiel even tells us the name of the leader, where he comes from, and something about the army he will lead. John the Revelator tells us how Satan will raise up a charismatic religious leader who will join with the great military leader, providing a supposed religious justification for the terrible havoc that they will wreak on the world. Other prophets also share much detail about what we can expect. Let's begin with Ezekiel's account and analyze what he tells us:

> And the word of the Lord came unto me, saying, Son of man, set thy face against Gog, the land of Magog, the chief prince of Meshech and Tubal, and prophesy against him (Ezekiel 38:1–2).

Ezekiel begins his prophecy by actually naming the leader, telling us where he comes from. His name, or more likely, his title, is Gog and he is from the land of Magog. Ezekiel was a contemporary with Lehi and Nephi and lived around 600 B.C. He was taken into captivity when the Babylonians conquered Jerusalem and took the population captive back to Babylon. So he uses names and titles that were common to his time but mean little to us today. Fortunately, historians and geographers can help us link many of the ancient names with current locations and peoples.

In Hebrew, *Gog* means "mountain." A mountain is a prominent thing in the landscape and is often used metaphorically, as in, "He was a mountain of a man." This is why some scholars think Gog may be a title rather than his given or familial name.

The King James translation suggests that Gog is from the land of Magog and a "chief prince," who also rules over two other countries. But some Bible scholars believe that the King James translation missed an important point here. The word that the KJV translators rendered as "chief" comes from the Hebrew *Rosh*. These scholars believe that it is not a title but the name of another land, along with Meshech and Tubal. They believe the more accurate translation of this verse should be: "Set thy face against Gog, *who is of* the lands of Magog, Rosh, Meshech, and Tubal." That change is more important than it may first appear.

To be clear, let us put it another way. Instead of saying that Gog is the chief prince of three countries—Magog, Meshech, and Tubal—these scholars say that he is the prince of four countries—Magog, *Rosh*, Meshech, and Tubal. A closer examination of those names helps us see why this is important.

Magog. This is the name of a son of Japheth, one of the three sons of Noah. And Magog is the land where he settled. Japheth, another of Noah's sons (see Genesis 10:2), is credited with fathering many of the early Gentile nations of the world, particularly those of Europe and central Asia.[1] We do have evidence that Magog is the name of a people who lived far to the north of the promised land. The ancient historian Josephus says that Magog was the land of the Scythians, a fierce barbaric people who occupied what is now eastern Europe and central Asia, primarily the area around Russia and its former Soviet satellite countries.

Rosh. This is thought to be an early form of *Rus* (pronounced Roos), which is the ancient root word for Russia. This is less certain, but there

---

[1] See Samuel Fallows, *The Popular and Critical Bible Encyclopedia and Scriptural Dictionary* (Chicago: Howard-Severance Company, 1911), 904.

is much to support this interpretation. Wilhelm Gesenius, a nineteenth-century German orientalist, who is still considered by many to be one of the premier scholars in Semitic languages, concluded that in this passage, Rosh was a proper name used for both a people and the place where they lived, rather than just a title. He said that both Byzantine and Arabic writers mention a people they call the *Rus*, who were part of the Scythian tribes, and concluded that there is no reason to question the existence of a people known as the *Ros* or *Rosh*, who are the early ancestors of the people we now call Russians.

Meshech was another of the sons of Japheth and therefore is the father of another group of what became Gentile nations (see Genesis 10:2). He and Tubal are typically mentioned together. Other scholars note that the ancient Assyrians called this people the *Moshki*. They too lived in the same general area around central and southern Russia, and eventually moved as far south as present-day Turkey. Moscow, the current capital of Russia, in Russian is pronounced *Moskvah,* and some believe that modern name comes from Meshech.

Tubal. Yet another of the sons of Japheth, whose tribe is assumed to have settled in the same general areas as his brothers. Remember that the landing place of Noah's ark was on Mount Ararat. Though we do not know for sure, a long tradition places the location of Mount Ararat in eastern Turkey near the Black Sea. Nearby countries are Iran, Armenia, Ukraine, Georgia, and Azerbaijan. Russia is to the north of these lands. Little more than that is known about these early peoples and their lands.

Let us now examine John's vision of this evil coalition of the last days.

A BEAST FROM THE SEA

John's vision also focuses on key players in the coming battle, as well as giving us considerable detail on the war itself and the army that brings it. John did not give us the name of the person, nor did he tell us where he's from. His focus was on the nature of this leader, and a religious leader who will join with him. It is a grim partnership that John describes after he saw the seventh seal opened (see Revelation 8:1). Though we are not told the duration of this massive war, Joseph Smith was taught that it will happen during an undefined period of time between the opening of the seventh seal and the Second Coming (see D&C 77:13).

In Revelation 9, John saw Satan (the star who fell from heaven) receive the key to the bottomless pit. That aptly describes Satan's kingdom—the depths of his evil works are unfathomable to us. When Satan opened the bottomless pit, John saw a great smoke come up out of the pit that became a vast cloud of locusts. This imagery seems to be symbolic of a mighty army that he saw in the last days. The locusts serve as a powerful image of a great army because they are virtually numberless and they destroy everything in their path. To make sure we understand that John is using locusts as a symbol of an actual army, he tells us that they have the "faces of men" (v. 7).

> *The things which John saw had no allusion to the scenes of the days of Adam, Enoch, Abraham or Jesus, only so far as is plainly represented by John. . . . John saw that only which was lying in futurity and which was shortly to come to pass.*
>
> JOSEPH SMITH,
> TEACHINGS OF THE PROPHET
> JOSEPH SMITH, 289

John then described what he next saw, and the imagery he used strongly evokes modern warfare, including airplanes, tanks, rockets, and so on (see verses 8–10). Then, as if to confirm our assumption that John was not seeing insects but a powerful, invincible army, John specifically states that he was told that the number of the army will be two hundred thousand thousand, or *two hundred million!*

To give us a perspective of how vast an army that is, here is a modern comparison. The total combatants from all countries on both sides of World War II is estimated to be between 40 and 60 million soldiers under arms! Armageddon will be three to five times greater than that, and that is just on one side of the combatants!

John's narrative of the battle breaks off at that point as the Lord showed him other important aspects of the latter days (see chapters 10–12). But he came back to his vision of the war in chapters 13–16. What he saw there were two fierce-looking beasts that seem to represent "degenerate earthly kingdoms controlled by Satan" (see the heading to chapter 13). John's description of both of these leaders is also filled with much imagery.

The first beast, who comes out of the sea, is a great military leader who makes war with the Saints (see Revelation 13:4, 7). He leads the world into captivity and kills many with the sword (see v. 10). Later, John specifically says that this leader "gathered them [his army] together into a place called in the Hebrew tongue Armageddon" (Revelation 16:16). His followers are also of the most wicked and vile and are loyal to their commander: "They worshipped the dragon [Satan] which gave power unto the beast [Gog]: and they worshipped the beast, saying, Who is like unto the beast? who is able to make war with him? And there was given unto him a mouth speaking great things and blasphemies" (Revelation 13:4–5).

A PARTNERSHIP OF EVIL

Something unique to John's account is a description of a second leader (a "beast from the earth") who operates in tandem with Gog, the military/political leader. In his epistles, John often spoke of an antichrist (see, for example, 1 John 2:18, 22; 4:3). It is a word that describes someone who is in open opposition to Christ and all who follow Him. Though John doesn't use the term antichrist in the book of Revelation, that is clearly this person's nature, and so in modern times many evangelical Christians commonly refer to this second beast as the antichrist. This seems clear from John's language:

- *He had two horns like a lamb but spake as a dragon* (see Revelation 13:11). The lamb invokes the imagery of the Lamb of God, another title for the Savior. Perhaps this is because the person pretends to be God's representative, but in reality fights against Christ and for Satan. That is his true nature.
- *He works great miracles*, including calling fire down from heaven as Elijah did (see v. 13).
- *He creates an image (probably a statue) of Gog,* which "miraculously" speaks, and somehow destroys anyone who refuses to bow down and worship the image of Gog (see v. 15). This partnership makes for a deadly combination—a powerful, charismatic military/political leader who seems invincible and leads a massive army of men. He is supported by and idolized by an equally charismatic religious leader, who works miracles and provides spiritual justification for his evil, and who carries out his master's will.

What John next says about this religious leader is puzzling and has caused much speculation: "And he causeth all, both small and great, rich and poor, free and bond, to receive a mark in their right hand, or in their foreheads: And that no man might buy or sell, save he that had the mark, or the name of the beast, or the number of his name. Here is wisdom. Let him that hath understanding count the number of the beast: for it is the number of a man; and his number is Six hundred threescore and six" (Revelation 13:16–18).

This enigmatic description is clearly puzzling and has generated much speculation—some of it far-fetched—about what the number 666 means.

John's description that no one can "buy or sell" without the "mark" of the beast clearly tells us that these two rulers have absolute dictatorial power over their citizens. This shouldn't surprise us too much, as we have seen such powerful dictatorships in our own times. Through extreme despotism, they control every aspect of the lives of their people. This rigid control has been enforced in many ways—the use of identity cards, rationing cards, ghettos, imprisonment, distinctive clothing, slave labor, and so on. It is also carried out with much violence, murder, rape, and military subjugation.

So that helps us better understand why John uses the concept of slavery to describe the people. But what is the significance of the number 666? Will we actually see people with a brand on their foreheads or the palms of their hands? It is possible, but a more plausible interpretation is that John uses this number in a symbolic or metaphorical way. Let us explain how that might be. We do know for sure that in John's day—when Rome was the most powerful empire in the world—it was common practice for Romans to brand their slaves with some kind of mark of ownership. Slaves had become so common by then that in some places they outnumbered the free citizens. Since one cannot discern who is or who is not a slave by simply looking at the individual, there had to be a way to clearly mark them as such. And to make that effective, the brand needed to be placed where it could not be easily hidden or removed.

The two preferred places for the branding of a slave were in the center of the forehead or on the palm of one hand. In addition to being very prominent, branding also connoted ownership, as in the branding of animals. Since this was a widely common practice in John's time, many Bible scholars believe he drew on this imagery to emphasize the point that the followers of these two men will be so totally devoted to them that it is as if they were their literal slaves. We can't safely assume that every person in Gog's army and the people in the countries he conquers will actually be branded.

Another thing we know about this time in history is that from this common practice of branding one's slaves, some devout followers of various religious sects saw that as a meaningful way to symbolize their own devotion to their gods. A few actually did brand themselves, but more commonly they would use paint or dye to mark themselves. Here is how one Bible scholar explains the mark on the forehead:

The classical idolaters used to consecrate themselves to particular deities on the same principle [of branding]. The marks used on these occasions were various. Sometimes they contained the name of the god; sometimes his particular ensign, as the thunderbolt of Jupiter, the trident of Neptune, the ivy of Bacchus, etc., or else *they marked themselves with some mystical number* whereby the god was described (Fallows, *Bible Encyclopedia*, 2:670).

That custom still prevails in some world religions.

Again, we're not suggesting that John is saying that sometime in the future millions of people will have three sixes branded or painted on their foreheads or the palms of their hand. His imagery could be a powerful way of saying that these followers of Gog and the antichrist will be the same as slaves to their masters. The imagery is quite compelling.

But why does John give us the enigmatic number of "six hundred three score and six." Two customs at that time can also help in our understanding. First, a common practice in the ancient world was to use what the Greeks called *gematria*, the same root from which we get our word *geometry*. In those times, each letter of the alphabet was also used to represent a numerical equivalent. For example, *alpha* = 1, *beta* = 2, *gamma* = 3, and so on. This was true in Hebrew as well: *aleph* was 1, *bet* was 2, *gimmel* 3. Thus, one could calculate the numerical equivalent of a person's name through the use of *gematria*.

It was also common in ancient times for some numbers to be symbolically associated with religious or other important concepts. For example, three was thought to symbolize the three members of the Godhead, also called the Trinity. Four was associated with the earth and our earthly, mortal life. For example, we speak of the four "corners" of the earth—an odd description for a globe—the four winds, and the four directions. By extension, the number forty came to suggest trials and challenges of life.

As noted earlier, one of the most important of the symbolic numbers was the number seven, representing completeness or perfection.

If we apply this symbolism to the number 666, we could say that it represents two spiritual concepts. There are three digits, which could imply that this person is somehow associated with deity. On the other hand, the number six falls one short of "perfection." Thus the number 666 would be an ironic and very negative way to describe Satan and his followers. They try to appear to be as the gods but are actually the epitome of imperfection. Or, as one person expressed it, the number 666 represents "imperfection triplified."

Here is how a conservative Christian scholar suggested that John's number could be interpreted:

> The number of the name "Jesus" in Greek [using *gematria*] *is 888*; [a number one greater than perfection]. . . . And according to this interpretation, the meaning [of 666] is that the beast falls as far short of "seven" (i.e., perfection and holiness) as Jesus goes beyond it (J. R. Dummelow, *A Commentary on the Holy Bible*, 1084).

AN ALLIANCE OF EVIL

We know that Gog, Ezekiel's title for the man who will lead this vast army, will likely lead the largest army in the history of the world. This strongly suggests future political and military alliances that draw on nations all over the world. The prophets have confirmed this. Ezekiel lists twelve nations or areas by name that come with Gog (see Ezekiel 38:5–6, 13). Jeremiah names twenty-one countries, then adds that it will be "all the kingdoms of the world" (Jeremiah 25:15–26). Daniel and John the Revelator give no specific countries but lump large areas together by referring to the "kings of the north," "the kings of the south," and "the kings of the east" (see Daniel 11:6–15, 40; Revelation 16:12).

Not all of those ancient names can be associated with modern countries, so we shall only note that many of them come from the Middle East and others are associated with current Europe, including the areas now controlled by Russia and her neighboring states. One of those named by Ezekiel and Daniel was the Persian Empire (see Ezekiel 27:10; 38:5; see also Daniel 10:13, 20; 11:2), which at that time stretched from India and China on the east to what we now call eastern and western Europe. Isaiah said: "Behold, these shall come from far: and, lo, these from the north and from the west; and these *from the land of Sinim*" (Isaiah 49:12). As we saw in an earlier chapter, *Sinim* was likely the ancient name for what we today call China and other countries of the Far East. No mention is made in the ancient texts about what we call the Americas, but that could easily be because at that time it had not been visited by people from the Old World.

From these references it seems clear that the prophets were trying to give us some idea of the vast scope of this future military alliance of a hundred thousand thousand. That is a sobering thought. But while numbers are important in measuring the threat of an army, many military experts would tell us that even more important is the training, the courage, and the morale of the troops, as well as how well equipped they are. How many times in history have we seen examples where a superior force was routed by a more determined and motivated enemy? Here too the prophets provide us a surprising amount of detail about what kind of soldiers Gog will lead.

> Thus saith the Lord God; Behold, I am against thee, O Gog, the chief prince of Meshech and Tubal [or prince of Rosh, Meshech, and Tubal]: . . . I will bring thee forth, and all thine army, horses and horsemen, all of them clothed with all sorts of armour, even a great company with bucklers and shields, all of them handling swords (Ezekiel 38:3–4).

The imagery Ezekiel uses here is very descriptive and conveys the idea of a superbly trained and well-equipped army. "Horses and horsemen" represent the two most dreaded things in ancient warfare: knights on horseback—what eventually came to be known as cavalry—and chariots. These struck great fear in a foot soldier because they could not stand against them. And Ezekiel describes them as superbly armed and equipped.

Note Joel's description of this force:

> A great people and a strong; there hath not been ever the like, neither shall be any more after it, even to the years of many generations. A fire devoureth before them; and behind them a flame burneth: the land is as the garden of Eden before them, and behind them a desolate wilderness; yea, and nothing shall escape them (Joel 2:1–11).

These are remarkable descriptors. No army before or after is its equal. In their wake is complete, total destruction, what some call a "scorched-earth" policy. The total desolation hints at the use of powerful weaponry, including the possible use of tactical nuclear weapons.

> The appearance of them is as the appearance of horses; and as horsemen, so shall they run. Like the noise of chariots on the tops of mountains shall they leap, like the noise of a flame of fire that devoureth the stubble, as a strong people set in battle array. Before their face the people shall be much pained. . . . They shall run like mighty men; they shall climb the wall like men of war; and they shall march every one on his ways, and they shall not break their ranks: Neither shall one thrust another; they shall walk every one in his path: and when they fall upon the sword, they shall not be wounded (Joel 2:4–8).

Here again we find the imagery of knights and chariots as symbols of the power and strength of this army. Faces that are "much pained" imply that others will be filled with sheer terror at the sight of them. Joel's imagery here shows that they are well trained and highly disciplined, for they do not break rank or panic even in the face of fierce resistance. "Climbing the walls" reminds us that before modern artillery and aerial bombardment, the only way to attack a fortified city was to batter open the gates or scale the walls. This often took place after a long siege that left the people weak and vulnerable. For a foot soldier, scaling the walls while the enemy rains down arrows, spears, stones, and boiling oil on his head was terrifying. And yet they "climb the wall like men of war." How they could fall upon the sword and not be wounded isn't clear. Modern body armor comes to mind, but it could just mean that it seems like they are invincible. This is a vivid depiction of a powerful, almost undefeatable army.

Earlier we mentioned John's description of the army as he saw it (Revelation 9). His choice of words is also very instructive.

- They "*were like unto horses prepared unto battle*" (v. 7). Powerful, invincible, unstoppable.
- They had "*hair as the hair of women*" (v. 8). At first we might think that John was seeing women in the army, which is no longer that uncommon. Perhaps this is a reference to the story of Samson, whose long hair gave him incredible strength in battle. That would be a powerful way of representing their strength and power.
- And the "*sound of their wings was as the sound of chariots of many horses running to battle*" (v. 9). His mention of wings and the deafening sound brings to mind the roar of many World War II bombers on their way to bomb whole cities into ruin, or modern jet aircraft and missiles.
- "*And they had tails like unto scorpions,* and *there were stings in their tails*" (v. 10). Does the image of tail gunners in World War II bombers come to mind? More modern weapons such as tanks, missile launchers, laser-guided bombs, etc., could also be part of what he saw.

SUMMARY AND CONCLUSIONS

There are many more things for us to learn about the battle of Armageddon, which we shall do in the next chapters. But let us remember this one thing: We have no specific idea how far into the future it will be when Gog is born and starts down that path that will bring so much sorrow and pain to the world. But we know that Satan isn't waiting for the time of Armageddon. It's not as though we're going to be sailing through smooth waters up until Gog is born, and then everything begins to collapse. All around us now, we see the battle raging, and, as Enoch saw, Satan throws back his head and laughs and his angels rejoice at the suffering they are causing.

This war even now rages all around us. But let us also remember that here we are only discussing one side of what is coming. Let us not forget that on the Lord's side there will be many wonderful things happening as well.

The Church has and is continuing to institute changes designed to strengthen our faith, fortify our families, and serve others more effectively. But there is much more yet to be done in preparation for what still lies ahead.

CHAPTER 25

THE BATTLE OF ARMAGEDDON

Gog and Magog are all the nations of the earth who take up the sword against Israel and Jerusalem in the day of Armageddon. Their identities remain to be revealed when the battle alliances are made. We can assume, however, that the United States, as the defender of freedom in all the world, will head one coalition, and that Russia, whose avowed aim is to destroy freedom in all nations, will head the enemies of God. (Bruce R. McConkie, *Millennial Messiah*, 481)

WHO SHALL STAND AGAINST THEM?

Now that we've seen who will be aligned with Gog in this grand alliance of nations and armies, the natural question that follows is who can possibly stand against such numbers and strength? Who can resist such an onslaught of power, backed by a determination to bring the entire world under their subjugation?

Ironically, though the scriptures on this last great war give us considerable detail on who will be in the powerful alliance of evil, only one name of a nation or a people that will stand against him is mentioned by the ancient prophets. And that nation is the homeland of ancient Israel. Both Joel and Zechariah specifically note that all nations will come against Jerusalem. Zechariah reports that the Lord said: "For I will gather all nations against Jerusalem to battle" (Zechariah 14:2). Joel promised a similar thing: "And in that time, when I shall bring again the captivity of Judah and Jerusalem [i.e., when they have returned from their captivity], I will also gather all nations, and will bring them down into the valley of Jehoshaphat [a valley in Jerusalem], and will plead with them there for my people and for my heritage Israel" (Joel 3:1–2).

However, the prophecy on war (D&C 87) states that war would be poured out on all nations beginning with the American Civil War. In the two global wars that have followed and several other wars thereafter, there have been coalitions of two great opposing forces—the armies who come from nations where democratic governments and principles of freedom are upheld, and those that come from nations where despotic, dictatorial leaders have put their peoples under virtual slavery. These include Nazism, Fascism, Communism, Socialism, and other radical regimes whose intent is to bring their people and others under full subjugation.

So does "all nations" include the United States of America? Will there be other allies on the side of the right? Why would we assume otherwise? Right now, the United States and its allies are leaders in supporting freedom and democracy around the world.

WHY DOES THIS WAR SEEM TO BE CENTERED IN THE MIDDLE EAST?

As we study what has been said about the battle of Armageddon, it quickly becomes clear that though in its early stages, the age of war will be a truly global conflict, and the scriptures are clear that the final battle will take place in the homelands of the original tribes of Israel. In addition to the scriptures cited above, note how specific Zechariah is about Gog's ultimate target:

> I will make Jerusalem a cup of trembling unto all the people round about, when they shall be in the siege both against Judah and against Jerusalem (Zechariah 12:2).

In a way, that is surprising. Modern Israel is a small country. Of the current 195 nations in the world, Israel ranks 149th in land size. Its capital of Jerusalem has a population of about 800,000, which falls far short of many other great cosmopolitan cities of the world. So, how is it that the last great and conclusive battle of Armageddon will take place in the state of Israel, and particularly in its capital city? While the scriptures don't answer that question specifically, there are details that can help us understand some of the possible reasons.

We have spoken much about the children of Abraham in this book, particularly about the house of Israel, who were descendants of Abraham through his grandson Jacob. But what is often overlooked is that Abraham had other children and grandchildren who were not in that direct covenant line. Both Ishmael and Esau were firstborn sons, but the covenant line went through Isaac and Jacob. Part of that was because they married outside of the covenant.

It shouldn't surprise us that they felt deep resentment about being cheated out of what they saw as their rightful place. They went on to have their own posterity, just as Isaac and Jacob did. We talk a lot about the twelve tribes of Jacob, or Israel, but we often overlook that Esau also fathered twelve tribes of his own (see Genesis 31). And Ishmael had a great posterity that stayed in that same general area. So many of the current animosities we see in the Middle East trace their roots back thousands of years. As one political observer noted, "Part of the problem in the Middle East is that this is a family feud that has been perpetuated through hundreds of generations."

Both sides claim a right to the land. Israelis say that this was their ancestral homeland for thousands of years and that they only left it when the Romans conquered them and scattered them throughout the empire. The Palestinians and other Arabic peoples counter with the fact that the Jews were not in that "homeland" for about two thousand years. And during that time, the Palestinians and other local peoples were there. So why would the world not recognize their right to the land?

And so it is that even today, the Middle East is one of the most politically turbulent areas of the world, with bitter clashes and full-scale wars still going on. As one Israeli prime minister said to naive outsiders who say they don't understand why the Israelis and the Arab peoples can't just get along and come to some kind of compromise: "Violence and bloodshed in the Middle East is a perpetual motion machine that requires no outside assistance to maintain itself or to threaten the peace and stability of other nations" (as cited in Joel C. Rosenberg, *Epicenter*, 42). The prophecies seem to indicate that this culture of tension and strife will continue right up until Armageddon.

Those cultural and political realities are profoundly influenced by a second major factor in understanding the realities of the Middle East. It can be described in one word: OIL! The discovery of huge petroleum reserves in the Middle East back in the early twentieth century was a major turning point in world history. And it would prove to have huge political ramifications. The discovery of the massive oil reserves in Saudi Arabia and other places throughout the region took place as the world was entering a new industrial, transportation, and technology revolution—a new age fueled by petroleum.

A tectonic shift in world finances and politics took place during those years. The Arab countries now became major players on the world stage. All around the world, nations began to align themselves based on what came to be known as "petro-politics."

With many nations heavily dependent on Arab oil, the state of Israel quickly found itself being more and more isolated politically. Ironically, those oceans of oil seemed to be everywhere in the Middle East except within the borders of the state of Israel.

But in the last few decades, new developments have changed the political landscape once again. Israel has now discovered large reserves of natural gas and petroleum. Experts now estimate that Israel's natural gas reserves are about 18 *trillion* cubic feet. In 2014, an Israeli subsidiary of a U.S. oil company discovered oil reserves in the Golan Heights, along the Israel/Syria border. That is predicted to be somewhere around one billion barrels (see "Israel's Never-Ending Search for Oil in Occupied Golan Heights," *Asharq al-Awsat*, aawsat.com/english/home/article/1676021/israel).

That puts Israel into the petroleum game and makes her an attractive target for potential conquest. But there is much more than oil. Like many other small nations, Israel has become a major science, medical, and technology center. They produce enormous amounts of food for the tables of Europe and the Middle East.

A final reason that could explain Gog's future interest in Israel and the Middle East is that Israel has a military prowess greater than its geographical size and population would normally warrant. So do many other countries in this region.

The possibility of war in the region has been a stark reality since the United Nations declared that the Jews and the Palestinians could have their homelands in 1947.

It would make sense that Gog would move on the Middle East because of its enormous oil reserves and other resources. They could not ignore the threat that military forces in the region would pose to their goals. So if we consider all of these factors—politics, oil, technology, food production, military capabilities, the political instability of the area, and vast tracts of lands in the region—we don't have to ponder overly long on why Gog and his armies would see this area as a "must" for conquest and subjugation.

WHEN JERUSALEM IS AGAIN ENCOMPASSED WITH ARMIES: THE FINAL DAYS

In chapter 1, we discussed in some detail a prophecy the Savior shared with the Twelve. One of the most amazing parts of what He said was both a prophetic warning and specific instructions about what to do when the people saw the prophecy being fulfilled: "And when ye shall see Jerusalem compassed with armies, then know that the desolation thereof is nigh" (Luke 21:20).

Just over thirty years later—still within the lifetime of those who had heard Him say it—the Savior's prophecy became a grim reality. When the Romans encircled the city and laid siege to it, then unexpectedly withdrew, the faithful Christians heeded the Savior's warning and escaped to a place not affected by the war. When the Romans returned in full force a few months later, there would be no mercy shown, and no further escape. All others were swept up in the total destruction of the Jews.

From the prophecies about Armageddon, we know that in the latter days Jerusalem shall once again be encompassed with armies—only this time they will be vastly more numerous. And they will come with far more sophisticated and dangerous weapons and far more disciplined troops than the Roman legionnaires.

In Hebrew, the name of Israel's capital is *Yerushalayim*, which means the city of peace. What an ironic name. Jerusalem has been besieged and completely conquered at least two dozen known times in history. The prophecies make it clear that there will be at least one more conquest added to that list before they find permanent peace. As Zechariah vividly describes it: "Behold, the day of the Lord cometh, and thy spoil shall be divided in the midst of thee. For I will gather all nations against Jerusalem to battle; and *the city shall be taken,* and *the houses rifled,* and the *women ravished;* and *half of the city shall go forth into captivity*" (Zechariah 14:1–2).

This time, however, the end will turn out very, very differently.

In the previous chapter, through the eyes of Ezekiel, Joel, and John, we saw that at some future time Gog and his innumerable army will sweep across the earth, eventually coming to the Middle East. He will encamp his armies in the valley of Megiddo and surrounding areas. The Holy City will once again be put under siege, which in this modern day could mean they would be subject to far more devastating weaponry than battering rams and catapults.

But this time, as John foresaw, a new element will be introduced into the equation of war. And it will make a profound difference:

> And there was given me a reed like unto a rod: and the angel stood, saying, Rise, and measure the temple of God, and the altar, and them that worship therein. But the court which is without

the temple leave out, and measure it not; for it is given unto the Gentiles: and the holy city shall they tread under foot forty and two months (Revelation 11:1–2).

For reasons not explained, John was commanded to use a rod and measure off the dimensions of the temple. Some believe it is a metaphor, conveying the concept of "taking one's measure," i.e., assessing strengths and weaknesses. But the measurement takes place on the Temple Mount and of the courtyards around the temple itself.

We know that the Temple Mount at the time of Jesus was a whole complex of buildings and other architecture. King Herod had the top of Mount Moriah leveled to create an area of almost forty acres. The temple was the centerpiece of the Mount of Moriah, and it had three courtyards directly in front of it to the east. Under the Mosaic law, nothing unclean was allowed into the temple's precincts, on penalty of death. The Romans allowed the Jews to enforce that law, so they put up a partition wall with signs at regular intervals stating that any Gentiles who passed through that wall would be executed. Otherwise, Gentiles were allowed elsewhere on the mount. This larger, nonrestricted area was known as the Court of the Gentiles.

Knowing that helps us understand this measuring process. What John seems to be suggesting is that Jerusalem will be invaded again and that the enemy will even get onto the Temple Mount, breach the inner courts, and totally desecrate the temple. This would have come as a terrible shock to John's listeners. This had happened three times before, when Babylon conquered Jerusalem in 587 B.C. and looted the temple, and again under the Seleucids, one of the Greek divisions of Alexander the Great's empire, who did the same around 179 B.C. The third time was prophesied by Jesus as part of the Olivet Discourse, which was fulfilled in A.D. 70 when Titus's legions breached the Temple Mount and not only tore down the altars of the temple but sacrificed to the pagan gods on that very site.

This utter desecration of the holy temple was considered to be the worst national tragedy that could fall upon them, and it came to be known as the abomination of desolation, or the "abomination that maketh desolate" (see Daniel 9:27; Matthew 24:15; Mark 13:14; JS—M 1:12). To hear John prophesy that it would happen again would have been deeply sobering to the Saints of his day, and should be the same for modern Latter-day Saints. In modern revelation, the abomination of desolation is referred to twice in the Doctrine and Covenant (see D&C 84:117; 88:85). The phrase has come to signify utter destruction.

What this verse does make quite clear is that the city of Jerusalem will be invaded in the latter days by the troops of Gog, who will show no reverence for this sacred site.

> And I will give power unto my two witnesses, and they shall prophesy a thousand two hundred and threescore days, clothed in sackcloth (Revelation 11:3).

Let's take the elements one by one. This chapter is the first and only mention by John of these two witnesses. The fact that he doesn't explain who they are could imply that his readers were already familiar with the concept, something that John could have taught them before his imprisonment on the Isle of Patmos. This would make sense because there are two Old Testament passages that refer to similar witnesses. The first is from Isaiah in a chapter that focuses on the last days and the restoration of Israel and their return to their homeland:

> There is none to guide her among all the sons whom she hath brought forth; neither is there any that taketh her by the hand [i.e., there are no prophets in the land to guide them]. . . . These two things are come unto thee; . . . Thy sons have fainted, they lie at the head of all the streets, as a wild bull in a net: they are full of the fury of the Lord (Isaiah 51:18–20).

Zechariah saw a candlestick (a seven-branched *menorah*, or Jewish lamp, which is often used as a symbol for Israel and Judaism) with two olive trees on either side of it. When he asked for its meaning, Zechariah was told that the two olive trees "are the two *anointed ones*, that stand by the Lord of the whole earth" (Zechariah 4:11, 14). That these two men are called "anointed ones" signifies they are servants of the Lord and perhaps invokes the concept of having received their temple covenants, which include washings and anointings (see D&C 124:39).

That both of these passages refer to the same two men was confirmed when Joseph Smith asked those fifteen questions about the book of Revelation. Here is question fifteen:

> Q. What is to be understood by the two witnesses, in the eleventh chapter of Revelation?
>
> A. They are two prophets that are to be raised up to the Jewish nation in the last days, at the time of the restoration, and to prophesy to the Jews after they are gathered and have built the city of Jerusalem in the land of their fathers (D&C 77:15).

This short answer is filled with helpful information. First, these are not just there to bear their testimony. They are prophets and will testify against Gog and his armies. And since the only place where we find prophets of God on earth today is within The Church of Jesus Christ of Latter-day Saints, then we can assume they will be leaders in the Church. Elder Bruce R. McConkie stated this emphatically:

> "In the mouth of two or three witnesses shall every word be established." (2 Cor. 13:1.) Such is God's eternal law. And these two shall be followers of that humble man, Joseph Smith, through whom the Lord of Heaven restored the fulness of his everlasting gospel in this final dispensation of grace. *No doubt they will be members of the Council of the Twelve or of the First Presidency of the Church* [those we sustain as prophets, seers, and revelators]. Their prophetic ministry to rebellious Jewry shall be the same in length as was our Lord's personal ministry among their rebellious forebears (McConkie, *Doctrinal New Testament Commentary*, 3:509–10).

Sometimes we hear members of the Church speak of these two men being "Jewish prophets." It does not say *two Jewish prophets* will be raised up, but that these two prophets will be *raised up to the Jewish nation*. This wording does not require that they be Jewish by lineage.

Note how John's words clearly show that this will happen in our day, the *last days*, particularly after the time of the Restoration. This confirms that John is not seeing his own day. But the timing is made even more precise when it says that this happens *after they [the Jews] are gathered and have built the city of Jerusalem in the land of their fathers*. The Jews began returning to their homeland in significant numbers in the late nineteenth century, but they didn't actually get their own country until May 1948.

One last note about these two witnesses. The Greek word translated here as *witness* is *martus*. As in English, the word can carry two meanings. The first is to testify to something after seeing it happen. In a deeper sense, particularly for Christians, witnesses were those who had proved that their faith or testimony was so strong that they would even give their life for it if necessary. These we call *martyrs*. At the time John wrote the book of Revelation, Christians, including John himself, were being severely persecuted by Rome. In the opening verses of the book of Revelation, John reminds us that the Savior was a faithful "witness," or martyr (Revelation 1:5), then tells his readers that he is their "brother, and companion in tribulation," and that currently he was on the Isle of Patmos, which was a Roman "prison island" because of His "testimony" (or witness) of Jesus (Revelation 1:9).

Thus John calls these two Apostles both prophets and witnesses. As we shall see, these two are to be witnesses in both senses of the word.

Finally, they wore sackcloth, which is a sign of mourning. It is likely that this symbolizes their sorrow for the evil and wickedness of the world and for the great suffering and devastation that is going on all around them at this time.

> These are the two olive trees, and the two candlesticks standing before the God of the earth (Revelation 11:4).

This confirms that these are the same two prophets that Zechariah saw. We have two different symbolic images here: two olive trees and two candlesticks. The "two" obviously suggests that they refer to the two prophets themselves. One Christian scholar summed up the imagery of the two witnesses in these words: "They are compared to two olive trees and candlesticks because they give forth the light of the truth of Christ and are fed with the oil of divine grace" (Dummelow, *One Volume Bible Commentary*, 1081). We could also say that they are fed by the oil of the Holy Spirit (see D&C 45:56–57).

> And if any man will hurt them, fire proceedeth out of their mouth, and devoureth their enemies: and if any man will hurt them, he must in this manner be killed. These have power to shut heaven, that it rain not in the days of their prophecy: and have power over waters to turn them to blood, and to smite the earth with all plagues, as often as they will (Revelation 11:5–6).

John now gives us an indication of how it is that these two prophets are able to hold back the mighty power of Gog and his armies. He notes three things: They emit fire that devours their enemies. They can call down drought upon the earth. And they have the power to turn water to blood and smite the earth with plagues.

Fire spewing from their mouths may be a symbolic expression referring to them speaking the word of God through the power of the Holy Spirit, which is likened unto fire (see D&C 45:56–57; see also Revelation 1:16).

Next it tells us that these two witnesses will have power to shut the heavens and stop the rains. Again this may have both literal and symbolic interpretations. To shut the heavens sometimes is a metaphor for a coming drought. It has also been used as a metaphor that the Lord is no longer speaking to and blessing His people. And finally, on the literal side, calling down fire from heaven was exactly what Elijah did with the priests of Baal, and he also brought on a drought just before that (see 1 Kings 17–18). Nephi was also given the power to bring on a drought to get the people to repent (see Helaman 11). This power to shut the heavens is one method the Lord uses to help bring His people back to the covenant.

Turning water to blood and calling down other plagues is a clear reference to another of the greatest of the Old Testament prophets. That's how Moses was able to get Pharaoh to free the children of Israel, calling down plagues, including turning the water to blood. Fire was also brought down to hold Pharaoh and his army back until the Israelites crossed over to the other side.

What a powerful promise these few verses hold. How is it possible that two mortal men could hold back the massive, powerful, fully equipped and superbly trained army described by Ezekiel and Joel? *They* can't! Not on their own. But when they are filled with the power of two of the greatest Old Testament prophets and use that power to carry out God's will, even the vast armies of Gog cannot stop them.

GOG TRIUMPHANT . . . GOG DESTROYED

John was shown how the power, the might, and the overwhelming numbers of Gog and his army were held back from defeat for three and a half years, which may be a literal amount of time or a symbolic one. These two ordained and anointed Apostles of The Church of Jesus Christ of Latter-day Saints bring with them power from on high to such a degree that the almost numberless army will be blocked from achieving their final goal—the conquest of Jerusalem.

> And when they shall have finished their testimony, the beast that ascendeth out of the bottomless pit [Gog and his armies] shall make war against them, and shall overcome them, and kill them. And their dead bodies shall lie in the street of the great city, which spiritually is called Sodom and Egypt, where also our Lord was crucified. And they of the people and kindreds and tongues and nations shall see their dead bodies three days and an half, and shall not suffer their dead bodies to be put in graves. And they that dwell upon the earth shall rejoice over them, and make merry, and shall send gifts one to another; because these two prophets tormented them that dwelt on the earth (Revelation 11:7–10).

Dead! Our two prophets are suddenly dead? How can that be? They are the salvation of Jerusalem, the only hope for what few of the Lord's people have survived the siege and the battles surrounding it. For that matter, it appears that they were the only hope for the world to avoid ending up as slaves in the first truly global dictatorship in history. It is a stunning turn of events. Let's examine what John describes more closely.

The title "the beast from the bottomless pit" is slightly different from the title for Gog ("the beast from the sea"), and the title for the ecclesiastical leader ("the beast from the earth"), and the title for Satan ("the angel of the bottomless pit"). So is not clear what John means here. Maybe he uses a term that includes all three, for all three are the leaders and are acting as one in this battle against the forces of good, led by these two witnesses.

Something that is surprising is that John describes Jerusalem at this time not as a holy city at all, likening it to Sodom and Egypt, two places in the ancient world that were so renowned for their wickedness that, like Babylon and Rome, they became types and symbols of gross evil. John makes it absolutely clear that this refers to Old Jerusalem when he adds, "where . . . our Lord was crucified." Does that mean that a majority of the Jews living there were no longer faithful to the covenant? Or could it be that by this time Jerusalem has largely become a Gentile city inhabited by the forces of Armageddon? It could imply that in those three and a half years of siege, Gog's army has taken over much of the city and now constitutes a large part of the population.

What John very clearly shows is that the death of these two prophets was a cause for great rejoicing and celebration, not just in Jerusalem but across the entire globe. That says much about the reach of Gog's influence and the state of the world at this time. They celebrate because the primary obstacle to their success has now been removed.

During the prophets' ministry of forty-two months, Gog and his godless followers have been held back by two men, men that they must despise and detest. Now it's over. Exultant at this sudden turn of events, Gog turns his troops loose on the city to loot, pillage, rape, burn, and murder with unrestricted abandon. But again, it is not just in Jerusalem that the celebrations go on. All the *people, kindreds, tongues,* and *nations* of the world rejoice.

Knowing what technology is today, we can suppose that at this time the news of the prophets' deaths would be sent out over the satellite systems of the world, probably accompanied with live video and on-the-spot reports. John says that all people, kindreds, tongues, and nations will join in the celebration. How many of the wildly celebrating members of Gog's followers who are there in Jerusalem will take "selfies" with the two bodies and post them on whatever social networks are in vogue at that time?

Zechariah also describes what that "celebration" will include. With the two prophets dead, Gog now seems to turn his troops loose on the city: "The city shall be taken, and the houses rifled, and the women ravished; and half of the city shall go forth into captivity" (Zechariah 14:2).

Evidently, the order is given—most likely from Gog himself—that the two bodies are to be left where they fell. That shouldn't surprise us. They provide dramatic, shocking, visible proof that the two are now dead. Feeds would go out worldwide so that all could join in the celebration, rejoicing, and debauchery going on in Old Jerusalem. And this will continue for three and a half days, which in this case, could be the actual time. What a horrible time that will be, for the bodies are left for all to see for three and a half days, and nothing restrains the horror going on in the city.

Isaiah seems to have been shown the same time, though he doesn't specifically tie it to Armageddon. What he saw is very similar to the horror that Zechariah saw. "Every one that is found *shall be thrust through;* and every one that is joined unto them *shall fall by the sword.* Their children also shall be dashed to pieces before their eyes; *their houses shall be spoiled,* and *their wives ravished*" (Isaiah 13:15–16).

Then, as abruptly as the celebration had begun, it comes to an abrupt and stunning end, and a shock wave races out across the whole world.

> And after three days and an half the Spirit of life from God entered into them, and they stood upon their feet; and great fear fell upon them which saw them. And they heard a great voice from heaven saying unto them, Come up hither. And they ascended up to heaven in a cloud; and their enemies beheld them (Revelation 11:11–12).

One moment the forces of evil are dancing around two dead bodies in a wild and most likely drunken celebration, then suddenly, even as their eyes refuse to believe what they see, the two bodies stir and get to their feet in plain sight of all that are there. John's description is an apt one, though understated: *"And great fear fell upon them."* Talk about a stunning moment. Talk about chills racing up and down your spine. Talk about being struck dumb. Some will certainly faint dead away. Wild panic would be another natural result.

But that's just the beginning. As the men get to their feet, the heavens themselves thunder out, "Come up hither." And all of those who haven't fainted will stand gaping as they watch the two figures ascend in a cloud.

We need to remember that most of those present at that moment will have embraced the philosophies of various antichrists and the philosophies of men. They don't believe in God. They don't believe in life after death. They don't believe there is any accountability for one's choices, that anything goes. So now, in one gut-wrenching moment, their shock will be greatly magnified as the realization that everything they have believed is now dramatically and irrefutably proven to be wrong. Surely this will be one of those times when they "would fain be glad if [they] could command the rocks and the mountains to fall upon [them] us to hide [them] from his presence" (Alma 12:14).

SUMMARY AND CONCLUSIONS

And what of those around the world who have kept the faith, who have stayed on the covenant path, who have been watching this global disaster unfold with heavy hearts. Think of the rejoicing that will be happening at this same time too. All the years of waiting and acting on faith that the prophecies will sometime be fulfilled, are now fulfilled.

And this miraculous rising from the dead is not the end of the remarkable events that are to take place at some future time in Old Jerusalem.

CHAPTER 26

"THEN SHALL THEY KNOW"

I hope we are all familiar with these words of the Lord and with his predictions concerning other coming events . . . because upon a knowledge of them, and an assurance of their reality . . . rests the efficacy of Christ's admonition, "be not troubled." . . . The Lord has given us no reason to think it will be easy to stay on course. As a matter of fact, he said that deception would become so persuasive that if it were possible, the very elect shall be deceived. Neither has he promised that the impending calamities will be miraculously turned aside nor that through the wisdom of men they can be averted. They are upon us because men have refused to be led by the living God. Generally speaking, men have rejected him and have chosen to put their trust in their own wisdom. In this they have made a terrible, tragic mistake. All history vindicates, and coming events will vindicate, the prophet's statement, "Cursed is he that putteth his trust in the arm of flesh." (Marion G. Romney, in Conference Report, October 1966, 52)

A GREAT EARTHQUAKE—PERHAPS THE GREATEST EVER

John the Revelator now completes his description of the events in Jerusalem of old by describing what happens immediately after the two prophets are seen being taken up into heaven. He provides details not found elsewhere in scripture:

> And the same hour was there a great earthquake, and the tenth part of the city fell, and in the earthquake were slain of men seven thousand: and the remnant were affrighted, and gave glory to the God of heaven (Revelation 11:13).

The *same hour* clearly refers to the taking up of the two prophets into heaven. John says that a "tenth part" of the city fell, which may suggest widespread but not totally devastating damage. As noted earlier, the number seven anciently was often used to symbolize fullness or completion, or even perfection. It is hard to tell if he uses that in this sense or if this is another "round" number.

"Remnants" may at first suggest anyone who survived the effects of the quake, good or evil. But there may be something more to John's choice of words here. The first thing to note is that those who were spared gave glory to God for their good fortune. One would expect that the truly wicked would give thanks for being "missed," but would not instantly turn back to religion.

One possible explanation is that the word *remnant* is often used to describe the surviving members of the house of Israel in the latter days. For example, in the Book of Mormon, "remnant" and "Israel" are linked together sixteen times, and in the Old Testament seventeen times, and many of those uses are speaking of Israel in the last days.

We're not saying that John was stating that the only ones killed were Gog's people. And seeing the two prophets raised from the dead and caught up to heaven, combined with experiencing an earthquake, could certainly have changed some pretty hard-hearted souls. It is difficult to say, because John says no more about them in this context, but goes on to describe the joy in heaven that the end has finally come. But from other prophecies that we shall examine now, we see that from this point on, it is a specific remnant of the house of Israel—that is, the Jews—that become the focus of what follows this massive earthquake.

A major earthquake just prior to Christ's coming is something that is described by numerous prophets. Some even speak of the heavens being shaken as well. Here is a sampling:

> And it shall come to pass at the same time when Gog shall come against the land of Israel, saith the Lord God, that my fury shall come up in my face. For in my jealousy and in the fire of my wrath have I spoken, Surely in that day *there shall be a great shaking in the land of Israel;* So that the *fishes of the sea,* and the *fowls of the heaven,* and the *beasts of the field,* and *all creeping things* that creep upon the earth, and *all the men that are upon the face of the earth, shall shake at my presence,* and the mountains shall be thrown down, and the steep places shall fall, and every wall shall fall to the ground (Ezekiel 38:18–20).

And he [Christ] shall utter his voice out of Zion, and he shall speak from Jerusalem, and his voice shall be heard among all people; And it shall be a voice as the voice of many waters [like a large waterfall], and as the voice of a great thunder, *which shall break down the mountains, and the valleys shall not be found* (D&C 133:21–22).

The details given here are quite remarkable and very sobering. Who would think that an earthquake could affect fish in the sea and birds in the air? "Creeping things" usually refers to insects, worms, snails, etc. And they are affected too? And note that this quake will be felt upon the whole face of the earth, not just in one location. How high will a quake like that register on the Richter scale? This could suggest that this is more than just a very powerful earthquake, but the most powerful quake the world has ever experienced.

Here are some other observations. We noted earlier in the book that history will repeat itself when Gog and his forces "compass Jerusalem," just as the Romans did three decades after Christ's death. Well, that seems to be the case here too. When Christ was crucified, an earthquake struck Jerusalem powerfully enough to rip open many graves and tear the veil of the temple (see Matthew 27:50–54).

At that same time in the Americas, massive natural disasters struck, including powerful earthquakes strong enough to bury coastal cities in the depths of the seas, to have mountains fall on cities—probably through massive landslides or volcanic activity—burying them in ash or lava or setting them on fire (see 3 Nephi 8). Immediately afterward, the resurrected Christ appeared to the Nephites, ushering in two hundred years of a Zion-like society.

And now, to bring an end to the war and awful wickedness of Armageddon, another earthquake (or perhaps series of earthquakes) strikes again, only this time it is powerful enough to shake the entire world and the heavens.

So let us see what else is associated with this moment in the future. A couple of things to note: The breaking down of the mountains and the raising of the valleys also suggests significant seismic activity. Most of us have never experienced a mega-quake and so do not fully understand the power that can be unleashed. In an 8.8 earthquake off the coast of Santiago, Chile, on February 27, 2010, the force was so powerful that seismologists estimate that it even shifted the earth slightly off its axis. They discovered later that the entire city of Concepción, with a population of about 750,000, was moved ten feet to the west.

The day after Christmas in 2004, the earthquake that struck in the

Indian Ocean off the coast of Indonesia caused a rupture along 900 miles of the fault line. It is still considered the largest known rupture in the earth's crust to have been caused by an earthquake. It was so powerful it triggered other quakes as far away as Alaska, about 7,600 miles to the north.

The key point to remember is that with it will occur what will be, without question, the greatest turning point in the history of the world, for what happens in Old Jerusalem following the earthquake is the immediate prelude to Christ's Second Coming and the ushering in of His reign on earth as King of kings and Lord of lords, as John saw in vision (see Revelation 19:11–16). Let us turn to the prophets and let them teach us what they foresaw through the visions of heaven.

THE SAVIOR MAKES AN APPEARANCE IN OLD JERUSALEM

There are billions of people around the world who know about the Second Coming of Jesus Christ—mostly the three Abrahamic religions. Fewer, but still a large number, believe that it is a real event that is coming in the future. Most think it is important to prepare themselves for that day, both spiritually and temporally. For Latter-day Saints, this is part of our core doctrine.

The Bible speaks of the Second Coming in both the Old and New Testaments. But it is through modern scripture that we are taught that there is not just one coming of Christ, but four comings, the last of which will be what we call *the* Second Coming. We are not speaking of what we might term "personal appearances," when He was seen by only one or two people, such as when He appeared in the Kirtland Temple to Joseph Smith and Oliver Cowdery. These are times when He makes an appearance to whole groups of people.

The first two, which we have already discussed, are His visit to His temple in New Jerusalem (see chapter 19) and His coming to the great council at Adam-ondi-Ahman (see chapter 23).

The Savior's third appearance is quite different from the first two. In those cases, He will come to gatherings of His faithful Saints, those we have designated as "true or covenant Israel." But this appearance will be to a group who do not even recognize Him at first. This will be such a startling experience for them that their first reaction will be one of deep shock, perhaps even fear. There is another surprising element of this third visit. He will come while the battle of Armageddon is still raging.

"Then Shall They Know"

In the appendix to the Doctrine and Covenants (section 133), we find many important teachings about the last days and Christ's Second Coming. It tells of glorious things to come before, during, and after that great event. In that revelation there is a specific invitation extended to His covenant people:

> Wherefore, prepare ye for the coming of the Bridegroom; go ye, go ye out to meet him. For behold, *he shall stand upon the mount of Olivet,* and upon the mighty ocean, even the great deep, and upon the islands of the sea, and upon the land of Zion. And he shall utter his voice out of Zion, and he shall speak from Jerusalem, and his voice shall be heard among all people (D&C 133:19–21).

This invitation suggests that His Saints will be found everywhere in the world in the last days, and that no matter where they may be, they are to go out to meet Him. This will be part of the actual Second Coming of Christ, for this is the "wedding supper," which symbolizes our joining into a covenant contract with Him, which is likened to the eternal commitment a husband and wife make with each other (see Matthew 22:1–14; Matthew 25:1–13).

As with the first two comings, here we are also told the exact location where He will appear. It will be on the "mount of Olivet," more commonly known to us as the Mount of Olives. The scriptures make it clear that the Mount of Olives is the actual place where this meeting will take place. Other prophets have also described this meeting.

In the closing chapter of his book, Zechariah described what we call the battle of Armageddon. In verse one, he states that "the day of the Lord cometh," then adds the description of the final days of Armageddon that we have already noted: "For I will gather all nations against Jerusalem to battle; and the city shall be taken, and the houses rifled, and the women ravished; and half of the city shall go forth into captivity, and the residue [another word for remnant] of the people shall not be cut off from the city" (Zechariah 14:2).

This seems to be happening during those awful three days when the two prophets lie dead in the streets of Jerusalem. But what immediately follows is a description of His third appearance:

> Then shall the Lord go forth, and fight against those nations, as when he fought in the day of battle. *And his feet shall stand in that day upon the mount of Olives,* which is before Jerusalem on the east, and the mount of Olives shall cleave in the midst thereof toward the east and toward the west, and there shall be a very great valley; and half of the mountain shall remove toward the north, and

half of it toward the south. And ye shall flee to the valley of the mountains; for the valley of the mountains shall reach unto Azal (Zechariah 14:3–5).

It is interesting that Zechariah saw the Lord *standing* on the Mount, not hovering in the air above it. This appears to be because of what follows. Earlier Zechariah gave us two other things that we can link to His coming to the Mount of Olives:

> I will pour upon the house of David, and upon the inhabitants of Jerusalem, the spirit of grace and of supplications: and *they shall look upon me whom they have pierced,* and they shall mourn for him. . . . In that day shall there be a great mourning in Jerusalem (Zechariah 12:10–11).

> And one shall say unto him, What are these *wounds in thine hands?* Then he shall answer, *Those with which I was wounded in the house of my friends* (Zechariah 13:6).

The Mount of Olives is one of several high ridges upon which the city of Jerusalem is built. Going from west to east, it is the last ridge before the land drops into the wilderness of Judea, the Jordan River, and the Dead Sea. Also, Olivet lies directly east of the Temple Mount, or Mount Moriah, and there is a deep valley—the Kidron Valley—between them. The Olivet ridge runs north to south for about two miles.

The earthquake creates a *"very great valley"* (Zechariah 14:4). This valley is not the Kidron Valley that is already there, but describes the split in the Mount of Olives itself. This rift divides Olivet into two sections, one to the north and one to the south, with this new "valley" running from west to east through what was before the Kidron Valley and the Mount of Olives. To confirm that, Zechariah specifically says that cleavage in the mountain ran east and west (see Zechariah 14:4).

This newly created valley would thus provide a natural escape route for those residents in the city trying to escape the rampages of Gog and his armies and the effects of the earthquake.

The *valley of the mountains* is likely a reference to the River Jordan Valley, which nestles between the hill country of Judea—where Jerusalem is—on the west and the mountains of Moab on the other side of the River Jordan.

Zechariah ends his narrative there. From his brief comments linked with other scriptures, we can come up with a possible reconstruction of what will happen once this split in the mount is discovered. Remember that just before the earthquake, there will be utter chaos in Jerusalem. Gog's army and followers will go on a wild rampage through the city, celebrating the death of the two prophets. After three days, just when it appears that all is lost, suddenly a great earthquake strikes the city, and the Mount of Olives is divided in two.

It appears that, on seeing the result of the quake, a group of surviving citizens of Jerusalem realize that suddenly there is a possible escape route. Fleeing desperately, they race out of the city. Since this was created in a massive quake, it is likely that the route will be filled with debris and the way will not be easy.

Though we are not told who will be part of that group, the likelihood that it includes families would be high. Fearful that their enemies might follow them, they would rush forward, all thoughts on getting free from the chaos behind them. As we shall see, the implication of what we are next told is that these are Jews,[1] residents of Jerusalem, who know of the idea of a Messiah but now are looking only for escape. There

> *Another appearance of the Lord will be to the Jews. To these beleaguered sons of Judah, surrounded by hostile Gentile armies, who again threaten to overrun Jerusalem, the Savior—their Messiah—will set His feet on the Mount of Olives, "and it shall cleave in twain." The Lord Himself will then rout the Gentile armies, decimating their forces. Judah will be spared, no longer to be persecuted and scattered. The Jews will then approach their Deliverer and ask, "What are these wounds in thine hands and in thy feet?" . . . What a touching drama this will be! Jesus—Prophet, Messiah, King—will be welcomed in His own country! Jerusalem will become an eternal city of peace. The sons of Judah will see this promise fulfilled: "After their pain, [the tribe of Judah] shall be sanctified in holiness before the Lord, to dwell in his presence day and night, forever and ever."*
>
> Ezra Taft Benson,
> Come unto Christ, 114

may be others who join them in this flight, but we are not given more details.

These next and most important details come from section 45 of the Doctrine and Covenants, another account of the Olivet Discourse. In this section, there are details not found anywhere else in scripture.

Then shall the arm of the Lord fall upon the nations. And then

---

1 Remember that "Jew" can be a descendant of the tribe of Judah, a generic term for anyone of the house of Israel, those who are of ethnic Jewish descent, or someone who accepts Judaism. The context here does not indicate how the term is used.

shall the *Lord set his foot upon this mount,* and it shall cleave in twain, and the earth shall tremble, and reel to and fro, and the heavens also shall shake. And the Lord shall utter his voice, and all the ends of the earth shall hear it; and the nations of the earth shall mourn, and they that have laughed shall see their folly. And calamity shall cover the mocker, and the scorner shall be consumed; and they that have watched for iniquity shall be hewn down and cast into the fire (D&C 45:47–50).

This clearly establishes that this is to take place in a future day. "Then" seems to refer to immediately after the resurrection of the two prophets, when the earthquake strikes the city. "Then" also includes that moment when the terrified citizens of Jerusalem discover that they now have a way to escape. And as they rush down that path to safety, it happens. They see a figure standing ahead of them, waiting for them. That would very likely create fear and panic. Is this someone there to block their escape?

And then shall *the Jews look upon me* and say: What are these wounds in thine hands and in thy feet? *Then shall they know that I am the Lord;* for I will say unto them: These wounds are the wounds with which I was wounded in the house of my friends. I am he who was lifted up. I am Jesus that was crucified. I am the Son of God (D&C 45:51–52).

What an incredible moment of shock and joy that will be. How we would love to have more details of that event. How wondrous it will be when someone there will record that moment for future generations.

The Jews have been waiting for their Messiah for thousands of years. They have been killed, captured, driven, and enslaved by their enemies. In the classic movie *Fiddler on the Roof,* Tevye was asked as they were being driven from their village, "Wouldn't now be a good time for our Messiah to come?" Certainly, this could be going through the minds of this remnant of the house of Israel as Gog ravages the city and its inhabitants.

Jesus evidently will extend His arms to welcome them. Do they immediately realize that this is their Messiah, come to save them? They know of the prophecies of the Old Testament prophets. It would be natural that in this grand miracle of deliverance, some at least would realize that the Messiah has finally come to save them.

But they are not ready for what they see: the scars on His hands and wrists, the scar in His side, and the scars on His feet. And they are stunned and cry, "What are these wounds?"

And then—most likely in a voice filled with love and compassion and not rebuke—He says, "These are the wounds with which I was wounded in the house of my friends, my people, the people that I came to earth to save."

And finally, so that there can be no mistake, no question, no uncertainty, He answers: *"I am he who was lifted up. I am Jesus that was crucified. I am the Son of God"* (D&C 45:52).

What a moment that will be. And what a turning point for the house of Israel.

Zechariah gives us some details in his prophecy: "And I will pour upon the house of David, and upon the inhabitants of Jerusalem, the spirit of grace and of supplications: and they shall look upon me whom they have pierced, and *they shall mourn* for him, as one mourneth for his only son. . . . In that day shall there be *a great mourning in Jerusalem*" (Zechariah 12:10–11).

Isaiah also seemed to be speaking of this time when he compared it to a whole nation being born in a day, reborn into the covenant they had abandoned so long ago:

> Who hath heard such a thing? who hath seen such things? Shall the earth be made to bring forth in one day? or *shall a nation be born at once?* for as soon as Zion travailed, she brought forth her children. . . . *Rejoice ye with Jerusalem, and be glad with her, all ye that love her: rejoice for joy with her, all ye that mourn for her* (Isaiah 66:8, 10).

AFTERMATH

We have now seen how the Lord intervened through His two prophets to hold off Gog and his monumental number of soldiers for three and a half years. We have seen the awful aftermath of what happened when those prophets were killed. And we have seen how a group of Jerusalemites escaped when an earthquake opened up an avenue that led to safety by splitting the Mount of Olives in two.

So, what do these dramatic events mean for Gog and his almost numberless armies? After the earthquake, then what? Are they all killed in the earthquake? Do any survivors simply realize they've lost and go home? Do they try to regroup and continue the battle?

There is always the aftermath of war that follows the end of hostilities. There is the rebuilding of homes, businesses, and even whole cities. There is farmland to reclaim, forests to restore, water sources to be purified, the dead to be buried, the restoration of law and order, caring for the victims of war until normalcy returns, *ad infinitum*. Do the prophets talk about this at all?

This is a key question because, as we shall see in the next chapter, the scriptures make it clear that the Second Coming of Jesus Christ follows very soon—perhaps even immediately—after Christ's appearance on the Mount of Olives. And as we shall also see, Christ's coming then ushers in His millennial reign. How can we have a world of peace with a Gog on the loose? Therefore, the conclusive event of the battle of Armageddon must signal his end and the end to the wickedness, depravity, and evil of the world. If that were not so, how would we set up enclaves of Zion across the world?

Do the prophets talk about this aftermath? Yes, some do. And it is not a pleasant thing, but it does answer some of our questions. They were commanded to make a record of what followed, the end of Gog and his mighty army. Here is what the prophets have said about what follows the death and resurrection of the two prophets. Some of these declarations specifically speak of the end of Gog, the antichrist who partners with him, and the army of the wicked that they bring with them. Others speak of the judgments that will prepare the world for the coming of Jesus Christ.

- *John the Revelator:* "And there fell upon men *a great hail out of heaven,* every stone about the weight of a talent: and men blasphemed God because of the plague of the hail; for *the plague thereof was exceedingly great*" (Revelation 16:21; see also 11:19).

    "I saw an angel . . . ; and he cried with a loud voice, saying to all the fowls that fly in the midst of heaven, *Come and gather yourselves together unto the supper of the great God;* That ye may eat the flesh of kings, and the flesh of captains, and the flesh of mighty men, and the flesh of horses, and of them that sit on them, and the flesh of all men, both free and bond, both small and great, . . . And the beast was taken, and with him the false prophet that wrought miracles before him. . . . *These both were cast alive into a lake of fire burning with brimstone*" (Revelation 19:17–18, 20–21).

- *Isaiah:* "For, behold, *the Lord will come with fire,* and with his chariots like a whirlwind, to render his anger with fury, and his rebuke with flames of fire. For *by fire and by his sword will the Lord plead with all flesh: and the slain of the Lord shall be many*" (Isaiah 66:15–16; see also Isaiah 34:2–10).

- *Zechariah:* "And this shall be the plague wherewith the Lord will smite all the people that have fought against Jerusalem; *Their flesh shall consume away while they stand upon their feet,* and their eyes shall consume away in their holes, and their tongue shall consume away in their mouth. . . . And they shall *lay hold every one on the hand of his neighbour, and his hand shall rise up against the hand of his neighbour"* (Zechariah 14:12–13).

- *Joseph Smith:* "And it shall come to pass, because of the wickedness of the world, that I will take vengeance upon the wicked, for they will not repent; for the cup of mine indignation is full; for behold, my blood shall not cleanse them if they hear me not. Wherefore, I the Lord God will send forth *flies upon the face of the earth,* which shall *take hold of the inhabitants thereof, and shall eat their flesh, and shall cause maggots to come in upon them;* And *their tongues shall be stayed* that they shall not utter against me; *and their flesh shall fall from off their bones, and their eyes from their sockets;* And it shall come to pass that *the beasts of the forest and the fowls of the air shall devour them up.* And the great and abominable church [which will be led by Gog and his "spiritual" cohort] . . . shall be cast down by devouring fire, according as it is spoken by the mouth of Ezekiel the prophet . . . , which have not come to pass but surely must" (D&C 29:17–21).
- *Ezekiel:* "It shall come to pass at the same time when Gog shall come against the land of Israel, saith the Lord God, that my fury shall come up in my face. For in my jealousy and in the fire of my wrath have I spoken, Surely in that day there shall be a great shaking in the land of Israel. . . . And I will call for a sword against him throughout all my mountains, saith the Lord God: *every man's sword shall be against his brother.* And I will plead against him with *pestilence* and with *blood;* and I *will rain upon him,* and upon his bands, and upon the many people that are with him, *an overflowing rain, and great hailstones, fire, and brimstone"* (Ezekiel 38:18–22).

"Therefore, thou son of man, prophesy against Gog, and say, Thus saith the Lord God; Behold, I am against thee, O Gog, the chief prince of Meshech and Tubal: And I will turn thee back, and *leave but the sixth part of thee* [five-sixths of two hundred million would be a death count of about one hundred and seventy million!]. . . . And I will smite thy bow out of thy left hand, and will cause thine arrows to fall out of thy right hand. *Thou shalt fall upon the mountains of Israel,* thou, and all thy bands, and the people that is with thee*: I will give thee unto the ravenous birds of every sort, and to the beasts of the field* to be devoured. . . . And I will send a fire on Magog [the land from which Gog came], and among them that dwell carelessly in the isles: and they shall know that I am the Lord" (Ezekiel 39:1–6).

These descriptions are so horrific, so awful, so dreadful, that the mind recoils from even dwelling on them. We therefore shall let them stand without further comment, except to make one clarification.

John said that the hailstones were about the size of a talent. In ancient times, most money was determined by weight. Even coins were minted by weight. Talents were the largest monetary measure of weight. Scholars estimate that generally a talent weighed between 45 and 75 pounds. Thus even one talent of gold represented a substantial fortune.

For our purposes here, let's say that a talent weighed 50 pounds. So if we had hailstones the size of a talent, how big would they be? Years ago, a meteorologist friend told me that he had calculated that if we are speaking of hail as being made of ice, a fifty-pound ice ball would be approximately the size of a basketball. Most of us have seen the extensive damage that hail the size of baseballs can do, so we can assume that basketball-sized hail would wreak enormous damage. Such a hail could devastate even an enormously large army in a very short amount of time.

One other thought on hailstones. In his description, Ezekiel linked these "great hailstones" to "fire and brimstone." *Brimstone* is an English word that does not really convey the original meaning of the Hebrew word. The better translation would be "resin," the gum that comes from various plants and trees and that is highly flammable. Because of that, the word *brimstone* came to be associated with any highly flammable materials, especially sulfur.

Figuratively, brimstone is associated with destruction and punishment, both of which would describe what is happening to Gog. We know that Sodom and Gomorrah were destroyed by fire and brimstone (see Genesis 19:24). We also know that sulfur and other flammable substances are found in volcanoes. This is often why rocks and debris are hurled from a volcano when it violently explodes, producing what could be described as fire raining down from heaven. That could also explain the phrases "the elements shall melt with fervent heat" (3 Nephi 26:3; 2 Peter 3:10, 12; D&C 101:25) and the "mountains flow down at thy presence" (D&C 133:44).

We shall close this chapter with Ezekiel's further description of the end of Gog and his vast armies of evil. Once again we are indebted to Ezekiel, who has taught us so much about Gog and the coalition of nations that led us to the final battle of Armageddon. As we noted above, trying to restore normalcy after a major war is a huge task. And this last great war will be the greatest war ever. So when it is over, think of the vastness of the cleanup efforts. What Ezekiel describes is the aftermath of the destruction of a massive army.

Ezekiel gives us some idea of the immensity of the task of putting things back together again. He is quite vivid in his descriptions of what followed the earthquake and Christ's appearing to the Jews. He obviously has to use words and concepts from his time to describe what he was shown in our modern day and age. For example, he describes the weapons of war left behind when the war is over as "bows and arrows and spears." We're pretty sure that Gog's army will come armed with all the modern weaponry and equipment available, but Ezekiel can only describe what he sees in words drawn from his own experience.

> It is done, saith the Lord God; this is the day whereof I have spoken. And *they that dwell in the cities of Israel* shall go forth, and shall set on fire and burn the weapons, both *the shields and the bucklers, the bows and the arrows, and the handstaves, and the spears,* and they shall burn them with fire *seven years* (Ezekiel 39:8–9).

Ezekiel uses the number seven several times in the chapter, which, as we have said before, could be used in a metaphorical way, as if he were saying, "The amount the weapons left behind was innumerable."

> So that they shall take no wood out of the field, neither cut down any out of the forests; for they shall burn the weapons with fire: and they shall spoil those that spoiled them, and rob those that robbed them, saith the Lord God (vv. 10).

The supplies of food, equipment, tools, and the many other materials required to support and sustain an army of that size would be enormous. So the survivors in Israel at that time will live off some of the spoils left behind for a long time afterward.

Next he turns to one of the grimmest of the cleanup tasks and one of the realities of war:

> And it shall come to pass in that day, that I will give unto Gog a place there of graves in Israel, . . . and there shall they bury Gog and all his multitude: . . . *And seven months shall the house of Israel be burying* of them, that they may cleanse the land. Yea, *all the people of the land shall bury them;* . . . And they shall sever out *men of continual employment,* passing through the land to bury with the passengers those that remain upon the face of the earth, to cleanse it: after the end of seven months shall they search. And the passengers [passersby] that pass through the land, *when any seeth a*

man's bone, then shall he set up a sign by it, till the buriers have buried it.... Thus shall they cleanse the land" (Ezekiel 39:11–16).

His vivid imagery here needs no further explanation on our part.

SUMMARY AND CONCLUSIONS

Ezekiel concludes his vision with a tribute to God, who had been mocked by Gog and his armies and most of the rest of the world. "Then shall [the house of Israel] know that I am the Lord their God, which caused them to be led into captivity among the heathen: but I have gathered them unto their own land, and have left none of them any more there" (Ezekiel 39:28).

As we end our study of the battle of Armageddon and the age of war that preceded it, we are left with a feeling of horror, but also awe at what is to come in the future. The horror comes in the descriptions that the prophets were inspired to share with us. But awe and a great feeling of reverential gratitude follows, because this story of the last great war gives us an explanation of the Lord's purposes. Many people have asked: "How is it possible that we can move from a world of wickedness, depravity, violence, corruption, immorality, war, suffering, and horror to a world of perfect peace, happiness, harmony, safety, prosperity, growth, advancement, and progress?"

Armageddon is one of the answers, along with other signs of the times. Just as the Lord gathers His covenant people out of the world into places of safety, refuge, and peace, so does He let the wicked gather themselves into an ever-expanding coalition of evil. And the consequences of their vile choices bring the sword of destruction upon them. Many in the world will certainly be turned from their wickedness as this evil spreads through all nations.

CHAPTER 27

GREAT AND MARVELOUS CHANGES

And he shall utter his voice out of Zion, and he shall speak from Jerusalem, and his voice shall be heard among all people; And it shall be a voice as the voice of many waters, and as the voice of a great thunder, which shall break down the mountains, and the valleys shall not be found. He shall command the great deep, and it shall be driven back into the north countries, and the islands shall become one land; And the land of Jerusalem and the land of Zion shall be turned back into their own place, and the earth shall be like as it was in the days before it was divided. (D&C 133:21–24)

AND THE EARTH SHALL BE AS IT WAS BEFORE IT WAS DIVIDED

In the book of Genesis, there is a rather astonishing tidbit of information buried within a genealogical table. After saying that Noah lived an additional three hundred and fifty years after the flood, there follows "the generations of . . . Noah" (Genesis 10:1). This table is only of the three sons whose families were taken into the ark—Shem, Ham, and Japheth. From these three sprang the nations of the earth, since all but Noah's immediate family either died before the flood, were killed in the flood, or were taken into heaven to join the city of Enoch.

One of the sons of Shem was named Eber, from whom the word *Hebrew* comes. Eber had a son named Peleg, whose name in Hebrew means "division." Moses then added this brief note explaining his name: "For in his days was the earth divided" (Genesis 10:25).

No further explanation is given for that rather startling thought. Note that it says the *earth* was divided, not the *world*. Though sometimes we use those two words interchangeably, in the Bible, "earth" typically describes the planet on which we live, while "world" generally refers to the people and human culture that exist on the earth. "Worldly" often refers to those people living on the earth who turn to the things of the world rather than the things of God. The passage in Genesis makes it clear that it was the sphere we call the earth that was being divided.

Obviously this cannot suggest that the globe itself, which forms our planet, will divide in two. Perhaps a better way to say what Moses was suggesting might be something like "the surface areas of the earth, the lands on which we live, will be divided." But even that raises numerous questions.

When I was in high school, there was much discussion in our science classes about what some geologists were calling the "continental drift theory." In 1912, a geophysicist and meteorologist named Alfred Wegler drafted a theory that once upon a time in ages far past, the earth had been one large super-continent. He postulated that since the continents rest on tectonic plates that "float" on the liquid magma that forms the core of the earth, over eons of time, the land masses of the earth have slowly "drifted" apart. As evidence, he cited the approximate match—much like a jigsaw puzzle—between the eastern coastlines of North, Central, and South America with the west coastlines of Africa and Europe. He also noted many similar animal and plant fossils are found in the matching areas, as well as similar rock formations.

In our geology textbook, the theory was briefly mentioned but openly scorned by the experts. Today, with the wide acceptance of plate tectonics theory, most geologists accept the theory as highly plausible. However, they state that this drift took millions of years and could not have happened within the history of modern man—which means they would reject that intriguing statement from Genesis.

We are not here to argue or defend one theory or another. Our purpose is to discuss prophecy. And it may come as a surprise to many that there are several prophecies that suggest that sometime in the future, the earth's land masses may come back together again. We share these ideas here only because in some ways they could tie in to the great earthquake discussed in the previous chapter. However, the scriptures do not give us enough detail to provide definitive answers, only enough to tantalize our minds. Here are other prophetic passages:

> Therefore I will shake the heavens, and *the earth shall remove out of her place,* in the wrath of the Lord of hosts, and in the day of his fierce anger (Isaiah 13:13; see also 2 Nephi 23:13).

Know ye not that ye are in the hands of God? Know ye not that he hath all power, and at his great command *the earth shall be rolled together as a scroll?* (Mormon 5:23).

And there were voices, and thunders, and lightnings; and *there was a great earthquake, such as was not since men were upon the earth, so mighty an earthquake, and so great.* And the great city [Jerusalem] was divided into three parts, and the cities of the nations fell: and great Babylon came in remembrance before God, to give unto her the cup of the wine of the fierceness of his wrath. And *every island fled away, and the mountains were not found* (Revelation 16:18–20).

Though these are specific promises, it is a challenge to grasp the enormous implications of what the Lord is saying. Nevertheless, those passages seem pretty unambiguous, and definitely do not feel like the Lord is speaking metaphorically.

We must remember that we are being told that the earth will come together again by the Lord's prophets, and that it is the Lord who created our earth and numberless others like it. So it seems like even the best scientists cannot describe what the Lord can or cannot do.

A FOUNTAIN OF WATER: THE DEAD SEA HEALED

This is another prophecy that comes from the pen of Ezekiel, and, as with his other prophecies, contains great specificity. He speaks of a fountain or spring of water that comes forth from beneath the temple in Jerusalem. Though he does not say that it is directly connected to the earthquake that splits the Mount of Olives in two, such a quake could explain the loosing of an underground water source. Remember, the Temple Mount is directly west of the Mount of Olives, separated from it only by the Kidron Valley. So it would be quite natural for a water source on the Temple Mount to flow east into the Kidron Valley, or possibly into the opening made by the Mount of Olives splitting in two. Mount Moriah is higher than Olivet, so water could naturally flow in that direction

Three prophets speak of this fountain, and all three are prophets who taught us the most about Gog and the battle of Armageddon. The first two—Joel and Zechariah—mention it only briefly. But in what seems to have been a stewardship for him, Ezekiel devotes almost a full chapter to it.

Joel: "And a fountain shall come forth of the house of the Lord, and shall water the valley of Shittim" (Joel 3:18). A fountain in the Old Testament is what we in America would call a spring. It is a source of fresh, potable water that flows from the ground through natural forces. There are two possible sites for the valley of Shittim (pronounced sheh-TEEM). Both are near the Jordan Valley east of Jerusalem, a natural place for the water to go.

Zechariah: "In that day there shall be a fountain opened to the house of David and to the inhabitants of Jerusalem for sin and for uncleanness. . . . And it shall be in that day, that living waters shall go out from Jerusalem; half of them toward the former sea, and half of them toward the hinder sea [the Mediterranean Sea to the west and the Dead Sea to the east]: in summer and in winter shall it be" (Zechariah 13:1, 14:8).

The "house of David" is another way of saying the Jews, since David was of the tribe of Judah. "To the inhabitants of Jerusalem" confirms that it is within the city, though Zechariah does not tie it specifically to the Temple Mount. It clearly is potable water and therefore could be used for washing ceremonies found in the Mosaic law, including the washing of sacrificial animals, which required "living" water. "Living waters" in the Old Testament generally signifies water from a running source, such as a creek, river, or spring, not standing water such as a pond or lake. From Zechariah we learn that the flow of this fountain is sufficient to create a double river, one flowing east to the Dead Sea and one flowing west to the Mediterranean Sea. This suggests that the output of the spring is prodigious. It also flows year-round and therefore is not dependent on the local rainfall.

Since Ezekiel's description is the fullest, the most detailed, and the most amazing, we shall summarize the main elements, leaving the reader to study the actual text more carefully (see Ezekiel 47:1–12).

Ezekiel is seeing this in vision. The prophet was brought to the door of the temple, where he saw water coming from under the threshold and running past the great altar where the sacrifices of the Mosaic law were performed. Lehi also saw a vision of a fountain of "living waters," which led to the tree of life (see 1 Nephi 11:25). It is probably not the same fountain, but it conveys the same idea of living waters that bring eternal life.

The angel then takes Ezekiel to where the water was flowing eastward, which would be toward the Mount of Olives. No mention is made of its breadth, depth, or swiftness at this point. He does not describe the course the water takes, but an eastward flow would naturally flow into the River Jordan and then into the Dead Sea.

Ezekiel was shown a man with a rod who measures the flow of water every thousand cubits of length, which is about 1,500 feet or a third of a mile. At first, the water is to their ankles, then to their knees, then to their loins (or waist), and finally it is so deep and so swift that they cannot cross it safely.

What happens next is perhaps the most amazing aspect of this vision. Ezekiel's "guide" calls Ezekiel to the brink of the river, where he points out many trees on both sides of the river. This surprises Ezekiel, for this is the Judean wilderness, which is currently a harsh desert area with little natural rainfall.

His guide then gives Ezekiel more stunning news. He says that eventually the waters of the Dead Sea "shall be *healed.*" That is astonishing. Most people are aware that the Dead Sea is currently the lowest spot on the face of the planet. It is nestled in the lowest area of what is called the Great Rift Valley. This is a gigantic seismic tear in the earth's surface that runs from Turkey on the north to eastern Africa on the south. Geologists say that it was made when some cataclysmic shift in the tectonic plates pulled apart, leaving a deep rupture on the earth's surface.

Most people also know that the Dead Sea is one of the saltiest—if not the saltiest—bodies of water in the world, with nearly 34% salinity. Most of its shoreline is caked with salt crust and salt pillars. Because of that, virtually no vegetation grows along its immediate shores.

So theoretically, there is only one way the Dead Sea could be healed naturally. A flow of fresh water into the sea could only heal it if there were an outlet to let the water continue on to the south. This would eventually replace the salt water with fresh water and also wash away the salt along its shorelines.

However, currently, the surface of the Dead Sea is about 1,400 feet *below* sea level. If no change is made in the current topography, bringing enough water in to find an exit to the south into the Gulf of Aqaba would back the water up for more than a hundred miles to the north, flooding the Jordan River Valley, which contains some of the richest farmland in Israel, Jordan, and possibly Syria.

If, on the other hand—and this is pure speculation—the great earthquake we have been discussing were to thrust the Jordan Valley upward dramatically, that problem would be solved. Ezekiel, of course, was not shown how it was done, only the effect on the arid and desolate landscape around the Dead Sea. And for anyone who has been to the Dead Sea, or bobbed like a cork in its waters, his description is astonishing:

> Every thing that liveth, which moveth, whithersoever the rivers shall come, *shall live:* and there shall be a very *great multitude of fish,*

because these waters shall come thither: for they shall be healed; and *every thing shall live whither the river cometh.* And it shall come to pass, that the *fishers shall stand upon it;* . . . they shall be a place to spread forth nets; . . . And by the river upon the bank thereof, on this side and on that side, shall grow all trees for meat, whose leaf shall not fade, neither shall the fruit thereof be [completely] consumed (Ezekiel 47:9–12).

What Ezekiel saw in vision is absolutely incredible!

SUMMARY AND CONCLUSIONS

Here is a good example of the great and terrible signs of the times often occurring side by side with each other. On the one hand we find incomprehensible numbers coming into the Holy Land to wage war, pillage, and destroy. The eventual destruction and death toll is staggering. On the other hand, prophets of God are holding back those forces from totally conquering the people. At the last, the army breaks through and ravishes the city. Then a great earthquake comes and provides an escape route for those in Jerusalem. And those who were about to die find their Messiah there waiting for them. The army is fully destroyed. A new river springs up in Jerusalem and a dead sea is healed. A thousand years of peace is ushered in.

What an amazing time that will be in the long history of our sojourn on this planet.

CHAPTER 28

HE COMES!

He comes! The earth shakes, and the tall mountains tremble; the mighty deep rolls back to the north as in fear, and the rent skies glow like molten brass. He comes! The dead Saints burst forth from their tombs, and "those who are alive and remain" are "caught up" with them to meet him. The ungodly rush to hide themselves from his presence, and call upon the quivering rocks to cover them. He comes! with all the hosts of the righteous glorified. The breath of his lips strikes death to the wicked. His glory is a consuming fire. The proud and rebellious are as stubble; they are burned and "left neither root nor branch." He sweeps the earth "as with the besom of destruction." He deluges the earth with the fiery floods of his wrath, and the filthiness and abominations of the world are consumed. Satan and his dark hosts are taken and bound—the prince of the power of the air has lost his dominion, for he whose right it is to reign has come, and "the kingdoms of this world have become the kingdoms of our Lord and of his Christ." (Charles W. Penrose, *Millennial Star*, September, 1859, 583)

THE END AND THE BEGINNING

At last we come to the central focus of all that has been said up to this point and all that will be said hereafter.

As human beings, there is something in our psyche that is intrigued with the ultimates in life—the biggest, the most famous, the fastest, the smallest, the most expensive, the highest peak, the lowest valley, the deepest ocean, the rarest, the most common, the most bizarre. The Guinness World Records company has made a profitable business of tracking these ultimates for us.

When it comes to the history of the world, historians might have a difficult time agreeing on what event would rank as the most significant, the most impactful, the most influential thing that has ever happened in human history. But after all that we have read and studied in the scriptures, and all that we have studied together in this book, we have no hesitation to boldly declare: Far and away, above all else that has happened since the Fall of Adam and Eve and the coming forth of the crucified Christ from the tomb, the Second Coming of Jesus Christ and the ushering in of the Millennium will be the most important event in history. It will be surpassed only when the world becomes a celestial orb where those who will live in the celestial kingdom will dwell. And once it takes place, even the most cynical skeptic, even the most hardened atheist, even the most learned scholars and sophisticated philosophers, yes, even the most worldly of the worldly, will have to acknowledge the truth and accuracy of that statement.

Because of the importance of the Second Coming, the Lord has given us enough information about it to fill its own book. There are literally hundreds of scriptural passages on this subject, so trying to summarize it is a little daunting. On the other hand, we can come to understand the essentials through a careful study of what the prophets have given us. We can do this for the most part by letting the prophets speak for themselves and commenting only briefly on what they have taught us.

One of the most popular of our Christmas hymns is "Joy to the World." It is truly a joyous hymn. The music was composed in the mid-1700s by the great George Frideric Handel, most famous for the *Messiah* oratorio. The lyrics were written earlier by an English poet and clergyman named Isaac Watts. However, Watts did not look to Matthew's and Luke's accounts of Christ's birth, as one might suppose. Rather, he took the text from Psalm 98 in the Old Testament, which is one of several messianic psalms that King David wrote. This makes for an interesting aspect of the hymn, which is often overlooked.

Originally the lyrics to "Joy to the World" were designed to be more about His *Second Coming* than His first. Then, as time passed, others took it upon themselves to make some minor changes and turn it into more of a Christmas carol. The most important difference was in the opening line of the first verse. A single word was changed. It now reads: "Joy to the world, the Lord *is* come." But Isaac Watts wrote it as, "Joy to the world, the Lord *will* come."

A careful analysis of many of the lines of this hymn shows that much of what we sing about is still in the future. That's not inappropriate for Christmas, but it also speaks to His Second Coming:

Let earth receive her King.
Rejoice, rejoice when Jesus reigns.
No more will sin and sorrow grow, nor thorns infest the ground [that's a Millennial promise].
He'll come [note the future tense] *and make the blessings flow.*
Far as the curse was found [this is the curse brought about by Adam's Fall, which only Christ's death and Atonement will make right].
Rejoice, rejoice . . . while Israel spreads abroad [which did not happen in His lifetime but is being fulfilled in our own time].

It is a wonderful hymn celebrating His coming to earth, but it also reminds us of the glorious events that will accompany His Second Coming. I have come to love singing it with both of His comings in mind.

In addition to the sheer volume of prophetic material on the Second Coming, there is another challenge. It is trying to put the various events associated with the Second Coming in some kind of sequential order. Which things will happen first? What precedes the actual coming? What follows it?

Is that information essential? Evidently not, for although the Lord has given us some indicators, in many cases He has not told us. While that can be frustrating, it does bring to mind a gentle reminder from Isaiah: "For my thoughts are not your thoughts, neither are your ways my ways, saith the Lord" (Isaiah 55:8). Which means that just because we don't see His purposes doesn't mean they are not there. We suppose that when all is said and done, it is more important to know *what* is going to happen than *when* it is going to happen.

With those givens, we shall now examine seven key aspects of this grand event known as the Second Coming.

1. Signs in the heavens
2. The actual Second Coming
3. Christ clothed in red raiment
4. The burning of the world by fire
5. The kingdom of God on the earth
6. The return of the city of Enoch
7. The Resurrection

SIGNS IN THE HEAVENS— THE SIGN OF THE COMING OF THE SON OF MAN

In chapter 14, as part of our discussion on natural disasters, we discussed various signs that will occur in the heavens as predicted in the prophecies.

Three of these are often mentioned together with wording that suggests they are closely connected to the actual Second Coming: (1) the sun is darkened; (2) the moon is turned into blood, or also darkened; and (3) stars fall from heaven (see, for example, D&C 29:14; 34:9; 45:42).

As we learn from Christ's visit to the Nephites, one natural way that the sun could be darkened and the moon not give her light—or appear to be blood red—might be due to severe air pollution, including but not limited to violent volcanic activity. The stars falling from heaven could be a natural description of what we call a meteorite shower. That doesn't seem too fearful, unless the meteorites are large enough that they don't burn out before they hit the earth.

Speaking on the Mount of Olives before His death, Jesus told His disciples that a time was coming when "this Gospel of the Kingdom shall be preached in all the world" (JS—M 1:31), which is definitely a last-days event. He then continued:

> And immediately after the tribulation of those days [part of the battle of Armageddon?], the sun shall be darkened, and the moon shall not give her light, and the stars shall fall from heaven. . . . Verily, I say unto you, this generation, in which these things shall be shown forth, shall not pass away until all I have told you shall be fulfilled (JS—M 1:33–34).

But after the mention of some of these other signs in the heavens, the Savior went on to speak of a single sign in the heavens that He called "the sign of the Son of Man." And in this case, He tied it directly to the Second Coming:

> After the tribulation of those days, and the powers of the heavens shall be shaken, then shall appear the sign of the Son of Man in heaven, and then shall all the tribes of the earth mourn; and they shall see the Son of Man coming in the clouds of heaven, with power and great glory (JS—M 1:36).

In section 88 of the Doctrine and Covenants, the Lord also spoke of one "great sign in heaven" just before His Second Coming: "And immediately there shall appear a great sign [note the singular] in heaven, and all people shall see it together" (D&C 88:93).

While teaching the Saints about some of the signs of the times, the Prophet Joseph spoke specifically of this one particular sign, using the same wording as did the Savior:

Judah must return, Jerusalem must be rebuilt, and the temple, and water come out from under the temple, and the waters of the Dead Sea be healed. It will take some time to rebuild the walls of the city and the temple, etc.; and all this must be done before the Son of Man will make His appearance. There will be wars and rumors of wars, signs in the heavens above and on the earth beneath, the sun turned into darkness and the moon to blood, earthquakes in divers places, the seas heaving beyond their bounds; *then will appear one grand sign of the Son of Man in heaven.* But what will the world do? They will say it is a planet, a comet, etc. *But the Son of Man will come* as the sign of the coming of the Son of Man, which will be as the light of the morning cometh out of the east (Joseph Smith, *Teachings*, 252–53).

While the world may not recognize it for what it is, Joseph tells us very clearly what that sign will be. It is so clearly stated that sometimes we don't see it. What is that sign? It is not a darkened sun, nor a blood moon, nor stars falling to earth. Those will precede it. Joseph makes it very clear. Let us read his words again: "*The Son of Man will come* AS the sign of the coming of the Son of Man." How simple and perfect. The great sign of the coming of the Son of Man *is* the actual Second Coming of Christ.

There is one more sign in the heavens that we often overlook. We know it well, but we don't associate it with the Second Coming because it happened during His first coming. A popular Primary song makes brief mention of it. The lyrics convey a person contemplating how the events preceding His Second Coming may be like those that preceded His first. Here are the words of the first verse as they lead up to the statement of interest to us here:

> I wonder, when he comes again,
> Will herald angels sing?
> Will earth be white with drifted snow,
> Or will the world know spring?
> I wonder if one star will shine
> Far brighter than the rest;
> *Will daylight stay the whole night through?*
> Will songbirds leave their nests?
> ("When He Comes Again," lyrics by Mirla Greenwood Thayne)

Latter-day Saints will immediately know that line refers to an event described in detail in the Book of Mormon. Five years before the birth of Christ in the Old World, Samuel the Lamanite was sent to call the backsliding Nephites to repentance. He made several prophecies, including this one:

> And behold, this will I give unto you for a sign at the time of his coming; for behold, there shall *be great lights in heaven,* insomuch that *in the night before he cometh there shall be no darkness,* insomuch that it shall appear unto man as if it was day. Therefore, there shall be *one day and a night and a day, as if it were one day and there were no night;* and this shall be unto you for a sign (Helaman 14:3–4).

Five years later, the wickedness of a large part of the Nephites had grown so dark that the enemies of the faithful announced that if the sign didn't appear that night, all the believers who would not deny Christ would be put to death. Gravely concerned, Nephi prayed and was assured that the time was at hand. And that night the sign was given:

> Behold, at the going down of the sun *there was no darkness;* and the people began to be astonished because there was no darkness when the night came. And there were many, who had not believed the words of the prophets, who fell to the earth and became as if they were dead. . . . And they began to know that the Son of God must shortly appear; yea, in fine, all the people upon the face of the whole earth from the west to the east, both in the land north and in the land south, were so exceedingly astonished that they fell to the earth (3 Nephi 1:15–17).

There is a profound type and symbol in that sign and its fulfillment. Those striving to remain faithful were facing death when daylight stayed through the night and spared them. To put it another way, because of the coming of Jesus Christ, the Light of the World, the faithful were spared from both a physical and a spiritual death.

This is all wonderful and marvelous, but what has it to do with Christ's Second Coming? Zechariah, the Old Testament prophet who lived about 400 years before Christ, made several remarkable prophecies about the time of the Savior's return, including the Savior's appearance to the Jews on the Mount of Olives. Here is one prophecy that is often overlooked:

> And it shall come to pass in that day, that the light shall not be clear, nor dark:[1] But it shall be one day which shall be known to the Lord, not day, nor night: but it shall come to pass, that at evening time it shall be light (Zechariah 14:6–7).

---

1 The phrase "the light shall not be clear, nor dark," is puzzling. In Hebrew the word means something that is "precious" or "rare." This could suggest that the light is plentiful enough to stay through the night and push back the darkness.

Bible scholars who do not have the advantage of access to modern prophecy try to explain this passage in various ways. One says that it is a metaphor of the light of the gospel pushing back the darkness as Christianity covered the world. Another thought it could represent the clearing of the skies after some natural disaster such as volcanic activity.

But the context for this specific prophecy by Zechariah is that it immediately follows his depiction of the visit of Christ to the Jews on the Mount of Olives, and therefore immediately precedes Christ coming as King of kings. Therefore, though we cannot say with absolute certainty that this is what Zechariah was foretelling, the evidence is persuasive enough that it is included here as another one of the signs in the heavens.

HE COMES! THE SECOND COMING OF JESUS CHRIST

Let us now turn to examine in detail what the prophets have said about the most sublime moment in all of human history. It is that moment when He, the Creator of worlds without number (see Moses 1:33–37); He who is King of kings and Lord of lords; He who suffered infinitely for the sins and sufferings of all mankind; He who broke the bands of death to make it possible for all of us to rise from the graves; He who is a glorious, resurrected, celestial Being, even He shall descend from heaven and stand on the earth once again.

We find one of the fullest descriptions of that moment in section 88 of the Doctrine and Covenants. It is a revelation that describes in detail the greatest event in human history, and, therefore, it is a revelation that we shall examine very closely. It should not surprise us that it too begins by mentioning the sign of the coming of the Son of Man:

> And immediately there shall appear a great sign in heaven, and all people shall see it together (D&C 88:93).

This is more than a sign that some people see in the sky. All the billions of the world's populations will not only see it, but will see it at the same time, "all together." The only way we humans can explain how the entire population of the world today could see the same event at the same time would be through a worldwide broadcast over extensive satellite networks. But God is not bound by our mortal limitations. And as already noted, His ways are not our ways. We do not know how it will happen. We do know unquestionably that it *will* happen.

What a stunning concept. In one blinding moment there will not be one person on all the earth who can say, "I don't believe there is a God. I don't believe in life after death."

> And another angel shall sound his trump, saying: That great church, the mother of abominations, that made all nations drink of the wine of the wrath of her fornication, that persecuteth the saints of God, that shed their blood—she who sitteth upon many waters, and upon the islands of the sea—behold, she is the tares of the earth; she is bound in bundles; her bands are made strong, no man can loose them; therefore, she is ready to be burned. And he shall sound his trump both long and loud, and all nations shall hear it (D&C 88:94).

Here will be another huge shock. Babylon—the ultimate image of the world's almost infinite love of wickedness—shall finally reap the consequences of her choices. And the wording here is very clear. No one is going to stop that from happening. The harvest is finally at hand. The time for the full separation of the wheat and the tares has come. Is this partially fulfilled with the final destruction of Gog's army? Will the great earthquake discussed earlier be selective in taking out the wicked, as happened in America at the time of the Crucifixion? Here, too, the Lord chooses not to give us specific answers. It boggles the mind to think that however it may happen, in one great swoop the wickedness of the world comes to an end. But the scriptures and the prophets have testified to us over and over that this is what is coming.

What follows next in section 88 is one of the most marvelous of all the things associated with the Second Coming. It has to do with the reopening of the first Resurrection. With the Savior's coming, the gates of death and hell will be once again opened. We shall discuss this more fully in a later chapter, so for now we shall leave section 88 and see what other prophets have said about the Second Coming.

> The time shall come when all shall see the salvation of the Lord; when every nation, kindred, tongue, and people shall see eye to eye and shall confess before God that his judgments are just. And then shall the wicked be cast out, and they shall have cause to howl, and weep, and wail, and gnash their teeth; and this because they would not hearken unto the voice of the Lord; therefore the Lord redeemeth them not (Mosiah 16:1–2).

> Prepare for the revelation which is to come, when the veil of the covering of my temple, in my tabernacle, which hideth the earth,

shall be taken off, and all flesh shall see me together. And every corruptible thing, both of man, or of the beasts of the field, or of the fowls of the heavens, or of the fish of the sea, that dwells upon all the face of the earth, shall be consumed; And also that of element shall melt with fervent heat; and all things shall become new, that my knowledge and glory may dwell upon all the earth (D&C 101:23–25).

Remember all thy church, O Lord, . . . that the kingdom, which thou hast set up without hands, may become a great mountain and fill the whole earth; That thy church may . . . be adorned as a bride for that day when thou shalt unveil the heavens, and cause the mountains to flow down at thy presence, and the valleys to be exalted, the rough places made smooth; that thy glory may fill the earth; That when the trump shall sound for the dead, we shall be caught up in the cloud to meet thee, that we may ever be with the Lord (D&C 109:72–75).

For behold, he cometh in the clouds with ten thousands[2] of his saints in the kingdom, clothed with the glory of his Father. And every eye shall see him; and they who pierced him, and all kindreds of the earth shall wail because of him (JST Revelation 1:7).

When thou comest down, and the mountains flow down at thy presence, thou shalt meet him who rejoiceth and worketh righteousness, who remembereth thee in thy ways. For since the beginning of the world have not men heard nor perceived by the ear, neither hath any eye seen, O God, besides thee, how great things thou hast prepared for him that waiteth for thee. And it shall be said: Who is this that cometh down from God in heaven with dyed garments; yea, from the regions which are not known, clothed in his glorious apparel, traveling in the greatness of his strength? . . . And the Lord shall be red in his apparel, and his garments like him that treadeth in the wine-vat. And so great shall be the glory of his presence that the sun shall hide his face in shame, and the moon shall withhold its light, and the stars shall be hurled from their places (D&C 133:44–49).

---

2 In Greek, the largest named number was *murias*, or ten thousand. Our word *myriad* comes from that word. Because it was the largest number, it was often used to convey an innumerable multitude.

> After these things I heard a great voice of much people in heaven, saying, Alleluia; Salvation, and glory, and honour, and power, unto the Lord our God: For true and righteous are his judgments: for he hath judged the great whore, which did corrupt the earth with her fornication, and hath avenged the blood of his servants at her hand. And again they said, Alleluia. . . . And I heard as it were the voice of a great multitude, and as the voice of many waters, and as the voice of mighty thunderings, saying, Alleluia: for the Lord God omnipotent reigneth.[3] Let us be glad and rejoice, and give honour to him: for the marriage of the Lamb is come, and his wife hath made herself ready. And to her was granted that she should be arrayed in fine linen, clean and white: for the fine linen is the righteousness of saints (Revelation 19:1–3, 6–8).

The human mind does not have the capacity to fully grasp what this day will be like, especially for those who have been faithful and will be among those caught up to meet Him.

"AND THEIR BLOOD HAVE I SPRINKLED UPON MY GARMENTS, AND STAINED ALL MY RAIMENT"

John used vivid imagery to convey to us the grandeur and glory of our Savior. And in that imagery we are taught something that may surprise a few people, for it describes something about the Savior's appearance when He comes:

> And I saw heaven opened, and behold a white horse; and he that sat upon him was called Faithful and True, and in righteousness he doth judge and make war. His eyes were as a flame of fire, and on his head were many crowns; and he had a name written, that no man knew, but he himself. And he was clothed with a vesture dipped in blood: and his name is called The Word of God (Revelation 19:11–13).

In many artistic renditions of the resurrected Savior, He is depicted in white robes. For example, in artists' renditions of Him at the Garden Tomb on that first Easter morning, He is almost universally dressed in white robes. And that is proper. White is the symbol of purity, holiness, and righteousness (see Revelation 6:11).

From another scripture, the imagery is confirmed in even more detail.

---

3 It is this verse that inspired George Frideric Handel's magnificent "Hallelujah Chorus."

Section 133 of the Doctrine and Covenants, which is devoted almost exclusively to the Second Coming, directly confirms what John saw in his vision. This makes it very clear that saying His raiment will be as red as blood was more than a simile describing the color of the cloth. John was teaching us something about the Savior and His Second Coming that was very important.

> And it shall be said: Who is this that cometh down from God in heaven with *dyed garments;* . . . And he shall say: I am he who spake in righteousness, mighty to save. And *the Lord shall be red in his apparel,* and his garments *like him that treadeth in the wine-vat.* And so great shall be the glory of his presence that the sun shall hide his face in shame, and the moon shall withhold its light, and the stars shall be hurled from their places. And his voice shall be heard: *I have trodden the wine-press alone,* and have brought judgment upon all people; and none were with me; And I have trampled them in my fury, and I did tread upon them in mine anger, and *their blood have I sprinkled upon my garments, and stained all my raiment;* for this was the day of vengeance which was in my heart (D&C 133:46–51; see also 63:2).

This is grim imagery—people being thrown into a winepress or onto a pressing floor. The Savior trampling them under His feet. Blood splattering on His clothing. And yet, in this passage, it is the Savior speaking directly to us. Knowing that Christ is perfect and that He wants only what is best for us, how do we reconcile this imagery with the Savior's invitation to all: "Come unto me, all ye that labour and are heavy laden, and I will give you rest" (Matthew 11:28)? What does this all represent? What lessons are we to learn from it?

One thing is clear. This is not a literal future event where human beings are going to be bound and thrown onto some great pressing floor to be trampled and crushed. Some would call it a metaphor or symbol. A more accurate word would be allegory. Because the difference is important, let's quickly define both terms. *Metaphor* comes from the Greek roots *meta*, over or across, and *pherein*, to carry or to bear. Therefore, a metaphor is a figure of speech by which a characteristic of one thing is transferred (or carried over) to another, e.g., "his temperament is the same as gunpowder and matches." Wearing bright red clothing could be seen as metaphorically having one's clothes dipped in blood.

Most allegories have some metaphoric attributes in them, but they differ in that allegories often involve some kind of story element that teaches important truths and principles, or a representation of future events. The allegory of the olive trees found in Jacob 5 in the Book of Mormon is an extensive and complicated allegory, teaching us about the scattering and gathering of Israel in the last days.

What makes it an allegory is the story itself, which weaves all of the elements together in order to teach a gospel principle or moral lesson. In the allegory of the olive trees, the lesson is that God, from the beginning, has offered His children the covenant that will bring them happiness and joy (the fruit of the tame olive trees) or sorrow, misery, and suffering (the bitter fruit).

The "story" we are examining here is not that extensive, but once we understand its spiritual parallels, the imagery becomes beautiful and profound. Yes, that's right. Even though it involves blood, it is a *beautiful* and *profound analogy*. There are four key elements of this allegory of the winepress. And as we shall see, they are based on deep, sacred, doctrinal principles.

1. *He who treads the winepress.* There is no ambiguity here. This is the Savior Himself. He made that very clear in both accounts cited above. He emphatically speaks in the first person, and tells us that no one else is with Him: "I have trodden the wine-press alone." This is because no one else could do what had to be done.

2. *The grapes.* The grapes represent people, but not all of humanity—one specific group in particular, the wicked and evil people of the world.

3. *The winepress and the process of pressing.* Grape juice, or wine, can only be found in the crushing of the grapes. This is what "presses" the juice out of the fruit. Citing the above passage from section 133, President Joseph Fielding Smith explained: "This earth is groaning today under the violence of corruption and sin. Wickedness is in the hearts of the children of men; and so it will continue according to the revelations of the Lord until that day when Christ shall come in the clouds of heaven, as he said, in red apparel, *coming in the spirit of vengeance to take vengeance on the ungodly, and to cleanse the earth from sin*" (Joseph Fielding Smith, *Doctrines of Salvation*, 3:55).

From this we learn that the process of pressing symbolizes a time of judgment upon the wicked, a time when the Savior and Redeemer comes down in a spirit of judgment and vengeance. Remember, these are those who have consistently fought against Christ, fought against His word, fought against His people, and fought against His work. These are those who have brought misery and suffering to millions—even billions—of people. In our day, *vengeance* has taken on a very negative connotation, suggesting a powerful urge to get revenge, no matter what the cost. Often the person seeking revenge becomes as evil and violent as the perpetrator of the original crime. But that is not what the word originally conveyed.

Vengeance comes from the Latin word *vindicare,* which means to vindicate, to make right, to claim that which is rightly owed or that which is just. If these wicked people, who have caused so much sorrow, so much pain, so much loss, so much suffering, were to be given a slap on the wrist and told not to do it again, then their victims would have every right to cry out, "This is not right! This is not just!"

And this is the key to understanding the analogy. Note carefully how Jesus said it: "I have trodden the wine-press alone, and have brought judgment upon all people; and none were with me." It is that last phrase that tells that in the judgment process, "none," i.e., none of those who are brought to the winepress, "were with me." They were not His disciples, they were not doing His work, they were not living in ways that blessed others. They followed another master and wreaked great havoc on the world. They certainly were not "with Him."

And when, as Amulek described, they are "brought to stand before God" having a "bright recollection of all our guilt" (Alma 11:43), the realization of what they have done will be like a great stone pressing down upon them. Alma graphically described that moment: "For our words will condemn us, yea, all our works will condemn us; we shall not be found spotless; and our thoughts will also condemn us; and in this awful state we shall not dare to look up to our God; and we would fain be glad if we could command the rocks and the mountains to fall upon us to hide us from his presence" (Alma 12:14).

This is a very important part of the allegory. It is not Christ that is crushing them under His feet; it is the weight of their own guilt, which comes when they realize with perfect remembrance just what they have done. The place of pressing is not some pressing floor in Israel, nor some great stone in a winepress. It is the weight of their own conscience that is pressing in upon them.

   4. *The blood.* This is the image that usually bothers people most. It is likened to the juice of the grapes, being pressed down until the juices burst forth, staining the garments of those treading the winepress. The Lord is very specific in how He stated it in D&C 133. He said, "I have trampled them in my fury, and I did tread upon them in mine anger, and *their blood have I sprinkled upon my garments, and stained all my raiment;* for this was the day of vengeance which was in my heart."

There were two foreshadowing events in Christ's mortal life that are symbolically related to the imagery of Christ wearing red in His apparel. The first happened when Pilate sent Jesus to King Herod to see if he would take responsibility for having Christ executed. Herod refused. However, in mockery of the fact that the citizens of Jerusalem were saying that Jesus was king of the Jews, Herod clothed Him in a scarlet robe and sent Him back to Pilate (see Luke 23:11; Matthew 27:28, 31). Many kings wore scarlet robes to signify blood, i.e., that they had power over life and death.

The second foreshadowing event took place in the Garden of Gethsemane. After the Last Supper in the Upper Room, the Savior took the Apostles out of the city to Gethsemane. There He left them and asked them to watch and pray with Him. He then went deeper into the garden to pray and prepare for what was about to happen.

Each of the four Gospel writers recorded this event. It was one of the great moments of eternity. But Luke shared details not found in the other three Gospels: "And there appeared an angel unto him from heaven, strengthening him. And being in an agony he prayed more earnestly: *and his sweat was as it were great drops of blood falling down to the ground*" (Luke 22:43–44).

Some scholars believe that this means His suffering was so intense that He broke into copious perspiration. Luke, they reason, wasn't actually saying that Jesus was bleeding, but rather that in the darkness of the night, His sweat looked as dark as blood. The flaw in that reasoning is that all of the Apostles, including Peter, James, and John, had fallen asleep after Jesus went off by Himself. So there were no eyewitnesses to His prayer. And Luke wasn't there at all. Which means that at some later time, Jesus shared details of His agony with His disciples.

In our dispensation we are taught that He literally did sweat blood. And He also explained what caused it. In a revelation given to Joseph Smith a short time before the organization of the Church (now D&C 19), the Savior spoke of eternal punishment and endless punishment. He taught Joseph an important doctrinal concept. "Eternal" and "endless" are not adjectives suggesting that there would never be an end to God's punishment. Rather, the two terms describe *God's attributes*. Therefore, they are used as titles for God. So what is really meant by those two terms is not that God's punishment has no end, but that it is called endless and eternal punishment because those are His names. *Endless* punishment means God's punishment. *Eternal* punishment means God's punishment.

What immediately follows this explanation of punishment is Christ's description of what took place that night in Gethsemane.[4] This provides powerful confirmation that Luke was not describing drops of sweat:

> Therefore I command you to repent—repent, lest I smite you by the rod of my mouth, and by my wrath, and by my anger, and your sufferings be sore—how sore you know not, how exquisite you know not, yea, how hard to bear you know not. [This is a description of what God's punishment is like. It may not go on forever, but while it lasts it will be very intense.] For behold, I, God, have suffered these things for all, that they might not suffer if they would repent; But if they would not repent they must suffer even as I; *Which suffering caused myself, even God, the greatest of all, to tremble because of pain, and to bleed at every pore, and to suffer both body and spirit*—and would that I might not drink the bitter cup, and shrink—Nevertheless, glory be to the Father, and I partook and finished my preparations unto the children of men. Wherefore, I command you again to repent, *lest I humble you with my almighty power;* and that you confess your sins, lest you suffer these punishments of which I have spoken, of *which in the smallest, yea, even in the least degree you have tasted at the time I withdrew my Spirit* (D&C 19:15–20).

Keep in mind that at this moment in the garden, the horrors of the cross were still waiting for the Savior. In less than twenty-four hours He would be dead. But at this point, Golgotha was still in His future.

So what was it that happened in the garden to create such extreme agony as to cause the blood vessels in His body to rupture? This passage in the Doctrine and Covenants was given to confirm the importance of repentance. And it does that by showing what the consequences will be if we don't come to Him. We need to repent because if we don't, then at some point we will come to understand in some small way the enormity of the suffering Christ endured that night in the garden, because *we will suffer to some degree some of His pain.*

And therein lies the key to understanding the allegory of the winepress. Why are His garments dyed in blood? Because in the garden He literally suffered for our sins to the point that *His* blood stained the clothing He was

---

4 Appropriately, the very name of the garden adds to the symbolic significance of this event. In Greek, *Gethsemane* means "oil press," and by extension, "a place of pressing." How fitting that it was there that the Christ was pressed down by the infinite weight of the sins of the world and that payment was made in blood.

wearing at that time. He died for our sins. He suffered as though He were guilty of them all.

Think about that for a moment. In this allegory, though He says that His raiment was stained with our blood, that is more than a metaphor. He took upon Him our *sins*, so that no one would have to suffer so infinitely intensely. But the price He paid was *literally His blood, not ours.*

Having bled at every pore, how red His raiment must have been in Gethsemane, how crimson that cloak! No wonder, when Christ comes in power and glory, that He will come in reminding red attire, not only signifying the winepress of wrath but also to bring to our remembrance how He suffered for each of us in Gethsemane and on Calvary!

The Neal A. Maxwell Quote Book, 22

Let us keep that doctrinal reality in our hearts when we think of Him who comes with "dyed garments" (D&C 133:46) when He comes to claim His rightful throne. This suffering, which was the price required to satisfy justice, made it possible for those who truly commit themselves to Him to be saved. In the garden and on the cross, and through the perfect life He lived, Jesus could come before the throne of His Father not only perfectly clean in His own right, but having paid the price in suffering for all the sins and wrongs in the world as if He were guilty of all. This is why He can say:

> Listen to him who is the advocate with the Father, who is pleading your cause before him—Saying: Father, behold the sufferings and death of him who did no sin [He is not talking about us. He is talking about Himself!], in whom thou wast well pleased; *behold the blood of thy Son which was shed* [in the garden and on the cross], the blood of him whom thou gavest that thyself might be glorified; Wherefore [because of that blood which He shed], Father, spare these my brethren *that believe on my name,* that they may come unto me and have everlasting life (D&C 45:3–5).

And for those who do not believe on His name, nor accept His covenant and strive to carry out His will in their lives, it shall be as though they are being crushed and pressed down by the weight of their sins in great sorrow and remorse. It is like they themselves are in the winepress, with their blood (the symbol of the lives they have lived) being sprinkled on His garments. But they cannot pay for their sins, even with that intensity of suffering. Only the Christ could do that.

SUMMARY AND CONCLUSIONS

That night in the garden, Jesus bled at every pore, pressed down by the weight of a world of sin, sorrow, injustice, inequity, suffering, *ad infinitum*. With that in mind, let us read again His words:

> *I have trodden the wine-press alone,* and have brought judgment upon all people; and none were with me; And I have trampled them [those who refuse to believe in Him] in my fury, and I did tread upon them in mine anger, and *their blood have I sprinkled upon my garments, and stained all my raiment;* for this was the day of vengeance which was in my heart (D&C 133:50–51).

When He comes again, He shall be clothed in a scarlet robe. And part of that color was shed for us.

CHAPTER 29

HE SHALL REIGN

At the Second Coming of the Lord, He will rule and reign from two world capitals. From the Old Jerusalem, He will rule as Lord of lords, and from the New Jerusalem, on this continent, He will rule as King of kings. At that great day, who may abide the day of His coming? Those who are armed with righteousness and with the power of God in great glory. Those who are called, chosen, and faithful, those who are prepared to offer unto the Lord an offering in righteousness, with records worthy of presentation to Him in His holy temple—a book containing the record of their dead, which shall be worthy of all acceptation. That is the purpose of temples, to provide ordinances that will unite our predecessors with us and with our posterity, that all the blessings promised to the seed of Abraham may be given, that the world may be prepared for the glorious Second Coming of the Lord. (Russell M. Nelson, *Teachings*, 350–51)

THE LORD WILL COME WITH FIRE

Another thing that is frequently tied directly to the Second Coming of Christ has to do with fire and burning. There are three passages that are the most specific—one from the Old Testament, one from the New Testament, and one from the Doctrine and Covenants. The first comes from the prophet Malachi, who lived about 400 years before Christ. His language is quoted or referred to by numerous other prophets:

> But *who may abide the day of his coming?* and who shall stand when he appeareth? for he is like a refiner's fire [as in "refinery," or smelter], and like fullers' soap [a fuller is one who prepares cloth; fullers' soap was some kind of strong cleansing agent]: . . . For, behold, the day cometh, that shall burn as an oven; and all

the proud, yea, and all that do wickedly, *shall be stubble:* and the day that cometh [seemingly a reference to the day of the Lord, or the Second Coming] shall burn them up, saith the Lord of hosts, that it shall leave them neither root nor branch (Malachi 3:2; 4:1; see also 1 Nephi 22:15; 2 Nephi 26:4; 3 Nephi 25:1; D&C 29:9; 64:24; 128:24; 133:64).

Peter spoke of Christ's Second Coming in his second general epistle, warning that in the last days there will be "scoffers" who ask, "Where is the promise of his coming?" (2 Peter 3:4). Peter then warns the Church members:

But the day of the Lord will come as a thief in the night, in the which the heavens shall shake, and the earth also shall tremble, and the *mountains shall melt,* and pass away with a great noise, *and the elements shall be filled with fervent heat;* the earth also shall be filled, and the *corruptible works which are therein shall be burned up.* . . . Looking unto, and preparing for the day of the coming of the Lord wherein *the corruptible things of the heavens being on fire, shall be dissolved, and the mountains shall melt with fervent heat* (JST 2 Peter 3:10, 12).

Finally, in section 133 of the Doctrine and Covenants, the Lord repeats some of what was said before but adds that the very presence of Christ, a celestial being whose glory is like that of the sun, is likened unto fire:

Calling upon the name of the Lord day and night, saying: O that thou wouldst rend the heavens, that thou wouldst come down, *that the mountains might flow down at thy presence.* And it shall be answered upon their heads; for the presence of the Lord shall be as the melting fire that burneth, and as the fire which causeth the waters to boil. O Lord, thou shalt come down to make thy name known to thine adversaries, and all nations shall tremble at thy presence—When thou doest terrible things, things they look not for; Yea, when thou comest down, and the mountains flow down at thy presence, thou shalt meet him who rejoiceth and worketh righteousness, who remembereth thee in thy ways (D&C 133:40–44).

We know that elsewhere in the scriptures, fire and burning are used as a metaphor for the shame that the guilty will experience when they come before God's presence for judgment. It is compared to a lake of fire (see, for example, 2 Nephi 9:16, 26; Jacob 3:11; D&C 63:17; Revelation 19:20). We also discussed fire as one of the dreadful signs of the times in Part III of this book. These fires could include wildfires, the fire associated with volcanic

> *Soon, however, all flesh shall see Him together. All knees shall bow in His presence, and all tongues confess His name. Knees that never before have assumed that posture for that purpose will do so then—and promptly. Tongues that never before have spoken His name except in gross profanity will do so then—and worshipfully. Soon, He who was once mockingly dressed in purple will come again, attired in red apparel, reminding us whose blood redeemed us. All will then acknowledge the completeness of His justice and His mercy. . . . Then we will see the true story of mankind. . . . The great military battles will appear as mere bonfires that blazed briefly, and the mortal accounts of the human experience will be but graffiti on the walls of time.*
>
> Neal A. Maxwell,
> *Even as I Am*, 120

eruptions, or fires that accompany natural disasters. These signs are all part of the preparation for the Second Coming in the last days, but they are not directly connected to it in the same way as suggested above.

However, the three scriptures cited above definitely talk about a burning of the wicked at His Second Coming, using metaphors like the "stubble" left after grain is harvested or "the tares" that are bound into bundles and burned (see D&C 38:12; 86:7; 88:94). Obviously some of that burning will come with the consciousness of guilt and shame as noted above. And some may actually die in the fires and other natural disasters sent by the Lord as warning voices to the wicked. Remember that the army of Gog will be destroyed when fire rains down from heaven upon them (see Ezekiel 38:22).

But the scriptures are quite explicit that there will be a burning and cleansing process connected directly with the Second Coming. And this seems to be directly connected to the actual presence of Jesus Christ. We're not given specifics on how this might work, but it seems to be tied to a Being whose glory is celestial and who is likened unto the sun itself. This sounds quite literal and not like symbolic fire. Note these passages:

- "Therefore, O Lord, deliver thy people from the calamity of the wicked; enable thy servants to seal up the law, and bind up the testimony, *that they may be prepared against the day of burning*" (D&C 109:46).
- "Prepare for the revelation which is to come, when the veil of the covering of my temple, in my tabernacle, which hideth the earth, shall be taken off, and all flesh shall see me together. And *every corruptible*

thing, both of man, or of the beasts of the field, or of the fowls of the heavens, or of the fish of the sea [even fish in the ocean!], *that dwells upon all the face of the earth, shall be consumed;* and also that of *element shall melt with fervent* heat; and all things shall become new" (D&C 101:23–25).

Modern revelation also speaks of a burning:

> Behold, now it is called today until the coming of the Son of Man, and verily it is a day of sacrifice, and a day for the tithing of my people; for *he that is tithed shall not be burned at his coming.* For after today cometh the burning—this is speaking after the manner of the Lord—for verily I say, tomorrow *all the proud and they that do wickedly shall be as stubble; and I will burn them up, for* I am the Lord of Hosts; and *I will not spare any that remain in Babylon* (D&C 64:23–24).

Isn't it interesting that the Lord includes those who are "tithed" as being among those who will escape the burning? Here is what President Hinckley had to say about this passage:

> Some years ago one of our brethren spoke of the payment of tithing as "fire insurance." That statement evoked laughter. Nonetheless, the word of the Lord is clear that those who do not keep the commandments and observe the laws of God shall be burned at the time of his coming. For that shall be a day of judgment and a day of sifting, a day of separating the good from the evil (Hinckley, *Teachings*, 576).

There is an interesting second confirmation of the importance of the law of tithing, and it comes from Malachi, whom we have already cited. We will remember that Malachi asked a question of his readers in chapter 3: "Who may abide the day of his coming? and who shall stand when he appeareth?" (Malachi 3:2). That's a key question we all want answered. Then in chapter 4, Malachi referred to being burned as stubble. So, what do we find in the rest of chapter 3, which is the text between the question on who shall abide the day and the description of the burning of the stubble?

> Bring ye all the tithes into the storehouse, that there may be meat in mine house, and prove me now herewith, saith the Lord of hosts, if I will not open you the windows [Hebrew, "sluices"] of heaven, and pour you out a blessing, that there shall not be room enough to receive it. And I will rebuke the devourer [fire is one thing that consumes everything before it] for your sakes, and he shall not destroy the fruits of your ground; neither shall your vine

cast her fruit before the time in the field, saith the Lord of hosts (Malachi 3:10–11).

This is probably the most quoted scripture on the principle of paying tithing, and here too it is found in the context of the burning.

There is much more we could say, but the summary is simple, plain, and very sobering. Christ's coming begins the Millennium, an age of unprecedented peace, prosperity, learning, growth, and righteousness! That would not be possible if the earth were not cleansed by that time. And the scriptures affirm that part of that cleansing will come by fire.

THE KINGDOM OF GOD ON THE EARTH

The prophets have also taught us about a tectonic shift in the political history of humanity that will occur when Jesus comes to earth again. Though we often speak of it in passing, we may not have thought about it in more detail.

George Frideric Handel composed one of the most familiar and beloved of all pieces of choral music. He drew on the words of ancient prophets for his inspiration. For example:

- "Then the moon shall be confounded, and the sun ashamed, when the *Lord of hosts shall reign in mount Zion, and in Jerusalem,* and before his ancients gloriously" (Isaiah 24:23).
- "And I heard as it were the voice of a great multitude, and as the voice of many waters, and as the voice of mighty thunderings, saying, *Alleluia: for the Lord God omnipotent reigneth*" (Revelation 19:6).
- "And he hath on his vesture and on his thigh a name written, KING OF KINGS, AND LORD OF LORDS" (Revelation 19:16; see also 1 Timothy 6:15).

Similar language is also found in modern scripture:

- "And the time cometh speedily that the righteous must be led up as calves of the stall, *and the Holy One of Israel must reign in dominion,* and might, and power, and great glory" (1 Nephi 22:24).
- "For I, the Lord, have put forth my hand to exert the powers of heaven; ye cannot see it now, yet a little while and ye shall see it, and know that I am, and *that I will come and reign with my people*" (D&C 84:119).
- "And the Lord, even the Savior, shall stand in the midst of his people, *and shall reign over all flesh*" (D&C 133:25).

He Shall Reign

Though other scriptures speak of Him ruling over His people, the last verse makes it clear that He will also reign over all the earth. John the Beloved, author of the book of Revelation, was privileged to see that time in vision with all of its splendor and glory:

> And I saw heaven opened, and behold a white horse; and he that sat upon him was called Faithful and True, and in righteousness he doth judge and make war. . . . And he was clothed with a vesture dipped in blood: and his name is called The Word of God. And the armies which were in heaven followed him upon white horses, clothed in fine linen, white and clean. . . . And he hath on his vesture and on his thigh a name written, *KING OF KINGS, AND LORD OF LORDS* (Revelation 19:11–16).

In six millennia of the world's history, we have had many, many kings and queens, and many, many lords and ladies. We have had presidents, prime ministers, chancellors, princes, exalted leaders, governors, generals, czars, and caesars. Thousands upon thousands of them.

One of those, whose title was Roman Procurator and who ruled over the small, backwater province of Judea in a forgotten corner of the Roman Empire, had Jesus brought before him, accused of sedition against Caesar, a capital crime. The Savior's enemies accused Him of claiming to be king of the Jews. That was anathema in the empire. But Pilate was puzzled by His demeanor. After questioning Him briefly, quite perplexed, Pilate asked: "Art thou the King of the Jews?"

Jesus asked him if he was asking this question for himself or because the Jews had said it.

Irritated, Pilate snapped back: "Am I Jew? Thine own nation and the chief priests have delivered thee unto me: what hast thou done?"

We look forward to the time . . . when God will assert his own right with regard to the government of the earth; when, as in religious matters so in political matters, he will enlighten the minds of those that bear rule, he will teach the kings wisdom and instruct the senators by the Spirit of eternal truth; when to him "every knee shall bow and every tongue confess that Jesus is the Christ." . . . Then shall the mists of darkness be swept away by the light of eternal truth. Then will the intelligence of heaven beam forth on the human mind, and by it they will comprehend everything that is great, and good, and glorious.

John Taylor,
Gospel Kingdom, 348

Jesus's answer was simple and straightforward: "My kingdom is not of this world."

"Art thou a king then?" Pilate asked again.

Jesus replied, "Thou sayest that I am a king," which meant, "You have spoken correctly. I am a king." Then Jesus calmly added: "To this end was I born, and for this cause came I into the world" (John 18:33–37).

Convinced that Jesus was no threat to Rome, Pilate tried to convince the Jewish leaders to free Him, but they would have none of it. Finally, Pilate washed his hands of it and delivered Jesus up to the legionnaires and the cross.

That was two thousand years ago. In some future day, people won't have to ask Him that question, for by that time, "every knee shall bow, and every tongue confess before him" (Mosiah 27:31). And there will be "the voice of a great multitude, and as the voice of many waters, and as the voice of mighty thunderings, saying, Alleluia: for the Lord God omnipotent reigneth" (Revelation 19:6).

In the chapter on the great council meeting held at Adam-ondi-Ahman, we learned that one of the things that will take place there will be the acceptance of Christ as the King of all creation, and He will be sustained as the rightful King of this world. Whether it will be then that He shall officially be crowned King or at some later time, we are not told. President Joseph Fielding Smith explains what that means:

> When our Savior comes to rule in the millennium, all governments will become subject unto his government, and this has been referred to as the kingdom of God, which it is; but *this is the political kingdom which will embrace all people* whether they are in the Church or not. . . . We must keep these two thoughts in mind. But the kingdom of God is the Church of Jesus Christ, and it is the kingdom that shall endure forever. When the Savior prayed, "Thy kingdom come," he had reference to the kingdom in heaven which is to come when the millennium reign starts (Joseph Fielding Smith, *Doctrines of Salvation*, 1:229).

This will be the fulfillment of a prayer that Joseph Smith said he had received by revelation. After speaking of the stone that the prophet Daniel saw cut out of the mountain and rolling forth until it filled the whole earth, Joseph wrote:

> Call upon the Lord, that *his kingdom may go forth upon the earth,* that the inhabitants thereof may receive it, and be prepared for the

days to come, in the which the Son of Man shall come down in heaven, clothed in the brightness of his glory, *to meet the kingdom of God which is set up on the earth.* Wherefore, *may the kingdom of God go forth, that the kingdom of heaven may come,* that thou, O God, mayest be glorified in heaven so on earth, that thine enemies may be subdued; for thine is the honor, power and glory, forever and ever. Amen (D&C 65:5–6).

In the year 2000, at the beginning of a new millennium, the First Presidency and the Quorum of the Twelve sent forth their testimony to the world. One of the things of which they testified was the Second Coming and Christ's reign as King of kings:

> We testify that He will someday return to earth. "And the glory of the Lord shall be revealed, and all flesh shall see it together" (Isaiah 40:5). He will rule as King of Kings and reign as Lord of Lords, and every knee shall bend and every tongue shall speak in worship before Him. Each of us will stand to be judged of Him according to our works and the desires of our hearts ("The Living Christ: The Testimony of the Apostles of The Church of Jesus Christ of Latter-day Saints").

THE ZION ABOVE MEETS THE ZION BENEATH

In Part IV: The Great Day, we discussed the concept of Zion in general and the city of New Jerusalem specifically. As we saw, Zion is a people, Zion is a land, Zion includes the stakes of the Church, Zion was the name of a city founded by Enoch, and Zion is another name for the city of New Jerusalem, which is yet to be built. We don't need to explore all of that again. Our focus here is on the events surrounding the Second Coming of Christ. And one of those joyous events will occur when the city of Enoch will descend from heaven to meet with the City of Zion here on earth.

We shall examine the two key scriptures that describe this amazing time. What makes this so remarkable is that the city of Enoch—the original Zion—was taken up into heaven before the flood, somewhere around 3000 B.C., or more than 5,000 years ago! So what we have is a whole city of translated beings.

The first passage comes from a vision given to Enoch. In the vision, Enoch saw a time of great wickedness when the power of Satan would rule on the earth. Seeing that, Enoch despaired, and, weeping, he asked the Lord when the earth would finally rest. The Lord assured him that the time was coming but that he would have to await a Restoration of the gospel in the last days (see Moses 7:58–62).

As part of his vision, Enoch saw when righteousness would "sweep the world as with a flood, to gather out mine elect from the four quarters of the earth, unto a place which I shall prepare, an Holy City . . . called Zion, a New Jerusalem" (Moses 7:62). So this is a latter-day Zion that Enoch saw. And then he was told:

> *This [the return of the city of Enoch] seems to be a time to come—near the great day of resurrection, and just preceding the time when the "arm of the Lord shall fall upon the nations." In that day the City of Enoch—the other City of Zion—will return and men shall again exercise perfect faith and have the guidance of divine power. Moreover, the thousand years of peace shall be ushered in.*
>
> JOSEPH FIELDING SMITH, SIGNS OF THE TIMES, 169–70

Then shalt thou and all thy city meet them there, and we [suggesting that the Savior will come with them] will receive them into our bosom, and they shall see us; and we will fall upon their necks, and they shall fall upon our necks, and we will kiss each other; *And there* [in New Jerusalem] *shall be mine abode*, And it shall be Zion, which shall come forth out of all the creations which I have made; and for the space of a thousand years the earth shall rest (Moses 7:63–64).

Here again we find words failing us. All we can do is ponder some of the more obvious questions. How does one describe such a sublime moment? How many will be coming down? How many will there be to meet them? Thousands? More? Will they need homes to stay in? Will they need to eat? What do translated beings look like? Will we have a chance to hear their stories, and they ours? If they had children, which is almost a given, are their children translated beings too? As fascinating as these things are to contemplate, the Lord has chosen to remain quiet on such details for the present.

One question that is especially intriguing relates to their current state. We know that there was no resurrection before Christ rose from the tomb. But we also know that when Jesus was resurrected, many others were too (see Matthew 27:52–53; D&C 138:12–19). Did the city of Enoch participate in the Resurrection? We are not told one way or the other. Enoch's name is not included in the names of the great and noble who were waiting there to greet Him. Does that mean Enoch and his people were left in their translated state? If they were resurrected too, that creates an interesting question. Because of their faithfulness, we can assume they would be gods now. Are gods allowed to mingle with mortals, to fall on their necks and kiss each other? It seems problematic. Elder Orson F. Whitney, a member of the Twelve in the early 1900s, gave it as his opinion that they were not resurrected at the time but still exist as translated beings somewhere:

> The city of Enoch is now on a terrestrial plane, awaiting its return to Earth, when the season shall be ripe and the preparation complete for its reception. The change wrought upon its inhabitants by translation not being equivalent to resurrection, they will undergo a further change to prepare them for celestial glory. The Saints remaining on earth to meet the Lord will likewise be changed, not by the "sleep" of death, but "in a moment, in the twinkling of an eye," at the time of the Savior's coming (Whitney, *Saturday Night Thoughts*, 117).

The other scripture passage about the city of Enoch comes from section 84 of the Doctrine and Covenants. We remember that this section opened with a promise of a temple being built in New Jerusalem (see vv. 2–5). Speaking of the new Zion, the Lord says that at that time, then "all shall know me, who remain, even from the least unto the greatest, and shall be filled with the knowledge of the Lord, and shall see eye to eye" (v. 98). It seems likely that this describes the time of reunion between Enoch's Zion and the new Zion. What a joyful time that will be. The Lord says that those who are on the earth at that time will "lift up their voice, and with the voice together [with the people of Enoch's Zion?] sing this new song" (see vv. 94–102):

We read in the Pearl of Great Price how Enoch gathered together those who were willing to make covenants to serve the Lord. They covenanted to obey the celestial law, or the law of consecration. They were willing to give all that they had—even their lives—to building the kingdom of God. They became so righteous that they walked with God, and He dwelt among them (see Moses 7:69). Consecration, catalyzed by righteousness, promotes inner peace. . . . Consecration will immunize you from unrighteous pride, anger, hatred, and other forms of spiritual self-degradation.

RUSSELL M. NELSON,
TEACHINGS, 89–90

The Lord hath brought again Zion;
The Lord hath redeemed his people, Israel,
According to the election of grace,
which was brought to pass by the faith and covenant of their fathers.
The Lord hath redeemed his people;
and Satan is bound and time is no longer.
The Lord hath gathered all things in one.
The Lord hath brought down Zion from above.

SUMMARY AND CONCLUSIONS

We have now discussed six of our topics that are associated with the Second Coming. Each of them describes a wondrous experience that awaits the faithful on both sides of the veil. In our next chapter, we shall move to the last culminating event that complete this remarkable time in history, and in some ways, it may be the greatest of all that is coming, other than the arrival of the Savior Himself.

CHAPTER 30

CAUGHT UP TO MEET HIM

The gift of resurrection is the Lord's consummate act of healing. Thanks to Him, each body will be restored to the proper and perfect frame. Thanks to Him, no condition is hopeless. Thanks to Him, bright days are ahead, both here and hereafter. Real joy awaits each of us—on the other side of sorrow. (Russell M. Nelson, Hope in Our Hearts, 65)

"HE IS NOT HERE, BUT IS RISEN"

Early in the morning of that first Easter Sunday, several women came to the tomb near Golgotha. On Friday, still reeling in deep shock, they had started to prepare the Savior's body for burial, but with the coming of the Sabbath at sundown, they had to leave before it was properly finished. Now they were back to complete their sorrowful task. To their surprise, the two Roman soldiers Pilate had left to guard the tomb were not to be seen. Then came an enormous shock. The great stone that had sealed the entrance to the tomb had been rolled back. They entered in and discovered that the body was gone. "And it came to pass, as they were much perplexed thereabout, behold, two men stood by them in shining garments: And as they were afraid, and bowed down their faces to the earth, they said unto them, *Why seek ye the living among the dead? He is not here, but is risen*" (Luke 24:4–6).

Had it been anyone else but two heavenly beings making that announcement, the women would likely not have believed it. But they did believe, and they rushed back to tell those who were still in mourning back in Jerusalem. The long-awaited Resurrection had begun, and word would quickly spread that the Garden Tomb was not the only grave that had been opened (see Matthew 27:52–53).

TRANSLATED BEINGS

Before we look more closely at the Resurrection that followed and will continue to follow Christ's coming out of the tomb on Easter morning, let us examine something that took place in the days immediately following the Resurrection of Jesus Christ.

In working with His closest followers—the remaining eleven Apostles in the Old World and the twelve disciples He chose when He visited the New World—Jesus did an interesting thing. In both cases, as He gave to the appointed leaders of His Church some final instructions and their charge to take the gospel to the world, He also granted them a personal request.

In his Gospel, the Apostle John recorded an enigmatic conversation between Jesus and Peter that took place shortly before Christ's final ascension. It is enigmatic because it gives us little context for what Jesus said. Peter, looking at John, asked, "And what shall this man do?" Christ replied, "If I will that he tarry till I come, what is that to thee?" Then John recorded: "Then went this saying abroad among the brethren, that that disciple should not die: yet Jesus said not unto him, He shall not die; but, If I will that he tarry till I come, what is that to thee?" (John 21:21–23).

Though it is not fully clear, this seems to be a direct indication that John would not die until Christ's Second Coming. Fortunately, we have a fuller account given to Joseph Smith as he worked on the Joseph Smith Translation:

> And the Lord said unto me: John, my beloved, what desirest thou? For if you shall ask what you will, it shall be granted unto you. And I said unto him: Lord, give unto me power over death, that I may live and bring souls unto thee. And the Lord said unto me: Verily, verily, I say unto thee, because thou desirest this thou shalt tarry until I come in my glory, and shalt prophesy before nations, kindreds, tongues and people. And for this cause the Lord said unto Peter: If I will that he tarry till I come, what is that to thee? For he desired of me that he might bring souls unto me, but

---

Behold, the bands of death shall be broken, and the Son reigneth, and hath power over the dead; therefore, he bringeth to pass the resurrection of the dead. . . . And now, the resurrection of all the prophets, and all those that have believed in their words, or all those that have kept the commandments of God, shall come forth in the first resurrection; therefore, they are the first resurrection.

MOSIAH 15:20, 22

thou desiredst that thou mightest speedily come unto me in my kingdom. I say unto thee, Peter, this was a good desire; but my beloved has desired that he might do more, or a greater work yet among men than what he has before done. Yea, he has undertaken a greater work; therefore I will make him as flaming fire and a ministering angel; he shall minister for those who shall be heirs of salvation who dwell on the earth. . . .Verily I say unto you, ye shall both have according to your desires, for ye both joy in that which ye have desired (D&C 7:1–8).

A similar thing took place as Jesus made His last visit with the twelve disciples He called to serve in the Americas. Only in this case, nine of the twelve desired the same thing that Peter and the other Apostles had asked for, while three asked that they too could tarry until the Second Coming (see 3 Nephi 28:1–12).

These two passages provide the most detail on what are known as translated beings. Other examples of such beings include the people of the city of Enoch (see Moses 7:18–21), some of the people who lived at the time of Melchizedek (see JST Genesis 14:32–36); and Moses and Elijah. We know that John and the Three Nephites were allowed to continue their ministry here on earth to help prepare for Christ's Second Coming.

We are not given any details in the scriptures of what the people of the city of Enoch and the people of Melchizedek have been doing since they were caught up to heaven. We know that had to be some form of translation, because the Resurrection would not begin for many centuries. But surely the Lord had a purpose in both of these cases.

Here is an interesting insight shared by President Harold B. Lee. In a conference session, one of the First Presidency members said that it was his belief that the priesthood of God had always been here on earth and would continue to be here until the end. Some members thought that was odd since there had been hundreds of years during the Apostasy when there was no Church and no priesthood on the earth. While going back to the Church Administration Building afterward, President Lee was walking with President Joseph Fielding Smith, who said:

> "I believe there has never been a moment of time since the creation but what there has been someone holding the priesthood on the earth to hold Satan in check." [Lee continues:] And then I thought of Enoch's city with perhaps thousands who were taken into heaven and were translated. They must have been translated for a purpose and may have sojourned with those living on the

earth ever since that time. I have thought of Elijah—and perhaps Moses, for all we know; they were translated beings, as was John the Revelator. I have thought of the three Nephites. Why were they translated and permitted to tarry? For what purpose? An answer was suggested when I heard President Smith . . . make the above statement. Now that doesn't mean that the kingdom of God has always been present, because these men did not have the authority to administer the saving ordinances of the gospel to the world. But these individuals were translated for a purpose known to the Lord. There is no question but what they were here (Lee, *Stand Ye In Holy Places*, 160–61).

This raises some questions about the Resurrection for those who have been translated. The scriptures clearly say that John and the Three Nephites were told that they would undergo a change that would allow them to tarry on earth without suffering death until Christ comes again. That means they have not been resurrected yet. And President Lee's statement clearly suggests that the people of the city of Enoch have not been resurrected yet either.

With that in mind, let us now examine the Resurrection itself.

THE FIRST AND SECOND RESURRECTIONS

Christ was the first human being to lay down His life and then pick it up again. We know that others were also resurrected at that time (see Matthew 27:50–52). That was part of what is known as the First Resurrection (see Alma 40:16; D&C 76:64). That phrase suggests that the Resurrection is not a one-time event, and this is what we shall now examine more closely.

Some of our prophets have used the phrase "the *morning* of the First Resurrection," signifying that this was the beginning of the resurrection process. This phrase is also found in the covenant language associated with certain temple blessings.

Judging by the names that President Smith was given in his vision, this first wave of resurrected beings was destined for the celestial kingdom, with many or all of them achieving the highest degree of the celestial kingdom. This signifies godhood, or what we also call *exaltation*. These were those called "saints," a word that means "those who have been sanctified." We also know from the scriptures that there will be a First and a Second Resurrection, and as we shall see, these two phrases describe an order in the Resurrection that is determined by our personal holiness and worthiness. The "morning of the First Resurrection" also tells us that this was only the first wave of those to be resurrected. But it did include all of the truly faithful who had died up to that time (see Mosiah 15:21–22). Joseph Fielding Smith confirmed that when he said: "The resurrection at the time of our Lord brought forth from the dead all those who had proved themselves worthy through the keeping of his commandments" (Smith, *Answers to Gospel Questions*, 3:86).

But in John's vision, we learn that the Resurrection that takes place at the time of the Second Coming of Christ is also part of the First Resurrection (see Revelation 20:6). Therefore, we know that the First Resurrection has two parts as far as timing goes.

For example, we know that Joseph Smith and others of this dispensation are still in the spirit world teaching the gospel (see D&C 138:53–54), which means that sometime after the resurrection of those who were resurrected with Christ, resurrection stopped for a time, and will not take place again until Christ comes.

How then do we explain the resurrection of the angel Moroni, who died about 400 years later? Again Joseph Fielding Smith reminds us of an important point: "While the scriptures speak of the First Resurrection and the second, . . . these expressions do not preclude the power and authority of our Lord to call forth from the dead any one whom he pleases without waiting for a general resurrection" (Smith, *Answers to Gospel Questions*, 3:86).

This leads us to why we are talking about the Resurrection in a chapter on the Second Coming of Christ. Our purpose here is to show that *when Jesus comes in His glory to take the throne that is rightly His, the morning of the First Resurrection will begin once again*, and those who will go to the celestial kingdom will be resurrected at His coming.

The prophetic teachings on this are very clear. Two primary scriptural sources give us the most complete picture of the Resurrection:

> And the remnant shall be gathered unto this place; And then they shall look for me, and, behold, I will come; and they shall see me in the clouds of heaven, clothed with power and great glory; with all the holy angels; and he that watches not for me shall be cut off. But before the arm of the Lord shall fall, an angel shall sound his trump, and the saints that have slept shall come forth to meet me in the cloud. Wherefore, if ye have slept in peace blessed are you; for as you now behold me and know that I am, even so shall ye come unto me and your souls shall live, and your redemption shall be perfected; and the saints shall come forth from the four quarters of the earth (D&C 45:43–46).

The Lord did not define who is meant by the "remnant," but "this place" has to be Old Jerusalem. We know that because section 45 is another version of the Olivet Discourse, which was given on the Mount of Olives in Jerusalem. So "this place" is Old Jerusalem. Therefore, the "remnant" seems to refer to the Jews who have returned to their ancestral homeland in our time. However, we note that He doesn't say that this is where His Second Coming will be, only that a remnant will be gathered there. We shall see in a moment that a more likely place for His coming is at the city of New Jerusalem.

The next statement is especially important, for it gives us a specific timing marker. "*Before* the arm of the Lord shall fall, . . . *the saints that have slept shall come forth to meet me in the cloud*" (D&C 45:45). Note again that it is the Saints who are participating here, not everyone. "Slept" refers only to their bodies being in the graves. We know that their spirits are in paradise and that they are actively preparing for the Second Coming of Christ and for the time of their own resurrection.

And in this we find a specific time marker. They will be caught up to meet the Savior just before He comes in His glory. This may surprise some, for we commonly think of the Resurrection as taking place *after* His Second Coming. As we study our second reference, we shall see that this is confirmed even more emphatically. This is of important significance, so let us say it once again. *The morning of the First Resurrection will resume just before Christ's coming.*

As we have discussed several times now, in the Lord's eyes only those who have been faithful to the covenants they have made with the Lord are considered to be true Israel, or called Saints, and only they will be saved in this morning of the First Resurrection. What rejoicing will be heard in the heavens at that hour! Speaking of those who have "slept in peace" is another way of saying that this renewal of the Resurrection is for those who have been faithful in this life. This is where the peace comes from. Our spirits are not resting in the grave with our bodies; they are in the spirit world, and what gives them peace as their bodies sleep is that they are in paradise, which Alma has described as "a state of rest, a state of *peace*, where they shall rest from all their troubles and from all care, and sorrow" (Alma 40:12).

"THEN SHALL THE ARM OF THE LORD FALL UPON THE NATIONS"

In chapter 26 we discussed the Lord's appearance on the Mount of Olives to the Jews of Jerusalem. This is another time marker. His arm falling on the nations could be a reference to that moment when the two witnesses in Jerusalem are resurrected and the armies of Gog and the wicked of the world feel the wrath of the Almighty God. This is supported by the Lord making reference to His appearance on the Mount of Olives to the Jews of Jerusalem, as discussed in chapter 26. And that suggests that the beginning of the First Resurrection will happen just *prior* to that time.

> And then [immediately after He shows Himself to the Jews] shall the heathen nations be redeemed, and they that knew no law shall have part in the first resurrection; and it shall be tolerable for them. And Satan shall be bound, that he shall have no place in the hearts of the children of men. And at that day, when I shall come in my glory, shall the parable be fulfilled which I spake concerning the ten virgins. For they that are wise and have received the truth, and have taken the Holy Spirit for their guide, and have not been deceived—verily I say unto you, they shall not be hewn down and cast into the fire, but shall abide the day. And the earth shall be given unto them for an inheritance; and they shall multiply and wax strong, and their children shall grow up without sin unto salvation. For the Lord shall be in their midst, and his glory shall be upon them, and he will be their king and their lawgiver (D&C 45:54–59).

"The heathen nations . . . that knew no law" refers to those people who never had the chance to hear the gospel in this life. This statement teaches us another important aspect of the Resurrection. From the Prophet's vision on the three degrees of glory we have a very clear description of what it takes to be accepted into the celestial kingdom when the Resurrection comes. "They are they who received the testimony of Jesus, and believed on his name and were baptized after the manner of his burial, being buried in the water in his name, and this according to the commandment which he has given" (D&C 76:50).

Note that this does *not* say this has to happen while we are still in mortality. This is why we search out the names of our ancestors and go into the temples and vicariously do their ordinances. If they died before receiving the gospel, they will be in spirit prison. If they fully accept the gospel there, then they become part of true Israel and have access to the same blessings as those who received the gospel in mortality. This must be so, or when and where we are born would become a discriminating factor in our eternal progression.

Also from D&C 76 we learn that those who will inherit the terrestrial kingdom are those "who are the spirits of men *kept in prison,* whom the Son visited, and preached the gospel unto them, that they might be judged according to men in the flesh; Who received not the testimony of Jesus in the flesh, but afterwards received it. *These are they who are honorable men of the earth, who were blinded by the craftiness of men.* These are they *who receive of his glory, but not of his fulness.* These are they who receive of the presence of the Son, but not of the fulness of the Father. Wherefore, *they are bodies terrestrial,* and not bodies celestial, and differ in glory as the moon differs from the sun. These are they *who are not valiant in the testimony of Jesus;* wherefore, they obtain not the crown over the kingdom of our God" (D&C 76:73–79).

We take the time to explore that subtle difference because in this sequence of events surrounding the Second Coming of Christ, we see that there are two main phases of the Resurrection of the dead, but with different, distinct aspects that are defined by their final assignment to a kingdom of glory.

The first to come forth from their graves will be those who have lived worthily enough to be exalted and go on to godhood, as described by the Lord: "If ye receive me in the world, then shall ye know me, and shall receive your exaltation; that where I am ye shall be also. This is *eternal lives*" (D&C 132:23–24). Eternal *lives*—plural—means that they will have the great privilege of creating spirit children just as our Heavenly Parents did.

But we also know that there will be people who lived faithfully enough to allow them to go to the celestial kingdom even though they will not be gods but will be "ministering servants" to those who are gods (see D&C 131:1–4; 132:16–17).

We take time to define these differences because these determine the order of the Resurrection. Since the covenant language that refers to the morning of the First Resurrection also refers to "eternal lives," we can conclude that the morning of the First Resurrection is for those destined for godhood. Those worthy of the celestial kingdom but not godhood will be resurrected next, but this too is part of the First Resurrection. Then comes those who will go to the terrestrial kingdom, as defined above. Elder McConkie referred to this as the "afternoon" of the First Resurrection. After citing D&C 88:99, he said: "Even the heathen who are without the law shall come forth in the afternoon of the First Resurrection and be blessed with a terrestrial inheritance that shall be tolerable for them" (*The Mortal Messiah,* 3:453).

We should keep in mind here that "morning" and "afternoon" define an order or sequence of the Resurrection rather than a specific time. In other words, the Lord does not seem to imply that those going to the terrestrial kingdom will have to wait hundreds of years before their resurrection. We are not given those specifics. What we are told is that three groups will be resurrected immediately before or during the Millennium—those being exalted, those going to the celestial kingdom but not as exalted beings, and those going to the terrestrial kingdom. Beyond that we are not given more details.

In a section where the Lord talks about the judgments of God coming upon the wicked—earthquakes, thunderings and lightning, the waves of the sea heaving themselves beyond their bounds, all things in commotion, etc.—once again the angels of heaven sound their trump. Drawing on the imagery of the parable of the ten virgins, they announce that the Resurrection is about to begin. What follows in section 88 of the Doctrine and Covenants not only describes the First Resurrection but gives us more details on the Second—or last—Resurrection. Again we shall emphasize specific time markers:

> And immediately there shall appear a great sign in heaven, and all people shall see it together. And another angel shall sound his trump, saying: That great church, the mother of abominations, . . . behold, she is the tares of the earth; she is bound in bundles; her bands are made strong, no man can loose them; therefore, she is ready to be burned. And he shall sound his trump both long and loud, and all nations shall hear it (D&C 88:93–94).

The "great sign" seems to be what Joseph Smith described as "the sign of the coming of the Son of Man," as discussed in chapter 28. Though the Lord uses different language here, the destruction of "Babylon," which is a metaphor of all the evil and wickedness of the world, could include the final events that destroy the armies of Gog at the time of the Lord's coming. It definitely tells us that the wicked and evil of the world will be bound—i.e., they will no longer be free to work their havoc on the world—and will await the fires of the Great Judgment.

> And there shall be silence in heaven for the space of half an hour; and immediately after shall the curtain of heaven be unfolded, as a scroll is unfolded after it is rolled up, and the face of the Lord shall be unveiled; And the saints that are upon the earth, who are alive, shall be quickened and be caught up to meet him. And they who have slept in their graves shall come forth, for their graves shall be opened; and they also shall be caught up to meet him in the midst of the pillar of heaven—They are Christ's, the first fruits, they who shall descend with him first, and they who are on the earth and in their graves, who are first caught up to meet him; and all this by the voice of the sounding of the trump of the angel of God (D&C 88:95–98).

Is this half an hour in our time or the Lord's time? We cannot say for sure. If it represents our time, it could signify several things. Is this a shocked silence over what has just happened with Armageddon? A reverent silence for the many dead? Or a breathless silence of anticipation that springs from knowing that after six thousand years, the world is about to have its first perfectly righteous King and enter an entire millennium of peace and righteousness? Again, we can only speculate.

But we have a definitive time marker in "immediately after." This describes the opening of the heavens to unveil the face of the Lord. Here the sequence of events closely follows that of D&C 45, with some omissions and some additional information.

The first thing described here, which once again has to do specifically with the Saints, was not mentioned in D&C 45. Those who are on the earth at this time, "who are alive," shall be "quickened" and caught up to meet Him. "Quickened" is a word that the Apostle Paul sometimes used. In the Greek it signifies "to cause to live, to arouse and invigorate." This may at first seem like an odd thing to say about people who are already alive, but this quickening suggests some kind of transformation that allows them to be caught up to heaven and endure the glory and presence of a celestial being.

> *When He comes again, unlike coming to the signifying meekness of the manger, He will come in overwhelming majesty and power. In at least one appearance, He will come in red apparel to remind us that He shed His blood for us. Among the astounding, accompanying events, stars will fall from the heavens. . . . What will we and those who witness these marvelous events speak of, then and later? . . . The more we come to know of Jesus and the Atonement, the more we shall praise and adore Him "forever and ever."*
>
> THE NEAL A. MAXWELL QUOTE BOOK, 301

Then follows what we also were taught in D&C 45. The graves of the Saints are opened, and they too are caught up to meet the Savior. It appears that these two things—the quickening of the living and the resurrection of the dead—happen either simultaneously or one immediately after the other. But it is clear that both of these groups are part of the "first fruits," i.e., the first ones to greet the Savior as He prepares to come again.

And after this another angel shall sound, which is the second trump; and then cometh the redemption of those who are Christ's at his coming; who have received their part in that prison which is prepared for them, that they might receive the gospel, and be judged according to men in the flesh (D&C 88:99).

This closely mirrors what we learn in D&C 45. That which follows the first part of the First Resurrection (those going to the celestial kingdom) is the second part of the First Resurrection, or the resurrection of those going to the terrestrial kingdom. They are described as those who were not valiant in their commitment to the Savior (see D&C 76:79).

THE SECOND RESURRECTION

The Second Resurrection will begin at the end of the Millennium and will be for those who are destined for telestial glory. They will have to wait for another thousand years of earth time to come forth from their graves. It is likely that they are kept in the spirit world that much longer in order for them to grow and learn and repent. Sons of perdition from this earth will also be resurrected, but only after all others have been (see D&C 76:37–39).

Turning again to the sequence of the Resurrection, note how the Lord describes what comes next:

> And again, another trump shall sound, which is the third trump; and then come the spirits of men who are to be judged, and are found under condemnation; And these are the rest of the dead; and they live not again until the thousand years are ended, neither again, until the end of the earth (D&C 88:100–101).

We learn two things from this verse. First, the Second Resurrection also has two parts to it, as does the First Resurrection. Next, we see that the Second Resurrection is reserved for the faithless people of the world. In another place, the Lord describes this group in greater detail:

> These are they who are liars, and sorcerers, and adulterers, and whoremongers, and whosoever loves and makes a lie. These are they who suffer the wrath of God on earth. These are they who suffer the vengeance of eternal fire. These are they who are cast down to hell and suffer the wrath of Almighty God (D&C 76:103–106).

And these are they who also will have to wait until the end of the Millennium for their resurrection. But this still is not the end. First come those destined for the telestial kingdom, which is still a kingdom of great glory that "surpasses all understanding" (see D&C 76:89). Then there follows one last and final phase of the Resurrection:

> And another trump shall sound, which is the fourth trump, saying: There are found among those who are to remain until that great and last day, even the end, who shall remain filthy still (D&C 88:102).

The second part of the Second Resurrection is reserved for those "who shall remain filthy still." Consider that for a moment. This is after all of that additional time in the spirit world, where they know of a certainty that God lives. And still they refuse to change. These are they who have been in the covenant and rejected it, who openly fought against the work of God (see D&C 76:25–42). They are called the sons of perdition (see D&C 76:32). These will be the very last to be resurrected, and they will not receive a kingdom of glory but will go to outer darkness for the rest of eternity.

One last thought on the Resurrection as it is connected to the Second Coming. As noted earlier, after Jesus ascended into heaven from the Mount of Olives and the two angels there promised that He would come again, virtually every age of believers has hoped theirs would be the one to see Christ's return.

We shall close with President Joseph F. Smith's explanation:

> It is our duty to make ourselves acquainted with those laws, that we may know how to live in harmony with his will while we dwell in the flesh, that we may be entitled to come forth *in the morning of the First Resurrection, clothed with glory, immortality and eternal lives,* and be permitted to sit down at the right hand of God, in the kingdom of heaven. And except we become acquainted with those laws, and live in harmony with them, we need not expect to enjoy these privileges (Joseph F. Smith, *Gospel Doctrine*, 435).

SUMMARY AND CONCLUSIONS

We have now examined seven aspects directly associated with the Second Coming of Jesus Christ. As we affirmed when we began this study, above all that has happened since the Fall of Adam and Eve and the Resurrection of Jesus of Nazareth, the Second Coming of Jesus Christ is far and away the most important event in the history of the earth. It will be surpassed only when the world becomes a celestial orb where those who will live in the celestial kingdom will dwell.

Now that we have concluded our study of those seven aspects, we add only two additional words: "Amen and amen!"

CHAPTER 31

THE GREAT MILLENNIAL DAY

We know that many worthy and wonderful Latter-day Saints currently lack the ideal opportunities and essential requirements for their progress. Singleness, childlessness, death, and divorce frustrate ideals and postpone the fulfillment of promised blessings. In addition, some women who desire to be full-time mothers and homemakers have been literally compelled to enter the full-time work force. But these frustrations are only temporary. The Lord has promised that in the eternities no blessing will be denied His sons and daughters who keep the commandments, are true to the covenants, and desire what is right. Many of the most important deprivations of mortality will be set right in the Millennium, which is the time for fulfilling all that is incomplete in the great plan of happiness for all of our Father's worthy children. We know that will be true of temple ordinances. I believe it will also be true of family relationships and experiences. (Dallin H. Oaks, With Full Purpose of Heart, 35)

BEAUTIFUL, BRIGHT MILLENNIAL DAY

Moral agency is a gift given to us from God. So is a world filled with opposites for us to choose between, such as good and evil, virtue and vice, pleasure and pain. These are two of the eternal realities of our existence. Without the freedom to choose, there could be no plan of happiness. But with that agency comes consequences.

One grim consequence of that reality is that a "third part" of the hosts of heaven chose to follow Lucifer in his rebellion against the Father and the Son and started a war in heaven. When they were cast out of heaven, they vowed to continue that war here on earth. That war has been raging now for about six thousand years. As Lehi said, these things "must needs be" to bring about the Lord's ultimate purposes. But the opposition that Satan has created is not part of what always "must needs be."

We know through revelation that the earth shall last for seven "days" of a thousand years each, with the final period being like the earth's Sabbath, a day of rest. As we have seen in the last few chapters, at the beginning of that last period of a thousand years, a "day" of rest will be ushered in by Christ's Second Coming. Three great things will take place at that time.

First, the wicked of the world will be destroyed. Much of that will come as they "war among themselves, and the sword of their own hands shall fall upon their own heads" (1 Nephi 22:13).

Second, Christ will return to take His place as King of kings and Lord of lords.

Third, Satan will be bound for a thousand years, allowing for a Millennium of peace, harmony, joy, and progress. That seems so far from where we are now that it is almost dreamlike. Yet the prophets of old and modern prophets have been shown what that coming time will be like. Since our attempts to describe the Millennial day will fall short of the prophetic word, we shall let the prophets speak for themselves.

ETHER 13:9–12

> *And there shall be a new heaven and a new earth; and they shall be like unto the old* save the old have passed away, and all things have become new. And then cometh the New Jerusalem; and blessed are they who dwell therein, for it is they whose garments are white through the blood of the Lamb; and they are they who are numbered among the remnant of the seed of Joseph, who were of the house of Israel. And then also cometh the Jerusalem of old; and the inhabitants thereof, blessed are they, for they have been washed in the blood of the Lamb; and they are they who were scattered and gathered in from the four quarters of the earth, and from the north countries, and are partakers of the fulfilling of the covenant which God made with their father, Abraham. And when these things come, bringeth to pass the scripture which saith, there are they who were first, who shall be last; and there are they who were last, who shall be first (Ether 13:9–12).

There shall be a new heaven and a new earth that are like our current heaven and earth. The phrase could be metaphorical, suggesting a complete change from what we have now. But a "new heaven" could suggest a different placement of the earth, which would make the stars in the sky at night appear to be in a different configuration. That seems less likely, but we noted that some scriptures speak of the heavens shaking. We're not sure what that means, but Isaiah specifically quotes the Lord, who said: "Therefore *I will shake the heavens,* and *the earth shall remove out of her place,* in the wrath of the Lord of hosts, and in the day of his fierce anger" (Isaiah 13:13; see also 2 Nephi 23:13; Isaiah 24:1; D&C 88:87). If the earth moves out of her place in the heavens, that would change the configuration of the night sky. One thing is for sure: things will drastically change when the Millennium comes, and that change will be profoundly for the better.

DOCTRINE AND COVENANTS 101:25–36

> *All things shall become new,* that my knowledge and glory may dwell upon all the earth. And in that day the enmity of man, and the enmity of beasts, yea, the enmity of all flesh, shall cease from before my face. And in that day whatsoever any man shall ask, it shall be given unto him. And in that day Satan shall not have power to tempt any man. And there shall be no sorrow because there is no death. In that day an infant shall not die until he is old; and his life shall be as the age of a tree; And when he dies he shall not sleep, that is to say in the earth, but shall be changed in the twinkling of an eye, and shall be caught up, and his rest shall be glorious. Yea, verily I say unto you, in that day when the Lord shall come, he shall reveal all things—things which have passed, and hidden things which no man knew, things of the earth, by which it was made, and the purpose and the end thereof—things most precious, things that are above, and things that are beneath, things that are in the earth, and upon the earth, and in heaven. And all they who suffer persecution for my name, and endure in faith, though they are called to lay down their lives for my sake yet shall they partake of all this glory. Wherefore, fear not even unto death; for in this world your joy is not full, but in me your joy is full (D&C 101:25–36).

All things shall become new so that His knowledge and glory can dwell on the earth.

The enmity of man, and the enmity of beasts . . . shall cease. This is something that is frequently mentioned, and usually with specific examples, such as children leading a lion or playing around the den of poisonous serpents.

Even beasts of prey will start eating grass. Perhaps some of that is also metaphorical imagery, but as we shall see, it is mentioned again and again, with very specific details.

Whatsoever any man shall ask, it shall be given unto him. This would be a natural result of a whole people who are faithful and true to their covenants.

Satan shall not have power to tempt any man. We can barely conceive of a world without Satan! We shall see what makes that possible in a few moments.

There shall be no sorrow because there is no death. This seems to mean death as we know it, not that everyone would be immortal. This is supported by the idea that babies won't die early, and when people do die in their old age, they won't go to the spirit world but will be resurrected in the twinkling of an eye. Their rest shall be glorious. How many tears have been shed over the untimely deaths of loved ones.

In that day when the Lord shall come, he shall reveal all things. The Lord shall reveal many precious things about the past and the world on which we live. It will be an age of great enlightenment, and not just in religious matters.

Those who suffered persecution for His sake will be given great glory.

2 NEPHI 21:4–9

> *With righteousness shall he judge the poor, and reprove with equity for the meek of the earth;* and he shall smite the earth with the rod of his mouth, and with the breath of his lips shall he slay the wicked. And righteousness shall be the girdle of his loins, and faithfulness the girdle of his reins. The wolf also shall dwell with the lamb, and the leopard shall lie down with the kid, and the calf and the young lion and fatling together; and a little child shall lead them. And the cow and the bear shall feed; their young ones shall lie down together; and the lion shall eat straw like the ox. And the sucking child shall play on the hole of the asp, and the weaned child shall put his hand on the cockatrice's den. They shall not hurt nor destroy in all my holy mountain, for the earth shall be full of the knowledge of the Lord, as the waters cover the sea (2 Nephi 21:4–9; see also Isaiah 11:4–9).

The Savior will *judge the poor, and reprove with equity the meek.* "Reprove" here sounds like some form of correction, but the Hebrew word used in Isaiah means to "show to be right, to prove or to judge," as well as to correct.

"Equity" is also a key word here. It conveys the idea of things being equal and fair. And this mortal life is anything but that. When we look at the differences people experience in such things as the quality of their lives, financial status, opportunities to progress, peace, intelligence, health, disease, birth defects, safety, education, the societies into which they are born, freedom, oppression, and a hundred other things, it is clear that this life is not fair. Some of these differences are caused by our own foolish choices, but many are neither caused by us nor can be fixed through our own efforts. Therefore, at the Judgment, many people can rightly say that life did not offer them a level playing field. We know that Christ paid the price for our *iniquities*, but we often overlook that He also suffered for our *inequities*. Who makes all of that right if there is to be true justice in the world?

> *Can we, even in the depths of disease, tell Him anything at all about suffering? In ways we cannot comprehend, our sicknesses and infirmities were borne by Him even before they were borne by us. The very weight of our combined sins caused Him to descend below all. We have never been, nor will we be, in depths such as He has known. Thus His Atonement made perfect His empathy and His mercy and His capacity to succor us, for which we can be everlastingly grateful as He tutors us in our trials.*
>
> Neal A. Maxwell,
> *Even as I Am*, 116

The answer is found in the Savior, because in addition to our sins, "he will take upon him the *pains*, and the *sicknesses* of his people. . . . and he will take upon him their *infirmities*" (Alma 7:11–12).

Isaiah was shown the future suffering of Christ and described Him as "a man of *sorrows*, and acquainted with *grief*. . . . Surely he hath borne our griefs, and carried our sorrows" (Isaiah 53:3–4). The Hebrew translation of that passage describes this specifically: "A man of *pains* and acquainted with *disease*. . . . Surely, *our diseases he did bear; and our pains he carried.*" If we think that suffering for the sins of the world caused Him infinite pain, what then does it mean that He also suffered added pain and sorrow caused by the inequities and injustices of life so that He could atone for injustices and inequities for all of us? In the end, none of us will be able to say that we were cheated.

Elder Jeffrey R. Holland tried to capture some sense of this broader view of His atoning sacrifice:

In a way that is as monumentally merciful as it is beyond our ability to comprehend, in a way that fills us with as much wonder as it does gratitude, Christ personally took upon himself, beginning in the garden of Gethsemane and continuing on to the cross at Calvary, both the spiritual and physical burden of the *transgressions and iniquities* of everyone in the human family, for all "like sheep have gone astray." Every accountable person who ever lived—except Jesus—has sinned "and come short of the glory of God." Furthermore, we know that Christ took upon himself other lesser but *still painful burdens* as well—sicknesses and afflictions, sorrows and discouragements and infirmities of every kind—that *these sufferings might be lifted* along with the suffering for sin and disobedience (Holland, *Christ and the New Covenant*, 91–92).

All of this too is what will be made right in that great Millennial day. As Christ so gently and yet firmly reminded Joseph Smith at the time of his deepest despair: "The Son of Man hath descended below them all. Art thou greater than he?" (D&C 122:8).

ISAIAH 65:17–24

I create new heavens and a new earth: and the former shall not be remembered, nor come into mind. . . . The voice of weeping shall be no more heard in her, nor the voice of crying. There shall be no more thence an infant of days, nor an old man that hath not filled his days: for the child shall die an hundred years old; but the sinner [being] an hundred years old shall be accursed. And they shall build houses, and inhabit [them]; and they shall plant vineyards, and eat the fruit of them. They shall not build, and another inhabit; they shall not plant, and another eat: for as the days of a tree are the days of my people, and mine elect shall long enjoy the work of their hands. They shall not labour in vain, nor bring forth for trouble; for they are the seed of the blessed of the Lord, and their offspring with them. And it shall come to pass, that before they call, I will answer; and while they are yet speaking, I will hear (Isaiah 65:17–24).

I create new heavens and a new earth. Is this another reference to some kind of literal change in the earth, or another way of saying that all will be made right? Elder McConkie stated: "All this was to be in the day of regeneration, the day when the earth would be refreshed and renewed and receive again its paradisiacal glory" (McConkie, *Mortal Messiah*, 4:306).

President Joseph Fielding Smith explained:

> When the reign of Jesus Christ comes during the Millennium, *only those who have lived the telestial law will be removed.* It is recorded in the Bible and other standard works of the Church that the earth will be cleansed of all its corruption and wickedness. Those who have lived virtuous lives, who have been honest in their dealings with their fellow man and have endeavored to do good to the best of their understanding, shall remain. . . . So we learn that all corruptible things, whether men or beasts or element, shall be consumed; but all that does not come under this awful edict shall remain. Therefore, the honest and upright of all nations, kindreds, and beliefs who have kept the terrestrial as well as the celestial law, will remain. Under these conditions people will enter the great reign of Jesus Christ, carrying with them their beliefs and religious doctrines (Joseph Fielding Smith, *Answers to Gospel Questions*, 1:108–11).

Old Jerusalem shall experience great rejoicing; *and the voice of weeping shall be no more heard in her.* Their Messiah now reigns. Jerusalem has been conquered about twenty-six known times in history. It has been virtually destroyed several times. Its peoples have been completely carried away into captivity at least three times. Today it is a city of unrest and ethnic tension between the Israelis and the Palestinians and surrounding countries. How ironic for a city whose names means "Peace." But there is a time coming when all of that shall cease. Who would not weep for joy when that day finally comes?

People will find their labors productive, not ending in vain. They shall build and inhabit, plant and eat the fruits of their labor. One only need think about how many people have been displaced through war, violence, famine, drought, or civil unrest. Currently in the world there are about seventy million refugees and displaced people, many of whom will never return to their homelands to rebuild what they have lost. Such will find rest and peace.

When they call on the Lord, He shall answer. Prayers offered will be prayers answered.

Even the animal kingdom may experience peace and harmony. No one will hurt or destroy in the Lord's holy mountain. It is hard for us to see how this could be, if this is literal and not just symbolic. But remember that Christ has promised us that it will be a new world.

ZECHARIAH 14:20–21

> In that day shall there be upon the bells of the horses, holiness unto the Lord; and the pots in the Lord's house shall be like the bowls before the altar. Yea, every pot in Jerusalem and in Judah shall be holiness unto the Lord of hosts: and all they that sacrifice shall come and take of them, and seethe therein: and in that day there shall be no more the Canaanite in the house of the Lord of hosts (Zechariah 14:20–21).

Holiness unto the Lord. Zechariah uses some lovely imagery here. The Old and New Jerusalems shall truly become holy cities through the righteousness of their people. Zechariah symbolizes that through the idea that something as trivial as the bells put on horses to let people know they are approaching will have "holiness to the Lord" written on them. Even the pots and pans we use to cook our meals will have the same.

This brings to mind the doorknobs of the Salt Lake Temple. Above the beehive, which symbolizes industry and thrift, are found the words "Holiness to the Lord."

DOCTRINE AND COVENANTS 43:31; 88:110

> For Satan shall be bound, and when he is loosed again he shall only reign for a little season, and then cometh the end of the earth (D&C 43:31).

> The seventh angel shall sound his trump; and he shall stand forth upon the land and upon the sea, and swear in the name of him who sitteth upon the throne, that there shall be time no longer; and Satan shall be bound, that old serpent, who is called the devil, and shall not be loosed for the space of a thousand years (D&C 88:110).

This has to be one of the most profound of all the promises. Satan bound! The numberless minions who followed after him, bodied and unembodied, will no longer be able to go about doing what they have done for a thousand years. Think of the effect that will have on the whole world!

Will this be a literal binding of Satan and his followers, as with chains? Nephi spoke of this and gave us a clear understanding that they will be bound in another way. After speaking of the time when the Lord's people would be blessed by the Holy One of Israel, Nephi goes on to say, "And he [the Lord] gathereth his children from the four quarters of the earth; and he numbereth his sheep, and they know him; . . . and *because of the righteousness of his people, Satan has no power; wherefore, he cannot be loosed for the space of many years; for he hath no power over the hearts of the people,* for they dwell in righteousness, and the Holy One of Israel reigneth" (1 Nephi 22:25–26).

It is enchanting to try to imagine what life will be like in the Millennium, but even with our most optimistic musings we will likely fall short of what it will be. Why? Because nothing in this world that we have seen comes close to approaching what a world without Satan shall be like.

And all thy children shall be taught of the Lord; and great shall be the peace of thy children. In righteousness shalt thou be established: thou shalt be far from oppression; for thou shalt not fear: and from terror; for it shall not come near thee (Isaiah 54:13–14).

In an age of social media with its bullying, shaming, pornography, with mass shootings, child abuse and child neglect, with sexual promiscuity, divorce, broken families, crime, war, violence, and dozens of other threats to our children and grandchildren, perhaps Isaiah's promise here is the sweetest of all: *"Great shall be the peace of thy children!"* And there are not many joys that are sweeter than that.

> *It will make a great difference when Satan will have his power taken away during that period, but the inhabitants of the earth will still have their agency. We are taught that during that thousand years, men will not be compelled to believe and that there will be many, at least in the beginning, who will belong to the Protestant and Catholic churches. The Lord will not take away from them their right to believe as they will. However, if they persist in their unbelief under the conditions which will prevail, they will be condemned.*
>
> JOSEPH FIELDING SMITH,
> ANSWERS TO GOSPEL QUESTIONS, 141

ANOTHER END AND ANOTHER BEGINNING

We shall conclude our discussion on the Millennium with a brief discussion of two more things that are sometimes overlooked. We have spoken much about the visions of John the Revelator in this book. As the Lord said, it was John's privilege to write of the last days of the world (see 1 Nephi 14:18–27). So it should not surprise us that it was through him that we learn of two great events that will take place at the end of the Millennium.

Though he mentioned it only briefly, John spoke of one last battle between good and evil at the end of the Millennium:

> And when the thousand years are expired, Satan shall be loosed out of his prison, and shall go out to deceive the nations which are in the four quarters of the earth, Gog and Magog, to gather them together to battle: the number of whom is as the sand of the sea. And they went up on the breadth of the earth, and compassed the camp of the saints about, and the beloved city: and fire came down from God out of heaven, and devoured them. And the devil that deceived them was cast into the lake of fire and brimstone, where the beast and the false prophet are, and shall be tormented day and night for ever and ever (Revelation 20:7–10).

This, at first, seems a little confusing, for Gog was the name Ezekiel gave to the leader of the vast armies of Armageddon, and Magog was the land from which he came. So how could John say that he will return at the end of the Millennium?

Remembering that John's writings are filled with symbolism and imagery, it should not surprise us that he uses Gog here as a type or symbol of a great military leader who sought to overthrow God's work and destroy His people. The invoking of the name of Gog tells us how terrible this war will be.

He doesn't give us more detail than that, but Joseph Smith confirmed that this is not that same Gog as described by Ezekiel: "The battle of Gog and Magog will be after the Millennium" ("History, 1838–1856, volume D-1 [1 August 1842–1 July 1843]," p. 1490, *The Joseph Smith Papers;* https://www.josephsmithpapers.org/paper-summary/history-1838–1856-volume-d-1-1-august-1842–1-july-1843/133).

But one question that quickly comes to mind is how that could happen when the people are so holy and have lived in righteousness for ten centuries.

There are three words to explain it. We find them used three times in the Book of Mormon, and in all cases they describe the children of righteous, covenant families. The three words are "the rising generation."

Note what happened after King Benjamin brought a whole people to Christ, bringing them to the point that they solemnly covenanted to take upon themselves the name of "the Lord Omnipotent . . . [for He] has wrought a mighty change in us, or in our hearts, that *we have no more disposition to do evil, but to do good continually"* (Mosiah 5:2). That was about 124 B.C.

Yet just four years later we read:

> Now it came to pass that there were many of *the rising generation* that could not understand the words of king Benjamin, . . . And now because of their unbelief they could not understand the word of God; and *their hearts were hardened.* And they would not be baptized; neither would they join the church. *And they were a separate people as to their faith, and remained so ever after,* even in their carnal and sinful state; for they would not call upon the Lord their God (Mosiah 26:1–4).

Here's another example. In 5 B.C., Samuel the Lamanite came among the Nephites, warning them against their wickedness and prophesying that the birth of the Messiah would be in five years. He told them that on the day of Christ's birth, there would be a day and a night and a day without darkness.

When the five years were up, a large number of Nephites had abandoned their faith. But as we know from the record of Nephi, on that very night of Christ's birth in the Old World, the sign was given. There was great fear, and many turned back to the Lord. That was in A.D. 1

Yet, we read that just three years later:

> And there was also a cause of much sorrow *among the Lamanites;* for behold, *they had many children who did grow up and began to wax strong in years, that they became for themselves,* and were led away by some who were Zoramites, by their lyings and their flattering words, to join the Gadianton robbers. And thus were the Lamanites afflicted also, and began to decrease as to their faith and righteousness, *because of the wickedness of the rising generation* (3 Nephi 1:29–30).

There is one more example. A large number of Nephites and Lamanites were converted to Christ after He personally visited the temple in the land Bountiful. The people were so thoroughly converted to Christ and His gospel that they *"were all converted unto the Lord,* upon all the face of the land, both Nephites and Lamanites, and there were no contentions and disputations among them, and every man did deal justly one with another. And they had all things common among them; therefore there were not rich and poor, bond and free, but they were all made free, and partakers of the heavenly gift" (4 Nephi 1:2–3).

This Zion society lasted for about two hundred years. And yet there came a point where they too started turning away. How could that happen? Here is what Mormon described for us: "And they did not dwindle in unbelief, but they did wilfully rebel against the gospel of Christ; *and they did teach their children that they should not believe*" (4 Nephi 1:38).

How is it that this greatest and grandest of all the Zion societies that will thrive during the Millennium turn away from the covenant? It is most likely that this same pattern will gradually creep in among the rising generation. Remember, Satan won't be bound in chains. He will be bound by the righteous hearts of the people. If the hearts of the people turn away from the Lord, then Satan's power once again begins to rise.

How long that final war will last we are not told. But in modern revelation we are told who will lead the armies of the Lord and how the battle will turn out:

> Satan shall be bound, that old serpent, who is called the devil, and shall not be loosed for the space of a thousand years. And then he shall be loosed for a little season, that he may gather together his armies. And Michael, the seventh angel, even the archangel [who is Adam], shall gather together his armies, *even the hosts of heaven.* And the devil shall gather together his armies; even the hosts of hell, and shall come up to battle against Michael and his armies. And then cometh the battle of the great God; and the devil and his armies shall be cast away into their own place, that they shall not have power over the saints any more at all. For Michael shall fight their battles, and shall overcome him who seeketh the throne of him who sitteth upon the throne, even the Lamb. This is the glory of God, and the sanctified; and they shall not any more see death (D&C 88:110–116).

A NEW HEAVEN AND A NEW EARTH

Another remarkable doctrine we received in the revelation that Joseph Smith described as "the 'olive leaf' . . . plucked from the Tree of Paradise" has to do with the final end of the earth. Note that we are speaking of the *earth* now, not the world. We said that the world, which describes the weaknesses and foibles of mankind, would eventually come to an end with the Second Coming of Jesus Christ. But the earth continues, moving from a telestial level of life to a terrestrial level. That's what makes the Millennium so remarkable.

The Great Millennial Day

But now we have come to the end—not just of our discussion of the Millennium, but also to the end of the seven thousand years of the world's temporal existence (see D&C 77:6–7). So then what? Is that it? Or is there more to follow? The Lord gave us the answer in section 88 of the Doctrine and Covenants.

The resurrection from the dead is the redemption of the soul. And the redemption of the soul is through him that quickeneth all things, in whose bosom it is decreed that *the poor and the meek of the earth shall inherit it.* Therefore, it must needs be sanctified from all unrighteousness, *that it may be prepared for the celestial glory;* For after it hath filled the measure of its creation, *it shall be crowned with glory, even with the presence of God the Father;* That bodies who are of the celestial kingdom may possess it forever and ever; for, for *this intent was it made and created,* and for this intent are they sanctified (D&C 88:16–20).

After the close of the millennial reign we are informed that Satan, who was bound during the millennium, shall be loosed and go forth to deceive the nations. Then will come the end. The earth will die and be purified and receive its resurrection. During this cleansing period the City Zion, or New Jerusalem, will be taken from the earth; and when the earth is prepared for the celestial glory, the city will come down according to the prediction in the Book of Revelation.

Joseph Fielding Smith.
Answers to Gospel Questions,
Vol. II, 106

There is not much in that statement that is ambiguous. And this is confirmed by what we know about the plan of salvation.

SUMMARY AND CONCLUSIONS

In the opening chapter of this book we said that we were going to undertake an extensive study of the prophecies of the last days and that our sources would be the word of the Lord as given to His chosen prophets, ancient and modern. We have done that now.

We also said that we were going to examine the idea of *preparation* and *separation*. We summarized that goal with the idea that what the Lord cares most about is our preparation for what will come. We know the future holds a great separation of the righteous from the unrighteous. So, in addition to our study of the events associated with the Second Coming, we need to focus on preparation. For it is preparation that gets us ready for the coming separation and allows us to "be not troubled."

With that in mind, the title for our closing section, Part VI, is a promise directly from the scriptures: *"If ye are prepared ye shall not fear"* (D&C 38:30).

Part VI

"If Ye Are Prepared Ye Shall Not Fear"

CHAPTER 32

WATCH AND BE READY

The Standard of Truth has been erected; no unhallowed hand can stop the work from progressing; persecutions may rage, mobs may combine, armies may assemble, calumny may defame, but the truth of God will go forth boldly, nobly, and independent, till it has penetrated every continent, visited every clime, swept every country, and sounded in every ear, till the purposes of God shall be accomplished, and the Great Jehovah shall say the work is done. (Joseph Smith, *Teachings of Presidents of the Church: Joseph Smith*, 142)

PREPARING FOR WHAT LIES AHEAD

We have come to the last section in the book. Earlier we identified the three most common questions people have about the Second Coming. *How soon will the end come?* That we answered in Part II. *What can we expect will happen?* We answered that using Elijah's description that it will be both a great and a dreadful day. Parts III, IV, and V discuss those two scenarios. *How do we prepare ourselves so it will be a great day and not a dreadful one?* Though this question is usually listed last, it is without a doubt the most important area of our study. So, in Part VI, we will explore how to win for ourselves one of the Lord's most comforting promises: "If ye are prepared ye shall not fear" (D&C 38:30).

In a way this will be a challenge, for it can truly be said that virtually *every* doctrine and principle of the gospel of Jesus Christ is designed to prepare ourselves, our families, and The Church of Jesus Christ of Latter-day Saints for the time of a great separation from the world. That could justify a book of its own. In addition, the standard works and messages of our living prophets, seers, and revelators are filled with counsel on what we need to do to prepare for this great separation.

While speaking to young adults of the Church, President Russell M. Nelson made reference to a title given to their age group. They are called Millennials because they came of age around the year 2000. President Nelson used that title to give them counsel that can be applied to all of us as well:

> Spiritual impressions I've received about you lead me to believe that the term Millennial may actually be perfect for you. But for a much different reason than the experts may ever understand. The term Millennial is perfect for you *if* that term reminds you of who you really are and what your purpose in life really is. A True Millennial is one who was taught and did teach the gospel of Jesus Christ premortally and who made covenants with our Heavenly Father there about courageous things—even morally courageous things—that you would do while here on earth. A True Millennial is a man or woman whom God trusted enough to send to earth during the most compelling dispensation in the history of this world. A True Millennial is a man or woman who lives now to help prepare the people of this world for the Second Coming of Jesus Christ and His millennial reign. Make no mistake about it—you were born to be a True Millennial! (Russell M. Nelson, "Becoming True Millenials," worldwide devotional for young adults, January 2016).

In separating ourselves from the world there will also be a great uniting and reuniting. The faithful will be gathered together into Zion societies that will last for a thousand years. Those whose bodies now lie in their graves shall come forth to join in the great wedding supper of the Lamb. The city of Enoch will come down and mingle with the faithful in a New Jerusalem.

This is what the future asks of us: *Preparation* for the coming *separation* and eventual reunion. Words cannot describe the joy of those who will be gathered to stand on the right hand of God, nor can they adequately depict the anguish of those who reject the light. Therefore, preparation for that coming separation and reunion should be one of the major purposes in life. To help us do that, the Lord has given us another commandment: "Watch, therefore, that ye may be ready" (D&C 50:46). Here are some of the things we should watch for.

UPON MY HOUSE SHALL IT BEGIN

Among the many promises of peace and joy and blessings for the faithful, we also find numerous warnings and admonitions. Some of them are directly tied to the last days and Christ's coming. For example, among the many wonderful things that await those who are on the covenant path in these last days, there is this very specific warning:

> Behold, vengeance cometh speedily upon the inhabitants of the earth, a day of wrath, a day of burning, a day of desolation, of weeping, of mourning, and of lamentation; and as a whirlwind it shall come upon all the face of the earth, saith the Lord. *And upon my house shall it begin, and from my house shall it go forth,* saith the Lord; *First among those among you, saith the Lord, who have professed to know my name and have not known me* (D&C 112:24–26).

In light of all the wonderful promises, those words are almost shocking. Upon His house? But, knowing of all our imperfections, should we really be surprised? The Lord has also reminded us that He cannot look upon sin "with the least degree of allowance" (Alma 45:16; D&C 1:31; 19:20). Sin and transgression are two of the great separating influences of life. Therefore, the Lord warns us sternly of their consequences.

He also states very clearly that those who have made solemn and sacred covenants with Him are held to a higher level of accountability than those who have not. This is because they were given the gift of the Holy Ghost after baptism, which gives them more light and knowledge than others. Thus, the Lord makes it emphatically clear that His elect are held to a higher standard:

> For of him unto whom much is given much is required; and he who sins against the greater light shall receive the greater condemnation. Ye call upon my name for revelations, and I give them unto you; and inasmuch as ye keep not my sayings, which I give unto you, ye become transgressors; and justice and judgment are the penalty which is affixed unto my law. Therefore, what I say unto one I say unto all: Watch, for the adversary spreadeth his dominions, and darkness reigneth (D&C 82:3–5).

Elder Dale G. Renlund and his wife, Sister Ruth L. Renlund, spoke in a world broadcast to young adults in January of 2019. They began with an allegory about a boat that makes us smile and wince at the same time. They titled their address "Doubt Not, but Be Believing."

Elder Renlund: Imagine having capsized in a boat while sailing in the ocean. You're wearing a life preserver and have been swimming for hours toward what you believe is the nearest shore, but you can't be sure. You've become extremely dehydrated, so that every time you start swimming, you become light-headed and fatigued. By your best estimates the shore is 30 kilometers, or 18 miles, away. You fear for your life because you can't swim that far. In the distance you hear a small engine. The sound seems to be coming toward you; your hope of rescue soars. As you look, you see a small fishing boat approaching.

Sister Renlund: "Oh, thank heavens," you think, "the captain sees me!" The boat stops and a kindly, weather-beaten fisherman helps you on board. Gratefully you crawl to a seat in the boat, breathing a sigh of relief. The fisherman gives you a canteen of water and some soda crackers. You consume them greedily. The water and soda crackers provide enough nourishment for you to recover. You are so relieved and so happy. You are on your way home. As you begin to revive and start feeling better, you start paying attention to some things you hadn't really noticed before. The water from the canteen is a bit stale and not what you would have preferred, like Evian or Perrier. The crackers tasted good, but what you really wanted was some delicatessen meat followed by a chocolate croissant. You also notice that the kindly fisherman wears worn boots and blue jeans. The sweatband on his hat is stained, and he seems to be hard of hearing.

Elder Renlund: You note that the boat is well-used and that there are dents in the right side of the bow. Some of the paint is chipped and peeling. You see that when the fisherman relaxes his grip on the rudder, the boat pulls to the right. You begin to worry that this boat and this captain cannot provide the rescue you need. You ask the fisherman about the dents and the rudder. He says he hasn't worried much about those things because he has steered the boat to and from the fishing grounds, over the same route, day in and day out, for decades. The boat has always gotten him safely and reliably where he wanted to go. You are stunned! How could he not worry about the dents and the steering? And why could the nourishment have not been more to your liking? The more you focus on the boat and the fisherman, the more concerned you become. You question your decision to get on board in the first place. Your anxiety begins to grow. Finally, you demand that the fisherman stop the boat and let you back into the water. Even though you are still more than 20 kilometers, or 12 miles, away from shore, you can't stand the idea of being in the boat. With sadness, the fisherman stops the boat and helps you back into the ocean. You are on your own again

(Dale G. and Ruth L. Renlund, "Doubt Not, but Be Believing," young adult broadcast, January 13, 2019).

The first reaction that some people will have to their parable will be, "That's not true to life. Surely no one would be so foolish as to jump back into the ocean." Maybe not into the actual ocean, but jumping into a life outside of the covenant? Unfortunately, that is happening all around us.

These members forget that the Church is the craft the Lord has given to help charter our way through troubled waters. We all know that members of the Church, including those in leadership, are not perfect. We all have our flaws and blemishes. We don't do things perfectly. And too often we may offend others to the point that they leave the boat, even though it is seaworthy and reliable. Sometimes these decisions are encouraged by people who have previously abandoned the boat or those who ridicule anyone who would get into any boat in the first place. These voices may come from a variety of sources that are highly biased or highly critical of the Church, its doctrines and policies, and/or its members. And sadly, some are too quick to abandon the boat and tread water while they wait for some other boat to come along and rescue them.

The world holds those same expectations. When people have been given more light, more truth, more blessings, more opportunities to learn, more affluence, more intellectual and physical gifts, we expect more of them and are disappointed when they don't measure up to the advantages that are theirs. We feel that is only just.

So knowing that God's justice is perfect, why would we expect anything different from Him? That is especially true of members of The Church of Jesus Christ of Latter-day Saints who have been given the gift of the Holy Ghost at their baptism. The Holy Ghost is a member of the Godhead who has numerous spiritual gifts for us. If we casually—or deliberately—turn our backs on Him, how can we not expect some loss of those privileges?

This applies not just to those who abandon the boat. Sadly there are members who stay on the boat and complain about all kinds of things—the captain, the speed at which to boat moves, the food, the water, the condition of the boat, the destination the captain has chosen.

How does the Savior feel about such members of the covenant? Here is what He said to members of the New Testament Church: "I know thy works, that thou art neither cold nor hot: I would thou wert cold or hot. So then *because thou art lukewarm, and neither cold nor hot,* I will spue thee out of my mouth" (Revelation 3:15–16).

That's pretty strong language from the Savior. But it is not the only place that He has given us this warning. Here are some other examples:

> For the indignation of the Lord is kindled against their abominations and all their wicked works. Nevertheless, Zion shall escape *if she observe to do all things whatsoever I have commanded her. But if she observe not to do whatsoever I have commanded her, I will visit her according to all her works, with sore affliction, with pestilence, with plague, with sword, with vengeance, with devouring fire* (D&C 97:24–26).

> If any man suffer as a Christian, let him not be ashamed; but let him glorify God on this behalf. For the time is come that *judgment must begin at the house of God* (1 Peter 4:16–17).

> I have decreed a decree which my people shall realize, inasmuch as they hearken from this very hour unto the counsel which I, the Lord their God, shall give unto them. Behold they shall . . . begin to prevail against mine enemies from this very hour. And by hearkening to observe all the words which I, the Lord their God, shall speak unto them, they shall never cease to prevail until the kingdoms of the world are subdued under my feet, and the earth is given unto the saints, to possess it forever and ever. But inasmuch as they keep not my commandments, and hearken not to observe all my words, *the kingdoms of the world shall prevail against them* (D&C 103:5–8).

When we remember that the Lord wasn't speaking to the wicked and faithless in these passages but to those who have agreed to take upon themselves His name, those are sobering warnings. Our prophets have also encouraged us to remember what our covenants require of us:

> The trouble with us today, is there are too many of us *who put question marks instead of periods after what the Lord says.* I want you to think about that. We shouldn't be concerned about why he said something, or whether or not it can be made so. Just trust the Lord. We don't try to find the answers or explanations. We shouldn't try to spend time explaining what the Lord didn't see fit to explain. We spend useless time. If you would teach our people to put periods and not question marks after what the Lord has declared, we would say, "It is enough for me to know that is what the Lord said" (Harold B. Lee, "Admonitions for the Priesthood of God," *Ensign*, January 1973).

MY PEOPLE WILL I PRESERVE

With that voice of warning ringing in our ears, let us now look at the promises the Lord has made to those who are His elect, to those who are not lukewarm in their commitments.

We took time to see some of the consequences of not being fully committed to the kingdom. But, as we saw in chapter 3, the Lord often speaks to us with both a voice of warning and a voice of promise. So, here are some of the promises the Lord offers to the faithful. These prophetic words are shared without further commentary, for the power in these promises is self-evident.

- "The keys of the kingdom of God are committed unto man on the earth, and from thence shall *the gospel roll forth unto the ends of the earth,* as the stone which is cut out of the mountain without hands shall roll forth, until it has filled the whole earth" (D&C 65:2; see also Daniel 2:44).
- "And it came to pass that I beheld the church of the Lamb of God, and its numbers were few, . . . nevertheless, I beheld that the church of the Lamb, who were the saints of God, were also upon all the face of the earth; and their dominions upon the face of the earth were small, . . . And it came to pass that I, Nephi, beheld *the power of the Lamb of God, that it descended upon the saints of the church of the Lamb,* and *upon the covenant people of the Lord,* who were scattered upon all the face of the earth; and *they were armed with righteousness and with the power of God in great glory*" (1 Nephi 14:12, 14).
- "What power shall stay the heavens? As well might man stretch forth his puny arm to stop the Missouri river in its decreed course, or to turn it up stream, *as to hinder the Almighty from pouring down knowledge from heaven upon the heads of the Latter-day Saints*" (D&C 121:33).
- "And all the inhabitants of the earth are reputed as nothing: and *he doeth according to his will in the army of heaven,* and among the inhabitants of the earth: and *none can stay his hand, or say unto him, What doest thou?*" (Daniel 4:35).
- "And every nation which shall war against thee, O house of Israel, shall be turned one against another, and they shall fall into the pit which they digged to ensnare the people of the Lord. *And all that fight against Zion shall be destroyed.* . . . For the time soon cometh *that the fulness of the wrath of God shall be poured out upon all the children of men;* for *he*

- *will not suffer that the wicked shall destroy the righteous*" (1 Nephi 22:14, 16).
- "The time soon cometh that the fulness of the wrath of God shall be poured out upon all the children of men; for *he will not suffer that the wicked shall destroy the righteous. Wherefore, he will preserve the righteous by his power,* . . . *Wherefore, the righteous need not fear; for thus saith the prophet, they shall be saved, even if it so be as by fire.* . . . Behold, *the righteous shall not perish;* for the time surely must come that *all they who fight against Zion shall be cut off.* And *the Lord will surely prepare a way for his people,* . . . *And the righteous need not fear, for they are those who shall not be confounded.* . . . And the time cometh speedily that *the righteous must be led up as calves of the stall,* and the Holy One of Israel must reign in dominion, and might, and power, and great glory" (1 Nephi 22:16–24).
- "*The Lord shall have power over his saints,* and shall reign in their midst, and shall come down in judgment upon Idumea, or the world" (D&C 1:36).
- "And *then shall the power of heaven come down among them; and I also will be in the midst*" (3 Nephi 21:25).
- "*I will rend their kingdoms;* I will not only shake the earth, but the starry heavens shall tremble. For *I, the Lord, have put forth my hand to exert the powers of heaven;* ye cannot see it now, yet a little while and ye shall see it, and know that I am, and that I will come and reign with my people" (D&C 84:118–19).
- "And by hearkening to observe all the words which I, the Lord their God, shall speak unto them, *they shall never cease to prevail until the kingdoms of the world are subdued* under my feet, and the earth is given unto the saints, to possess it forever and ever. But *inasmuch as they keep not my commandments, and hearken not to observe all my words, the kingdoms of the world shall prevail against them*" (D&C 103:7–8).

Here too we shall share counsel that those we sustain as prophets, seers, and revelators have taught us. Speaking to the youth in a worldwide broadcast, President Nelson made a promise:

> I promise you—not the person sitting next to you, but you—that, wherever you are in the world, wherever you are on the covenant path—even if, at this moment, you are not centered on the path—I promise you that *if you will sincerely and persistently do the spiritual work needed to develop the crucial, spiritual skill of learning*

how to hear the whisperings of the Holy Ghost, you will have all the direction you will ever need in your life. You will be given answers to your questions in the Lord's own way and in His own time (Russell M. Nelson, "Hope of Israel," worldwide youth devotional, June 3, 2018, 2–3).

Elder Neil L. Andersen spoke of a "compensatory power" that comes from obedience:

> *As evil increases in the world, there is a compensatory spiritual power for the righteous.* As the world slides from its spiritual moorings, *the Lord prepares the way for those who seek Him,* offering them greater assurance, greater confirmation, and greater confidence in the spiritual direction they are traveling. The gift of the Holy Ghost becomes a brighter light in the emerging twilight. . . . This added blessing of spiritual power does not settle upon us just because we are part of this generation. . . . As with all spiritual gifts, it requires our desiring it, pursuing it, and living worthy of receiving it. . . . I emphasize once again: *As evil increases in the world, the Lord does not leave us on the same footing.* In a world that would diminish or discard or impair belief, *there is an added spiritual power for those who are willing to set their course on increasing their faith in Jesus Christ* (Neil L. Andersen, "A Compensatory Spiritual Power for the Righteous," BYU Education Week devotional, August 18, 2015, 4–6).

Many of us worry about keeping our families safe in a world that is ever spiraling downward:

> We face the challenge of raising families in the world in darkening clouds of wickedness. Some of our members are unsettled, and sometimes they wonder: Is there any place one can go to escape from it all? Is there another town or a state or a country where it is safe, where one can find refuge? The answer generally is no. The defense and the refuge is where our members now live. . . . *We are not to be afraid, even in a world where the hostilities will never end.* The war of opposition that was prophesied in the revelations continues today. *We are to be happy and positive. We are not to be afraid. Fear is the opposite of faith.* . . . We speak of the Church as our refuge, our defense. There is safety and protection in the Church. It centers in the gospel of Jesus Christ. *Latter-day Saints learn to look within themselves to see the redeeming power of the Savior*

of all mankind (Boyd K. Packer, "A Defense and a Refuge," *Ensign*, November 2006).

President Gordon B. Hinckley warned about the age of pessimism in which we live:

> This is an age of pessimism. Ours is a mission of faith. To my brethren and sisters everywhere, *I call upon you to reaffirm your faith*, to move this work forward across the world. You can make it stronger by the manner in which you live. Let the gospel be your sword and your shield. Each of us is a part of the greatest cause on earth (Gordon B. Hinckley, "Stay the Course," *Ensign*, November 1995).

When he was President of the Church, Howard W. Hunter also made a promise:

> I promise you in the name of the Lord whose servant I am that *God will always protect and care for his people*. We will have our difficulties the way every generation and people have had difficulties. But with the gospel of Jesus Christ, you have every hope and promise and reassurance. *The Lord has power over his Saints and will always prepare places of peace, defense, and safety for his people* (Howard W. Hunter, *That We Might Have Joy*, 94).

SUMMARY AND CONCLUSIONS

If one ever needed the motivation to break loose from being lukewarm in the faith or from being lukewarm in the covenant, this combination of warnings and promises can provide that motivation. All of us need to get a little more fire into our testimonies, a few more thermal units into our commitment to the kingdom. All of us need the compensatory power that allows us to call down the blessings of heaven for ourselves and our families.

So let us take this counsel to heart. We are looking for ways to increase our preparation for Christ's Second Coming. In this chapter we have two introductory concepts. First, we cannot be lukewarm in our commitment to the kingdom. Second, if we are fully committed, the promises from the Father and the Son are so powerful that they become a strong motivating factor in and of themselves.

As we said at the beginning, this section is on preparing ourselves (and others) for the days ahead. We are especially concerned about being properly prepared for the day of His coming. Therefore, we shall now examine four areas of preparation that will bless our lives. These are:

    1. Increase in our knowledge and understanding of the world around us.

    2. Increase in our knowledge and understanding of the gospel.

    3. Prepare ourselves temporally.

    4. Prepare ourselves spiritually.

CHAPTER 33

INCREASE IN KNOWLEDGE

We live in a time of turmoil. Earthquakes and tsunamis wreak devastation, governments collapse, economic stresses are severe, the family is under attack, and divorce rates are rising. We have great cause for concern. But we do not need to let our fears displace our faith. We can combat those fears by strengthening our faith. . . . Why do we need such resilient faith? Because difficult days are ahead. Rarely in the future will it be easy or popular to be a faithful Latter-day Saint. Each of us will be tested. The Apostle Paul warned that in the latter days, those who diligently follow the Lord "shall suffer persecution." That very persecution can either crush you into silent weakness or motivate you to be more exemplary and courageous in your daily lives. (Russell M. Nelson, "Face the Future with Faith," *Ensign*, May 2011)

THE SCHOOL OF THE PROPHETS

In a revelation given on December 27, 1832, while The Church of Jesus Christ of Latter-day Saints was still in its infancy, the Lord gave the Prophet Joseph Smith a very direct and very explicit commandment: "And as all have not faith, seek ye diligently and *teach one another words of wisdom;* yea, *seek ye out of the best books* words of wisdom; *seek learning,* even by study and also by faith" (D&C 88:118). In the same section, after naming several areas of study they should be learning about, the Lord added, "that ye may be prepared in all things" (v. 80).

This was at a time when the American nation was barely fifty years old. Much of the country was rural, with many isolated hamlets and villages. Often, schools were primitive, limited or nonexistent and the three

Rs—reading, 'riting, and 'rithmetic—often had to be taught at home. This revelation made it very clear that the Lord values education and learning for His people. But what followed a few verses later must have come as a surprise.

The Lord said that they were to set up a "school of the prophets, established for their instruction in all things that are expedient for them" (D&C 88:127). The first "school," which was held in one of the rooms above the Newel K. Whitney Store in Kirtland, Ohio, began about a month later. At this point, however, this educational effort was not aimed at the whole Church but to selected Church leaders, and there were never more than about twenty-five students. Its purpose was primarily to help them prepare to serve missions and build up the Church. Instruction focused on the scriptures and Church doctrine, though some time was devoted to secular subjects, especially English grammar, which would help make them more effective missionaries.

The school continued for about three months until spring planting began. Then many of the brethren left on their missions and others went to work preparing their land. It never reconvened, but other "schools" were initiated in Missouri and Kirtland. It was to set a pattern for the Church regarding education. A deep appreciation for the value of education was woven into the cultural fiber of the Church. Wherever the Saints gathered, they remembered that initial commandment to "teach one another." Once they arrived in Utah, elementary and secondary schools were started, often held in tents or log homes. As the Church grew, so did their educational efforts. Elementary and secondary schools sprang up in virtually every community. Academies of higher learning were organized throughout the territory. Just three years after they arrived in Salt Lake City, Brigham Young created the University of Deseret, which eventually became the University of Utah. The Brigham Young Academy in Provo also went on to become a major university, and is still operating today as Brigham Young University.

Why pause to review this history in a chapter on preparing ourselves for the coming of Jesus Christ? First, an educated people are a people much better equipped to deal with life and its challenges. Second, through learning we can better understand what the future holds and the implications of that for ourselves and our families.

That learning consists of two separate but interlocking tracks: education in the things of the world, and education in things of God. Both are important if we are to be better prepared for the Second Coming.

INCREASING OUR KNOWLEDGE AND UNDERSTANDING OF THE WORLD AROUND US

It has never been part of the Lord's plan that His people should withdraw from the world into isolated communities, conclaves, monasteries, or convents. We are to be *in* the world but not *of* the world. And that is by the Lord's design so that we can be a positive influence in the world. In addition to asking that we be good citizens and good neighbors, the Lord has used many metaphors to describe what He expects of His Saints. We are to be a light on a candlestick. A city on a hill. Leaven in the lump of bread. The salt of the earth. A seed planted in good soil. The wheat but not the tares. A treasure hid in a field or a pearl of great price. Virgins with extra oil in their lamps.

And as part of our being in the world, the Lord has specifically directed us to be aware and knowledgeable of the world in which we live. We previously cited the Lord's admonition to "seek learning by faith" (see D&C 88:118).

It is of interest that the Lord gave Joseph Smith a specific revelation about learning more of the world than just our own limited fields of labor and sociality. And part of that seems to be directly linked to our overall preparation for the days that are ahead.

Perhaps this is not something that is high on our list of priorities as we think about preparing for the Second Coming, but it is something that the Lord has specifically asked of us. And part of the reason could go back to what the Savior said about the leaves of the fig tree and the signs of the times.

The Lord promised that we would "be not troubled" if we recognized the signs of the times when we see them. Knowing about the "dreadful" signs of the times won't make all of our anxiety go away, but there is comfort in knowing what God has warned us about so we can "watch and be ready" (see D&C 50:46).

AN INFORMED PEOPLE

Sometimes, the news media focuses so much on all the troubles of the world—and there is plenty to fill up the time—that we may get discouraged and decide to just turn it off. This is understandable, but we also have this very clear directive from the Lord to learn and gain knowledge, and not just in spiritual matters. President Russell M. Nelson also reminded us of that dual expectation when he said, "Increase in learning includes spiritual as well as temporal knowledge" (*Teachings*, 210).

Perhaps when we strive to seek out of the best books, we should also strive to seek out of the best media. We live in an amazing age of information. We even have a new verb in our vocabulary: "Google it." Of course much of it is spiritual trash, even pure evil. But that doesn't mean we should shut down all access to the resources we now have. With all of the negative media that is out there, there are still many wonderful sources of information readily available. There are educational channels, balanced news reporting, special interest groups, clubs and organizations, many excellent books and periodicals, lecture series, podcasts, and blog sites that are informative, helpful, and uplifting.

President Dallin H. Oaks reminds us of our responsibility to carefully select what we watch and listen to:

> We live in a time of greatly expanded and disseminated information. But not all of this information is true. We need to be cautious as we seek truth and choose sources for that search. We should not consider secular prominence or authority as qualified sources of truth. We should be cautious about relying on information or advice offered by entertainment stars, prominent athletes, or anonymous internet sources. Expertise in one field should not be taken as expertise on truth in other subjects (Dallin H. Oaks, "Truth and the Plan," *Ensign*, November 2018).

On the other hand, we have been counseled to be aware of the world around us. That includes the wonders of our world and the positive side of the human experience. But part of that awareness will also include some things that are disturbing and even depressing. We are expected to pick and choose wisely, but not to shut ourselves away from the world.

President Gordon B. Hinckley talked about the importance of balance in various areas of our lives, including how much time we spend even on things that are good:

> Nor can you afford to idle away your time in long hours watching the frivolous and damaging programming of which much of television is comprised. There are better things for you to do (Gordon B. Hinckley, "A Chosen Generation," *Ensign*, May 1992).

It is interesting that the Lord doesn't tell us in detail what we should watch or not watch, what we should read or not read, what we should study or not study. As the Prophet Joseph taught, the Lord teaches us correct principles, then leaves us to govern ourselves. And one of those principles is to seek learning.

INCREASE OUR KNOWLEDGE AND UNDERSTANDING OF THE GOSPEL

President Jedediah M. Grant of the First Presidency asked the following question and then gave the answer: "Why is it that the Latter-day Saints are perfectly calm and serene among all the convulsions of the earth—the turmoil, strife, war, pestilence, famine and distress of nations? It is because the spirit of prophecy *has made known to us that such things would actually transpire upon the earth*. We understand it, and view it in its true light. We have learned it by the visions of the Almighty" ("The Hand of God in Events on Earth," *Improvement Era*, February 1915, 286).

It is very likely that some readers are exclaiming: "Calm and serene? Who is calm and serene?" Perhaps that's one of the reasons they have stopped watching the nightly news. But President Grant's point is a good one. Knowing that God knows of the "convulsions of the earth" and that He will help us get through them is greatly comforting. Here we are seeing an emphasis on a different kind of learning. What President Grant spoke of was gospel knowledge, doctrinal knowledge, scriptural knowledge, prophetic knowledge. This is the other side of preparing ourselves through learning. We are not to ignore learning about our world. But neither are we to ignore our knowledge of the gospel in doing so.

Elder David A. Bednar also reminded us that gaining gospel knowledge is a serious obligation on the part of all members of the Church:

> Each and every member of The Church of Jesus Christ of Latter-day Saints *bears a personal responsibility to learn and live* the truths of the Savior's restored gospel and to receive by proper authority the ordinances of salvation. We should not expect the Church as an organization to teach or tell us all of the things we need to know and to become devoted disciples and endure valiantly to the end. Rather our individual responsibility is *to learn* what we should learn, *to live* as we know we should live, and *to become* what the Master would have us become. As young Joseph Smith returned to his home from the Sacred Grove immediately after the appearance of the Father and the Son, he spoke first with his mother . . . [and said to her] "I have learned for myself" (David A. Bednar, *Increase in Learning*, 1).

Marion G. Romney, of the First Presidency, gave an important insight on why we need to know and understand what is happening on both sides of this equation—the worldly and the spiritual. We have spoken of this before. It is what Jesus taught the Twelve on the Mount of Olives.

> It was in the light of Christ's *foreknowledge* of this glorious consummation [the Second Coming] that he said to his disciples, "be not troubled." . . . I hope we are all familiar with these words of the Lord and with his predictions concerning other coming events, such as the building of the new Jerusalem and the redemption of the old, the return of Enoch's Zion, and Christ's millennial reign. *Not only do I hope that we are familiar with these coming events; I hope also that we keep the vision of them continually before our minds.* This I do *because upon a knowledge of them, and an assurance of their reality and a witness that each of us may have part therein, rests the efficacy of Christ's admonition, "be not troubled"* (Marion G. Romney, in Conference Report, October 1966, 51–52).

This is a reminder that part of the gospel knowledge the Lord has given us and expects us to study includes the events surrounding the Second Coming. Joseph Fielding Smith, then a member of the Quorum of the Twelve Apostles, gave a series of lectures in Salt Lake City shortly after World War II began. After describing some of the terrible things associated with the battle of Armageddon, President Smith said:

> I know these are unpleasant things. It is not a pleasant thing even for me to stand here and tell you that this is written in the Scriptures. If the Lord has a controversy with the nations, He will put them to the sword. Their bodies shall lie unburied like dung upon the earth. That is not nice, is it, *but should we not know it? Is it not our duty to read these things and understand them? Don't you think the Lord has given us these things that we might know and we might prepare ourselves* through humility, through repentance, through faith, that we might escape from these dreadful conditions that are portrayed by these ancient prophets? (Smith, *The Signs of the Times*, 154–55).

There is one aspect of gospel knowledge that is especially important in our preparation for the Second Coming. It is knowing and understanding a key part of the overall gospel. That part is called the doctrines of the gospel.

Over my years as a teacher and administrator in the Church Educational System, in my various callings and Church service, and with my own family and friends, I have gradually come to understand how important the doctrines of the gospel are to our spiritual health. They are actually foundational to all that we believe, and if our knowledge and understanding of the doctrine is weak, then our spiritual foundations may also be weak.

Sometimes we are not clear on the difference between a *doctrine* of the gospel and a *principle* of the gospel. Elder Bednar clearly explains what each one is, how they differ, and how one flows from the other:

> A gospel *doctrine is a truth—a truth of salvation* revealed by a loving Heavenly Father. Gospel *doctrines are eternal, they do not change,* and pertain to the eternal progression and exaltation of Heavenly Father's sons and daughters. . . . *Gospel doctrines answer the question of "why?"* For example, the doctrine of the plan of happiness answers the questions of *why* we are here on earth, *why* marriage between a man and a woman is ordained of God, and *why* the family is central to the Creator's plan. . . .
>
> A *gospel principle is a doctrinally based guideline* for the righteous exercise of moral agency. Principles are subsets or components of broader gospel truths. *Principles provide direction.* Correct principles always are based upon and arise from doctrines (Bednar, *Increase in Learning,* 151–52, 154; italics in original).

Everything that we believe in and act upon in the Church, including all gospel principles, is based on and springs from the doctrines of the gospel. In D&C 101:78, we find the phrase "that every man may *act* in doctrine and principle." From that, Elder Bednar makes a point often overlooked:

> Please note in this verse the phrase "act in doctrine." We might ordinarily think of doctrine as something we study, something we learn, and something we strive to remember. However, the Lord indicates in this revelation that *doctrine is something that you and I should act in. Ultimately, the Savior is interested not in just what we know,* but in . . . how we apply what we know for righteous purposes (Bednar, *Increase in Learning,* 73–74; italics in original).

This is an enormously important concept for our study here because we may not fully understand the importance of doctrine in our spiritual development. Over the years, I have come to realize that very often, those who are wavering in their testimony or questioning their commitment to the Church lack a deep understanding of the doctrines of the gospel. That lack can contribute to muddled thinking. And that is very often the root cause for them leaving the Church, although they may give other reasons for their action.

A good example of that today is found in those who are offended by the

Church's stance on same-gender marriage. Even some who have grown up in the Church, attended seminary, served missions, and have converted others to the gospel have been blinded by the philosophies of the world. We accept the fact that with court and government rulings around the world, same-gender marriage is now not only widely accepted but also fully legal. But one doctrine that is often set aside is that God's law takes first priority, and the world's law cannot override that.

The world would have us believe this is a social issue, a fairness issue, a "rights" issue. But all of those are secondary to God's laws, which are eternal. And, as it states in the Family Proclamation, "Marriage between a man and a woman is ordained of God" and "the family is central to the Creator's plan for the eternal destiny of His children." When members of the Church forget or ignore that this is God's law, they are then troubled when our leaders don't just accept what the world has said is both legal and lawful. And in that small drifting away from the doctrine, many members of the Church walk themselves out of the Church.

> [Some] Church members know just enough about the doctrines to converse superficially on them, but their scant knowledge about the deep doctrines is inadequate for deep discipleship. Thus uninformed about the deep doctrines, they make no deep change in their lives. . . . Such members move out a few hundred yards from the entrance to the straight and narrow path and repose on the first little rise, thinking, "Well, this is all there is to it."
>
> NEAL A MAXWELL, *MEN AND WOMEN OF CHRIST*, 2

Another example of doctrinal muddiness or confusion that is quite popular, both in and out of the Church, has to do with the belief that God's love and Christ's love is unconditional in the sense that it has no limitations or restrictions. It is a lovely idea that comes from the depths of a believing heart. But unfortunately, it is based on a misunderstanding of God's nature. Or better, a misunderstanding of the *doctrine* of God's nature. In short, it is doctrinally flawed.

Many passages clearly show that God's love for us comes with very clearly defined conditions. For example, here are just a few passages that show us how Jesus defines what He asks of us:

- "Not every one that saith unto me, Lord, Lord, shall enter into the kingdom of heaven; *but he that doeth the will of my Father*" (Matthew 7:21).

- "He that hath my commandments, *and keepeth them,* he it is that loveth me: and he that loveth me shall be loved of my Father" (John 14:21).
- "*If ye keep my commandments,* ye shall abide in my love" (John 15:10).
- "Ye are my friends, if ye do whatsoever I command you" (John 15:14).

We could post an equal number of scriptures where the Lord condemns certain behaviors and warns that unless there is repentance, the person will alienate himself or herself from God. Yes, that's right. We can do things that alienate us from God. Nephi saw our day and described many of the problems and challenges that we would face. One of them is this very idea we are speaking of, that God's nature is like that of doting parents who think that their children can do no wrong.

> Yea, and there shall be many which shall say: Eat, drink, and be merry, for tomorrow we die; and it shall be well with us. And there shall also be many which shall say: Eat, drink, and be merry; nevertheless, fear God—he will justify in committing a little sin; yea, lie a little, take the advantage of one because of his words, dig a pit for thy neighbor; there is no harm in this; and do all these things, for tomorrow we die; and if it so be that we are guilty, God will beat us with a few stripes, and at last we shall be saved in the kingdom of God. Yea, and there shall be many which shall teach after this manner, *false and vain and foolish doctrines* (2 Nephi 28:7–9).

Even in the Church we find some who have embraced this idea of unconditional love to the point where they believe that if they choose to violate the Word of Wisdom, or take off their temple garments, or live with their partner, or ask to have their name removed from the Church, this does not affect their personal relationship with Jesus or the Father. This represents a dangerous doctrinal drift. And that is only aggravated by what we noted before: "He who sins against the greater light shall receive the greater condemnation" (D&C 82:3).

Two members of the Twelve taught the importance of the doctrine in simple language. But they did more than that. They defined what comes of knowing and accepting true doctrine:

> True doctrine, understood, changes attitudes and behaviors. The study of the doctrines of the gospel will improve behavior quicker than a study of behavior will improve behavior. Preoccupation with unworthy behavior can lead to unworthy behavior. This is why we stress so forcefully the study of the doctrines of the gospel (Boyd K. Packer, "The Meaning of Maturity," *Ensign,* November 1986).

Elder Neal A. Maxwell stated very succinctly: "Doctrine drives discipleship" ("Glorify Christ: An Evening with Neal A. Maxwell," February 2, 2002, 6).

There are two promises in those statements: True doctrine changes us. It changes how we feel and it changes what we do. It also defines our discipleship. And the implication is clear. If we do not know the doctrine, then our behavior will change, and not for the good, which weakens our discipleship.

In virtually every list of things we should do to increase our testimony, deepen our faith, etc., we find this counsel expressed in some form or another: We need to read and study the scriptures and words of the prophets. And, of course, that is not incorrect. But it is interesting that the phrase "study the scriptures" is not found anywhere in the scriptures. And "reading the scriptures" is found only once—in Alma 22:12, when Aaron is reading the scriptures to the king of the Lamanites.

So, what verbs *are* used in the scriptures that describe how we should approach them? The answer is very enlightening.

- "Thou shalt *meditate* therein day and night" (Joshua 1:8).
- "He shall read therein *all the days of his life*" (Deuteronomy 17:19).
- "*Give attendance* to" (1 Timothy 4:13). The Greek word there means to hold in your mind, to give heed to, to pay special attention to.
- "*Meditate upon* these things; *give thyself wholly* to them" (1 Timothy 4:15).
- "*Hold fast unto*" (1 Nephi 15:24).
- "*Liken all scriptures unto us*" (1 Nephi 19:23).
- "*Feast upon the words of Christ*" (2 Nephi 32:3). That's a great verb. Not nibble, not snack upon, not even eat heartily from. *Feast* carries the connotation of a celebration where food is served as part of that celebration.
- "*Lay hold* upon" (Helaman 3:29).
- "*Search . . . diligently*" (3 Nephi 23:1).
- "*Treasure up* in your minds continually" (D&C 84:85).

And here are some from the Brethren:

- "Do you have *a daily habit* of reading the scriptures? If we're not *reading the scriptures daily*, our testimonies are growing thinner, our spirituality isn't increasing in depth" (Harold B. Lee, *Teachings*, 152).
- "When you begin to *hunger and thirst after those words*" (Ezra Taft Benson, *Teachings*, 54).

- *"Immerse* yourself in the scriptures" (Jeffrey R. Holland, *However Long and Hard the Road*, 9).
- "Faith is nurtured through knowledge of God. It comes from prayer and *feasting upon the words of Christ through diligent study of the scriptures*" (Russell M. Nelson, *Perfection Pending*, 109).

Now let us look at a sampling of the promises that come when we go into the scriptures as directed above. As we do so, keep in mind our context. We are talking about how to prepare ourselves and others for the Second Coming:

- "Then thou shalt make thy way prosperous, and then thou shalt have good success" (Joshua 1:8).
- "The law of the Lord is perfect, converting the soul" (Psalm 19:7).
- "Thy word is a lamp unto my feet, and a light unto my path" (Psalm 119:105). Think of camping in the woods on a night without a moon. Where do you shine your flashlight as you move toward your tent?
- "That it might be for our profit and learning" (see also 2 Timothy 3:16; 1 Nephi 19:23).
- "Tells [us] all things what [we] should do" (2 Nephi 32:3).
- "Healeth the wounded soul" (Jacob 2:8).
- Brings us spiritual power (see Alma 31:5).
- "Will point to you a straight course to eternal bliss" (Alma 37:44).
- "Divide[s] asunder . . . the snares . . . of the devil, and lead[s] the man of Christ in a strait and narrow course" (Helaman 3:29–30).
- Gives us what to say in the very hour we need it (see D&C 84:85).
- "When I get casual in my relationships with divinity and . . . it seems that no divine ear is listening and no divine voice is speaking, that I am far, far away. *If I immerse myself in the scriptures the distance narrows and the spirituality returns*" (Spencer W. Kimball, *Teachings*, 135).
- "I feel certain that if, in our homes, parents will read from the Book of Mormon prayerfully and regularly, both by themselves and with their children, *the spirit of that great book will come to permeate our homes and all who dwell therein. The spirit of reverence will increase; mutual respect and consideration for each other will grow. The spirit of contention will depart. Parents will counsel their children in greater love and wisdom. Children will be more responsive and submissive to that counsel. Righteousness will increase*" (Marion G. Romney, in Conference Report, April 1960, 110).
- "There is a power in the book [the Book of Mormon] *which will begin*

to flow into your lives the moment you begin a serious study of the book. You will find greater power to resist temptation. You will find the power to avoid deception. You will find the power to stay on the strait and narrow path. . . . When you begin to hunger and thirst after those *words, you will find life in greater and greater abundance.* These *promises—increased love* and *harmony* in the home, *greater respect* between parent and child, *increased spirituality and righteousness*—these are not idle promises, but exactly what the Prophet Joseph Smith meant when he said the Book of Mormon will help us draw nearer to God" (Russell M. Nelson, *Teachings*, 54).

- "To feast means more than to taste. To feast means to savor. We savor the scriptures by studying them *in a spirit of delightful discovery and faithful obedience.* When we feast upon the words of Christ, *they are embedded 'in fleshy tables of the heart.' They become an integral part of our nature*" (Russell M. Nelson, *Teachings*, 346).

SUMMARY AND CONCLUSIONS

The Lord has not left us alone. Truly it is, as Elder Maxwell said, a time of high adventure in the Church and for its members. We should rejoice in being born in this day and having the privilege of being part of this dispensation.

But if we are to be ready for what is coming, we must be prepared. One of the key ways to prepare is to increase our knowledge, particularly with regard to world events. The other is to increase our gospel knowledge.

CHAPTER 34

TEMPORAL PREPARATION

Hearken, O ye people of my church. . . . Hearken ye people from afar; and ye that are upon the islands of the sea, listen together. . . . Prepare ye, prepare ye for that which is to come, for the Lord is nigh. (D&C 1:1, 12)

INDEPENDENT ABOVE ALL THINGS

The next aspect of our personal preparation for the Second Coming involves *temporal* preparation. *Temporal* is defined as relating to this earth, the world in which we now live. The Lord has given us temporal guidance to further prepare us for the separation that is coming. To do that, we shall closely examine a revelation given to the Church in March 1832.

As part of the law of consecration and stewardship (see chapter 17), the Lord gave some very clear directions for the Saints:

> This is the *preparation wherewith I prepare you,* and the foundation, and the ensample [example] which I give unto you, whereby you may accomplish the commandments which are given you; That through my providence, notwithstanding the tribulation which shall descend upon you, that *the church may stand independent above all other creatures beneath the celestial world* (D&C 78:13–14).

The more one considers that statement, the more remarkable it becomes. And in some ways, the more perplexing. In the first place, it sounds more like a sweeping generalization for the whole Church and not something that applies only to the law of consecration and stewardship.

Next, it raises some interesting questions. The goal is to stand independent of everything beneath heaven, which is a nice way of saying "everything in your world." Though we know this was given back then for a specific purpose, we also know that, like most of the revelations in the Doctrine and Covenants, this one also has direct application for our time too.

The first thing the Lord says is that He expects the Church and its members to be independent of all other things in our world. That is a sweeping statement. Does that mean He expects the Church to free itself from all other ties? If so, does that mean Church members need to grow and process our own food? Cut down trees to build our cabins? Think of the services that the various levels of society and government provide for us—highways and transportation, law enforcement, judicial systems, medical facilities, entertainment, education, water and sewage systems, military protection, social services, and on and on. Are we to be independent of all of that? And if so, how do we do that?

We live in a highly complex social system where we rely on others to help us meet our everyday needs. Is the Lord suggesting that we sever all such connections? Clearly that cannot be the Lord's intent, for human beings have always depended on each other for their existence. So, let us study this passage closely so we can better understand what the Lord has asked us to do.

Let us begin by taking a closer look at the word itself. Again, Noah Webster's 1828 *American Dictionary of the English Langugae* helps us determine what the word meant back in Joseph's time. That is helpful because we know that the meaning of words can change over time. "Independence" literally means "without dependence," so we shall examine the definition of "dependence." Here are some of the key definitions from Webster: *A state of being where one is at the disposal of another. Unable to subsist or to perform anything without the aid of someone or something else. One who is sustained by or relies upon another for support or favor* (see Webster, s.v. "dependence").

This helps, for we see that independence does not necessarily mean there are no connections whatsoever. Rather, it suggests that we should not be totally reliant for our support on someone or something else. For if we are, and that someone or something fails, then we go down with it.

Let's use an example of this principle from real life. In recent years, we have seen prosperous mining regions in the U.S. gradually die. The mines were so rich in minerals, such as coal, that when they were first discovered, they quickly drew in enough people that new towns and cities were created to support them. Everyone in the city—not just the miners—prospered because of the mines. Then, after a time, the coal ran out, or power plants started running on natural gas, or people began pressing for cleaner air, and the mines began to close. If a town had diversified its economy, there was a chance it might survive, although greatly diminished. But if it was totally dependent on the coal industry, the town died.

With that, let us now examine more closely the scripture that tells us to be independent of—or not totally reliant on—other things in this world. It is a principle that has much to teach us about our own temporal preparation.

Here is the context of that verse about independence. In the beginning of the revelation, the Lord told the leaders of the Church—Joseph Smith, Sidney Rigdon, and Newel K. Whitney—that it was time to organize a bishop's storehouse so they could better care "for the poor of my people" (D&C 78:3). The Lord then made it clear that this caring for the poor was to be an everlasting order in the Church. And this would help Church members to be "equal . . . in earthly things." And the Lord made it clear that this equality is necessary if the Church and its members are to have a place in the celestial world (see vv. 4–7).

After telling the leaders to counsel with the Saints, the Lord told them that they were to set up this order by covenant, and warned them of the consequences if they did not follow His counsel. All of this was prelude to the two verses cited on page 410. Let's break these two verses down into their component parts so that we can better understand what the Lord was trying to teach those brethren—and us!—about becoming independent from "all other creatures beneath the celestial world."

- The first thing the Lord makes clear is that what He is about to give them is to help prepare them. It will give them a foundation for what they do and be an example to others.
- This example will help them and Church members accomplish the commandments He has given them, i.e., to care for the poor.
- This can happen through His providence, i.e., what He will provide for them. This is a reminder that we are all dependent upon the love and mercy of God. This dependence is good because God is perfect and all He does is for the benefit of His children.
- This is to happen notwithstanding the tribulation that will come. This is almost certainly a reference to what will soon befall the Saints in Jackson County. And if they do as instructed, this will help them, even in the face of that tribulation, to stand independent *above* all others in our world.
- The Lord then goes on to talk about other blessings that await them if they are faithful.

This is the context of the charge to be independent from, or not totally reliant on, earthly things, earthly ways, or earthly systems.

PREPARING TEMPORALLY FOR WHAT IS TO COME

It will be helpful in this discussion to examine how the world strives to care for its poor and those in need.

President Dallin H. Oaks once wrote a book called *The Lord's Way*. His purpose was to contrast the ways of the world with the ways of the Lord. It is a book filled with insights about how the Lord works.

One of the chapters in the book is titled "Care for the Poor." In a brilliant and thought-provoking analysis, President Oaks contrasted the Lord's way with the world's way of caring for the poor. After clearly establishing that the Lord has given His people in all ages a specific charge to watch over and care for the poor, the needy, the widows, the orphans, the sick, the afflicted, etc., President Oaks showed how government efforts that set out to accomplish the same purposes—to help the poor—often fall far short of their goal.

Acknowledging that their intent is usually good, President Oaks states:

> *The responsibility for each person's social, emotional, spiritual, physical, or economic well-being rests first upon himself, second upon his family, and third upon the Church if he is a faithful member thereof. No true Latter-day Saint, while physically or emotionally able will voluntarily shift the burden of his own or his family's well-being to someone else. So long as he can, under the inspiration of the Lord and with his own labors, he will supply himself and his family with the spiritual and temporal necessities of life.*
>
> Spencer W. Kimball, "Welfare Services: The Gospel in Action," *Ensign*, November 1977

> There is widespread dissatisfaction with government welfare programs. Critics include not only the taxpayers who finance the assistance and resent the fact that it seems to fall far short of its stated aims, . . . but also the persons who receive assistance and who resent the extent and nature of the aid and the administrative controls that accompany it (Dallin H. Oaks, *The Lord's Way*, 104–5).

We know that literally hundreds of billions of dollars have been spent by governments around the world to aid the poor and help those in need, but over and over, a large share of that money goes not to the poor but to those who build and maintain and administer the programs, which creates a huge and usually inefficient bureaucracy.

In contrast to these well-meaning but counterproductive programs, let us look at a better way. During the height of the Great Depression, millions lost their jobs, and subsequently, millions of families forfeited their farms and homes and faced a crisis of survival. In 1936, the Church launched a formal effort to help their members in this crisis, but in a way that was in harmony with the revelation to maintain independence from the world and also to avoid idleness (see D&C 68:30–32). In April general conference of that year, the First Presidency announced the beginning of what they called a "Church Security Plan." (This name was later changed to the "Church Welfare Plan.") The First Presidency explained why they were undertaking this new program:

> Our primary purpose was to set up, in so far as it might be possible, a system under which the curse of idleness would be done away with, the evils of a dole abolished, and independence, industry, thrift and self respect be once more established amongst our people. The aim of the church is to help the people to help themselves. Work is to be re-enthroned as the ruling principle of the lives of our Church membership (in Dallin H. Oaks, *The Lord's Way*, 109).

In a follow-up message from the First Presidency to the Church issued in October general conference, the First Presidency further stated that "the real purpose of the Church Security Plan is to assist each individual *to secure independence* to *help make him self-supporting*" (in James R. Clark, *Messages of the First Presidency of The Church of Jesus Christ of Latter-day Saints*, 6:240). Obviously, the Brethren were making reference to the counsel in D&C 78.

In the ensuing years, as economic stability gradually returned, the welfare program was continued in the Church. Many things have changed since then, but the basic principles are still the same.

Two key doctrinal elements of the effort have been consistent since the beginning. First, its purpose is to help its members to become independent and self-reliant (another word for being independent). And that is not just independence from the government, but financial independence from the Church as well. The second principle is to encourage all members to show love for their neighbor, especially those that are in need.

Note that the first of those goals is a temporal goal, which is to stay independent from the world. Again, "temporal" is defined as things relating to mortality and this world.

The second is a spiritual goal, to obey the commandment to love our neighbors as ourselves. That often will involve some kind of temporal help, but the driving motivation is a spiritual one. These two goals may seem to suggest separate efforts, but that is not so with the Lord. He says: "Verily I say unto you that *all things unto me are spiritual, and not at any time have I given unto you a law which was temporal*" (D&C 29:34).

If we lose sight of that spiritual perspective and see temporal preparation as something completely separate from our spiritual development, then we miss the mark, and probably the blessings that go with being on the mark. So to repeat a core concept, when we help others become independent of the world, then they are blessed both temporally and spiritually, as are those who extend that help.

The principles of welfare upon which we work [are]:
1. We strive for self-reliance, temporally and spiritually. This includes a reserve supply of basic items needed to sustain life.
2. When additional aid is needed, the family comes first. The immediate and extended family will be blessed as they rally around their loved one(s) and lend a helping hand.
3. If the individual and the family cannot meet the challenges, then the Church constitutes the next line of defense.
4. Church welfare is administered by the bishop, who reports to his stake president. . . . Providing in the Lord's way humbles the rich, exalts the poor, and sanctifies them both.

Russell M. Nelson,
Teachings, 265–66

PREPARING TEMPORALLY FOR AN UNCERTAIN FUTURE

President Harold B. Lee once referred to what he called "the inevitable tragedies of life" (*Decisions for Successful Living*, 220). Those of us who have lived very long know exactly what he means by that. In the scriptures, the Lord commonly uses two words that describe these tragedies. The first is *tribulation* (see, for example, D&C 58:2–4) and the other is *adversity* (see, for example, D&C 121:7).

Tribulation comes from a Greek word that means "to press or to squeeze." It is derived from what was known as the *tribulum*. This was the heavy stone used in the threshing of grain.

That is a perfect way to describe life sometimes. It is like having a great millstone pressing down on us, turning round and round, grinding us down little by little, pressing the breath and life and joy out of us. It can come in many forms—a debilitating or fatal disease, a terrible accident with severe injury or death, termination of employment, fire, earthquake, war. We could name dozens of other possibilities.

Let us now look at the word *adversity*. Common synonyms include misfortune, calamity, distress, affliction, misery, woe, suffering, and bereavement. One is tempted to quip, "Wow! No wonder I am depressed."

However, though we cannot avoid these things—they are "inevitable," as President Lee reminds us—we can greatly mitigate their effects by preparing for them in advance. Knowing this, the Church has set four strategic goals or initiatives to help its members prepare in advance for just such contingencies. If they do this faithfully, they can cope much more effectively with challenges when they come.

The Church has also developed numerous resources to help us meet those goals. They are simple things, but they can increase our ability to cope, and also reduce the ancillary side effects that so often accompany a tragedy. These efforts to prepare will not automatically eliminate all of the shock and trauma of the loss, but at least they do not add to the already grueling pressure of the *tribulum*.

To illustrate how temporal preparation and following spiritual principles work together to help individuals and families without taking away their independence, let's create a hypothetical Latter-day Saint family.

It is a family of six—husband, wife, and four children, ages three to fourteen. They live far away from their extended families. The husband has a good job with good benefits and opportunities for advancement. The wife supplements their income by teaching piano lessons in the home. They are a happy, well-adjusted family, striving to be faithful to their covenants. From the beginning of their marriage, the couple determined they were going to follow the Church's counsel to prepare for future emergencies. Over the years they accumulated a basic supply of food, established a comfortable "rainy day" savings account, avoided all but essential debt, and determined to live within their means.

One day the father is involved in a terrible accident and is severely injured. He will end up being hospitalized for six to eight weeks and undergo rehabilitation for six to seven months after that. He will not be able to work at all during that time.

This is a terrible tragedy and a very difficult time for the family. But think how much more stress and anguish there would be if, in addition to caring for her injured husband, the wife had to:

- Go to work to sustain the family
- Find childcare for her younger children
- Face possible foreclosure on their home
- Ask the bishop for food and money to pay their monthly bills
- Tell the children there is no money for extras
- Take out a second mortgage on the house
- Leave the state and move in with extended family

I'm not saying that it's wrong to go to the bishop or to take out a temporary loan. The Church recognizes that life comes with its challenges, and they are prepared to help. But sometimes our poor choices—such as extravagant living, excessive debt, get-rich-quick investments, or financing a new business by leveraging our home equity—can create their own crises and make us dependent on others.

A bishop friend who described his ward as "comfortably affluent" once expressed frustration with some members who were seeking aid from the Church. They were quite offended when he suggested they sell their boat and their motor home and buy a less expensive car before they asked the Church to help them meet their debt obligations. He described them as "the wealthy poor." That is just the opposite of what the Church has asked of us. Such people come to the Church for aid because they have lost their independence to excessive debt and poor management.

BEING INDEPENDENT TODAY

In the years since the welfare program was first initiated, our society and our way of living have changed dramatically. Therefore, the Church's response to these changes has required adjustments as well. For example, when the program first began, a substantial number of Church members lived in rural or semi-rural circumstances. Many of those had gardens and raised much of their own food. Canning—or bottling—fruits and vegetables was commonplace among many people, and not just Church members.

Now, large agribusinesses are common, and as much as 95% of a nation's population live in urban areas. They often live in large residential complexes where the residents have no private land of their own. Many others live in small homes or apartments that have little or no space for food storage. Thus these families face real challenges in preparing temporally, even when they want to do so.

The changes in our modern way of life have required the Church to adjust its welfare outreach. For example, some countries have strict laws against "hoarding." Storing more than a week or two's worth of food is defined as hoarding and is considered illegal. So in a global church and a changing world, the Brethren continue to adapt, but always with those same principles at the foundation.

Yet even with all of these changes, we still hear members talk about having a two-year supply of food or having enough fuel on hand to warm their houses through the winter. These were once the preparations that were asked of our members, but that has changed *under the direction of our prophets, seers, and revelators*. Therefore, it is important that we understand what it is that we are now being asked to do in order to be prepared temporally.

In a pamphlet prepared by the Church entitled "All Is Safely Gathered In: Family Home Storage," the First Presidency gives this wise counsel:

> We encourage Church members worldwide to *prepare for adversity in life by having a basic supply of food and water and some money in savings*. We ask that you *be wise* as you store food and water and build your savings. Do not go to extremes; it is not prudent, for example, to go into debt to establish your food storage all at once. *With careful planning, you can, over time, establish a home storage supply and a financial reserve*. We realize that some of you may not have financial resources or space for such storage. Some of you may be prohibited by law from storing large amounts of food. We encourage you to store as much as circumstances allow. May the Lord bless you in your home storage efforts ("All Is Safely Gathered In," churchofjesuschrist.org/all-is-safely-gathered-in-family-home-storage).

The First Presidency then outlined four basic goals, with some brief but very practical ways to achieve those goals. They are:

- *Three-month supply:* Build a small supply of your food that is part of your normal, daily diet. Purchase a few extra items each week and gradually increase your supply until it is sufficient for *three months*. Rotate regularly to avoid spoilage.
- *Drinking water:* Store drinking water for circumstances in which the water supply may be polluted or disrupted. Store water in sturdy, leak-proof, breakage-resistant containers. Keep water containers away from heat sources and direct sunlight.
- *Financial reserve:* Establish a financial reserve by saving a little money each week and gradually increasing it to a reasonable amount (see "Prepare Every Needful Thing: Family Finances Guide").

- *Longer-term supply:* For longer-term needs, where permitted, *gradually* build a supply of food that will *last a long time and that you can use to stay alive,* such as wheat, rice, and beans. These items can last thirty years or more when properly packaged and stored in a cool, dry place.

Note that these recommendations are simple, practical, clear, relatively inexpensive, and doable. And if we follow that counsel, we will be much better prepared when a crisis strikes.

While these four initiatives were first set forth in 2007, they are still current on the Church's website. They are based on the same simple principles that have guided the Church from the beginning, and they are designed to help keep us independent from all things beneath the celestial world.

FINANCIAL RESERVES AND THE MANAGEMENT OF DEBT

The third area of preparation discussed in the pamphlet "All Is Safely Gathered In," is financial preparation: "Establish a financial reserve by saving a little money each week and gradually increasing it to a reasonable amount." At the end of that sentence, there is a reference to another resource provided by the Church. It is called "Family Finances." It too contains a message from the First Presidency:

> Latter-day Saints have been counseled for many years to prepare for adversity by having *a little money set aside.* Doing so adds immeasurably to security and well-being. *Every family has a responsibility to provide for its own needs to the extent possible.* We encourage you wherever you may live in the world to *prepare for adversity by looking to the condition of your finances.* We urge you to *be modest in your expenditures; discipline yourselves in your purchases to avoid debt. Pay off debt as quickly as you can,* and free yourselves from this bondage [another way of saying, stay independent]. Save a little money regularly to gradually build a financial reserve. If you have paid your debts and have a financial reserve, even though it be small, you and your family will feel more secure and enjoy greater peace in your hearts ("Prepare Every Needful Thing: Family Finances").

Two things are emphasized in their statement: First, set aside some financial resources, and second, get out of debt as quickly as possible.

In the accompanying inset quote, President Thomas S. Monson dryly noted that too many members have a year's supply of debt but no food.

Though his comment does make us smile, it should also cause a twinge of guilt too, for too many members of the Church are in that very circumstance.

Debt is a double burden. One part of the burden is paying back the money we borrowed. The other is paying the interest that comes with it. To give an idea of how much that is, on a $400,000, 30-year mortgage with an interest rate of 4%, the borrower will end up paying $287,478 in interest. They call that a 4% loan, when in reality it is a 71.8% interest rate.

And what should be of great concern to all of us is the debt crisis the world is now facing. In 1971, the year that the first edition of this book was published, the U.S. national debt was $427 billion dollars, or about 34% of the gross domestic product, i.e., the worth of goods produced by the country in that same year. In 2019, our national debt was $22.8 trillion dollars, which was 106% of the GDP! We owed more debt than the total value of what the entire U.S. economy produced!

> *Many more people could ride out the storm-tossed waves in their economic lives if they had their . . . supply of food . . . and were debt-free. Today we find that many have followed this counsel in reverse: they have at least a year's supply of debt and are food-free.*
>
> THOMAS S. MONSON,
> CHURCH NEWS, MAY 12, 2001, 7

The coronavirus pandemic that began to sweep across the world as this book was being prepared for publication has had a huge impact on the economic stability of millions of people. Unemployment is approaching levels not seen since the Great Depression, and debt obligations are rising rapidly. Many governments, already with great debt loads, are borrowing billions more. This has created an economic *and* health crisis. These disasters cannot be avoided, but they can be prepared for.

The danger is that at some point, the system can no longer support the debt, and the whole system begins to collapse, as it did in 2007–2009 and back in the 1930s.

Though many of the prophets have warned us against debt over the generations, President Gordon B. Hinckley was particularly persistent in issuing those warnings.

> We have witnessed in recent weeks wide and fearsome swings in the markets of the world. . . . The *time has come to get our houses in order.* So many of our people are living on the very edge of their incomes. . . . *There is a portent of stormy weather ahead to which*

we had better give heed. . . . I am troubled by the huge consumer installment debt which hangs over the people of the nation, including our own people. . . . We are carrying a message of self-reliance throughout the Church. Self-reliance cannot be obtained when there is serious debt hanging over a household. . . . I urge you, brethren, to look to the condition of your finances. I urge you to be modest in your expenditures; discipline yourselves in your purchases to *avoid debt to the extent possible. Pay off debt as quickly as you can, and free yourselves from bondage. . . .* That's all I have to say about it, *but I wish to say it with all the emphasis of which I am capable* (Hinckley, "To the Boys and to the Men," *Ensign*, November 1998).

Occasions of this kind [the terrorist attacks on the United States on 9/11/2001] pull us up sharply to a realization that life is fragile, peace is fragile, civilization itself is fragile. The economy is particularly vulnerable. *We have been counseled again and again concerning self-reliance, concerning debt, concerning thrift. So many of our people are heavily in debt for things that are not entirely necessary. . . . I urge you as members of this Church to get free of debt where possible and to have a little laid aside against a rainy day* (Hinckley, "The Times in Which We Live," *Ensign*, November 2001).

Though it has been about twenty years now since President Hinckley gave that talk, I can still clearly remember that night. I was sitting in a stake center, watching the priesthood broadcast with two of my sons. President Hinckley spoke with such solemnity and such gravity, I was struck with a strong impression that I remember to this day: "You have just heard a prophet prophesy." Six years and two months later, beginning in December 2007, what would soon be called the Great Recession began when an 8-trillion-dollar bubble of debt in the housing market suddenly burst. Chaos in the financial markets swiftly followed.

A short time after that I got a glimpse of the personal fallout of the crash. I was visiting another ward on a fast Sunday. The last person to get up and bear his testimony was a man who was obviously troubled. With a lot of emotion, he bid farewell to the ward members, announcing that this was his family's last day in the ward. The person I was with leaned over and explained that three years earlier, this man and his wife had started a business together. It was a big success and they were doing well. So the previous year, they had decided to mortgage their company *and* their home so they could expand the business to keep up with the growth. This was in late November of 2007. "They lost everything—their house and their business," my friend explained. "That's why they're moving."

Struggling to speak through his tears, the man closed with this statement: "The hardest thing I have ever had to do in my life is to try to explain to my sixteen-year-old son why our family is moving in with Grandma and Grandpa."

PREPARING FOR THE FUTURE

Financial crises come and go, some mild, some devastating. Natural disasters strike with stunning swiftness. War or significant social upheaval may happen in the country where we live. Long employment with the same company may end when the human resource manager calls us in, hands us a box, and tells us to be out of our office in the next half an hour.

In large measure, for most of us, life is good. Life is stable. But it can also be highly volatile and unpredictable. In recent times we have had members of the Church lose their homes to a massive fire in California. Some lost their homes to floods in Texas. Many have been driven from their homes by hurricanes or other violent storms. How many times in recent years have we read of our local meetinghouses being opened up as community shelters in times when disaster has struck?

From numerous prophecies and the signs of the times being fulfilled all around very swiftly, we know that our situation could quickly grow much worse than it is now. About forty-five years ago, Bishop Victor L. Brown, then Presiding Bishop of the Church, summarized possible conditions the Church might face in the future and described the Church's ability—or inability—to handle the needs of people under each of those conditions. Obviously much has changed since this was given in 1976, both for the world and the Church. In 1976, the number of Church members was about 3.7 million members, with 798 stakes and 148 missions. In 2018 we had 16.3 million members (a 4.5-fold increase), 3,383 stakes (a 4.2-fold increase), and 407 missions (a 2.8-fold increase). So while the Church has many more resources, there are also many more members who may be facing these coming conditions. Some might suppose that this assessment is now long outdated. But note that this was not an assessment of the Church's current resources. It was an assessment of possible conditions in society that could impact the Church's temporal resources. And that assessment still has relevance for us today.

Presiding Bishop Victor L. Brown said in his report:

Let me share the panorama of conditions that *could befall* each of us individually and the Church collectively. I would like you to see what *might* happen under *three hypothetical but potentially real conditions.*

Condition One is characterized by a relatively stable economy, modest unemployment, and only limited natural disasters—a condition much like that which we now experience in this and many other countries. Only a small number of families or individuals in the Church would need to call upon their bishops for temporary health, emotional, or economic assistance. For those families or individuals unable to fully care for themselves, we would use our production projects, storehouses, employment efforts, and fast offering funds to help meet their needs. Appropriate health and social services capabilities of the Church would support the priesthood in administering to these special needs. *Our present state of Church preparedness allows us to meet the claims on the Church which Condition One seems to imply.*

Condition Two is characterized by more serious health, social, and economic stress. This could include a depressed economy with serious unemployment, or perhaps localized natural disasters. *Society would be unstable and disunited.* In order for the Church to meet the needs of those who could not care for themselves, we would be required to produce the maximum from our production projects, reduce the variety of items produced and distributed, provide broad-scale work opportunities, and organize special quorum relief efforts. Health and social services would be needed in many places. *Clearly, the material resources of the Church would be taxed heavily to meet this burden, particularly if Condition Two lasted very long or were very widespread.*

Under *Condition Three,* circumstances would be *very serious.* The economy would be very depressed, perhaps even suffering a near breakdown. Unemployment would be widespread. There would probably be widespread social disunity. This condition could be the result of either economic problems such as severe crop loss, broad-scale natural disasters, or possibly international conflict. *Under such circumstances, the Church, relying on its present resources, would very likely not be able to provide any more assistance than that rendered under Condition Two, and therefore could not meet the total welfare needs of the people.* . . .

Therefore, if the time comes that we move out of Condition One into a widespread Condition-Two situation, we are well beyond the current capacity of the Church alone to meet the temporal needs of the Saints.

I would like to stress that this preparedness includes more than temporal preparedness. *Particularly in Conditions Two and Three we would encounter social disunity, worry, fear, depression, and all the emotional stresses that accompany such economic and social conditions. Health conditions would be precarious. Families and individuals would need to be prepared emotionally and physically to weather this condition. Members would have greater need than ever to rely on each other for strength and support. . . .*

Our temporal salvation will come only in following the counsel of the Brethren to be prepared as families and individuals, as wards and as stakes. As we apply their counsel, we make of Zion a refuge and a standard of righteous living as commanded by the Lord (Victor L. Brown, "The Church and the Family in Welfare Services," *Ensign*, May 1976).

Ironically, as this book is going to press, the world is largely facing a Condition-Two situation, with some closer to Condition Three. So this is not just prophecy we are discussing—it is reality.

SUMMARY AND CONCLUSIONS

This concludes our study of temporal preparation. If nothing else, it is hoped that this has opened your eyes to the reality that temporal preparation is much more than having three months' worth of food in the pantry and some water in the basement. It is not a change of behavior that some of us need as much as it is a change of perspective, a change of mindset, if you will. If we can make that happen, we can work out the details of what we need to do and how to do it.

In D&C 78:14 the Lord said that through His providence the Church could "stand independent above all other creatures beneath the celestial world." As we approach the Second Coming, that independence will become more and more critical.

But remember, it is not just the Second Coming we are preparing for. We are preparing for life. We are preparing for that day when the *tribulum* comes into our lives and begins to press down upon us. How grateful we will be if we have prepared ourselves in such a way that we can maintain our independence. How grateful we will be if our preparation is such that the resources of the Church can be used to help those less fortunate than ourselves.

CHAPTER 35

STRENGTHEN THE BRIDGES: PREPARING OURSELVES SPIRITUALLY

President Gordon B. Hinckley taught, "There is concern that some people in the Church have mental but not spiritual conversion. The gospel appeals to them, but real conversion is when they feel something in their hearts and not just in their minds. There is mental assent, but not spiritual conviction. They must be touched by the power of the Holy Ghost, which creates a spiritual experience. The power and deep conversion of the Spirit is needed by our members to get into their hearts to confirm what they agreed to in their minds. This will carry them through every storm of adversity." The great task, the great challenge of the First Presidency and the Twelve is to get the spirit of the gospel from people's minds into their hearts, to where they have spiritual experiences, and those spiritual experiences are enough that they change feelings, they change our view of life. (M. Russell Ballard, given at Martin's Cove, July 11, 2001)

A DILEMMA

We come now to the third and final aspect of our section on preparation—spiritual preparation. Without hesitation we can say that this is the most critical of all the areas of preparation. For if we are not spiritually ready for what is coming, a library full of knowledge and a basement full of food storage will not see us through the days ahead.

But this creates a dilemma. How do we write just one chapter on spiritual preparation, when the whole message of the gospel is how to prepare ourselves spiritually for this world and the next? We are not talking about dozens of scriptures on this topic. There are literally hundreds of them! And every prophet, seer, and revelator of this dispensation, from Joseph Smith to our current First Presidency and Quorum of the Twelve, has given us wise counsel on this topic.

How do we sift through that mountain of counsel and condense it down to a few key principles that will be the most helpful to us?

HIGH ADVENTURE

In 1979, Elder Neal A. Maxwell, speaking to a symposium of teachers from the Church Educational System, made a statement that was both exhilarating and deeply sobering:

> Now we are entering times wherein there will be for all of us as Church members, in my judgment, some special challenges which will require of us that we follow the Brethren. *All the easy things that the Church has had to do have been done.* From now on, it's high adventure. *And followership is going to be tested in some interesting ways* ("The Old Testament: Relevancy within Antiquity," Church Educational System symposium, 1979, 12).

That is exciting in a way, but it is also somewhat discouraging. Some of us were not ready for the high adventure that the world is experiencing now. High panic has been more prevalent. What do we do? How do we prepare?

Some years ago, an article came into my hands. It is a true story of an experience that two Christian missionaries had, but it is also somewhat of an allegory. And it provides an answer to our question.

A Christian missionary couple were called by their church to serve in Africa. Their assignment would be for several years at a missionary outpost deep in the heart of the continent. They came by ship, bringing with them a truck and a truckload of heavy machinery. They were to build a small factory that would provide both employment for the native people and also raise the overall economic level of the area.

When the couple disembarked and unloaded their equipment, someone pointed out that they had a serious problem. When loaded with all of the materials they had brought, their truck weighed about eight tons. The missionary outpost was several hundred miles inland, and most of the roads to get there were primitive and rough and went through some pretty wild country. The biggest problem, however was the weight of the truck. The locals told the missionary couple that the road to their destination passed over many rivers and streams and numerous deep ravines. The bridges at those sites were made by the local tribes and were typically made of logs tied together with vines. Each bridge had signs set up next to it indicating the maximum load it could bear. Some signs said 3T, meaning it could handle up to three tons. Some had 4T and a few had 6T. But none of the bridges had an 8T sign beside it. Their truck was too heavy.

The missionary and his wife were deeply concerned. They had neither the time nor the resources to make more than one trip. Discouraged, they thought at first, "We shall just have to leave some things behind." But then they had another idea. "We need every piece of machinery we brought if we are to build that factory," they agreed. *"So we cannot lighten the load. Our only option is to strengthen the bridges."*

And that's what they did. At each bridge they would stop, and with considerable effort, which was often dangerous because the rivers were infested with crocodiles and poisonous snakes, they would cut down trees and fortify each bridge to the point that it could carry the full eight-ton load. Though the journey took them much longer than they had expected, in this manner they carried all that they had brought with them to the missionary outpost and built the factory as they had been charged to do (see Virginia Law Shell, "The Bridge," *Guideposts*, January 1975, 10–11).

That is a wonderful description of our dilemma. We have a long journey to make, and much of it is through wild and dangerous country. And some of the bridges are not very safe. Unfortunately, it is not going to be possible to lighten the load that is placed on us and our families. Therefore, our only option is to strengthen our spiritual bridges.

PARABLES OF PREPARATION

That is a powerful metaphor and one that seems to describe what is coming in our lives. However, while it tells us *what* we need to do, it doesn't give us a lot of help on *how* to do it. For that, we shall turn to the Savior and learn from Him.

During the last days of His mortal life, Jesus taught the Twelve three parables. He taught them one right after the other with little or no comment on each. And, He gave those parables immediately after He gave a lengthy talk on the last days and His Second Coming.

We have spoken of the Olivet Discourse several times now in the book. Found in Matthew 24 (see also JS—M 1), it qualifies as one of the greatest discourses on the Second Coming found in all of scripture. We have spoken several times in this book about preparation for separation. Ironically, these three parables, which many people do not associate with Christ's sermon on the last days, actually are parables of preparation. And in each parable we shall see that if we neglect our preparation, we could end up being part of the separation process.

In the Joseph Smith Translation, we learn that the parables are linked together with this introductory statement: "And then, *at that day, before the Son of man comes,* the kingdom of heaven be likened unto . . ." (JST Matthew 25:1). This makes it very clear. Matthew 25 is a continuation of the Olivet Discourse and teaches three great principles on how to prepare for what still lies ahead.

THE PARABLE OF THE TEN VIRGINS (MATTHEW 25:1–13)

> Then [JST "at that day, before the Son of man comes"] shall the kingdom of heaven be likened unto ten virgins, which took their lamps, and went forth to meet the bridegroom. And five of them were wise, and five were foolish. They that were foolish took their lamps, and took no oil with them: But the wise took oil in their vessels with their lamps. While the bridegroom tarried, they all slumbered and slept. And at midnight there was a cry made, Behold, the bridegroom cometh; go ye out to meet him. Then all those virgins arose, and trimmed their lamps. And the foolish said unto the wise, Give us of your oil; for our lamps are gone out. But the wise answered, saying, Not so; lest there be not enough for us and you: but go ye rather to them that sell, and buy for yourselves. And while they went to buy, the bridegroom came; and they that were ready went in with him to the marriage: and the door was shut. Afterward came also the other virgins, saying, Lord, Lord, open to us. But he answered and said, Verily I say unto you, I know you not. [The JST changes that to "ye know me not"]. Watch therefore, for ye know neither the day nor the hour wherein the Son of man cometh (Matthew 25:1–13).

This well-known and oft quoted parable draws on the wonderful imagery of a wedding celebration at the time of Christ. Though we find some remnant of those traditions in modern times, the culture has changed in many ways. George Mackie, a Christian minister who spent much of his life in the Holy Land, described what a wedding ceremony was like in Palestine in the nineteenth century. It greatly enriches our understanding of what Jesus described in the parable and thus helps us better learn the lesson taught in the parable. This was imagery His disciples were very familiar with, and it is in that imagery that we too are taught one of the three key principles of spiritual preparedness.

Oriental [Middle Eastern] marriages usually take place in the evening. . . . The whole attention is turned to the public arrival of the bridegroom to receive the bride prepared for him and waiting in the house among her female attendants. . . . During the day the bride is conducted to the house of her future husband and she is there assisted by her attendants in putting on the marriage robes and jewellery [sic]. During the evening, the women who have been invited congregate in the room where the bride sits in silence, and spend the time commenting on her appearance, complimenting the relatives, etc. . . . As the hours drag on their topics of conversation become exhausted, and some of them grow tired and fall asleep. There is nothing more to be done, and everything is in readiness for the reception of the bridegroom, when the cry is heard outside announcing his approach.

The bridegroom meanwhile is absent, spending the day at the house of one of his relatives. There, soon after sunset, that is between seven and eight o'clock, his male friends begin to assemble. . . . The time is occupied with light refreshments, general conversation and the recitation of poetry in praise of the two families . . . and of the bridegroom in particular. After all have been courteously welcomed and their congratulations received, the bridegroom, about eleven o'clock, intimates his wish to set out. Flaming torches are then held aloft by special bearers, lit candles [or small lamps] are handed at the door to each visitor as he goes out, and the procession sweeps slowly along toward the house where the bride and her female attendants are waiting. A great crowd has meanwhile assembled on the balconies, garden-walls, and flat roofs of the houses on each side of the road. . . . The bridegroom is the centre of interest. Voices are heard whispering, "There he is! there he is!" From time to time women raise their voices in the peculiar shrill, wavering shriek by which joy is expressed at marriages and other times of family and public rejoicing. The sound is heard at a great distance, and is repeated by other voices in advance of the procession, and thus intimation is given of the approach half an hour or more before the marriage escort arrives. . . . As the house is approached the excitement increases, the bridegroom's pace is quickened, and the alarm is raised in louder tones and more repeatedly, "He is coming, he is coming!"

Before he arrives, the maidens in waiting come forth with lamps and candles a short distance to light up the entrance, and do honour to the bridegroom and the group of relatives and intimate friends around him. These pass into the final rejoicing and the marriage supper; the others who have discharged their duty in accompanying him to the door, immediately disperse, and the door is shut (George Mackie, *Bible Manners and Customs*, 123–26).

The word *parable* in the Greek means to place two things side by side. Let us do that to help us better understand the parable.

- The *marriage* ceremony—or marriage supper as it is called in other parables—represents the covenant relationship between the Savior and those who become His covenant people. The Savior is the *Bridegroom* and the Church and its members are His *bride*. Just as marriage is a covenant between a man and woman wherein they join their lives together, and in many cultures the wife then takes upon herself the name of her husband, so it is with the members of the Church. We take upon ourselves the name of Christ and covenant to be "faithful" to Him. The covenant between husband and wife involves much more than just living together. It is a commitment to love and cherish each other through all of life, to be faithful to one another, to work together to create a home and family, and to prepare each member of the family for the life to come. Notice that in the imagery of the Old Testament, the prophets likened turning away from the worship of the only true God and worshiping idols to adultery. Israel was often accused of "going a whoring" after false gods (see, for example, Exodus 34:15).

  One more thing about the wedding supper. Though it does represent the covenant between Jehovah and Israel—ancient and modern—in another sense, the marriage supper specifically signifies the Second Coming of Jesus Christ. That will be the culminating moment when He becomes the literal king and His marriage to Israel will last for a thousand years.

- The *guests* invited to the wedding supper were usually extended family and close friends. They would represent those who have made the covenant with God. In our day that means members of the Church, and we are likened unto a great family. For example, in the Church today, we still call each other brother and sister. This is partly because we all come from the same Heavenly Parents, but it also signifies that we are brothers and sisters in the covenant.

- The *lamps* are a source of light. In the time of Christ, there were larger lamps for inside the house and smaller ones that could be carried in the palm of a hand to provide light when one had to go out at night.

- The *oil* in the lamps was olive oil. Olives, and the oil squeezed from them, were an everyday part of life in the Middle East. Olive oil was used in many ways, including as a cooking oil, a dressing for salads, a dip for bread, and so on. But oil was also used to anoint the sick, in the coronation of kings, and in the anointing of priests. In the parable, the oil was used for light, and the lamps were almost certainly the little hand lamps already mentioned. Small hand lamps were made from clay then fired in a kiln. They were small enough to fit in the palm of the hand and were hollow so they could be filled with oil. One end was pinched and a small hole made in it. Here a wick was laid so that one end of it was in the oil. In a time when there was no city-provided lighting, and when a moonless night was very dark, these small lamps became the "flashlights" of the ancient world. However, due to their size, they would only burn for about an hour before more oil was needed. Therefore, what made the five virgins foolish was not that they didn't have lamps, nor oil in their lamps. It was that they hadn't thought to bring extra oil. Keep that in mind as we explore the imagery of the oil further.

- We are told very specifically in modern revelation that the *oil* in the lamps is symbolic of *the light and truth we receive through the gift of the Holy Ghost.* This interpretation comes directly from the Lord:

> At that day, when I shall come in my glory, shall the parable be fulfilled which I spake concerning the ten virgins. For they that are wise and have received the truth, and *have taken the Holy Spirit for their guide,* and have not been deceived—verily I say unto you, they shall not be hewn down and cast into the fire, but shall abide the day (D&C 45:56–57).

- The *virgins*—which was the common term for an unmarried woman—are a symbol of purity and worthiness and of those who have not made a "marriage" with someone else. In this case they represent Church members. As we shall see, the parable is not about the world, but about those in the covenant.

With these elements in place, let us examine the parable more closely, especially to see what it teaches us about preparing ourselves spiritually for the Second Coming, represented by the wedding supper. President Spencer W. Kimball gave a lengthy discourse on this parable that is especially helpful as we seek to understand it more fully.

I believe that *the Ten Virgins represent the people of the Church of Jesus Christ and not the rank and file of the world.* All of the virgins, wise and foolish, had accepted the invitation to the wedding supper; they had knowledge of the program and had been warned of the important day to come. They were not the gentiles or the heathens or the pagans, nor were they necessarily corrupt and reprobate, but *they were knowing people who were foolishly unprepared for the vital happenings that were to affect their eternal lives.* . . .

Hundreds of thousands of us today are in this position. Confidence has been dulled and patience worn thin. It is so hard to wait and be prepared always. But we cannot allow ourselves to slumber. The Lord has given us this parable as a special warning.

At midnight, the vital cry was made. . . . At midnight! Precisely at the darkest hour, when least expected, the bridegroom came. When the world is full of tribulation and help is needed, but it seems the time must be past and hope is vain, then Christ will come. The midnights of life are the times when heaven comes to offer its joy for man's weariness. But when the cry sounds, there is no time for preparation. . . .

In the daytime, wise and unwise seemed alike; midnight is the time of test and judgment. . . . The foolish asked the others to share their oil, but *spiritual preparedness cannot be shared in an instant.* . . . The kind of oil that is needed to illuminate the way and light up the darkness is not shareable. How can one share obedience to the principle of tithing; a mind at peace from righteous living; an accumulation of knowledge? How can one share faith or testimony? How can one share attitudes or chastity, or the experience of a mission? How can one share temple privileges? *Each must obtain that kind of oil for himself.* . . .

In the parable, oil can be purchased at the market. In our lives *the oil of preparedness is accumulated drop by drop in righteous living.* Attendance at sacrament meetings adds oil to our lamps, drop by drop over the years. Fasting, family prayer, home teaching, control of bodily appetites, preaching the gospel, studying the scriptures—each act of dedication and obedience is a drop added to our store. Deeds of kindness, payment of offerings and tithes, chaste thoughts and actions, marriage in the covenant for eternity—these, too, contribute importantly to the oil *with which we can at midnight refuel our exhausted lamps* (Spencer W. Kimball, *Faith Precedes the Miracle*, 253–56).

Over the years, we occasionally hear of a global oil crisis, where petroleum is in such short supply that the cost at the gas pump skyrockets precipitously. But here in this parable is the real oil crisis of our generation, remembering that the oil represents having the Spirit in our lives. This is an individual thing and doesn't show up in the newspaper headlines. And "crisis" is not too strong of a word. Think of the sorrow and heartbreak that comes when we see our children or fellow members of the Church moving away from the Lord, turning their backs on the Church, or going off on "forbidden paths," as Lehi described. All of these desensitize our ability to receive the Spirit.

As parents, wouldn't it be wonderful if we could stick a dipstick in the ears of our children and check the level of their spirituality for that day? If we see it's a little low, how nice it would be if we could get a can of light and truth and "top them off" for the day. Wouldn't it be wonderful if we could do that for ourselves?

If the ten virgins represent the Lord's covenant people, or those He calls His "elect," then the fact that half of them were not prepared with extra oil is sobering indeed. But here's another thought. Worldwide, we know we have a significant percentage of members who never come to church, who are members only because their names are on the records of the Church. They are as yet not true Israel, for true Israel is covenant Israel.

As we saw earlier, the Lord's definition of Church membership is not whether or not there is a membership record or whether someone has a temple recommend, but it is defined by Christ specifically as "whosoever repenteth and cometh unto me, the same is my church" (D&C 10:67). So does this say that only about half of those who are active members will have enough oil in their lamps?

President Harold B. Lee, citing a statement made much earlier by Heber C. Kimball, talked about the importance of having oil in our lamps, and drew on the imagery of this parable:

> Let me say to you, that many of you will see the time when you will have all the trouble, trial and persecution that you can stand, and plenty of opportunities to show that you are true to God and his work. This Church has before it many close places through which *it will have to pass before the work of God is crowned with victory.* To meet the difficulties that are coming, it will be necessary for you to have a knowledge of the truth of this work *for yourselves.* The difficulties will be of such a character that *the man or woman who does not possess this personal knowledge or witness will fall. . . .* The time will come when *no man nor woman will be able to endure*

on borrowed light. Each will have to be guided by the light within himself. *If you do not have it, how can you stand?* (Harold B. Lee, in Conference Report, October 1965).

Borrowed light is, of course, a direct reference to the five foolish virgins, who raced out to find light at midnight.

Let us hold that thought for a moment and put this in the context of our "preparation for the separation" concept. We have already seen that the five foolish virgins are members of the Church. All have been invited to the wedding. All have been given the gift of the Holy Ghost. All have lamps and all have brought oil in their lamps. So they have some degree of spiritual light with them. What they don't have is enough oil to see them through until the Bridegroom actually comes. And this brings us to the separation.

The five foolish virgins must have found some oil, for they returned to the house, eagerly expecting to be given entrance. But they found that the door was shut. When they knocked and begged for entry, the Lord's answer was, "I know ye not." That's in the King James Version. In the Joseph Smith Translation, there is a significant change. The Lord says, "*Ye know me not*" (JST Matthew 25:12). That is a very different thing. The problem lies within the foolish virgins, and this is what excludes them from the wedding supper. Another time, President Lee said:

> How I wish I could impress you who must daily walk out on the swaying bridge of worldliness and sin, . . . when you have twinges of doubt and fear that cause you to lose the rhythm of prayer and faith and love, . . . I would fervently pray that you could feel the love flowing from my soul to yours, and know of my deep compassion toward each of you as you face your problems of the day. The time is here when every one of you must stand on your own feet. The time is here *when no man and woman will endure on borrowed light. Each will have to be guided by the light within himself. If you do not have it, you will not stand* (Harold B. Lee, *Decisions for Successful Living*, 234).

With that phrase in mind—we cannot live on borrowed light—take notice of how often President Russell M. Nelson has spoken to the Church about the importance of having this light and spiritual power in our lives:

> I urge you to *stretch beyond your current spiritual ability to receive personal revelation.* . . . Nothing opens the heavens quite like the combination of increased purity, exact obedience, earnest seeking, daily feasting on the words of Christ in the Book of Mormon. . . .

> *In coming days, it will not be possible to survive spiritually without the guiding, directing, and comforting influence of the Holy Ghost. . . . I plead with you to increase your spiritual capacity to receive revelation. . . .*
>
> Pray in the name of Jesus Christ about your concerns, your fears, your weaknesses—yes, the very longings of your heart. And then listen! Write the thoughts that come to your mind. Record your feelings and follow through with actions that you are prompted to take. As you repeat this process day after day, month after month, year after year, [we could also insert "drop by drop" here] you will *"grow into the principle of revelation."* . . .
>
> Our Savior and Redeemer, Jesus Christ, will perform some of His mightiest works between now and when He comes again. We will see miraculous indications that God the Father and His Son, Jesus Christ, preside over this Church in majesty and glory. *But in coming days, it will not be possible to survive spiritually without the guiding, directing, comforting, and constant influence of the Holy Ghost.* My beloved brothers and sisters, *I plead with you to increase your spiritual capacity to receive revelation* (Russell M. Nelson, "Revelation for the Church, Revelation for Our Lives," *Ensign*, May 2018).

> When you reach up for the Lord's power in your life with the same intensity that a drowning person has when grasping and gasping for air, power from Jesus Christ will be yours. When the Savior knows you truly want to reach up to Him—when He can feel that the greatest desire of your heart is to draw His power into your life— *you will be led by the Holy Ghost to know exactly what you should do. When you spiritually stretch beyond anything you have ever done before, then His power will flow into you* (Russell M. Nelson, "Drawing the Power of Jesus Christ into Our Lives," *Ensign*, May 2017).

In summary, while there are dozens of things we can do to increase our spiritual readiness, if we could choose only one thing to do, or one principle to focus on, or one effort to undertake, it would be to live so as to *receive, recognize, and respond to personal revelation*. As President Nelson has said, if we do not do this, we will not survive spiritually in the days that are coming.

THE PARABLE OF THE TALENTS (MATTHEW 25:14–30)

The second parable given by the Savior in Matthew 25 is also well known. Though it is usually given the name in the heading above, a more accurate title might be "the parable of the three servants," for this story is more about the men than the money. As we read and study it, remember that it too was given to help us know how to better prepare spiritually for what lies ahead.

> For the kingdom of heaven is as a man travelling into a far country, who called his own servants, and delivered unto them his goods. And unto one he gave five talents, to another two, and to another one; to every man according to his several ability; and straightway took his journey. Then he that had received the five talents went and traded with the same, and made them other five talents. And likewise he that had received two, he also gained other two. But he that had received one went and digged in the earth, and hid his lord's money. After a long time the lord of those servants cometh, and reckoneth with them. And so he that had received five talents came and brought other five talents, saying, Lord, thou deliveredst unto me five talents: behold, I have gained beside them five talents more. His lord said unto him, Well done, thou good and faithful servant: thou hast been faithful over a few things, I will make thee ruler over many things: enter thou into the joy of thy lord. He also that had received two talents came and said, Lord, thou deliveredst unto me two talents: behold, I have gained two other talents beside them. His lord said unto him, Well done, good and faithful servant; thou hast been faithful over a few things, I will make thee ruler over many things: enter thou into the joy of thy lord. Then he which had received the one talent came and said, Lord, I knew thee that thou art an hard man, reaping where thou hast not sown, and gathering where thou hast not strawed: And I was afraid, and went and hid thy talent in the earth: lo, there thou hast that is thine. His lord answered and said unto him, Thou wicked and slothful servant, thou knewest that I reap where I sowed not, and gather where I have not strawed: Thou oughtest therefore to have put my money to the exchangers, and then at my coming I should have received mine own with usury. Take therefore the talent from him, and give it unto him which hath ten talents. For unto every one that hath shall be given, and he shall have abundance: but from him that hath not shall be taken away even that which he hath. And cast ye the unprofitable servant into outer darkness: there shall be weeping and gnashing of teeth (Matthew 25:14–30).

In the parable, the lord, or master, of these men represents Jesus Christ, our Master. The *far country* where He would be going was heaven, and He would be there for a very long time. The *three men* are called His servants, which again suggests that this parable was also directed to those of the covenant, not the people of the world.

The word *talent* can be a little misleading, for we use it now to mean a gift or an ability of some kind. But in New Testament times, a talent was a form of money. At that time, all money came from precious metals—gold, silver, and brass. And the worth of the money was determined by weight. The talent was the largest form of money. A good estimation for this talent would be around fifty pounds. We can get an idea of its worth by comparing it to money that we understand. For example, if it was a fifty-pound talent, that means it weighed 800 of our ounces. If they were talents of gold, and gold was selling for $500 an ounce, one talent would be worth $400,000 today. So a single talent was a substantial fortune. Five talents would be a staggering fortune. It says a lot about how much confidence the lord had in his servants.

So what do the talents in the parable represent? Obviously something of great worth—but of spiritual worth, not just temporal worth. We note that the talents were not given to the three servants as a salary, nor as a personal gift. It was the lord's money, and they were to invest it for his purposes. So what things of worth does God give to us that He expects we will use to further His work? The list is long but include things such as life itself, a mortal body, a bounteous earth on which to live, families, the gospel, the Church, and much, much more. These are the talents given to us. And in return He asks that in addition to living our lives, we labor to do His work, expand His kingdom, and increase His influence in the world.

Of special interest to us is the fact that our "several ability," as the Lord called it, is not what determines the reward we are given. This is an interesting phrase, for it acknowledges that each of us has different gifts, different talents, different resources, different opportunities, different strengths, and different weaknesses. What matters to the Lord is how we use and develop what we are given. Though the first servant made his master $2,000,000 in profit (using our $400,000 per talent as a measure) and the second servant made only $1,200,000, the praise for both men, and the promise to them, was exactly the same. Therefore, we can assume that if the third servant came back and said, "I was only able to make you $400,000," his reward would have been the same. It was when he admitted that he had done nothing with what he had been given, but buried his talent out of fear and then tried to put the blame on the master—he was a "hard man"—that the master called him a "wicked and a slothful servant" and cast him out.

So what does the parable of the talents, or the parable of the three servants, teach us about spiritual preparation for the coming separation? What happened to the slothful servant? He was cast out. In modern revelation, the Lord reminds us that since He created all things on this earth, "all things therein are mine," and that we are only "stewards"—or caretakers—of His properties (D&C 104:14, 55–56). This life is a stewardship. We are not to live just for ourselves. We have obligations to others, and we have obligations to God. We are to use whatever we are blessed with to further His work and His purposes.

Here is what the Brethren have said we should learn from the parable of the talents:

> Each man holding the priesthood should learn his duty from the Parable of the Talents. . . . We are under obligation as men holding the priesthood to put to service the authority which we have received. If we do this, then we shall have other responsibilities and glory added, and we shall receive an abundance, that is, the fullness of the Father's kingdom; but if we bury our priesthood, then we are not entitled to receive any reward—we cannot be exalted (Joseph Fielding Smith, in Conference Report, April 1966, 102).

President Spencer W. Kimball suggested that the implications of this parable were for all Church members:

> The Church member who has the attitude of leaving it to others will have much to answer for. There are many who say: "My wife does the Church work!" Others say, "I'm just not the religious kind," as though it does not take effort for most people to serve and do their duty. But God has endowed us with talents and time, with latent abilities and with opportunities to use and develop them in His service. He therefore expects much of us, His privileged children. The parable of the talents is a brilliant summary of the many scriptural passages outlining promises for the diligent and penalties for the slothful (Spencer W. Kimball, *Teachings*, 149).

Here is another interesting thing to note about this parable. If we take this second charge seriously—to strive to use whatever we have been given to further God's work—this willingness not only builds the kingdom and blesses others; it also opens our hearts and greatly increases the likelihood that the Spirit will come into our lives, as promised in the first parable. Light and truth come to us drop by drop, and one of the spigots is our consecration to build up His work and His kingdom. Note how Nephi directly connected the effort to build Zion to having greater access to God through the Spirit:

"And blessed are they *who shall seek to bring forth my Zion* at that day, for *they shall have the gift and the power of the Holy Ghost*" (1 Nephi 13:37).

THE PARABLE OF THE SHEEP AND THE GOATS (MATTHEW 25:31–46)

This is the last parable in this threesome of the parables of preparation and separation. It is likely the best-known and the least ambiguous of the three. It sounds less like a parable and more like an actual description that awaits us all sometime in the future. But it, like the other two, has direct implications for our examination of spiritual preparation. It teaches us a third principle of spiritual preparation.

> When the Son of man shall come in his glory, and all the holy angels with him, then shall he sit upon the throne of his glory: And before him shall be gathered all nations: and he shall separate them one from another, as a shepherd divideth his sheep from the goats: And he shall set the sheep on his right hand, but the goats on the left. Then shall the King say unto them on his right hand, Come, ye blessed of my Father, inherit the kingdom prepared for you from the foundation of the world: For I was an hungred, and ye gave me meat: I was thirsty, and ye gave me drink: I was a stranger, and ye took me in: Naked, and ye clothed me: I was sick, and ye visited me: I was in prison, and ye came unto me. Then shall the righteous answer him, saying, Lord, when saw we thee an hungred, and fed thee? or thirsty, and gave thee drink? When saw we thee a stranger, and took thee in? or naked, and clothed thee? Or when saw we thee sick, or in prison, and came unto thee? And the King shall answer and say unto them, Verily I say unto you, Inasmuch as ye have done it unto one of the least of these my brethren, ye have done it unto me. Then shall he say also unto them on the left hand, Depart from me, ye cursed, into everlasting fire, prepared for the devil and his angels: For I was an hungred, and ye gave me no meat: I was thirsty, and ye gave me no drink: I was a stranger, and ye took me not in: naked, and ye clothed me not: sick, and in prison, and ye visited me not. Then shall they also answer him, saying, Lord, when saw we thee an hungred, or athirst, or a stranger, or naked, or sick, or in prison, and did not minister unto thee? Then shall he answer them, saying, Verily I say unto you, Inasmuch as ye did it not to one of the least of these, ye did it not to me. And these shall go away into everlasting punishment: but the righteous into life eternal (Matthew 25:31–46).

In the Near East, shepherds commonly allow sheep and goats to graze together, but when it comes time for bedding them down for the night, or for shearing them, or for taking them to the market to be sold, the sheep and the goats are separated.

We know this story well. Where the other two parables were clearly tied to mortality, this parable takes place at some future time of judgment.

In both cases, the individuals are surprised when the Lord either praises them or accuses them for how they treated Him in this mortal life. They ask when they ever saw Him and either did or did not do what He accused them of. His answer is the same in both cases: "Inasmuch as ye have done it [or not done it] unto one of the least of these my brethren, ye have done it unto me" (v. 40).

This parable teaches our third area of spiritual preparation, which is quite simple. And it ties in to the second great commandment to love our neighbors as ourselves. In this life, we are expected to treat one another justly, and to look on others' tribulations with compassion and to help them. And how we do that will determine whether we will have joy or misery in the next world. This is a principle taught in many places throughout the scriptures, and it is the core doctrine behind the law of consecration and stewardship and the more recent program of ministering.[1] King Benjamin put it very simply when he taught, "When ye are in the service of your fellow beings ye are only in the service of your God" (Mosiah 2:17). In the preface to the Doctrine and Covenants, the Savior said that He would "recompense unto every man according to his work, and measure to every man *according to the measure which he has measured to his fellow man*" (D&C 1:10).

Not long before his death, Joseph Smith spoke to a large crowd outside of the Nauvoo Temple and "prophesied in the name of the Lord, concerning the merchants in the city; that if they, and the rich did not open their hearts and contribute to the poor, they would be cursed by the hand of God, and be cut off from the land of the living" (see "History, 1838–1856, volume C-1 Addenda," p. 71, *The Joseph Smith Papers;* https://www.josephsmithpapers.org/paper-summary/history-1838–1856-volume-c-1-addenda/71).

In April general conference, 2018, a realignment of Melchizedek Priesthood quorums was announced. In the letter from the First Presidency that announced those changes, they stated: "The separate programs of home teaching and visiting teaching are now a coordinated effort referred to as 'ministering.' . . . *Ministering is Christlike caring for others and helping meet*

---

[1] Note that the word "minister" is used by the Savior in verse 44 of the parable.

their spiritual and temporal needs" (Letter from the First Presidency, April 2, 2018).

In the priesthood session that Saturday evening, President Nelson said: "A hallmark of the Lord's true and living Church *will always be an organized, directed effort to minister to individual children of God and their families.* Because it is His Church, we as His servants will minister to the one, just as He did. *We will minister in His name, with His power and authority, and with His loving-kindness*" ("Ministering with the Power and Authority of God," *Ensign*, May 2018). In the closing session on Sunday, he described this approach as a "newer, holier approach to caring for and ministering to others" (Russell M. Nelson, "Ministering," *Ensign*, May 2018). Sister Jean B. Bingham, Relief Society General President, also spoke by assignment on that topic, summing it up with these words:

> *In remembering together before the Lord the poor, the needy, and the oppressed, there is developed, unconsciously but realistically, a love for others above self, a respect for others, a desire to serve the needs of others. One cannot ask God to help a neighbor in distress without feeling motivated to do something toward helping that neighbor. What miracles would happen in the lives of the children of America, and of the world, if they would lay aside their own selfishness and lose themselves in the service of others.*
>
> GORDON B. HINCKLEY,
> BE THOU AN EXAMPLE, 31

After all is said and done, *true ministering* is accomplished *one by one with love as the motivation.* The value and merit and wonder of sincere ministering is that it truly changes lives! *When our hearts are open and willing to love and include, encourage and comfort, the power of our ministering will be irresistible.* With love as the motivation, miracles will happen, and we will find ways to bring our "missing" sisters and brothers into the all-inclusive embrace of the gospel of Jesus Christ (Jean B. Bingham, "Ministering as the Savior Does," *Ensign*, May 2018).

SUMMARY AND CONCLUSIONS

The prophecies are clear. We have a lot of bridges to cross before we reach our destination. Some have a 3T sign, and some have a 6T sign. None have an 8T sign.

There is no way that we can lighten that load. But there are three simple and yet profound principles that will help us strengthen the bridges. And there are not many aspects of the gospel that don't fit comfortably under one or more of these principles.

So when someone asks, "What can I do to strengthen the bridges in my life?" the answer may be summed up with three simple recommendations:

1. Live so as to have the Holy Spirit.
2. Consecrate yourself to building the kingdom.
3. Minister to those in need.

EPILOGUE

As we come to the end of this book, let us go back to where we began. In the preface, I shared with the readers how this book first began fifty years ago now. As a young teacher with the Church Educational System, I developed an interest in the prophecies of the last days and the signs of the times. As I gathered scriptural passages and quotes from those we sustain as prophets, seers, and revelators, eventually I felt impelled to write a book about this topic. It was published in 1971 as *The Coming of the Lord*.

Now, fifty years later, we have come to the end of a new edition whose title includes one additional change from the original: *The* Second *Coming of the Lord*. As I think back on those early years and the decades that have passed since then, my mind and heart are full of many thoughts and emotions.

I find it especially significant that after all those years of reading and studying the signs of the times, we are now seeing those signs being fulfilled just as the prophets—ancient and modern—have foretold.

In the last few months, we have watched with astonishment as a worldwide pandemic has swept around the globe, with hardly a nation that has not been hit. We have countries with millions of citizens who have closed their borders and quarantined their citizens. Millions of businesses of all kinds have been closed or have had to send their workers home to work remotely. Major events of all kinds have been canceled, including the Olympic Games. As this book goes to press, we have over ten million people infected with COVID-19 and have surpassed 500,000 deaths. Those numbers will surely be even more sorrowful by the time this book is printed and you are reading it.

We have entered an era when the Church of Jesus Christ has instituted programs and protections to help its members stay safe in these troubled times. These are ways we've never before seen in the history of the Church. Home gospel worship, including the administration of the sacrament in the home. Baptisms curtailed except in rare, special cases. Temples closed and thousands of marriage sealings postponed until they reopen. Tens of thousands of missionaries released early, quarantined in place, or brought home until the crisis passes. All Missionary Training Centers around the world closed, and missionaries being prepared through online training. All family history centers closed, and ordinance work for the dead postponed until the temples can safely reopen.

And with those profound and intensive changes in mind, let us not forget to see another promised sign of the times. Enoch saw our day and said of it: "The day shall come that the earth shall rest, but before that day the heavens shall be darkened, and a veil of darkness shall cover the earth; and the heavens shall shake, and also the earth; and great tribulations shall be among the children of men, *but my people will I preserve*" (Moses 7:61). That too is a promised sign of the times.

For years now, those leaders whom we sustain as prophets, seers, and revelators have been seeking revelation and inspiration on how to better prepare the Church for what is coming in the future. And now at least one part of the prophesied future in upon us. And look what those years of preparation have created, and how the Lord has undertaken His own preparation for this time. For example:

- We have the communications technology that we could broadcast the general conference of April 2020 to all the world, even though only a few people at a time were actually together for the broadcast.
- With that technology, a truly global Church could participate in the sacred Hosanna Shout together, with President Russell M. Nelson leading us.
- A few years ago, we started a program of home-centered, Church-supported gospel learning, with every family receiving Come, Follow Me manuals to help us better teach the scriptures in the home. Think what a blessing that is to us now when "home-centered" has become a stark reality.
- The Sunday meeting schedule was reduced so that we could spend more time with our families in gospel study and Sabbath worship. Now we have even more time to do that.
- The home and visiting teaching programs were replaced by a new ministering effort that asks us to more consistently and more carefully reach out and care for others. How prescient for what is happing in our wards and branches now.
- The Church has recently increased its emphasis on being more

self-reliant and self-sufficient and getting out of debt. With millions of people left without employment, those are critical blessings now.
- Significant changes in youth programs now allow more of our youth to have leadership experience, participate in temple ordinances, and serve more directly in the Church.
- The Church itself has practiced the very things it asks of its members, including provident living and staying out of debt. That has given the Church the resources to be a positive force in this world crisis. They have the resources to charter numerous flights to help bring missionaries home, to help members who have lost their jobs or have critical health needs, and to give generous humanitarian service aid to numerous countries around the globe.

These and other examples of advanced preparation are reaping great blessings for Church members and others. This is yet another evidence that the Lord watches over His children and blesses those who are striving to be faithful.

Just before His death, Jesus spoke to His disciples about the signs of the times in the last days. Here is one thing that He warned them of: "And there shall be men standing in that generation [the generation living in the last days], that shall not pass until they shall see an overflowing scourge; for a desolating sickness shall cover the land" (D&C 45:31).

This is not the first pandemic the world has experienced, nor is it likely to be the last. But the point is, though those words were spoken over two thousand years ago, they perfectly describe what we are seeing all around us this very day. And that is true of other signs of the times as well. A few are still in the future, but we have been seeing signs of the times fulfilled around us for generations now—increasing wickedness and evil, war, the collapse of civil order, famine, pestilence, plagues, earthquakes, tsunamis, fierce storms, and floods.

And, as just noted, we have also seen the "great" side of the great and dreadful day unfolding. The Church has become a truly global church. We are blessed with great advances in knowledge, science, technology, medicine, communications, transportation, and so on. More than two millennia ago, Christ told His Apostles to take the gospel to all the world (see Mark 16:15). He gave the same charge early in our day (see D&C 18:28). It has taken us almost two hundred years of patient laboring, but now, as a truly global crisis strikes the world, the Church is present in a large majority of the countries of the world. As a clue to how many countries that involves, we know that the

Church now publishes its materials in 188 languages! More than 80% of all members now have a temple within a few hundred miles of their homes. The blessings of the gospel are open to all.

So, in closing, as this new edition of *The Second Coming of the Lord* prepares to go to press, I should like to share the following observations and reflections with the readers.

- When it comes to knowing what the future holds for us, we are truly a blessed people. We love the prophecies of the Old and New Testaments. To that precious treasure is added hundreds of pages of scripture, which are also filled with prophecies.
- For almost two hundred years now, we have been led and blessed by living prophets, seers, and revelators, and this will continue right up to the Second Coming.
- The Savior wants us to know what the future holds, and how to prepare for it, for He wants us there at His coming.
- The gathering of Israel is far more important, and far more urgent, than many of us understood.
- Though there are terrible things in our future, the Lord has prepared a way for His people to "be not troubled." He will prepare places of peace, safety, and refuge for us.
- Many things that were prophecies in 1971 are now history, or are in the process of being fulfilled.
- No unhallowed hand can stop the work of God from progressing. The evidence of this is everywhere around us and increases almost daily.
- If we are prepared, we shall not fear.
- Fear is a fickle motivator. If fear and anxiety is the only thing that drives us to change, once the threat is gone, our determination can easily melt away.
- We are truly part of "a marvelous work and a wonder" (2 Nephi 25:17).
- Our primary task is not to put everything in our lives in order in some panicky, frenzied rush, but to daily assess where we are and where we need to be, then move steadily forward.
- Remember that two of the most important questions we can add to our prayers are: "What am I doing right now that I need to change so I can bring more revelation into my life?" And, "What am I *not* doing right now that the Lord would have me start doing?"

As we close this book, we do so with the words of the prophet of God who was chosen to open this dispensation, the dispensation of the fulness of times, and whose vision saw the fulfillment of that day. We have cited his words before, but it is fitting that we read them once again:

> The building up of Zion is a cause that has interested the people of God in every age; it is a theme upon which prophets, priests and kings have dwelt with peculiar delight; they have looked forward with joyful anticipation to the day in which we live; and fired with heavenly and joyful anticipations they have sung and written and prophesied of this our day; but they died without the sight; we are the favored people that God has made choice of to bring about the Latter-day glory; it is left for us to see, participate in and help to roll forward the Latter-day glory, "the dispensation of the fullness of times, when God will gather together all things that are in heaven, and all things that are upon the earth, even in one" (Joseph Smith, *History of The Church of Jesus Christ of Latter-day Saints*, 4:609–10).

BIBLIOGRAPHY

Ballard, M. Russell. *Our Search for Happiness.* Salt Lake City: Deseret Book, 1991.

Bednar, David A. *Increase in Learning: Spiritual Patterns for Obtaining Your Own Answers.* Salt Lake City: Deseret Book, 2011.

Bell, Jim. *In the Strength of the Lord: The Life and Teachings of James E. Faust.* Salt Lake City: Deseret Book, 1999.

Benson, Ezra Taft. *Come unto Christ.* Salt Lake City: Deseret Book, 1983.

———. *Teachings of Ezra Taft Benson.* Salt Lake City: Deseret Book, 1988.

———. *The Constitution, A Heavenly Banner.* Salt Lake City: Deseret Book, 1986.

Bloxham, V. Ben, et al., eds. *Truth Will Prevail: A History of The Church of Jesus Christ of Latter-day Saints in the British Isles 1837–1987.* Germany: The Church of Jesus Christ of Latter-day Saints, 1987.

Clark, James R. *Messages of the First Presidency of The Church of Jesus Christ of Latter-day Saints,* 5 vols. Salt Lake City: Bookcraft, 1965.

Clarke, Adam. *The Holy Bible Containing the Old and New Testaments with Commentary and Critical Notes.* Nashville: Abingdon Press, 1972.

Daughters in My Kingdom: The History and Work of Relief Society. Salt Lake City: The Church of Jesus Christ of Latter-day Saints, 2011.

Dummelow, J. R. *A Commentary on the Holy Bible.* New York: MacMillan Publishing Company, Inc., 1908.

Fallows, Samuel. *The Popular and Critical Bible Encyclopedia and Scriptural Dictionary,* 3 vols. Chicago: Howard-Severance Company, 1911.

Grow, Matthew, et al., eds. *Saints: The Story of the Church of Jesus Christ in the Latter Days,* Vol 1. Salt Lake City: The Church of Jesus Christ of Latter-day Saints, 2018.

Hastings, James, ed. *Dictionary of the Bible.* New York: John Scribner's Sons, 1909.

Hinckley, Gordon B. *Be Thou an Example.* Salt Lake City: Deseret Book, 2000.

———. *Discourses of President Gordon B. Hinckley,* 2 vols. Salt Lake City: The Church of Jesus Christ of Latter-day Saints, 2004.

———. *Teachings of Gordon B. Hinckley.* Salt Lake City: Deseret Book, 1997.

Holland, Jeffrey R. *Christ and the New Covenant.* Salt Lake City: Deseret Book, 1997.

Hunter, Howard W. *Teachings of Howard W. Hunter.* Salt Lake City: Deseret Book, 1997.

Huntington, Ellsworth. *Bulletin of the American Geographical Society,* Vol. 34, No. 4, 304.

Jannsen, Sarah, et al., eds. *The World Almanac and Book of Facts.* New York: Simon and Schuster, 2018.

Bibliography

Josephus, Flavius. *Josephus: Complete Works.* William Whiston, trans. Grand Rapids, MI: Kregel Publications, 1960.

Kimball, Spencer W. *The Teachings of Spencer W. Kimball.* Edward L. Kimball, ed. Salt Lake City: Bookcraft, 1982.

———. *Faith Precedes the Miracle.* Salt Lake City: Deseret Book, 2001.

Lee, Harold B. *Decisions for Successful Living.* Salt Lake City: Deseret Book, 1973.

———. *Stand Ye in Holy Places.* Salt Lake City: Deseret Book, 1974.

———. *The Teachings of Harold B. Lee.* Clyde J. Williams, ed. Salt Lake City: Bookcraft, 1996.

———. *Ye Are the Light of the World.* Salt Lake City: Deseret Book, 1974.

Ludlow, Daniel H., ed. *Encyclopedia of Mormonism: The History, Doctrine, and Procedures for the Church of Jesus Christ of Latter-Day Saints*, 5 vols. New York: MacMillan Publishing Co., 1992.

Mackie, George M. *Bible Manners and Customs.* Grand Rapids, MI: Fleming H. Revell Co., 1898.

Maxwell, Neal A. *Men and Women of Christ.* Salt Lake City: Bookcraft, 1991.

———. *Not My Will, but Thine.* Salt Lake City: Deseret Book, 2008.

———. *The Neal A. Maxwell Quote Book.* Cory H. Maxwell, ed. Salt Lake City: Deseret Book, 2009.

McConkie, Bruce R. *Doctrinal New Testament Commentary*, 3 vols. Salt Lake City: Bookcraft, 1965.

———. *Millennial Messiah: The Second Coming of the Son of Man.* Salt Lake City: Deseret Book, 1982.

———. *A New Witness for the Articles of Faith.* Salt Lake City: Deseret Book, 1985.

Nelson, Russell M., *Hope in Our Hearts.* Salt Lake City: Deseret Book, 2009.

———. "The Love and Laws of God." BYU devotional, September 17, 2019.

———. *Perfection Pending and Other Favorite Discourses by Russell M. Nelson.* Salt Lake City: Deseret Book, 1998.

———. *The Power within Us.* Salt Lake City: Deseret Book, 1988.

———. *Teachings of Russell M. Nelson.* Salt Lake City: Deseret Book, 2018.

Oaks, Dallin H. *The Lord's Way.* Salt Lake City: Deseret Book, 1991.

———. *With Full Purpose of Heart.* Salt Lake City: Deseret Book, 2002.

Packer, Boyd K. *The Holy Temple.* Salt Lake City: Bookcraft, 1980.

———. *Let Not Your Heart Be Troubled.* Salt Lake City: Bookcraft, 1991.

———. "Let Not Your Heart Be Troubled." BYU devotional, October 1966.

———. *Mine Errand from the Lord: Selections from the Sermons and Writings of Boyd K. Packer.* Salt Lake City: Deseret Book, 2008.

———. "On the Shoulders of Giants." BYU J. Reuben Clark Law Society devotional, February 2004.

———. "Steady as She Goes." BYU devotional, January 1969.

———. "To Those Who Teach in Troubled Times." Address to CES religious educators, 1970.

Rosenberg, Joel C. *Epicenter.* Carol Stream, Ill.: Tyndale House Publishers, Inc., 2008.

Scharffs, Gilbert. *Mormonism in Germany: A History of The Church of Jesus Christ of*

Latter-day Saints in Germany between 1840 and 1970. Salt Lake City: Deseret Book, 1970.

Smith, Eldred G. "Patriarchal Blessing," in *Lectures in Theology: "Last Message Series,"* University of Utah Institute of Religion, April 30, 1971.

Smith, George Albert. *Teachings of George Albert Smith*. Robert and Susan McIntosh, eds. Salt Lake City: Bookcraft, 1996.

Smith, Hyrum M. and Janne M. Sjodahl. *Doctrine and Covenants Commentary*. Salt Lake City, Deseret Book, 1970.

Smith, Joseph. *Teachings of the Presidents of the Church: Joseph Smith*. Salt Lake City: The Church of Jesus Christ of Latter-day Saints, 2007.

Smith, Joseph F. *Gospel Doctrine: Selections from the Sermons and Writings of Joseph F. Smith*. Salt Lake City: Bookcraft, 1998.

Smith, Joseph Fielding. *Answers to Gospel Questions*, 5 Vols. Salt Lake City: Deseret Book, 1957–1972.

———. *Church History and Modern Revelation*. Salt Lake City: The Church of Jesus Christ of Latter-day Saints, 1947.

———. *Doctrines of Salvation*, 3 Vols. Bruce R. McConkie, ed. Salt Lake City: Bookcraft, 1954.

———. "Predicted Judgments." BYU devotional, March 1967.

———. *The Progress of Man*. Salt Lake City: Deseret Book, 1936.

———. *The Signs of the Times*. Salt Lake City: Deseret Book, 1942.

Taylor, John. *Gospel Kingdom*. Salt Lake City: Bookcraft, 1964.

Unger, Merrill F. *Unger's Bible Dictionary*. Chicago: Moody Press, 1952.

Vincent, M. R. *Word Studies in the New Testament*, 2 Vols. MacDill Airforce Base, Florida: MacDonald Publishing Co.

Webster, Noah. *Noah Webster's First Edition of an American Dictionary of the English Language. 1828*. Facsimile First Edition. San Francisco: Foundation for American Christian Education, 1995.

Whitney, Orson F. *Saturday Night Thoughts*. Salt Lake City: Deseret News Press, 1921.

Widtsoe, John A. *Evidences and Reconciliations*. Salt Lake City: Bookcraft, 1943.

———. *Joseph Smith—Seeker after Truth, Prophet of God*. Salt Lake City: Deseret News Press, 1951.

Wilson, William. *Old Testament Word Studies*. Grand Rapids, MI: Kregel Publications, 1978.

Woodruff, Wilford. *The Discourses of Wilford Woodruff*. G. Homer Durham, ed. Salt Lake City: Bookcraft, 1946.

———. *Wilford Woodruff: History of His Life and Labors*. Matthias F. Cowley, ed. Salt Lake City: Bookcraft, 1964.

Wright, George Ernest, et al., eds. *The Westminster Historical Atlas to the Bible*. Philadelphia: The Westminster Press, 1956.

Ye Shall Be Witnesses unto Me: New Testament Reading Guide for Religion 212–213. Salt Lake City: Church Educational System, 1975.

Young, Brigham. *Discourses of Brigham Young*. John A. Widtsoe, ed. Salt Lake City: Deseret Book, 1954.

INDEX

Abomination of desolation, 303
Abortion, 15
Abraham, descendants of, 39, 299–300
Abrahamic Covenant, 36–39, 43–44, 103
Accountability, 92, 389, 391
Adam and Eve: covenants of, 37; LDS views on, 268–69; and conference of the faithful, 269–72, 274; and great conference yet to come, 275–79. *See also* Fall of Adam
Adam-ondi-Ahman: conference of the faithful held at, 269–72; valley of, 272–75; great conference yet to come at, 275–79, 354
Adams, John, 183
Adversity, 416. *See also* Trials
Africa, 117
Agency: and consequences, 30–31; in premortal world, 34–35, 371–72; and consecration, 205; during Millennium, 379
Allegory: of winepress, 341–47; of strengthened bridges, 426–27
American Constitution, 169–71, 175, 177–78, 179–80, 183–84, 217
American West: gathering to, 51–52; early Saints' migration to, 196; and gathering in New Jerusalem, 239
Ancient of Days, 274, 275–76. *See also* Adam and Eve
Andersen, Neil L.: on preparation for Second Coming, 12; on compensatory power for righteous, 18–19, 137, 154, 395; on commotion preceding Second Coming, 23; on last days, 61; on signs of the times, 73–74
Angels: ministering of, 90–93; of judgment, 93–96, 100–101; release of, 96–98;

of destruction, 98–100; and Israelites' escape from Egypt, 213–14
Animals, during Millennium, 373–74
Anti-Christs, 135–36, 291–94
Apocrypha, 248–51
Apostasy, 59, 93, 94, 137
Apostles: martyrdom of, 93; as sowers, 93; charge given to, 108
Armageddon, 283–85, 296–97, 324; battle of, 147–48, 286–87; meaning of term, 286; leader of great army in, 287–89; John's vision of evil coalition, 289–91; evil religious and military/political leaders in, 291–94; alliance of evil in, 294–96; resistance against alliance of evil in, 298–99; as centered in Middle East, 299–301; Jerusalem to be encompassed with armies during, 301–7; triumph and destruction of Gog in, 307–10; and great earthquake, 311–14; and Christ's appearance in Old Jerusalem, 314–19; aftermath of, 319–24
Army of the Lord, 215–17
Assyria, 25, 242, 247, 248–49
Atonement, 375–76

Babylon, 25, 93–94, 242, 338, 367
Ballard, Melvin J., 70, 161, 165
Ballard, M. Russell, 131–32, 173, 199
Bearded darnell, 91
Beast, mark of, 291–93
"Beast from the bottomless pit," 308
Beck, Julie B., 127–28
Bednar, David A., 402, 404
Bedouin tent, as metaphor for Zion, 197–99
Benson, Ezra Taft: on preparations in spirit world, 16; on blessings of obedience, 30; on spirits reserved for last days, 101; on times of the Gentiles, 103; on

signs of the times, 141; on endurance of United States, 171; on challenges to Constitution, 180; on Book of Mormon as keystone, 181; on redemption of Zion, 210; on gathering to New Jerusalem, 224; on Christ's appearance in Old Jerusalem, 317; on scripture study, 407
Bering Strait, 262
Bill of Rights, 169–70
Bingham, Jean B., 441
Blood: moon to be turned to, 164; Jesus sweats, 344–46
Blood Israel, 39
Book of Enoch, 272
Book of Mormon: as type and shadow of America and world, 180–83; publication of, 192–93; power of, 408–9
Book of Revelation: and Nephi's vision, 78–79; writing of, 79–80; understanding, 80–85; and opening of seventh seal, 85–88; vision of battle of Armageddon in, 289–91
Borrowed light, 433–34
Branch Davidians, 60
Branding, 292–93
Bridges, strengthening, 426–27
Brightness, before Second Coming, 335–37
Brimstone, 322
Brown, Victor L., 422–24
Bubonic plague, 163, 167
Burning, 348–52

Caldwell County, Missouri, 273
Camp Fire, 100
Cavalry, 295–96
Celestial kingdom, 362–63, 365, 377
Chariots, 295–96
Children: protecting, 227–28; during Millennium, 379
China, 253, 294
Christians: in Jerusalem, 6–8; persecution of, 305–6
Christofferson, D. Todd: on voice of warning, 30; on covenants and spiritual growth, 34; on building up of Zion, 219; on joining of earthly and spirit world Zions, 221, 233; on Zion, 228
Church of Jesus Christ (early church), 103–4, 269–70

Church of Jesus Christ of Latter-day Saints, The: views on House of Israel, 38; and gathering of Israel, 48–49; growth of, 51, 108–17; and migration of Saints, 115–16; involvement of members of, in wars, 153–54; persecution of, 170–73, 175, 195–96, 209–11; organization of, 192–93; and inhabitants of New Jerusalem, 237–38; during Millennium, 239; and return of lost tribes of Israel, 264–65; and two prophets raised up to Jewish nation, 305; warnings and admonitions given to Saints, 388–92; finding fault with, 389–91; safety in, 395–96; educational efforts in, 398–99; preparedness of, 410–13, 444–45; conditions impacting financial resources of, 422–24; as worldwide organization, 445–46
Church of the Lamb, Nephi's vision of, 78–79
Church Security Plan / Church Welfare Plan, 414–15, 417
City of Enoch, 188–90, 193, 202, 271, 355–58
City walls, attacking, 296
Civil War, 138–39, 141, 142–47, 154, 218
Clark, J. Reuben, 179, 180, 207
Class distinctions, 182
Clay, Henry, 172
Cold War, 69
Compensatory power, 18–19, 137, 154, 395
Consecration, 201–5, 207–8
Consecration and stewardship, law of, 203–4, 205–7
Consequences, 30–31
Constitution of the United States, 169–71, 175, 177–78, 179–80, 183–84, 217
Continental drift theory, 326
Conversion, 425
Cook, Quentin L., 46, 136
Core documents, 192–93
Coronavirus/COVID-19 pandemic, x, 13, 88, 167, 236, 420, 443–45
Corruption: as Satan's strategic goal, 134; in Nephite government, 182
Covenant lineage, 42–43
Covenant people, 38. *See also* Elect; House of Israel; Israel; Israelite(s)
Covenant(s): defined, 32–33; conditions

concerning, 33–34; in premortal world, 34–36; and elect of God, 35–36; Abrahamic Covenant, 36–39, 43–44, 103; of patriarchs, 36–39; and house of Israel, 37–43; gathering and, 43–44
Cowdery, Oliver, 245, 258–59
Creation, and natural disasters, 160–61

Danger: warning others of, 29–30; warnings of, 68. *See also* Warning(s)
Daniel, 275–76
Darkness: maintaining hope in, 9; caused by volcanic eruptions, 163–64, 165; and signs in the heavens, 164, 334
Darnell, 91
David, 191
Daviess County, Missouri, 273–74
Daylight, before Second Coming, 335–37
Dead, ordinance work for, 224–25, 365. *See also* Resurrection(s)
Dead Sea, healing of, 327–30
Death, during Millennium, 374. *See also* Resurrection(s)
Debt, 419–22
Deep, highway cast up in midst of, 261–62
Degrees of glory, 365–67, 369
Deism, 160
Democracy, as in decline, 145
Desolation, abomination of, 303
Destruction, angels of, 98–100
Dictatorships, 151–52
Discipleship, doctrine and, 406–7
Disease, 165–67
Disobedience, curses of, 23–29
Dispensation of the fulness of times, 49–51, 105–6
Doctrine and Covenants 77, 80–84
Doctrines of the gospel, 403–7
Douglas, Stephen A., 175
"Dreadful," 72, 126
Drought, 76, 167, 306–7
Dummelow, J. R., 294

Earth: temporal existence of, 84–85; cleansing of, by fire, 148–49; as belonging to Lord, 203; division of, 325–26; to come together again, 325–27; new, 372–73, 382–83; sanctification of, 382–83

Earthquakes, 99, 157–58, 163–64, 165, 311–14, 316–17
Eber, 325
Ebola virus, 167
Eden, 271
Egypt, 308
Einstein, Albert, 66
Elect, 35–36, 101, 393–96. *See also* Covenant people; House of Israel; Israel; Israelite(s)
Elias, 245
Elijah, 27, 245, 361, 362
Elite, teaching of false prophecies by, 135–37
Enoch, city of, 188–90, 193, 202, 271, 355–58
Enoch, vision of Satan, 11, 133
Ephraim, 40, 43, 246, 263–64
Equity, 375–76
Esau, 299–300
Euphrates River, 250–51
Eusebius, 7
Eve, 269. *See also* Adam and Eve
Event markers, 87. *See also* Signs of the times
Exaltation, and First Resurrection, 362–63
Excommunication, 95–96
Exodus, 211, 212–14
Experience, learning through, 31
Exploitation, as Satan's strategic goal, 134

Faith: facing latter days with, 16–19; sustaining, 31; and trials of latter days, 131, 154; and compensatory power for righteous, 154; strengthening, 398
Fall of Adam, 82, 84, 87
False philosophies, teaching of, 135–37
Famine, 76, 165–67
Faust, James E., 21, 31, 263–64
Fear, of last days, 123–24
Fig tree, signs of the times likened to, 71–72
Financial crisis of 2008, 11–12, 421–22
Financial preparation, 419–22
Fire: cleansing by, 148–49; pillar of, 214; Jesus Christ to come with, 348–52; as sign of the times, 350
Firebombing, 141–42
First Resurrection, 338–39, 362–64, 366, 368–69, 370
Flight, turbulent, 124–25
Flooding, 100
Food storage, 417–19

Forty, 83–84
Fountain of water, 327–30
Fulness of the Gentiles, 104–6

Gallus, Cestius, 4–5, 7
Garden of Eden, 271
Gathering of Israel: in last days, 28, 32, 45–47, 48; in spirit world, 36, 45, 118; and covenants, 43–44; and restoration of all things, 45–47; through missionary work, 46, 51, 118; importance of, 46–49; scriptural references to, 48–49; and dispensation of the fulness of times, 49–51; policy change regarding, 51–53, 196–97; phases of, 52–53; charge concerning, 117–18; places for, 233–34; inclusivity of, 237; and return of lost tribes of Israel, 244–47, 255–56; two aspects of, 247. *See also* Lost tribes of Israel
Gematria, 293
Generation: length of, 106–7; and population growth, 253–54; rising, 380–82; of Millennials, 388
Gentiles: defined, 41; gospel restored to, 102; and house of Israel, 102–3; times of the, 103–4; fulness of the, 104–6; fulfillment of times of the, 106, 111, 116; and seed of Joseph, 108
Geologic disasters, 163–65
Germany, 141–42
Gesenius, Wilhelm, 289
Gethsemane, 344–47
Glory, degrees of, 365–67, 369
God: trusting in, 12–13, 392; voice of, 20–22; covenants with, 32–34; elect of, 35–36; perception of time of, 64–66, 84–85; loving and tender concern of, 75; and natural disasters, 158, 159, 160–61; sermons on natural disasters, 162–63; and lost tribes of Israel, 258; love of, 405–6; nature of, 405–6
Gog, 288, 290–95, 298, 302, 304, 306, 307–10, 319–21, 323, 380
Gospel: increasing knowledge about, 402–9; doctrines of, 403–7
Grant, Jedediah M., 77, 176, 177, 402
"Great," 126
Great and dreadful day of the Lord, 123–28, 279–80

Great Britain: and World War II, 141–42; and Civil War, 144
Great Rift Valley, 329
Guilt, 343, 349–50

Hailstones, 322
Haran, 249
Hawaii, 111
Heart, pure in, 225, 240–41
Heaven(s): signs in, 159, 164–65, 333–37; powers of, to be shaken, 165; shutting, 306–7; opening of, 368; war in, 371–72; new, 372–73, 382–83; shaking, 373
Herod, 344
Hinckley, Gordon B.: on peace through perilous times, 26; on natural disasters, 95; on last days, 127; on September 11 terrorist attacks, 138; on war, 148; on debt to early pioneers, 196; on burning at Second Coming, 351; warns against pessimism, 396; on wisely spending your time, 401; on financial debt, 420–21; on spiritual conversion, 425; on serving others, 441
HIV/AIDS epidemic, 167
"Holiness to the Lord," 378
Holland, Jeffrey R., 9, 58, 375–76, 408
Holy Ghost: importance of, 18; and accountability of Saints, 389, 391; and spiritual guidance, 394–95; and oil in parable of ten virgins, 431, 433; and increasing capacity to receive revelation, 434–35
Hope: maintaining, 9; and positive events in last days, 15–16; Thomas S. Monson on, 16; facing latter days with, 16–19
Horses and horsemen, 295–96
House of Israel, 38; Jew as generic term for, 41–42; remnants of, 42; Gentiles and, 102–3. *See also* Israel
Hunter, Howard W., 33, 396
Hurricane Katrina, 95, 99
Hurricane Maria, 99
Hyde, Orson, 141

Ice, 260
Independence, 410–12. *See also* Self-reliance; Temporal preparedness

INDEX

Independence, Missouri, 209–11. *See also* Jackson County, Missouri
Indonesia: earthquake in, 99, 157–58, 313–14; volcanic eruption in, 163–64
Inequity, 375–76
Inspiration, and sacred sites, 275
Intellectual elite, teaching of false prophecies by, 135–37
Intercessory prayer, 344–47
Ishmael, 299–300
Israel: and Abrahamic covenant, 37–38; terms related to, 38–43; times of, 103–4; and battle of Armageddon, 299–300. *See also* Gathering of Israel; House of Israel; Lost tribes of Israel
Israel (kingdom), 40, 246–47
Israel (land), 39
Israel (political), 40
Israel (state): creation of, 106; and battle of Armageddon, 299–300; natural gas and petroleum reserves of, 301
Israel, True, 41
Israelite(s), 38–43, 211, 212–14, 260

Jackson County, Missouri: return to, 214–16, 234–36; temple in, 221–23; plan for, 230–33; as location of New Jerusalem, 239; as location of Garden of Eden, 271. *See also* Independence, Missouri
Jacob, remnant of, 42
Jaredites, 14, 26, 173
Jehovah, Israel to be led by, 213–14. *See also* Jesus Christ
Jeremiah, 25–26, 47, 242, 257
Jerusalem: destruction of, 3–8, 24, 25, 301–2; Christians in, 6–8; as Zion, 190–92; as capital city during Millennium, 234; as destination of lost tribes of Israel, 256; encompassed by armies during Armageddon, 301–7; likened to Sodom and Egypt, 308; great earthquake in, 311–12, 316–17; Jesus Christ to make appearance in, 314–19; and Resurrection, 363–64; and Christ's Millennial reign, 377; as holy city, 378. *See also* New Jerusalem
Jerusalem Temple: destruction of, 3, 6, 303; fountain of water from beneath, 327–30
Jesus Christ: prophesies of Jerusalem's destruction, 3–4, 6, 301–2; coming unto, 10; calms Sea of Galilee, 13, 17; voice of, 20–22; covenants with, 32–34; teachings on signs of the times, 71–74; opens seals, 81; and establishment of gospel, 103–4; prophecies concerning, 212; Moses as type for, 213; Israel to be led by, 213–14; to appear in New Jerusalem, 224; testimony of, 259; appears at conference of the faithful, 270; to be installed as rightful Ruler of earth, 277, 278; works of, 287; natural disasters at time of death of, 313; Millennial reign of, 320, 348, 352–55, 377; appearance of, at Second Coming, 340–47; dressed in scarlet robes, 344; intercessory prayer of, 344–47; to come with fire, 348–52; acknowledgment of, 350; resurrection of, 359; appearance on Mount of Olives, 364–65; empathy of, 375–76; trusting, 392; love of, 405–6
Jew(s): defined, 41–42, 317n1; reject gospel, 104
Joel, 327–28
John the Beloved, 78, 79, 360–61. *See also* Book of Revelation
Joseph: remnant of seed of, 42; seed of, 108
Joseph Smith Translation, 80, 193
Josephus, 24, 25, 288–89
Joy, through difficulties, 127
"Joy to the World," 332–33
Judah (Southern Kingdom), 25, 40, 41–42, 242, 246–47
Judges, government by, 174
Judgment: and ministering angels, 91–93; angels of, 93–96, 100–101; natural disasters as part of, 98, 161–62; at great conference yet to come, 277; of wicked, 342–45; during Millennium, 374–75

Katrina (hurricane), 95, 99
Kimball, Heber C., 239
Kimball, Spencer W.: and policy change regarding gathering, 52; on bringing again Zion, 207–8; on gathering of Israel, 255; on records of lost tribes of Israel, 265; on scripture study, 408; on self-reliance, 413; on parable of ten virgins, 431–32; on parable of talents, 438

King, Martin Luther Jr., 219
Kingdom of God, 352–55
Kingship, 181, 182
Kirtland Temple, 222, 245
Knights, 295–96
Knowledge: and educational efforts in Church, 398–99; increasing, about world, 400–401; increasing, about gospel, 402–9
Kolob, 65
Koresh, David, 60
Korihor, 135–36

Lakes, drying up, 167
Lamanites, 381–82
Land of promise, 173–74
Last days: conditions and events in, 13–17, 168, 227–28; facing, with faith, 17–19; peace in, 26; gathering in, 28, 32, 43–44, 45–47, 48; as dispensation of the fulness of times, 49–51; spirits saved for, 51, 88–89, 101; progression of gospel in, 54; fear of, 123–24; and great and dreadful day of the Lord, 123–28; joyful anticipation for, 128; Satan's pervasive influence in, 129–32; scope of Satan's efforts in, 132–37; Zion to be established in, 193–94
Latin America, 116
Law, rule of, 179
Lee, Ann, 60
Lee, Harold B.: on signs of the times, 68, 101; on importance of strong testimony, 92, 433–34; on failing of elect, 101; on gathering of Saints, 240–41; on priesthood and translated beings, 361–62; on trusting Lord, 392; on scripture study, 407
Lehites, 253
Life spans of patriarchs, 270
Light: before Second Coming, 335–37; borrowed, 433–34
Locusts, 290
Longsuffering, 95–96
Lost tribes of Israel: return of, 242–43, 244–47, 266–67; speculation on location of, 243; questions concerning, 243–44; travels and fate of, 247–52; current location of, 252–54; self-knowledge concerning identity of, 254; destination of, at time of return, 255–56; journey of, at time of return, 256–65; scriptures and records of, 265–66. *See also* Gathering of Israel
Love: of God and Jesus Christ, 405–6; for neighbor, 440

Mackie, George, 428–30
Magog, 288–89, 298, 321–22, 380
Maria (hurricane), 99
Mark of the beast, 291–93
Marriage rates, 15
Marriages, Middle Eastern, 428–31
Marsh, Thomas B., 49
Martus, 305
Materialism, as Satan's strategic goal, 133–34
Maxwell, Neal A.: on signs of the times, 72–73; on unifying House of Lord, 285; on Christ's red attire at Second Coming, 346; on acknowledgment of Lord, 350; on Second Coming, 368; on Christ's suffering and mercy, 375; on gospel knowledge, 405; on doctrine and discipleship, 407; on following General Authorities, 426
Mayan calendar, 60
McConkie, Bruce R.: and policy change regarding gathering, 52–53; on phases of Church growth, 108; on natural disasters, 162; on Zion, 189–90; on consecration, 202; on return of ten tribes versus gathering of Israel, 245; on ten tribes of Israel, 252; on scriptures and prophets of lost tribes, 258; on prophets of lost tribes, 259–60; on Adam-ondi-Ahman, 268; on great conference yet to come, 279; on Armageddon, 283, 298; on two prophets raised up to Jewish nation, 305; on First Resurrection, 366
McKay, David O., 71, 226
Media, 401
Megiddo, 286
Melchizedek, 190–92, 361
Meshech, 289
Metaphor, 341–42
Michael, 269, 272–73. *See also* Adam and Eve
Middle East: Armageddon as centered in, 299–301; marriages in, 428–31

INDEX

Migration of Saints, 51–52, 115–16, 235–36
Millennials (generation), 388
Millennium: duration of, 66; as "final day," 84; and timing of Second Coming, 85–86; timing of, 87; ordinance work in, 224–25; capital cities during, 234; status of Church in, 239; Christ's reign during, 320, 348, 352–55; importance of ushering in of, 331–33; mortal deprivations set right in, 371; ushering in of, 372; prophecies concerning, 372–79; battle between good and evil at end of, 380–82; sanctification of earth following, 382–83
Miller, George, 60
Mining, 411–12
Ministering, 440–41
Ministering angels, 90–93
Miracles, through forces of nature, 261
Missionary work: and gathering of Israel, 46, 51, 256; in Russia, 71; charge concerning, 108, 118; Church growth through, 109–10
Mocking, 127–28
Money, obsession with, 133–34
Monson, Thomas S., 16, 170, 419–20
Moon, to be turned to blood, 164
Morals, collapse of, 133
Mormon, 26–27
Moroni, prophecies of, 62–63
Moses: last sermon of, 22–29; prophecies concerning prophets like unto, 212, 234; as type for Christ, 213; and restoration of priesthood keys, 245, 258–59; and Israelites' escape from Egypt, 260; as translated being, 361, 362
Moshki, 289
Mosiah, 173–74, 181
Mount of Olives, 315–18, 364–65

Natural disasters, 156–58, 168; drought, 76, 167, 306–7; famine, 76, 165–67; pestilence, 76, 165–67; hurricanes, 95, 99; as part of mortality, 95; and angels of destruction, 97–98; increase in frequency and intensity, 98–100; geologic disasters, 99, 157–58, 163–65, 311–14, 316–17; tsunamis, 99, 157–58; flooding, 100; causes of, 101; warnings of, 158–59; signs in the heavens, 159, 164–65, 333–37; doctrines and principles associated with, 160–62; service during, 161; as form of judgment, 161–62; Lord's sermons on, 162–63; desolating scourge, 165–67; as sign of Second Coming, 311–14, 316–17; at time of Christ's death, 313; and temporal preparedness, 422
Nauvoo, Illinois, 187–88
Nauvoo Temple, 222
Neglect, as Satan's strategic goal, 134
Neighbors, commandment to love, 440
Nelson, Russell M.: on preparation for Second Coming, 3, 10; on trusting in God, 12; on need for Holy Ghost, 18; on prophets, 25; on gathering in last days, 28, 43–44, 45–47, 48; on gathering in spirit world, 36; on Abrahamic covenant, 37; on perspective on covenant path, 41; on dispensation of the fulness of times, 51; on progression of gospel, 54; on timing of Second Coming, 60; on spirits reserved for last days, 88–89; on restoration of gospel, 105–6; on joy through difficulties, 127; on trials of latter days, 131, 132; on challenges of latter days, 168; on gathering in Zion, 200; on lineage and gathering of Israel, 263; on importance of revelation, 287; on works of Christ, 287; on Christ's Millennial reign, 348; on city of Enoch, 357; on resurrection, 359; on Millennials, 388; on spiritual guidance, 394–95; on strengthening faith, 398; on increasing learning, 400; on scripture study, 408–9; on Church welfare, 415; on increasing capacity to receive revelation, 434–35; on ministering, 441
Nelson, Wendy, 266–67
Nephites, 26–27, 173–74, 181–83, 228–29, 381–82
New heaven and new earth, 372–73, 382–83
New Jerusalem, 239–41; and army of the Lord, 215–16; peace, refuge, and safety in, 218–19; Jesus Christ to appear in, 224; life in, 225–27; prophecies concerning, 233; gathering in, 234–36; inhabitants of, 237–38; impact on current Missouri residents, 238–39; location of,

239; as destination of lost tribes of Israel, 256; as holy city, 378; to be taken from earth, 383. *See also* Zion
Noah, 74, 325
Northern Kingdom (Kingdom of Israel), 40, 246–47
Nuclear holocaust, 148–50, 295
Numbers: round, 82–83; symbolic and numerical significance of, 83–85, 293–94, 312, 323

Oaks, Dallin H.: on preparation for Second Coming, 14; on signs as calls to repentance, 22; on perspective on covenant path, 41; on signs of Second Coming, 69; on signs of the times, 73, 98; on ethnic diversity in Church, 117; on spiritual causes of commotion, 123; on understanding Constitution, 179; on consecration, 205; on Millennium, 371; on media selection, 401; on caring for poor, 413
Obedience: need for courageous, 21; blessings of, 22–23, 30; curses of disobedience, 23–29; compensatory power from, 395
Oceans, 261–62
Oil, 300–301, 430–31, 432–33
Olive leaf revelation, 139, 230
Olive oil, 430–31
Olivet Discourse, 3–4, 71–73
Olive trees, allegory of, 342
Oppression, as Satan's strategic goal, 134

Packer, Boyd K.: on spiritual preparedness, 17; on hope for future, 18; on spirits reserved for last days, 51; on endurance of world, 57; on trials of latter days, 131; on horrors of World War II, 142; on preservation of Constitution, 183–84; on Independence temple site, 222; on sacred sites, 275; on raising families in wicked times, 395–96; on doctrine and behavior, 406
Palestine, partitioning of, 106
Parable(s): of wheat and tares, 91–96, 285; concerning spiritual preparedness, 427–28; of ten virgins, 428–35; of talents, 435–39; of sheep and goats, 439–41

Passover, 213
Patriarchal blessings, 40, 42–43, 246, 254, 270
Patriarchs: covenants with, 36–39; and establishment of Church, 269–70; life spans of, 270
Paul, 58–59, 104–5
Peace: in perilous times, 26; in New Jerusalem, 218–19
Peleg, 325
Pella, 7–8
Penrose, Charles W., 90, 126–27, 223–24, 331
Perdition, sons of, 369–70
Persecution: of early Saints, 170–73, 175, 195–96, 209–11; of Christians, 305–6
Pessimism, 396
Pestilence, 76, 165–67
Petro-politics, 300–301
Pilate, 353–54
Pillar of fire, 214
Pillar of smoke, 213–14
Plague, 163, 167
Polynesian Saints, 116
Poor and needy, 413–15
Population growth, 253–54
Pornography, 228
Positive events, 15–16
Poverty, as slavery, 145
Powers of heaven, to be shaken, 165
Pratt, Orson, 153
Premortal world, 34–36, 371–72
Preparation for Second Coming, 387–88; spiritual, 16–17, 425–44; linking of separation and, 92–93; and warnings and admonitions given to Saints, 388–92; and Lord's promises to His elect, 393–96; and increasing knowledge about world, 400–401; and increasing knowledge about gospel, 402–9; temporal, 410–24
Present, 65, 66
Pride, 136, 182
Priesthood: restoration of, 245, 258–59; given to Adam, 269; and translated beings, 361–62
Principles: associated with natural disasters, 160–62; versus doctrines, 404
Promise, voice of, 21–22, 27, 30
Promised land, 173–74

Prophecy / prophecies: concerning Jerusalem's destruction, 3–4, 6, 301–2; purpose and value of, 6–8; teaching of false, 135–37; concerning war, 139–41, 146; concerning Civil War, 142–47, 218; concerning United States, 174–78; concerning Constitution, 180, 183–84; concerning prophets like unto Moses, 212, 234; concerning New Jerusalem, 233; spirit of, 259; concerning battle of Armageddon, 287–88; concerning Second Coming, 338–40; concerning Millennium, 372–79. *See also* Revelation(s); Vision(s)

Prophets: foresight of, 25; of lost tribes of Israel, 258–60; two witnesses as, 304–5

Ptolemy, 253

Pure in heart, 225, 240–41

Quickening, 368

Rainbows, 74–77
Red garments, 341–47
Refuge: in New Jerusalem, 218–19; places of, 240
Refugees, 15, 145
Relativity, 66
Remnant of Jacob, 42
Remnant of seed of Joseph, 42
"Remnants," 146, 312
Remnants of house of Israel, 42
Renlund, Dale G., 389–90
Renlund, Ruth L., 389–90
Repentance: signs as calls to, 22; importance of, 345–46
Restoration: as ongoing, 3; and fulness of the Gentiles, 105; and founding of United States, 169–70
Restoration of all things, 45–47
Resurrection(s): First Resurrection, 338–39, 362–64, 366, 368–69, 370; and meeting of city of Enoch and Zion, 355–56; of Jesus Christ, 359; and Lord's arm falling upon nations, 364–69; Second Resurrection, 367, 369–70
Revelation(s): on war, 138–39; on Civil War, 142–47; concerning Apocrypha, 248; concerning return of lost tribes, 257–58; importance of, 287; during Millennium, 374; increasing capacity to receive, 434–35. *See also* Prophecy / Prophecies; Vision(s)

Reynolds, George W., 251

Righteous: separation of wicked and, 8–9; compensatory power for, 18–19, 137, 154, 395; promises concerning, 219–20; to gather in New Jerusalem, 224; Armageddon and gathering of, 285

Righteousness: to sweep world as flood, 355; and spiritual preparedness, 432

Rioting, 150–52, 218–19

Rising generation, 380–82

Roman Empire: and destruction of Jerusalem, 4–6, 24, 25, 302; slavery under, 292

Romney, Marion G., 310, 402–3, 408

Rosh, 288, 289

Round numbers, 82–83

Rule of law, 179

Russia, 69–71, 298

Ryegrass, 91, 94

Sacrament: covenants in, 34; at great conference yet to come, 279
Safety: in New Jerusalem, 218–19; places of, 240; in Church, 395–96
Salem, 191
Salt Lake Temple, 96–97
Same-gender marriage, 404–5
Santayana, George, 6
Satan: Enoch's vision of, 11, 133; evil of, 11; pervasive influence of, 129–32; scope of efforts of, 132–37; strategic goals of, 133–34; resisting, 137; John's vision of, 290; current efforts of, 296–97; to be bound during Millennium, 372, 374, 378–79
Scarlet robes, 344
School of the Prophets, 398–99
Scourge, 165–67
Scriptures: of lost tribes of Israel, 265–66; studying, 407–9
Sea of Galilee, 13, 17
2 Esdras, 248–51
Second Coming: preparation for separation at time of, 8–9; speculation on timing of, 57–61; scriptures concerning timing of, 61–62; and our time versus God's time, 65–66; timing of, 86–88; sense

INDEX

of urgency concerning, 88–89; Christ's appearance at time of, 314–19, 340–47; importance of, 331–33, 370; events of, 333; scriptural descriptions of, 337–40. *See also* Preparation for Second Coming

Second Resurrection, 367, 369–70

Seed of Joseph, 108; remnant of, 42

Seers, 70

Self-reliance, 413, 414–15. *See also* Independence; Temporal preparedness

Separation: at Second Coming, 8–9; and parable of wheat and tares, 91–96; linking of preparation and, 92–93; from worldliness, 237; preparation for, 388; of sheep and goats, 440

September 11 terrorist attacks, 138

Service: during natural disasters, 161; for others, 440–41

Seven, 83, 85, 312, 323

Seven seals of the apocalypse, 80, 84, 86, 87–89. *See also* Book of Revelation

Sexually transmitted diseases, 167

Shame, 349–50

Sheep and goats, parable of, 439–41

Shittim, 327–28

Shutting the heavens, 306–7

Sickness, 165–67

Sign of the Son of Man, 334–35, 367

Signs in the heavens, 159, 164–65, 333–37

Signs of the times, 68–71, 77; Jesus's teachings on, 71–74; rainbows as, 74–77; as event markers, 87, 88; and seven seals of the apocalypse, 87–88; increase in frequency and intensity, 98–100, 141, 166–67; causes of, 101; and Gentiles and House of Israel, 102–3; fulfillment of, 113–17, 443–45; beginning of, 125; purpose of, 129; war as, 139; fire as, 350

Sin: cleansing of earth from, 342; as separating influence, 389

Sinim, 253, 294

666, 291–94

Slaves: uprising of, 144–46; branding of, 292–93

Smith, Eldred G., 42

Smith, Emma, 35

Smith, George Albert, 70–71, 169

Smith, Hyrum Mack, 227

Smith, Joseph F.: on natural disasters, 156, 160, 161; on return to Zion, 214–15, 236; on women's role in kingdom and future events, 278; on obedience and coming forth in First Resurrection, 370

Smith, Joseph Fielding: on Wilford Woodruff and parable of wheat and tares, 97; on gospel preached to Gentiles, 104; on fulfillment of times of the Gentiles, 107; on war, 140; on Zion, 194; on consecration, 201; on work for dead during Millennium, 224–25; on location of New Jerusalem, 239; on blessings of Ephraim, 264; on great conference yet to come, 276–78; on Armageddon, 286–87; on cleansing of earth from sin, 342; on Christ's Millennial reign, 354, 377; on meeting of Zion and city of Enoch, 355; on priesthood and translated beings, 361–62; on Resurrection, 363; on Satan's binding during Millennium, 379; on sanctification of earth, 383; on gospel knowledge, 403

Smith, Joseph Jr.: on gathering in last days, 32; on dispensation of the fulness of times, 50; on rainbow, 75, 76–77; and Joseph Smith Translation, 80, 193; and understanding Revelation, 80–84; on signs of the times, 125; on last days, 128; on corruption of current generation, 129; prophesies of wars, 146; on suffering of Saints, 154; petitions for redress for persecution, 172; prophesies concerning United States, 175–78; on Constitution, 179; on building up of Zion, 187, 447; and consecration, 202; vision of redemption of Zion given to, 212; and plat for Jackson County, 231–33; and restoration of priesthood keys, 245, 258–59; on prophets, 259; and valley of Adam-ondi-Ahman, 273–74; on great conference yet to come, 276; on John's vision of Armageddon, 290; on signs in the heavens, 334–35; on kingdom of God, 355; on progression of gospel, 387; and School of the Prophets, 398–99; and temporal preparedness of Church, 412

Smith, Joseph Sr., 164

Smoke, pillar of, 213–14

Snow, Eliza R., 177–78

Snow, Lorenzo, 218, 238
Social contracts, 150–51
Social upheaval, 134–35, 150–53, 218–19, 262
Societal morals and values, collapse of, 133
Sodom, 308
Solemn assembly, 278
Son of Man, sign of the, 334–35, 367
Sons of perdition, 369–70
Sorrow, during Millennium, 374
Southern Kingdom (Judah), 25, 40, 41–42, 242, 246–47
Soviet Union, 69–71
Spanish flu epidemic, 167
Spiritual power, for righteous, 18–19, 137, 154, 395
Spiritual preparedness, 16–17, 425–26; allegory for, 426–27; parables concerning, 427–28; and parable of ten virgins, 428–35; and parable of talents, 435–39; and parable of sheep and goats, 439–41
Spirit world: preparations for Second Coming in, 16; gathering in, 36, 45, 118
Stakes, 110–12, 196–99
Stars, to fall from heavens, 164–65, 334
Stevenson, Edward, 274
Stewardship, 204. *See also* Consecration and stewardship, law of
Suffering: in Gethsemane, 344–47; and mercy of Jesus Christ, 375–76
Sumatra earthquake, 99, 157–58, 313–14

Talents, 322, 437; parable of, 435–39
Talmage, James E., 251, 266, 268–69
Tares, 91–96, 285. *See also* Wheat and tares, parable of
Taurus Mountains, 250, 251–52
Taylor, John, 177, 225, 237–38, 353
Telestial kingdom, 369, 377
Temple Mount, 3, 5–6, 302–3, 327
Temporal preparedness, 410–13; for poor and needy, 413–15; for tribulation and adversity, 415–17; and modern way of life, 417–19; financial, 419–22; and future conditions impacting Church resources, 422–24
Tent, as metaphor for Zion, 197–99
Ten virgins, parable of, 428–35

Terrestrial kingdom, 365–67, 377
Testimony: importance of strong, 92, 433–34; of Jesus Christ as spirit of prophecy, 259
Thessalonians, 58–59
Three, 83
Three Nephites, 361, 362
Time: problem with our perception of, 62–65; ours versus God's, 65–66, 84–85; wise use of, 401
Times of Israel, 103–4
Times of the Gentiles, 103–4; fulfillment of, 106, 111, 116
Timing: of Lord, 33; of Second Coming, 57–61, 86–88; scriptures concerning, of Second Coming, 61–62; and problem with our perception of time, 62–65; and our time versus God's time, 65–66, 84–85
Tithing, 204, 351–52
Titus, 5–6
Tornadoes, 100
Totalitarian governments, 15
Translated beings, 360–62. *See also* City of Enoch
Transportation, for journey to New Jerusalem, 236–37
Trials: joy through, 127; faith and, 131, 154; comfort through, 375–76; temporal preparedness for, 415–17
Tribulation, 415–16. *See also* Trials
"Trouble" / "Troubled," 72–73
True Israel, 41
Trust, in Lord, 12–13, 392
Tsunamis, 99, 157–58
Tubal, 289
Turbulence, 124–25
Two witnesses, 304–10, 311–12

Uchtdorf, Dieter F., 124
United Order, 204
United States of America: founding of, 169–70; and persecution of early Saints, 170–73; warnings concerning, as promised land, 173–74; prophecies concerning, 174–78; Book of Mormon as type of, 180–83; prophecy concerning war to save, from destruction, 217; and battle of Armageddon, 298, 299

INDEX

US Constitution, 169–71, 175, 177–78, 179–80, 183–84, 217
USSR, 69–71

Van Buren, Martin, 172
Vengeance, 343
Vespasian, Flavius, 5
Vision(s): of Satan given to Enoch, 11, 133; given to Nephi, 78–79; of temple complex in New Jerusalem, 223; of Daniel, 275–76; given to John concerning battle of Armageddon, 289–91; of two witnesses, 304–6; of healing of Dead Sea, 328–30. *See also* Prophecy / Prophecies; Revelation(s)
Voice of promise, 21–22, 28, 30
Voice of warning, 20–21, 22, 27–30, 68
Volcanic eruptions, 163–64, 165

War in heaven, 371–72
Warning(s): voice of, 20–21, 22, 27–30, 68; of natural disasters, 158–59; given to Saints, 388–92
War(s), 154–55; and withdrawn rainbow, 77; as Satan's strategic goal, 134–35; age of, 138–42, 217; as sign of the times, 139; prophecies concerning, 139–41, 146; as result of wickedness, 146–47; and battle of Armageddon, 147–48, 286–87; and possibility of World War III, 148; and possibility of nuclear holocaust, 148–50; and possible collapse of social order, 150–53; involvement of Saints in, 153–54; and army of the Lord, 215–16; poured out on all nations, 298–99. *See also* Armageddon
Water, fountain of, 327–30
Watts, Isaac, 332
Wealth, obsession with, 133–34
Wegler, Alfred, 326
Welfare, 413–15
Wheat and tares, parable of, 91–96, 285
White robes, 340–41
Whitney, Orson F.: on book seen by John, 79; on time periods on earth, 80; on war, 141; on revelation concerning Civil War, 143; on return of Adam, 274; on faithfulness and spiritual survival, 280; on city of Enoch, 357
Whore, 93–94

Wicked: separation of righteous and, 8–9; and natural disasters, 95; Armageddon and gathering of, 285; judgment of, 342–45; to be bound, 367; destruction of, 372
Wickedness: prevalence of, 10–11; in last days, 13–15; during last dispensation, 50–51; Babylon as type for, 93–94; and natural disasters, 95; war as result of, 146–47; destruction of, 367, 377; safety from, 395–96
Widtsoe, John A., 203, 206, 264
Wight, Orange L., 274
Winepress, allegory of, 341–47
Witnesses, two, 304–10, 311–12
Women: mocking of LDS, 127–28; at great conference yet to come, 277–78; role of, in kingdom and future events, 278
Woodruff, Wilford: on release of destroying angels, 96–98; on gospel restored to Gentiles, 102; on temple in New Jerusalem, 223; on life in New Jerusalem, 226–27; on plat for Jackson County, 232
World, increasing knowledge about, 400–401
World War I, 141–42
World War II, 141–42, 286–87
World War III, 148

Young, Brigham, 177, 225–26, 230

Zion, 199–200, 227–29; building up of, 187, 447; redemption of, 187–88, 209–12; city of Enoch as, 188–90, 193; old Jerusalem under David as, 190; ancient Jerusalem under Melchizedek as, 190–92; established in last days, 193–94; location of, 194–95; and early Saints, 194–96; stakes of, 196–99; and consecration, 202, 207; bringing again, 207–8; return to, 211–15, 216, 234–36, 240; and army of the Lord, 215–17; peace, refuge, and safety in, 218–19; meeting of city of Enoch and, 221, 233, 355–58; temple in center of, 221–23; temple complex in, 223–25; life in, 225–27; purpose of, 227; and plat for Jackson County, 231–33; city of, 233–39
Zion's Camp, 209–10, 222